Deep Weird

Deep Weird

The Varieties of High Strangeness Experience

EDITED BY
JACK HUNTER, PhD.

www.augustnightpress.com

Deep Weird

This compilation, Copyright © 2023 by Jack Hunter. All rights reserved.
Published by August Night Press; an imprint of White Crow Productions Ltd.

The right of Jack Hunter to be identified as the author of this work has been asserted by them in accordance with the Copyright, Design and Patents act 1988.

No part of this book may be reproduced, copied or used in any form
or manner whatsoever without written permission, except in the
case of brief quotations in reviews and critical articles.

A CIP catalogue record for this book is available from the British Library.
For information, contact White Crow Books by e-mail: info@whitecrowbooks.com.

Cover Design by Astrid@Astridpaints.com
Interior design by Velin@Perseus-Design.com

Paperback: ISBN: 978-1-78677-224-4
eBook: ISBN: 978-1-78677-225-1

Non Fiction / BODY, MIND & SPIRIT / Parapsychology /
ESP, Clairvoyance, Precognition, Telepathy.

www.augustnightpress.com
www.whitecrowbooks.com

Dedicated to the memory of Dr Carlos Alvarado (1955-2021) whose warmth, scholarship and exploratory spirit are a continuing inspiration.

PRAISE FOR *DEEP WEIRD*

Carl Gustav Jung wrote about "synchronicities," while Rhea White dubbed them "exceptional human experiences." Rudolf Otto discussed "the numinous" and Alan Watts cited "these things." Jack Hunter uses the umbrella terms "deep weird" and "highly strange," proposing that they be the topic of disciplined inquiry. In this remarkable volume Dr Hunter and his chapter authors provide numerous examples of events that at first glance seem to be absurd, bizarre and surreal. The result is a collection of anecdotes, vignettes, and descriptions that beg for explanation, especially when Occam's Razor cannot cut to the quick, when the Gordian Knot cannot be sliced, and when mainstream science can only offer reductionism. Readers may react with skepticism to some of these tales, but they will never be bored as they peruse this extraordinary anthology.

~ STANLEY KRIPPNER, PhD., CO-EDITOR OF *VARIETIES OF ANOMALOUS EXPERIENCE: EXAMINING THE SCIENTIFIC EVIDENCE.*

Deep Weird features some of the best minds today researching the witness experience of the surreal made real. This book reiterates the rule that the more unbelievable an account of the uncanny is, the more we should pay attention to the details, and the effects on the witness. The world of the numinous is not for the binary-minded.

~ GREG BISHOP, AUTHOR OF *IT DEFIES LANGUAGE: ESSAYS ON UFOS AND OTHER WEIRDNESS.*

This book is a delight to read and timely as both a science and experience based assessment of how consciousness and perception are integral to experiencing weird events. It represents an important step along the yellow brick road that hopefully leads to better understanding. I am still investigating the subtle forces within consciousness that build a bridge between an extraordinary perception and the constructs around it that we seem to create, asking if that resulting 'strange experience' provides real meaning within our lives, or is just an illusion. Every now and then something perceptive or insightful can illuminate the way towards better awareness of how and why things happen as they do. The Oz Factor did that for me. I hope this book proves to be that spark for you.

~ JENNY RANDLES, AUTHOR OF *MIND MONSTERS: INVADERS FROM INNER SPACE?*

Talk about high weirdness! In this potent collection, the intrepid Jack Hunter stakes out an expansive conceptual zone for the paranormal keyed to our anomalous times. Gathering texts between (and beyond) sociology and subjectivity, science and magic, scholars and experiencers, *Deep Weird* unsettles the borderlands and gets under your skin.

~ ERIK DAVIS, PHD., AUTHOR OF *HIGH WEIRDNESS: DRUGS, ESOTERICA* AND *VISIONARY EXPERIENCE IN THE SEVENTIES.*

There is a public face to the paranormal, where Bigfoot is an undiscovered primate and UFOs are visiting scientists from a distant planet. These mainstream conclusions are tidy and logical, all of it above the waterline in bright sunshine. Yet anyone who truly looks into these dark mysteries will confront a baffling strangeness, a shadow realm where real events play out with enigmatic dream logic. The authors in this book have journeyed into the deepest waters, and what they share will stretch the mind of any seeker brave enough to listen. This collection is a testament to the unsettling weirdness that permeates our reality. It's not just that things are weird – it's that they're too weird.

~ MIKE CLELLAND, AUTHOR OF *THE MESSENGERS: OWLS, SYNCHRONICITY* AND THE *UFO ABDUCTEE*

CONTENTS

Praise for *Deep Weird* vii

Foreword: The Implied Projector - Jeffrey J. Kripal 1

Introducing the Deep Weird: High Strangeness, Boggle Thresholds and Damned Data in Academic Research on Extraordinary Experience - Jack Hunter 5

PART 1: DEEP WEIRD PHENOMENA 47

1. Synchronicity – Sharon Hewitt Rawlette 49
2. Near-Death Experiences: Unpeeling the Universal, Cultural, and Individual Layers – Gregory Shushan 75
3. Out-of-Body Experiences in the Screen Age – Samantha Lee Treasure 89
4. Superhumanity: An Exercise of Active Imagination – Michael Grosso 113
5. Ectoplasm: Where Biology Meets Imagination – Zofia Weaver 129
6. Poltergeists and High Strangeness – Alan Murdie 149
7. Disembodied Eyes Revisited: An Investigation into the Ontology of Entheogenic Entity Encounters – David Luke 169
8. Fairy Ain't What It Used to Be: Traditional vs Contemporary Fairies – Simon Young 189
9. Anything-but-Standard: High Strangeness Entity Encounters – Zelia Edgar 211

ix

PART 2: RESEARCHING THE DEEP WEIRD 227

10. Strange Talk: Epistemological, Methodological and Ethical Aspects of Conducting Interviews about Anomalous Experiences – Leonardo Breno Martins 229

11. The Extraordinary Encounter Continuum Hypothesis – Peter M. Rojcewicz 243

12. Creating Project Hera: Application of Deep Neural Networks and Database Architectures to Albert Rosales' Humanoid Encounter Datasets – Barbara A. Fisher & Christopher Diltz 259

PART 3: MODELLING THE DEEP WEIRD 271

13. "The Projectionist's Booth": High Strangeness Viewed Through the Lens of Cinema – Joshua Cutchin 273

14. An Introduction to the Egregorial – Anthony Peake 291

15. Minds in Nature: Panpsychism – Peter Sjöstedt-Hughes 307

16. Through A Magickal Lens: Towards an Experimental Model of Conjuring – Susan Demeter 317

17. Jiisakiiwigaan: Shaking Tent Ceremony as Sacred Metamorphosis – Renée E. Mazinegiizhigo-kwe Bédard 335

Biographies 359

References 367

Index 405

FOREWORD

The Implied Projector

JEFFREY J. KRIPAL

> "2020 is so fucking wild that the Pentagon just confirmed UFOs and it's barely news."
> TWEET OF SANTIAGO MAYER,
> EXECUTIVE DIRECTOR OF *VOTERS OF TOMORROW*

The damned. High strangeness. The sacred. The numinous. The boggle threshold. The Oz factor. The deep weird. We learn the original coiners and meanings of all of these phrases in these carefully curated and collected pages (Jack Hunter has done it again). Whatever we want to call it, the present topic has received little academic attention for a fairly simple reason: it deconstructs academic attention. But it also deconstructs sensory attention, rational attention, scientific attention, and pretty much any other kind of attention that we want to name. That is kind of the whole point.

Still, *these things happen*. It seems utterly pointless, and rather a waste of time, to argue that they do not happen. It seems far more interesting, and far more efficient, to begin with a simple "they happen," and then work from there to theorise why or how they happen. Those are two very different steps in the process or project. I think we can and should debate and discuss the second one. I think we are long past debating or discussing the first. I am, anyway. I have had quite enough. I think the present essayists have as well. In any case, that is what makes each of these chapters so valuable and so provocative – they do not begin by rehearsing the same old arguments, the same old matter/anti-matter debate that ends up with, well, nothing in the end. And isn't that the whole point of that old, tired debate? To end the conversation? To keep it from going anywhere? To end up with nothing at all?

It is not that the essayists have a definitive answer or place to go. They in fact propose many different ways forward but no definite end or answer: the philosophical analysis of moments of synchronicity, a most astonishing focus on ectoplasm as embodied imagination, evolutionary advance, psychedelic revelations, entity encounters, the near-death experience across cultures and times, indigenous knowledge and ritual, comparative folklore, the cinematic model, and magical conjuration, to name a few of the paths into the forest.

It is quite the forest. And we never get out.

Allow me to tell a simple story that I have told many times. It goes like this. When I was young (and naïve), I thought that someone somewhere knew the truth of things. The task, then, became reading as many people in as many languages and translations as I could. I had to find that author, you know. He or she would explain everything, and then I would have the truth of things too.

It never happened. The more I searched and read and travelled and talked, the more I began to realise that *no one has the truth of things*. Oh, sure, some had the truth to this or that. They might have even had some kind of realisation or enlightenment experience. I do not doubt that. But that is hardly the truth of all things. And it is not what I was trying to understand anyway, which was just the entire history of religions. The latter looked more and more like a gigantic phantasmagoria, a millennia-long running science fiction movie, a "nonfiction narrative with a science fiction nervous system," to quote my friend John Philip Santos (2017, p. 392).

This is why I really like Joshua Cutchin's view – itself based partly on Jacques Vallée (itself based on Plato's Cave) – that one way to look at the whole shebang is through the metaphor of film and the projector. But, whoa, what a projector! What wild, crazy, absurd movies! My own academic mentor, Wendy Doniger, has written about the entire history of mythology as a gigantic spider web, with an unknown spider sitting in the centre (Doniger, 1998). That works, too, although it may make some of us the flies. Seems about right. Wendy, by the way, could also think and write metaphysically, especially with and through Hindu mythical and mystical literature (Doniger, 1986). Which is all to say: academics are people, too, and sometimes they are really, *really* interesting.

Still, I get the critique of the academy. I also share it and have advanced it myself, mostly to stand up for people. It happened like this. As I began to get to know and work with extreme experiencers a few decades ago, someone would tell me a story, say, about a phone call from the dead, or a monstrous spectral presence attempting to possess the person as he slept, or driving (a car) into another dimension off a state highway, or getting radiated by a coloured light or plasma that kills the household cat (wait, *what*?). I would wait for the punchline, for the story to get simpler, for something to make sense. It never did. As the person came to trust me and tell me more and more of the story, it *never* got simpler or more reasonable, much less explainable. It just got stranger, and stranger, and then stranger still. As human trust develops and secrecy wanes, the truth of these matters gets deep weird, to use Jack's elegant phrase. They *never* "make sense" (which implies that the evolved senses are adequate to reality, which they are not).

I eventually learned to accept this confusion, mostly by coming to terms with the deep weird *by not coming to terms with it*. I no longer think it can be explained by any of our academic methods, be they scientific, social scientific, or humanistic (so many boxes we put ourselves in), *or* our popular mythologies, much less our military or national interests. *None* of them work. I had finally to conclude that human consciousness and embodiment *are* strange, *are* weird, other, or alien in relationship to all of our understandings and assumptions, and likely to any and all understandings or cognitive frameworks that we can possibly have. I had to learn to exoticise the human condition for a simple reason: because the human condition *is* exotic.

It is *wild.* It is *deep weird.*

And that, of course, is what I think this book is ultimately about – our own exoticisation, our own fundamental, irreplaceable, irreducible queerness. The authors who write in this book, many of whom I know and have had the honour of reading in other contexts, are some of the most eloquent and erudite commentators writing today. Please read them, and please consider seriously and long what they have to say. But please do not read them to find "the answer" or "the truth of things." There is no such thing to have.

And that itself, I suppose, is the truth I should have been looking for all along.

DEEP WEIRD

High Strangeness, Boggle Thresholds and Damned Data in Academic Research on Extraordinary Experience

JACK HUNTER

This introductory chapter is about the stranger reaches of psychical research and why it is that some of the most unusual paranormal reports often come to be neglected in the academic study of extraordinary experiences, even within what is already a relatively fringe field of inquiry. Some of the reasons are methodological in nature – deliberate choices made by researchers to exclude certain cases – while others are rooted in deeper ontological, cultural and personal attitudes toward anomalous data. The academic aversion to the most unusual forms of extraordinary experience has resulted in a gulf between the kinds of experiences discussed in the scholarly literature – which are often neatly separated into distinctive types and categories (OBE, NDE, voice hearing, encounters with light, spirit possession, religious experience, apparitions and so on) – and the writings of Fortean[1] and popular paranormal researchers, who have more frequently been able to discuss a much broader range of extraordinary experiential accounts (from UFO encounters to monster flaps, time-slips, haunted houses, humanoid interactions, Bigfoot and fairy sightings, and everything in

---

[1] Named after the famed collector of anomalies Charles Hoy Fort (1874-1932).

between). Fortean researchers have also had much more freedom to explore the overlaps and intersections that interweave this diversity. This book, then, is an attempt to 'cross the streams' of the academic and Fortean traditions of extraordinary experience research, each of which has its insights, strengths and limitations. The Fortean approach is inclusive and exploratory, while the academic approach is careful and critical.

In spite of the differences between these perspectives, there are some significant themes that run throughout *both* the established academic literature on religious and extraordinary experience *and* the canon of popular paranormal research. These similarities suggest that even the most unusual experiences, which have often been ignored in academic and scientific research, contain elements that seem to connect them to other forms of extraordinary experience that *are* more broadly accepted (such as certain kinds of spiritual, mystical, transpersonal, psychedelic and religious experiences, about which there is an abundant academic literature). What this book suggests, then, is that the 'highly strange' might in fact be a central feature of extraordinary experiences more generally, and that instead of being neglected the 'deep weird' should be granted greater and renewed scholarly attention.

The Wyrd and The Deep Weird

Before going any further, I want to take a moment to unpack what I mean by the term 'Deep Weird.' I will discuss the phenomenology of the weird – what the weird *feels* like and how it is experienced – later on in this chapter, but the etymology of the word is also important, and provides a revealing backdrop for the explorations that are presented in this book.

The word 'weird' has its origins in the Germanic and Old English word 'wyrd,' referring to the idea of destiny, or fate. This understanding of the term is clearly seen in Shakespeare's evocative depiction of the Three Witches in Macbeth – popularly known as the 'Weird Sisters' – who could see into the future, and who predicted Macbeth's demise. This image draws on ancient understandings of the weird that go back to pre-Christian Anglo-Saxon traditions (Jeler, 2020). In his influential book *The Way of Wyrd* (2012 [1983]), psychologist Brian Bates presented a hybrid of fiction and non-fiction to portray an image of the wyrd worldview of an Anglo-Saxon sorcerer over a thousand years ago. Here the wyrd is understood as a deep and interconnecting structure that gives shape and meaning to reality. Bates explains that:

> [...] in its archaic original sense, [wyrd] meant that aspect of life which was so deep, so all-pervasive and so central to our understanding of ourselves and our world that it was inexpressible. Wyrd refers to our personal destiny. It connects us to all things, thoughts, emotions, events in the cosmos as if through the threads of an enormous, invisible but dynamic web (Bates, 2012, p. ix).

Like anthropologist E.E. Evans-Pritchard's (1902-1973) famous description of Sudanese Azande witchcraft beliefs (Evans-Pritchard, 1976), or Carl Jung's (1875-1961) notion of synchronicity (Jung, 2010), the Wyrd was understood by the Anglo-Saxons as a 'connecting principle' – something that linked seemingly un-related phenomena and events in a meaningful way. This is a particularly interesting connotation in light of the discussions that follow, which seem to point in the direction of the interconnectivity of extraordinary experiences. But the modern term 'weird' has also come to have a much broader meaning in popular usage, incorporating ideas to do with the 'strange,' 'uncanny,' 'bizarre,' 'abnormal,' 'surreal,' and so on, and this is often the sense in which the term is used by paranormal experiencers today ('I had a weird experience last night,' for example). It is in this broad sense that the term 'weird' is primarily employed here. Nevertheless, it is interesting to note that the archaic sense of the term – of an invisible, dynamic web that interweaves reality, connecting disparate phenomena – is a theme that continues to emerge through contemporary 'weird' experiences, as we shall see. It also goes to show that the weird has always been deep.

By 'Deep Weird,' then, I mean to refer to some of the *most* unusual, bizarre and uncanny experiences and phenomena documented in the paranormal literature – experiences that are stranger, perhaps, than the 'average' ghost sighting (if there can be such a thing) – poltergeists, ectoplasmic materialisations, non-human and humanoid entity encounters, improbable synchronicities, religious miracles, UFO waves, near-death and out-of-body experiences, cryptid sightings, psychedelic journeys to alien other-worlds, and all manner of combinations and intersections of the above. These are experiences that push, and often far-exceed, the boundaries of what the dominant models of Western science and culture allow for, and yet are relatively commonly reported worldwide.

The term 'Deep Weird' also implies that the contributors to this book 'think deeply' about the weird in all of its guises, taking it seriously (but not always *too* seriously) from a variety of different perspectives – anthropological, psychological, philosophical, parapsychological, indigenous, Fortean, and so on – in order to consider its broader implications critically, rather than simply excluding or dismissing it. My final intended meaning of the term is, therefore, to suggest that far from being trivial, these experiences and phenomena *might* actually tell us something important about ourselves and the deep structures and processes of reality.

The Varieties of Extraordinary Experience

In 1902 – 120 years ago by the time the book you hold in your hands was released – William James' (1842-1910) hugely influential work *The Varieties of Religious Experience* was first published. It collected together his Gifford Lectures on 'natural theology' given at the University of Edinburgh between 1901-1902. Over the course of this series of talks, written up for the purposes of his book, James analysed 'religious' experiences that he had gathered from literary sources and clinical case notes, often using examples from famous or influential figures and religious leaders (Taves, 1999, p. 273). James' emphasis on 'celebrity' experiences was likely part of an effort to suggest their worthiness for study in the first place (appealing to the respectability of his informants), though in effect it narrowed his sample size and drew attention away from extraordinary experiences in the general population. Despite some minor limitations, however, James' study was pioneering and opened up a range of extraordinary experiences for serious consideration in the academy. He included in his discussion, for example, the following account from one of his informants, which possesses several features that will become recurrent themes in the pages that follow:

> Quite early in the night I was awakened [...] I felt as if I had been aroused intentionally, and at first thought someone was breaking into the house [...] I then turned on my side to go to sleep again, and immediately felt a consciousness of a presence in the room, and singular to state, it was not the presence of a live person, but of a spiritual presence [...] I felt also at the same time a strong feeling of superstitious dread, as if something strange and fearful were about to happen (cited in James, 2004, p. 64).

It is clear from the above extract that James' definition of religious experience was very broad, encompassing types of experience that do not necessarily include traditional religious themes or imagery. Rather, common phenomenological motifs are highlighted across a range of experiential accounts from different contexts. In this case there is: a sense of intentional awakening, the sense of a 'spiritual' presence, and the growing feeling of 'superstitious dread.' For James, and those scholars who followed in his footsteps, extraordinary experiences such as these were thought to represent the primary origin of the world's religious beliefs, doctrines and traditions: 'core experiences' interpreted through different philosophical frameworks. Historian of Religion Ann Taves has suggested that it was James' *Varieties of Religious Experience* that first constituted the concept of '"religious experience" in a technical sense as an object of study,' and first defined it as a 'generic "something" that informed "religion-in-general" apart from any tradition in particular' (Taves, 1999, p. 271).

But it is James' emphasis on *varieties* of experience – as opposed to 'religious experience' as a single monolithic category – that is crucial for the purposes of *this* book, and provides a firm foundation for the explorations that follow. For example, James gives a summary of the *varieties* of what he calls the 'religious sentiment' – which may include sensations such as 'religious fear, religious love, religious awe, religious joy, and so forth' (James, 2004, p. 36) – that is, different *forms* that religious feelings can take from one individual to the next. He explains:

> One [...] allies it to the feeling of dependence; one makes it a derivative from fear; others connect it with the sexual life; others still identify it with the feeling of the infinite; and so on. Such different ways of conceiving it ought of themselves to arouse doubt as to whether it possibly can be one specific thing; and the moment we are willing to treat the term 'religious sentiment' as a collective name for the many sentiments which religious objects may arouse in alternation, we see that it probably contains nothing whatever of a psychologically specific nature (James, 2004, p. 36).

For James, then, there was not a single 'religious experience' – 'nothing whatever' resembling anything 'specific' – rather there are many different religious *experiences,* which on the surface have little to do with traditional religious motifs. Despite this fundamental diversity, however, James also recognised some important themes that seem to run centrally throughout the rich variety of experiential narratives that he described and analysed in his lectures. Chiefly, these included the qualities that he referred to as:

- *Ineffable* – such experiences cannot adequately be put into words.
- *Noetic* – they impart knowledge, often of God or the ultimate reality.
- *Transient* – they are short-lived and temporary.
- *Passive* – they feel like they are coming from outside of the experiencer, beyond their control.

What this would seem to suggest – right from the very beginning of the formal academic investigation of these experiences – is that there is *both* a wide variety of religious experiences *and* a sense of their interconnectedness through certain properties, qualities and processes. The dominant tendency has been to think of these two polarities as binary opposites: *either* there is one core experience that is interpreted in different ways, *or* there are many different kinds of unrelated, culturally constructed experiences. This has created a tension between *universalist* and *particularist* approaches in religious experience research. Most notably, debates rage between those who adopt a so-called 'common-core' approach to religious experience and those who reject the idea in favour of cultural particularism (cf. Proudfoot, 1987). Similar schisms also emerge between those who adopt the experiential source hypothesis, and those who favour the cultural source hypothesis (see Hufford, 1982) in the study of folklore, for example.[2] But the real world is not quite so black and white: *both perspectives*, it would seem, need to be taken into consideration. The universal and the particular, the experiential and the cultural. As a useful illustration, psychologist of religion Lucy Bregman gives a revealing example of this relationship in the context of a pan-human experience – dying. She writes:

---

[2] The experiential source hypothesis suggests that traditions of supernatural belief often have an experiential origin, e.g. anomalous experiences give rise to systems of belief. The cultural source hypothesis, on the other hand, suggests that supernatural beliefs are purely cultural in origin, and have no underlying reality beyond that (Hufford, 1982).

> What could be more obviously a universal human fact than death and, therefore, dying? Perhaps with the exception of those persons whose deaths are instantaneous, or occur without warning in sleep, all of us will experience some lead-in or lead-up to our actual deaths. In this sense, dying is probably as nearly universal as anything imaginable. But [...] Even though men and women have died at all times and places, they have not suffered through the anticipation of their own deaths in necessarily similar ways. They may or may not be experiencing a fundamentally universal psychological process called "dying" (Bregman, 1989, p. 58).

Even something as fundamental to human life as death, then, can be experienced in an enormous variety of different ways from one individual to the next, and from one situation to another, while nevertheless sharing essential underlying features and processes. Death is not a singular experience – though it is universal – and can take many different forms, and be interpreted in many different ways.

Arguing along similar lines, the philosopher David E. Cooper emphasises the plural in his discussion of what he calls the 'senses of mystery,' he writes:

> [...] it is possible and helpful to distinguish different aspects or modes of mystery. It is not exactly that there are several separate mysteries on which to reflect. The ineffable way of things is not anything we can describe and articulate so as to then divide it up into discrete compartments. But there are different faces or aspects of mystery that offer themselves to attention and reflection (Cooper, 2018, p. 21).

Compartments dissolve in the face of the great mystery, and reveal much more variety, diversity and interconnection than any kind of neat taxonomy might suggest. William James' recognition of the many forms, modes or aspects that religious experiences can take, would later go on to influence emerging approaches in the study of other kinds of extraordinary experience. Robert Masters (1927-2008) and Jean Houston, for example, continued the theme in the 1960s with their *The Varieties of Psychedelic Experience* (1966), which although dealing only with LSD (itself just one among many other varieties of psychedelic substances), emphasised the *diversity* of experiences occasioned by the consumption of the drug. There is no single monolithic LSD experience, just as there is no single monolithic religious experience. Masters and

Houston explain, in relation to the experiential reports documented in their book, that:

> [...] it is not possible to say that they are "typical." Every such experience is in many significant ways very *individual* and depends for its structure and content upon what the subject brings to the session in the way of personal history and frame of reference (Masters & Houston, 1966, p. 6).

This is what Timothy Leary (1920-1996) and colleagues referred to as 'set and setting' – individual mindset and environmental setting – particularly in the context of their early research on the perceptual effects of psilocybin, the main psychedelic component of magic mushrooms (Leary, Litwin & Metzner, 1963). Extraordinary experiences – including those that are not induced by psychedelic substances – are modulated by these factors and shaped by our cultural frameworks, beliefs and expectations (though they can undoubtedly still surprise us, which perhaps also suggests the involvement of extra-psychological, or pre-cultural, processes or agents). Individual differences therefore play an important role in contributing to the variety of extraordinary experiences that human beings report. Though again, as with James, Masters and Houston do emphasise some key threads that run through the spectrum of LSD experiences they collected. The book, for instance, is structured according to the following phenomenological criteria, each section containing illustrative clinical examples of alterations in:

- Experiencing the body and body image.
- Experiencing other persons.
- Experiencing the world of the non-human.

They also include chapters on other themes that seemed to recur in their sample population, including:

- The voyage inward.
- Psyche and symbol.
- Religious and mystical experience.

Psychedelic experiences therefore may take on a rich variety of forms – with vastly different contexts and contents – but there are also common themes that seem to repeat from one report to the next on a regular basis.

These phenomenological themes also connect psychedelic experiences to other kinds of extraordinary, ecstatic, religious and paranormal experiences, which often share similar features and characteristics (Luke, 2020), as well as possible underlying processes. In the year 2000, psychologists Etzel Cardeña, Steven Lynn and Stanley Krippner ensured the continuation of James' 'varieties' tradition into the twenty-first century with the publication of their edited volume on the *Varieties of Anomalous Experience*. Here, the varieties of anomalous experience is expanded from the religious and psychedelic to include everything from:

> [...] commonly documented sensations and perceptions like synesthesia, lucid dreaming, out-of-body experiences, and auditory and visual hallucinations, to rarer and more seemingly inexplicable experiences such as anomalous healing, past-lives, near-death, mystical experiences, and even alien abductions (Cardeña, Lynn & Krippner, 2000).

These are amongst the most common categories and varieties of extraordinary experience discussed (and experienced) today. While it might seem that each of these is a discrete 'kind' of experience – with its own symptoms, aetiology, and so on – in fact they might best be thought of as existing on a sliding scale, or spectrum, of phenomena and experiences with no solid distinctions between them. Nevertheless, the segregation of research agendas in the academy, as well as in popular paranormal research, frequently leads to the 'damning,' to use Charles Fort's terminology, of certain experiences that blur – or collapse – these neat categories. Complex or problematic experiences are frequently excluded from the conversation (Hunter, 2021a), and it is precisely to these kinds of experiences that I now want to turn.

High Strangeness

In the annals of research on extraordinary experience there are certain cases that are so strange that they stand out from the crowd. These are stories of experiences and events that are far weirder than, for example, the slightly above chance evidence for psi revealed in parapsychological experiments (cf. Parker & Brusewitz, 2003; Radin, 2006), or the 'average' ghost encounter or UFO sighting. These experiences are utterly bizarre, and cannot be neatly classified or easily understood – they are experiences that *fall between* the established categories of paranormal researchers and academics. The strange events documented by John Keel in the 1960s, building up to the collapse of the Silver Bridge in Point Pleasant, which included psychic dreams, premonitions, strange lights and sightings of the 'Mothman' by many residents of the area (Keel, 2002 [1975]), weird encounters with hovering telepathic robots emitting noxious fumes (Edgar, 2022, pp. 9-13), meetings with thousand-eyed threshold guardians in psychedelic reveries (Luke, 2008), strange UFO sightings and observations of apparent inter-dimensional portals (amongst other things) reported on the Skinwalker Ranch in Utah (Kelleher & Knapp, 2005), and sinister gnomes in miniature cars chasing children in 1970s Nottingham (Young, 2022a). This is just a small selection of some of the most unusual examples, but deeply weird experiences and phenomena can also be more subtle, though no less profound. UFO experiencer and researcher Mike Clelland, for instance, describes how real-life paranormal experiences are often enmeshed in a "tangled knot of implausibility" in which "synchronicity spills over the edges like an unattended sink" (Clelland, 2020, p. 44). In Clelland's case, his own UFO experiences were synchronistically intertwined with numerous uncanny encounters with owls.[3]

Seemingly distinct paranormal events and experiences, then, often appear to merge and overlap in the real world. Indeed, so common is

---

[3] While in the process of writing and editing this introduction, I had my own synchronistic experience with with an owl. While driving to the next village, along the edge of the Tanat Valley (see Hunter, 2022) listening to a radio programme on BBC Radio 4 about poetry, I suddenly had the thought that I might see an owl (I had recently seen a few). I looked up and saw a big white barn owl swoop down and over the car, just as a line from Edward Fitzgerald's translation of *The Rubaiyat of Omar Khayyam* was read out, which said "The Bird of Time has but a little way To fly – and Lo! the Bird is on the Wing." When I arrived at my destination, I told a friend that I had seen an owl (holding back on the weird synchronistic elements), and he proceeded to tell me about a strange experience he had had with a very large owl while driving one time that seemed to disappear right from the middle of the road as the car approached. Then I mentioned the weirdness. On the way home I saw a hare. One of the most unusual things about this particular experience was that, because I know that this kind of thing happens to people (e.g. from reading Mike Clelland's book), I was very aware that it was happening to me, so it just sort of played out in front of my eyes (and ears), and I was just wondering what to expect next while observing the event unfold. Very weird.

this kind of paranormal cross-pollination in the life-worlds of many experiencers, that Clelland considers it "a sign to trust the event as legitimate," arguing that "[t]he more complicated the interwoven details, the more valid it seems" (Clelland, 2020, p. 44). In the popular UFO and paranormal literature this element of paranormal experience is referred to as the 'High Strangeness' factor. The term was coined by the pioneering UFO researcher and astronomer Dr J. Allen Hynek (1910-1986) in the context of his 'Strangeness Rating' for reported UFO encounters. He explains:

> A light seen in the night sky the trajectory of which cannot be ascribed to a balloon, aircraft, etc., would [...] have a low Strangeness Rating because there is only one strange thing about the report to explain: its motion. A report of a weird craft that descended within 100 feet of a car on a lonely road, caused the car's engine to die, its radio to stop, and its lights to go out, left marks on the nearby ground, and appeared to be under intelligent control receives a high Strangeness Rating because it contains a number of separate very strange items, each of which outrages common sense [...] (Hynek, 1979, p. 42).

In other words, the strangeness rating is a measure of "the number of information bits the report contains, each of which is difficult to explain in common sense terms" (ibid.). Computer scientist and UFOlogist Dr Jacques Vallée later expanded Hynek's rating, elaborating seven distinct levels of strangeness: ranging from the lowest level of a simple sighting of a light in the night sky all the way up to abduction experiences and the psychic side of the UFO phenomenon, accounts of which contain the highest number of anomalous information bits (Vallée, 1977, pp. 114-119). It is precisely these highly strange cases that collapse the neat categorisations of experiences discussed above. Through his work, for example, Vallée has demonstrated that the UFO experience is far stranger than the standard 'nuts-and-bolts' and extraterrestrial hypothesis (ETH) perspectives would often like to admit, and suggests that UFO experiences have a great deal in common with other forms of extraordinary experience reported throughout history – from ghosts to magic and fairies (cf. Graham, 2017). More recent writings from the popular paranormal field have also begun to highlight the high strangeness that permeates other areas of the paranormal, such as in the case of Bigfoot encounters – and other cryptozoological interactions

– which often cannot be adequately distinguished from accounts of poltergeist, fairy and UFO experiences (Cutchin & Renner, 2020). A Bigfoot sighting is not always *just* a Bigfoot sighting, and is often much more, and may include telepathic communications, dream visitations and other kinds of psychic experiences.

In a 1991 survey of the work of the independent psychical researcher D. Scott Rogo (1950-1990), George P. Hansen commended Rogo's willingness to tackle even those elements of the paranormal 'that most consider "subversive"' (Hansen, 1991, p. 33). Hansen goes on to list many of the complex overlaps that characterise high strangeness experiences, the most 'subversive' aspects of the already marginalised paranormal, which Rogo was willing to consider under the banner of psychical research:

> [...] demonic experiences, bigfoot sightings, poltergeist action, and phenomena suggesting survival of bodily death have all been reported in conjunction with UFOs. Strange animal mutilations have been reported in poltergeist cases as well as with UFO sightings. Striking ESP experiences [...] have been reported by UFO contactees. Some of the contactees claim bedroom visitations by angels, extra-terrestrial aliens, and mythical creatures. Similar experiences have been reported for thousands of years. These are unsettling claims not only because of their innate strangeness, but also because they fall between the discrete categories most people assume to be valid, and thus most researchers (even those in parapsychology) prefer to ignore them (Hansen, 1991, p. 33).

Because the more outlandish elements of paranormal experience are often ignored or dismissed, even by parapsychologists, Hansen suggests that the responsibility to investigate them has often fallen to journalists and other popular writers. Charles Fort's collections of 'Damned Facts' (Fort, 2008), John Keel's investigations of the Mothman, Men in Black, monsters and UFOs (see Keel, 1971; 2002; 2013), the hugely influential books of Jenny Randles on the alien abduction phenomenon and other mysteries (see, for example, Randles, 1988; 1990), Albert Rosales' recent epic compendia of humanoid encounters (Rosales, 2016), and Greg Bishop's writings on the UFO phenomenon (Bishop, 2016), are good examples of popular researchers who have embraced High Strangeness in their writings. Despite its acceptance as an almost defining feature of paranormal experience in the popular and Fortean research communities, however, very little attention has been paid to the High Strangeness factor in the context of academic or scientific research on extraordinary experience more generally. The writings of Jeffrey J. Kripal over the last decade (Kripal, 2010; 2011; 2020; see also Strieber & Kripal, 2016), not to mention the work of his students and the recent establishment of the Archives of the Impossible at Rice University,[4] have certainly paved the way for further academic engagement with the highly strange (cf. Davis, 2019). Nevertheless, high strangeness research remains a fringe activity in parapsychology, psychical research and the study of extraordinary, religious and spiritual experiences more generally.

Why, then, has High Strangeness historically received such little scholarly attention?

Boggle Thresholds and Academic Research on Extraordinary Experience

One possible explanation has been offered by the historian of psychical research Renée Haynes (1906–1994), who coined the term 'Boggle Threshold' to refer to the point at which an extraordinary experience, phenomenon or event is deemed to be so outlandish and unlikely that it is entirely dismissed by the researcher. She explains that:

> Individual boggle thresholds will vary [...] with individual temperament, history, training, and aptitude. They will also be influenced by [...] the groups to which each individual is linked: family, friends, school, employment, university. In people brought up in the discipline of the physical sciences the levels of boggledom are likely to differ considerably from the levels found in those brought up in the humanities (Haynes, 1980, p. 94).

Boggle Thresholds also play their part in academic fields that actively engage in research on extraordinary experience (as opposed to simply ignoring it), such as parapsychology and religious experience research. Boggle Thresholds may, for instance, place limits on the kinds of experiences that a study will take into consideration – and there might

---

[4] https://impossiblearchives.rice.edu

well be pragmatic reasons for excluding certain phenomena from a research project. For example, in their pioneering study, published as the *Census of Hallucinations* in 1889, philosopher Henry Sidgwick (1838-1900) and colleagues in the early Society for Psychical Research (SPR) made use of what qualitative research methodologists call a 'filter question' at the beginning of their survey (Krosnick & Presser, 2018, p. 264), specifically to filter out certain kinds of experiences that might 'muddy the waters' in their study of hallucinatory experiences. Their filter question was:

> Have you ever, when believing yourself to be completely awake, had a vivid impression of seeing or being touched by a living being or inanimate object, or of hearing a voice; which impression, so far as you could discover, was not due to any external physical cause? (Sidgwick, 1891, p. 52).

Sidgwick explains that this 'last sentence is intended to exclude, as far as possible, a class of experiences which are liable to confound with hallucinations' (Sidgwick, 1891, p. 52). The implication is that there are certain experiences, such as those that occur in dreams, or visual illusions when not 'completely awake,' for instance, that should be ruled out of a study of auditory and visual hallucinations. But what about experiences that fall between these categories – those peculiar times when we are between waking and sleeping, in hypnagogic and hypnopompic states that we now know are rich in hallucinatory experiences (Ohayon *et al.*, 1996)? A whole plethora of extraordinary experiences is potentially ruled out from the start. As sociologist David Yamane suggests: 'by using a […] a filter […] qualitative researchers run the risk of filtering out those who do not understand their experiences in the terms given by the researcher' (Yamane, 2000, p. 180). Real-world experiences may entirely exceed the researcher's terms and criteria for inclusion, and so might end up being ignored completely.

The Religious Experience Research Unit at Oxford University also took a similar approach to the collection of its data on contemporary religious experiences in the 1960s, using a combination of public calls for experiential narratives in newspapers, pamphlets and via widely distributed questionnaires (Hardy, 2006, pp. 17-25). This research employed the now famous 'Hardy Question' – named after the founder of the research unit, marine biologist Sir Alister Hardy (1896-1985) – to try to keep the focus of the enquiry firmly on certain types of extraordinary experience, namely 'religious'[5] ones:

> Have you ever been aware of or influenced by a presence or power, whether you call it God or not, which is different from your everyday self?

Hardy notes in his own analysis of the data collected by the RERU, however, that in spite of the use of the filter question the general public continued to send in 'accounts of the more ecstatic experiences,' and as such the research team ultimately decided against trying to restrict the kinds of experiences that people could submit to the collection (Hardy, 2006, p. 19). This is perhaps indicative of the 'wilder' nature of real-world religious experiences, which do not necessarily fit neatly into simplistic classificatory schemes. Hardy's decision to allow the incorporation of heterodox accounts of religious experiences, therefore, has led to the creation of a very rich resource for researchers, containing all manner of extraordinary experiences. The Religious Experience Research Centre (RERC), as it is now called, is currently based at the University of Wales Trinity Saint David and houses over 6,000 self-submitted reports of 'religious experiences' from the general population. The contents of the archive are ripe for research on the overlaps between paranormal, religious and other kinds of extraordinary experiences.

Damned Experiences

The archive has provided the source material for several studies of religious experience over the years, and various different approaches to categorising them into distinctive types have been attempted, but this work has often also continued to perpetuate a distinction between certain kinds of experiences, and to exclude others. In his 1977 phenomenological study, for example, Timothy Beardsworth focussed in particular on experiences of a 'sense of presence' drawn from the first one-thousand submitted reports in the archive. He explains

---

[5] Religion itself is a particularly slippery phenomenon to define. What makes an experience religious? If it is just the interpretation of the experience that makes it religious, then any experience might be considered a religious experience, or perhaps there is some sort of ontological difference?

how he classifies these experiential narratives in the introduction to his analysis:

> The episodes I shall quote involve "sensory" phenomena – visions, voices, and the like. I classify the phenomena under separate [headings] according to the "sense" involved: (1) visual, (2) auditory, (3) tactile, (4) inward sensations. There is also (5) the sense of a "presence," the feeling that someone is there, based on no sensory evidence at all. This feeling, I think, so far as being out on a limb, somehow underlies the other "sensory" categories (Beardsworth, 1977, p. ix).

It is interesting to note Beardsworth's suggestion that the 'sense of presence' might underly the various categories of experience he discusses, again pointing to the interconnectivity of extraordinary experiences. He then goes on to give numerous fascinating accounts from the RERU archive, categorising them according to the criteria listed above. The following extract is a randomly-selected, though more or less representative example from Beardsworth's study that shares similar features with many of the experiences submitted in response to Hardy's question, and is the kind of account commonly featured in analyses of the archive's contents. You could say it is a reasonably standard, or straight forward, 'religious' experience (broadly defined):

> Male 60: "There was no sensible vision, but the room was filled by a Presence which in some strange way was both about me and within me. I was overwhelmingly possessed by Someone who was not myself, and yet I felt I was more myself than I had ever been before [...]" (cited in Beardsworth, 1977, p. 122).

Experiential accounts such as this give very intimate insights into what are often powerfully transformative, and deeply personal, moments in peoples' lives, and are a rich source of data for research. It also accords very well with the experience described by William James earlier – a textbook experience, if you will. These are extraordinary experiences to be sure – they include encounters with beings of light, hearing disembodied voices, out-of-body experiences, transfiguration of landscapes, and many interactions with entities interpreted as angels and so on – but there are also experiences contained in the RERC archive that do not often appear in such studies – out-lying accounts that cannot quite fit into the ordered frameworks put together by academic researchers. The following account, for example, which I found during my own perusal of the archive, has the reference number 000235 so was presumably included in the first one-thousand accounts surveyed by Beardsworth in the 1970s. The experience is undoubtedly a sensory (visual) one, and includes a very distinctive sense of presence, though for some reason the account does not appear in his examination of sensed presences in the archive:

> On the Friday a man came to clean the carpet and curtains in the drawing room. Later on there was a complete fusing of everything electrical. Clocks, radios, refrigerator, freezer, T.V. all the lights etc. In the evening I lay down on a sofa, closed my eyes and tried to relax. I then saw several little green men with very unpleasant expressions. They were looking at me. They seemed to be at a distance. I suppose "gnomes or goblins" would be an adequate description. I didn't like what I saw, and I was reminded of the time I had a rheumatic illness when I was seven, and had been very alarmed by the "little green men" I had seen then. Hallucinations, presumably.

Date of Experience: 1951, Female.
RERC Archive Reference: 000235.

This is clearly an experience with a high strangeness rating – what Alister Hardy might have called one of 'the more ecstatic experiences' – perhaps to the extent that it exceeded Beardsworth's boggle threshold, leading to its exclusion from his study. But there are many different elements of this experience that resonate with other features of high strangeness: the man coming to clean the carpets (who has clearly been mentioned for a reason), the fusing of electrical devices, the 'little green men,' the 'unpleasant' feeling, the life-time of similar experiences, and so on. Put in these terms it carries many of the hallmarks of a UFO, abduction or Men in Black experience (see discussion below). Perhaps, then, it is not a religious experience after all, but a paranormal experience, so it belongs in a different category? On the other hand, the direct reference to "gnomes or goblins" in the account also has clear parallels with the body of research related to encounters with fairies and other folkloric entities. Simon Young's recent *Fairy Census* (2018), for instance, contains numerous descriptions of similar contemporary interactions with small green humanoids (amongst others), so maybe it is a fairy experience – and yet, the report was explicitly self-submitted as a religious experience, in response to Hardy's question.

Regardless of the way the experience is ultimately categorised, it is clear that a distinction is being made between those experiences that *are* suitable for inclusion in academic publications concerned with religious and extraordinary experience, and those accounts that do not quite fit the mould. Such accounts – and there are other high strangeness experiences in the archive (see Hunter, 2019a for a couple of other examples) – are unlikely to be found in scholarly research publications because of their high strangeness rating. To use Charles Fort's terms they become 'damned data,' even in an already damned field like parapsychology or religious experience research. There are, however, some investigators from the canon of academic research on extraordinary experience, as well as from the Fortean traditions, who *have* commented on the deep weirdness that underlies and interconnects many such experiences, and these scholars provide useful foundations for studies of high strangeness going forward.

Deep Weird Phenomenology: Men in Black, the Numinous, the Weird, the Oz Factor and More

The German theologian Rudolf Otto (1869-1937) is perhaps most famous for his notion of the 'numinous' experience, which he took to be the foundational religious impulse, making a similar argument to William James' perspective discussed above. Otto suggested that the sense of the numinous is conjured through our interactions with what he terms "the wholly other" – "something which has no place in our scheme of reality but belongs to an absolutely different one" (Otto, 1958, p. 29). For Otto the numinous experience was non-rational – pre-existing any kind of religious doctrine – but could be broadly understood through two overlapping characteristic 'feeling-responses' that he labelled *mysterium fascinans* and *mysterium tremendum*, the beautiful and frightening aspects of the numinous respectively. Otto also highlights the occasional tendency of numinous experiences to slip over into a state of what he calls "daemonic dread" – the *mysterium horrendum*, or the "negative numinous" – which can be utterly terrifying for the experiencer, though no less powerful or significant. Otto elaborates on the nature of the numinous in the following extract from his *The Idea of the Holy* (1958), emphasising its multiplicity:

> The feeling of it may at times come sweeping like a gentle tide, pervading the mind with a tranquil mood of deepest worship [...] It may burst in sudden eruption up from the depths of the soul with spasms and convulsions, or lead to the strangest excitements, to intoxicated frenzy, to transport, and to ecstasy. It has its wild and demonic forms and can sink to an almost gristly horror and shuddering [...] It may become the hushed, trembling, and speechless humility of the creature in the presence of [...] that which is a mystery inexpressible [...] (Otto, 1958, p. 13).

Immediately obvious, again, is that the numinous is not a monolithic experience, but rather comprises of a spectrum of different responses – from the beautiful to the terrifying, and from the ecstatic to 'speechless humility.' Otto's emphasis on the 'wholly other,' the 'non-rational' and the numinous, effectively drew academic attention back towards some of the stranger features of religious experience – as well as to its darker dimensions – and his analysis is a good starting point for a scholarly approach to High Strangeness as a feature of extraordinary experience. As we will see later on, Otto's characteristic feeling-responses (combining wonder and dread) are frequently reported in a wide variety of extraordinary experiences.

The folklorist Peter Rojcewicz (1987) – whose work is featured in this book – is another example of an academic researcher of extraordinary experience who has faced up to the highly strange and the wholly other, especially in his analysis of the bizarre Men in Black (MIB), who have been reported mysteriously turning up to question and intimidate UFO experiencers since the 1950s. Rojcewicz understands the MIB both in terms of a modern folk-tradition – that is, as a system of beliefs and narratives told and re-told about the mysterious humanoids – and as a particular kind of deeply weird extraordinary experience. Take, for example, his summary of the highly unusual behaviour of the Men in Black:

> Often dressed in black clothing that may appear soiled and generally unkempt or unrealistically neat and wrinkle-free, MIB have on occasion displayed a very unusual walking motion, moving about as if their hips were swivel joints, producing a gliding or rocking effect, often with the torso and legs seemingly moving off into opposite directions [...] (Rojcewicz, 1987, p. 151).

Encounters with the MIB, then, can clearly have a very high strangeness rating. They are often bizarre interactions, and evoke the numinous in the sense of being simultaneously fascinating to observe and yet deeply troubling for the experiencer. Such encounters are frequently ignored in academic studies of UFO experiences, despite their relatively widespread reporting by witnesses. As Rojcewicz points out, such accounts are unlikely to be examined in the scholarly literature on extraordinary experiences (or even within folklore studies), precisely because they are *so weird*. What I am suggesting here, however, is that it is precisely *the experience of weirdness* that we should be paying attention to, which clearly connects MIB encounters to other kinds of extraordinary experience. The cultural theorist Mark Fisher (1968-2017) suggests that the 'weird' is – like Rudolf Otto's notion of the numinous – a kind of feeling-response that results from an interaction with an anomalous stimulus (the 'wholly other' in Otto's terminology), such as an encounter with the Men in Black, Mothman or creepy gnomes. Fisher explains that:

> [...] the weird is a particular kind of perturbation. It involves a sensation of wrongness; a weird entity or object is so strange that it makes us feel that it should not exist, or at least it should not exist here. Yet if the entity or object is here, then the categories which we have up until now used to make sense of the world cannot be valid (Fisher, 2016, p. 15).

Weird experiences, then, seem to imply that reality far exceeds the comfortable limits of our established scientific worldviews. The 'weird fiction' writer H.P. Lovecraft (1890-1937) also provides a useful exposition of the weird as a particular kind of feeling-response in his 1927 essay 'The Supernatural in Fiction.' He explains that true weird fiction has the capacity to induce in the reader a 'certain atmosphere of breathless and unexplainable dread of outer, unknown forces.' He continues:

> [...] there must be a hint, expressed with a seriousness and portentousness becoming its subject, of that most terrible conception of the human brain – a malign and particular suspension or defeat of those fixed laws of Nature which are our only safeguard against the assaults of chaos and the daemons of unplumbed space (Lovecraft, 1927, p. 107).

This admittedly ultra-gothic perspective nevertheless captures the idea of the weird as something that is 'non-rational.' In a weird experience the fixed laws of nature dissolve. It is, perhaps, one of the essential features of effective horror and weird fiction stories that they are able to induce such feeling-responses in the reader (Hunter, 2021c). Lovecraft's understanding of the weird also echoes Otto's realisation that the numinous often arises through interaction with the 'wholly other,' which is perhaps the perfect description of Lovecraft's pantheon of inter-dimensional extraterrestrial gods. This feeling of 'deep weirdness,' which Otto described and Lovecraft sought to induce in his readers, seems to run right throughout many of the varieties of reported anomalous experience – from ghost sightings and interactions with Bigfoot and Mothman, through to angelic visitations, UFO encounters and mystical visions. It is a feeling response that seems to connect disparate phenomena to each other.

Further terms that are often used to refer to bizarre experiences and strange states of arousal include 'uncanny,' 'surreal' and 'absurd,' and these are also worth taking a moment to unpack before going any further, particularly for what they can tell us about the phenomenology of the deep weird. For the founder of psychoanalysis, Sigmund Freud (1856-1939), the sense of the 'uncanny' "belongs to the realm of the frightening, of what evokes fear and dread" (Freud, 2003, p. 123). But, just as Lovecraft suggests in his essay, the uncanny is much more than *simple* fear:

> [...] one may presume that there exists a specific affective nucleus [...] which allows us to distinguish the 'uncanny' within the field of the frightening (Freud, 2003, p. 123).

In particular, Freud points to experiences and phenomena that seem to dissolve our usually assumed (predominantly Western) frameworks for making sense of the world – experiences that are 'creepy' and 'unsettling' as well as frightening. In his essay he gives examples that include inanimate objects seeming to become animate (dissolution of the animate/inanimate dichotomy), ghostly encounters (life/death), seeing your own double, or doppelgänger (self/other), as well as countless examples taken from imaginative literature and fairy tales.[6] Encountering phenomena that break down these dichotomies

---

[6] But Freud is quick to dismiss the possible reality of such uncanny phenomena and their implications, writing: "We – or our primitive forefathers – once believed that these possibilities were realities, and were convinced that they actually happened. Nowadays we no longer believe in them, we have *surmounted* these modes of thought; but we do not feel quite sure of our new beliefs, and the old ones still exist within us ready to seize upon any confirmation. As soon as something *actually happens* in our lives which seems to confirm the old discarded beliefs we get the feeling of the uncanny"

can give rise to a sense of the uncanny in the experiencer. The French writer André Breton (1896-1966), was a great early admirer of Freud, and took inspiration from his psychoanalytic approach in his own efforts to establish the Surrealist movement in the 1920s. In his 1924 'Manifesto of Surrealism' Breton defined surrealism as:

> Psychic automatism in its pure state, by which one proposes to express [...] the actual functioning of thought. Dictated by thought, in the absence of any control exercised by reason, exempt from any aesthetic or moral concern (Breton, 1990, p. 26).

Free association techniques had been employed by Freud, and the psychoanalytic school that followed on from him, as a means of revealing unconscious, usually repressed, drives and motivations, and this was interpreted and practiced by Breton and the Surrealists in the form of automatic writing and drawing (Esman, 2011, pp. 173-174). For the Surrealists, some of whom were as much influenced by Spiritualist automatic writing and the occult as Freudian free-association (Choucha, 1992), these techniques became a method for allowing other elements of the unconscious to bubble to the surface of awareness for the purposes of artistic and literary creation (Campion, 2002; Thompson, 2004). It is also of interest to note that Breton was in regular communication with eminent psychical researchers of the time, including Charles Richet (1850-1935) and Théodore Flournoy (1854-1920) (Alexandrian, 1970, p. 47). The deconstruction of the boundary between the conscious and the unconscious mind was a key concern in the Surrealist movement. The philosopher and historian Sarane Alexandrian (1927-2009) elaborates, explaining that the aim of the Surrealists was:

> [...] to reconcile reality with the illogical processes which arise in ecstatic states or in dreams, with the aim of creating a super-reality. Surrealism cannot accurately be described as fantasy, but as a superior reality, in which all the contradictions which afflict humanity are resolved as in a dream (Alexandrian, 1970, p. 48).

A truly surreal experience, then, would be one in which a sort of dream logic prevails, where the barriers between conscious and unconscious

---

(Freud, 2003, p. 247–248).

processes are dissolved, and where the distinction between internal (psychological/subjective) and external (physical/objective) reality dissipates. Breton's suggestion that the surreal is 'exempt from any aesthetic or moral concern,' and is characterised by an 'absence of any control exercised by reason,' is also particularly resonant with the bizarre nature of many high strangeness experiences, which often seem to 'play out' irrationally – and sometimes quite shockingly – in front of the experiencer according to their own logic, like dreams, nightmares, or surrealist films (see Joshua Cutchin's chapter in this book).[7]

Finally, a brief word on the absurd. In his short book *The Myth of Sisyphus*, existential philosopher Albert Camus (1913-1960) suggests that 'absurdity' is not necessarily a characteristic of the world itself, but rather is a response that arises as a consequence of human efforts to make sense of, categorise and rationalise it – that is to fit it into neat boxes. Camus writes:

> The world in itself is not reasonable, that is all that can be said. But what is absurd is the confrontation of the irrational and the wild longing for clarity whose call echoes in the human heart. The absurd depends as much on [humans] as on the world. For the moment is all that links them together. It binds them one to the other as only hatred can weld two creatures together. This is all I can discern clearly in this measureless universe where my adventure takes place (Camus, 2000 [1942], p. 26).

A sense of the absurd, then – like the numinous and the weird – emerges when our taken-for-granted human models are revealed to be

---

[7] There is a very interesting intertwining of surrealism and high strangeness in the case of the 'Owlman' (owls again) spotted in the Cornish village of Mawnan Smith. The first sighting of the huge owl-like-humanoid was reported by a group of school boys in 1926, and was reported in the local and national media. The strange story attracted the attention of Max Ernst (1891-1976) and Leonora Carrington (1917-2011), two occult-minded surrealist painters, who travelled to the village to conduct rituals to summon the cryptid in the1930s. Both artists would go on to include bird-man imagery in their paintings for years to come (Dale, 2019). Further sightings of the Owlman have since been reported in the woods around Mawnan Smith, notably after 1976, beginning just a few weeks following Max Ernst's death (Gerhard, 2013, pp. 62-69).

incomplete, or little more than illusion, incapable of accommodating the chaos and complexity of the real world.[8]

The philosopher of mind Bernardo Kastrup might agree with Camus about the absurd, and has referred to anomalous phenomena – such as UFO sightings – as 'calls to the absurd' (Kastrup, 2011, p. 7). They are phenomena that refuse to 'bend the knee' to our established models and hint at something more. As we have already seen with James and others, Kastrup detects amongst the many varieties of 'calls to the absurd' some common themes and phenomenological motifs that seem to emerge and recur in vastly different contexts, including:

> [...] their defiance not only of the known laws of physics but – and much more significantly – those of logic and common sense as well; their highly symbolic, metaphorical, psychological character; strong and unexplained intuitions seizing the subject at a deep emotional level; and the occurrence of common motifs such as fairy-like entities (aliens, dwarves, elves), aerial phenomena, zigzagging motion, the sun, and other radiating light sources (Kastrup, 2011, p. 7).

When approached from a comparative perspective, bizarre experiences – such as encounters with the Men in Black – reveal a number of features that connect them to broader motifs in the phenomenology of extraordinary and religious experience (Evans, 1987), and are also shown to induce similar characteristic feeling-responses in experiencers. For example, Peter Rojcewicz gives a detailed narrative description of an MIB encounter given to him by an informant that includes an eerie sense of quiet stillness surrounding the interaction, reminiscent of what paranormal investigator Jenny Randles has called the 'Oz Factor.' The Oz Factor is common in a range of paranormal experiences, and often seems to precede the climactic encounter – whether with a UFO in the sky, Bigfoot in the woods, a gnome-like entity in the garden or an angel in your bedroom. Randles defines it as:

---

[8] This, of course, raises the issue of the influence of different cosmologies/worldviews/ontologies on the experience of the paranormal. For those whose worldview allows for the possibility of spirits, for example, it is not necessarily absurd to encounter one. See Renee Bedard's chapter in this volume, and her comments on the lack of fear of supernormal beings in Anishinaabeg worldview.

> [...] a set of symptoms [...] which [create] the impression of temporarily having left our material world and entered another dream-like place with magical rules [...] It tells us [...] most notably that the percipient has changed their state of consciousness [...] The result is a dreamy and weirdly silent state of mind that is recognised as peculiar [...] even though they do not appreciate what it implies (Randles, 1988, p. 22).

Rojcewicz's MIB account also highlights the strange and awkward movements of the mysterious figures as a trigger for this dreamlike state, and the growing sense of the *mysterium tremendum/horrendum* that eventually engulfs the experiencer: "Within, say, ten seconds, great fear overwhelmed me and for the first time I entertained the idea that this man was otherworldly. Really, I was very frightened" (Rojcewicz, 1984, pp. 163).

As a further illustration of these overlapping high strangeness traits, the following narrative was sent to me by an informant who was looking for help making sense of an extraordinary encounter he and a friend had while walking in the wilderness as teenagers, not far from his friend's home. My informant has given permission for the following extracts from his initial message to me to be included in this chapter. He explains how he and his friend were walking away from the house, down a path toward the surrounding woodland, when:

> [...] both of us immediately saw something out of place [...] below about 30-40 feet away from us in between the trees [there was something] tall, white and three dimensional. It appeared to be completely white and soft like light, but it did not illuminate the trees or ground around it [...] it was shaped in [an] upside down V or U [...] It was so white that you could see the shadow being cast on it while it was swaying like it was a real animal [...]

Instantly apparent in the context of this discussion is the anomalous 'sense of presence' noticed by my informant and his friend – both recognised 'something out of place' in their immediate environment. It is also, therefore, a shared experience, suggesting an objective (or at least inter-subjective) anomalous presence in the woods. That the encounter was with a being of light is also a classical feature of many forms of religious and spiritual experience. The unusual behaviour of the light itself – such as the fact that it did not illuminate the surrounding trees – is also a widely noted theme across a range of extraordinary experiences, including UFO encounters and near-death experiences, during which light often behaves in peculiar ways (cf. Fox, 2003; Puhle, 2013). Perhaps strangest of all is the bizarre shape of the entity, described as 'an upside down V or U' that swayed 'like it was a real animal.' The description is, to use Otto's terminology, of something 'wholly other' – at odds with the morphology of any known living creature. My informant continues his description of the entity he and his friend witnessed:

> [...] It was making creepy swaying movements with its (whole body) [...] It was moving left to right in a specific motion standing on the forest floor in the same area between the trees making absolutely no sound, and there was absolutely no wind. It was beautiful to look at but terrifying at the same time. We watched it in silence as it was swaying and I started to feel impending doom (the sinking feeling in your chest) "set in" and it felt like I was going to die or something bad was going to happen. I told my friend specifically "I don't like this," he agreed, and we immediately left the forest [...]

This extract contains several features that further resonate with other elements of high strangeness experiences that we have been discussing. The 'creepy swaying movements' of the entity, for instance, are reminiscent of the bizarre motions of the otherworldly MIB discussed above. The fact that there was "absolutely no sound, and there was absolutely no wind" recalls the 'Oz Factor' described by Jenny Randles in conjunction with UFO sightings and alien abductions; and Otto's sense of the dual-natured numinous is captured vividly in the way that the swaying entity is described as 'beautiful to look at but terrifying at the same time,' with the experience gradually slipping into the feeling of 'impending doom' and what Otto called *mysterium horrendum*. This is an account with a high number of anomalous information bits "each of which outrages common sense" (Hynek, 1979, p. 42), which might be summed up as:

* An encounter with a non-human entity.
* A sense of the numinous – wonder to begin (*mysterium fascinans*) gradually giving way to fear (*mysterium tremendum/horrendum*).
* The Oz Factor.
* Unusual behaviour of light.
* A sense of the uncanny, surreal, absurd – dream logic pervades.

Other phenomenological elements could likely also be drawn in here, such as the kinds of olfactory phenomena documented by Joshua Cutchin, with sulphurous, burning or ozone smells often being associated with paranormal experiences (Cutchin, 2016). Distinctive sounds are also important – we have already noted the absence of sound in the Oz factor, but rapping, booming and buzzing sounds are also associated with all manner of paranormal experiences, from OBEs and abductions to hauntings and NDEs (Parsons & Cooper, 2015). The following account from my own collection was submitted by a past student of mine, who has given permission for it to be reproduced here. The strange experience was initiated by the sound of a booming but incomprehensible voice. He explains:

> I was around seven years old when my cousin [...] was staying over for the night. My bed was positioned to the right of the window in my bedroom and the curtains were drawn, my cousin was reading [...] A strange deep toned voice with a kind of distorted resonance sounded from the window, capturing both our attention. My cousin told me not to go [...] I was too curious and slowly walked towards the window before opening the curtains. In the centre of the window was a face of light, the bright light seemed to be pulsating inside of the face. It was large enough to engulf the entire centre of the window. The mouth began moving and the deep vibrating muffled voice started to speak [...] I was unable to understand most of it and was too in shock to pay close enough attention [...] I felt locked in place during the event and was in disbelief of what was happening, my cousin jumped off the bed and we both ran downstairs [...] When we approached the window again it had completely gone.

Another shared childhood experience, this time an encounter with a strangely luminous face apparently trying to communicate through a closed window. It is, in some ways, a very different experience, though with many connecting features. Weird sounds, the odd behaviour of pulsing light, the feeling of being 'locked in place.' It is precisely this coming together of numerous highly strange threads that makes the two experiential narratives I have just shared so compelling, in spite of their downright weirdness, and why I think they should be taken seriously. As Mike Clelland suggests: "The more complicated the interwoven details, the more valid it seems" (Clelland, 2020, p. 44).

Parapsychology and High Strangeness

In addition to the phenomenological features discussed in the previous section, psi phenomena also represent another of the central threads running through the apparent diversity of highly strange experiences. Mind-to-Mind communication (telepathy), for example, is a common motif in many varieties of extraordinary experience – from mystical and religious communications with God (Luhrmann, 2012), through to interactions with Bigfoot (Cutchin & Renner, 2020, p. 71), and telepathic communications from alien entities (Mack, 1994, pp. 38-39). As already mentioned, John Keel's famous study of high strangeness, *The Mothman Prophecies*, also covered accounts of a wide range of other psychic experiences leading up to the collapse of the Silver Bridge, including precognitive dreams and prophetic visions (Keel, 2002). Experimental parapsychology has demonstrated statistically compelling evidence for the existence of psi phenomena (Parker & Brusewitz, 2003; Radin, 2006). Given that these phenomena have been repeatedly documented in controlled laboratory conditions, it also seems reasonable to suggest that they might be active in the context of real-world paranormal experiences as well. What contribution does parapsychology make to understanding high strangeness?

One point of contact with the pluralistic themes discussed in this chapter are the well known varieties of psi phenomena revealed in parapsychological experiments over the years. Indeed, 'psi' itself is a catch-all label that encompasses a variety of different ostensible phenomena:

- *Extrasensory Perception*, or ESP (itself an umbrella term incorporating telepathy, clairvoyance, remote viewing, and so on).
- *Psychokinesis*, or PK (further subdivided into micro-PK and macro-PK effects, as well as RSPK – recurrent spontaneous psychokinesis – an alternative to the spirit hypothesis in poltergeist cases).
- *Precognition* (accessing information from the future).
- *Retrocognition* (accessing information from the past).
- *Psychometry* (accessing information from objects).

There are also phenomena and experiences discussed in parapsychology that are clearly related to psi in some way, but that also apparently involve the action of non-physical, and sometimes non-human, agents (e.g. spirits), such as mediumship, which further complicates matters. Psi, like extraordinary experiences more generally, then, is multiple, varied and diverse, and like the other crossovers discussed above, its different strands frequently overlap in lived experience, rendering these neat categories of phenomena difficult to disentangle in the real-world. Parapsychologists Michael Thalbourne and Lance Storm have attempted to address the entanglement of psi phenomena with their concept of 'psychopraxia,' which effectively suggests that both ESP and PK are inseparable from one another, as well as from other 'normal' and 'paranormal' processes of information gathering, or action in the world. They explain that:

> The reason for the ambiguity comes from the fact that ESP and PK are discourse-dependent concepts that have emerged out of a fundamentally dualistic framework – any kind of paranormal cognition is automatically labelled ESP because it largely manifests mentally, and any kind of paranormal action is automatically labelled PK because it largely manifests physically. Researchers tend to avoid any attempt at disambiguation or clarification (Storm & Thalbourne, 2019, p. 9).

What this implies is that there is, perhaps, no real distinction between ESP, PK and the other forms of psi, rather they are all aspects of the same life processes reaching out into the world for information, interaction and communion. It is clear that parapsychology alone does not provide an *explanation* for high strangeness experiences, but the subtle processes that parapsychologists have investigated for the last century *do* seem to play a central role in the enormous variety of highly strange experiences. As such, they are an important part of the puzzle. They also suggest that diversity and the complex interconnectivity of phenomena seems to run all the way down, from the large scale phenomenology of real-world high strangeness experiences, down to the deeper level functioning of psi.

Fundamental Diversity: Cosmology and Consciousness

To briefly summarise where we are at so far: William James highlighted the 'varieties of religious experience,' psychedelic researchers emphasised the role of individual differences in modulating extraordinary experience, (giving rise to more diversity!), parapsychologists have revealed a variety of intersecting psi phenomena, and more recent efforts have brought a broader array of extraordinary experiences into respectable scholarly discourse. As we have seen, high strangeness experiences frequently collapse neat scholarly categories, suggest deeper interconnectedness of extraordinary experiences and phenomena, and are damned in the academy. Psi phenomena are often important features of high strangeness experiences – facilitating communication with extraordinary entities, for example. But like high strangeness experiences, psi also refuses to be put into neat categories, or indeed to provide solid evidence of itself. There might also, therefore, be deeper structures underlying *both* psi and high strangeness, as well as the varieties of extraordinary experience. George Hansen's trickster theory, for example, suggests that the boundary dissolving characteristics of paranormal experiences and phenomena belie a deeper, weirder interconnectedness (Hansen, 2001). This trickster-like quality is also seemingly inherent in other natural systems, and so may represent an even deeper feature or characteristic of the natural world (Hunter, 2020a). Could this trickster-like tendency perhaps represent the *personality* of a cosmic mind, or the personalities of many cosmic minds?

Diversity might also be a deep feature of consciousness itself – just as biological systems tend towards increased biodiversity, so too might consciousness tend towards psychodiversity – and this may have important implications for our understanding of the varieties of high strangeness experiences, amongst other things (cf. Hunter, 2019b; 2021b). Not only does this suggest that there is a broad range of different states of consciousness involved in high strangeness experiences (altered states, trances, and so on), but it also implies that there are a great many different forms of mind and consciousness out there in the world, with which we might interact during such experiences. In a *world of many minds* we might expect to encounter ways of being that are 'alien' to our own particular sensibilities every once in a while (Holroyd, 1979). We might even expect to encounter non-human parts of our own minds. As such, perspectives like panpsychism (the notion that consciousness is a fundamental aspect of reality, see Sjöstedt-Hughes, 2022), and animism (which suggest that the world is made up of persons, not all of which are human, and with whom we must establish good relationships, cf. Harvey, 2005), might provide useful frameworks for contemplating some high strangeness experiences. Encounters with the non-human, then, could be considered one of the defining features of the high strangeness experiences discussed in this book,[9] and their collective implication is that we are embedded within a vastly complex ecosystem of different interacting minds and intelligences (see Hunter, 2019b; Cutchin, 2022).

Furthermore, this vast network of interacting minds may exist across multiple worlds and dimensions – what indigenous scholar Lance Foster has called 'The Invisible Ecosystem' (Foster, 2019). This is an idea that resonates with John Keel's famous notion of the 'superspectrum' – the suggestion that all manner of paranormal entities exist on different frequency ranges, which occasionally interact with our own (Keel, 2013). Paranormal researcher David Scott Rogo also came to a similar conclusion, arguing that the varieties of high strangeness experiences recorded throughout history point in the direction of multiple co-existent realities. In his book *Beyond Reality* (1990), which surveys a range of paranormal and spiritual experiences, he explains his intention:

> [...] to show that the existence of psychic, spiritual, and so-called 'extraterrestrial' forces points to the possibility of multiple realities [...] such phenomena as ghosts, UFOs, and religious miracles reflect the existence of parallel realities probably coexisting in time/space with our everyday reality (Rogo, 1990, p. 11).

This sentiment is also echoed in Jacques Vallée's 1988 book *Dimensions: A Casebook of Alien Contact*, in which he argues that:

> [...] the UFO phenomenon *represents evidence for other dimensions beyond spacetime*; the UFOs may not come from ordinary space, but from a *multiverse* which is all around us, and of which we have stubbornly refused to consider the disturbing reality in spite of the evidence available to us for centuries (Vallée, 1988, p. 284).

Multiple dimensions were also one of the possible explanations put forward by researchers to explain the weird phenomena observed at the Skinwalker Ranch in Utah (Kelleher & Knapp, 2005), and have been evoked in recent years to help make sense of some of the more unusual

---

9   It is for this reason that I propose the 'Non-Humanities' as a parallel to Jeffrey Kripal's 'Superhumanities,' and as a way of making sure that we do not fall into too much of an anthropocentric mode in our explorations of the extraordinary.

aspects of the psychedelic experience, such as their tendency to transport the experiencer to labyrinthine alien 'otherworlds' (Luke, 2019; Sjöstedt-Hughes, 2022). Indeed, the notion of higher dimensional spaces has long been of interest to those seeking to make sense of unusual experiences. As historian of religion Christopher White explains, 'these ideas [...] restore a sense that the world is greater than anything our eyes can see, helping to forge an unexpected kind of spirituality' (White, 2018).

Multiplicity, fractal diversity and a capricious[10] resistance to any kind of neat classification appear to be core features of extraordinary experience – and perhaps of reality more generally – and the deeper into the weird that we descend the more complex, multifarious, interdimensional and interconnected things seem to become.

Ontological Flooding and the Deep Weird

Given the mind-boggling varieties, dimensions and trickster-like characteristics we have been exploring over the preceding pages (not to mention what is yet to come), it seems crucial to develop a framework that is able to embrace the complexity of high strangeness.

In previous publications I have argued that the reductionist approaches that are usually applied to extraordinary experiences and phenomena in the academic context have generally been unsuccessful in providing satisfactory accounts of them. In my ethnographic work on spirit mediumship at the Bristol Spirit Lodge (Hunter, 2020b), for example, it became clear that none of the dominant explanatory models in anthropology or psychology were able to accommodate the complexity of the mediumistic practices and experiences that I observed and participated in. Anthropologists have tended to interpret spirit possession in terms of the dominant paradigm of social functionalism, for example – that is that spirit possession practices exist solely because they perform important functions in the societies where they take place, especially in helping to maintain social cohesion and to provide socially acceptable modes of expression for repressed members of society. Cognitive, psychological and psychopathological interpretations are also common, essentially explaining mediumship

---

[10] In some respects the figure of the Great God Pan would seem to be a fitting archetype for high strangeness – capricious, half-human, fun, terrifying, all at once (Robichaud, 2021).

and possession in terms of faulty processing of cognitive information, as a psychological defence mechanism in the face of mortality, or as the product of physiological or psychological pathology, respectively. All of these explanatory frameworks sit comfortably within mainstream science's dominant materialist ontology, and provide a neat way for such experiences and phenomena to be explained away, but none of them quite live up to the complexity of the real-world experience of mediumship and possession as it plays out in the field.

For instance, social functionalist accounts tend to ignore the role and importance of personal experience in mediumship – what it actually feels like, phenomenologically, for mediums and those who engage with them – in favour of abstract social functions. Cognitive approaches attempt to explain possession in terms of the ways that human beings process information and make sense of the world, but do not adequately account for the other elements of possession, such as the subjective experience of the possessed and its socio-cultural significance. Pathological approaches have been shown to be flawed by the fact that in many societies becoming a medium is a positive life choice that may be desirable, and is clearly differentiated from illness. The physiological evidence also suggests that mediumship should not be considered pathological – mediumistic states appear to have quite different neurological correlates to pathological conditions (Bastos, *et al.*, 2016). The reduction of mediumship to pathology is also problematised by the fact that in the Western context people who claim to be mediums are often more psychologically 'healthy' than non-mediums (Roxburgh & Roe, 2011). Further to all of this, none of these dominant frameworks take into consideration the (damned) evidence from psychical research and parapsychology, which suggests that some mediums (at least) *are* able to access accurate information from anomalous sources (Beischel & Schwartz, 2007), and have been observed to produce extraordinary séance phenomena under controlled conditions. No account of mediumship and possession can be complete, then, if it ignores the data from parapsychology, or the meaning of the experience for the experiencer, as well as for their wider socio-cultural milieu.

This is not to say, of course, that mediumship does not perform social functions (it really does), or that cognitive factors are not involved (of course they are), or that mediumship does not perform important psychological functions (it does), or that there is a clear boundary line between mediumship and mental illness (there is not). All of these factors *are* involved, but the crucial point is that the phenomenon of mediumship cannot be reduced to any single one of them. Indeed, as the parapsychological data suggests, there may be many more factors simultaneously in action (such as psi and the possibility of discarnate spirits), that need to be taken into consideration for modelling and theory construction (Winkelman, 1982). This is not a problem that is limited to the study of mediumship or the paranormal. The real world is complex, and as such requires equally complex ways of thinking about it.

In a sense what is needed is a 'systems' approach to extraordinary experience – a way of understanding the interaction of multiple contributing processes in any given event or experience, including psychological, physiological, socio-cultural, ecological, parapsychological, non-human, and many other factors. Explaining the systems view of nature, theoretical physicist Fritjof Capra writes:

> The new vision of reality we have been talking about is based on an awareness of the essential interrelatedness and interdependence of all phenomena – physical, biological, psychological, social and cultural. It transcends current disciplinary boundaries and will be pursued within new institutions (Capra, 1985, p. 285).

My own term for an approach that is able to transcend current disciplinary and theoretical boundaries, and entertain multiple concurrent theories and processes, is 'ontological flooding' (Hunter, 2015a; 2016; 2017a; 2017b). The idea emerged over the course of my doctoral research (Hunter, 2020b), and partially in response to the dominance of ontological bracketing in phenomenological social science research on the paranormal. The standard approach in the social sciences is to bracket out questions about the reality of the paranormal in order to get on with the business of researching the social processes that are going on – social facts. In other words, it allows researchers to study those aspects of the paranormal that do not contradict the dominant materialist models of the social and physical sciences, but not those aspects that might threaten this, such as its potential reality (Northcote, 2004). This essentially turns the paranormal (as well as any other worldview, excepting the dominant view) into a system of erroneous beliefs about the world. It excludes the experiential components of the life-worlds of informants, and any consideration of their implications. Again, they become 'damned facts.' Ontological flooding is an effort to overcome this problem. Here is how I explained the term in *Manifesting Spirits*, the book based on my doctoral research on mediumship at the Bristol Spirit Lodge:

Ontological flooding is essentially a position that emphasises complexity and the interaction of multiple contributing factors in any given situation or phenomenon. From this perspective, no single explanatory framework or ontological scheme is able to give a fully satisfying account of what is taking place in a given ethnographic context, though they may give indications of particular contributing processes of *becoming* (Hunter, 2020b, p. 4).

Furthermore:

[...] we do not begin our investigation from the position of certainty that our ontology [whatever that might be] is the only one that can really be taken seriously. "We" might have it all wrong. Everything is equally possible, everything is equally questionable, and nothing is certain. This is not a rejection of science or the scientific method, but an expansion of it. What I am calling for is a return to awe and wonder in science (Hunter, 2020b, p. 164).

Ontological flooding has also been recognised by others working in the paranormal field as a useful framework for grappling with high strangeness and expanding the scope of paranormal research. Sean Esbjörn-Hargens (2020), for example, writes that the "engagement and development of new paradoxical and integrative methods (e.g., Jack Hunter's [...] ontological flooding, Jeff Kripal's [...] comparative practices, Jacque Vallée's [...] recursive unsolvability, Karen Barad's [...] agential cuts: cutting together/apart, Jenny Rice's [...] gorgoylian methods: making something new via strange juxtapositions)" can be used to "invite ambiguity, synchronicity and the trickster as core components of the research and data" (Esbjörn-Hargens, 2020, p. 4).

An ontologically flooded perspective also suggests that we should look beyond the confines of the dominant models of Western science to try to make sense of the world, and not to exclude phenomena or experiences that resist our categorisation. This would entail an exploration of other modes of understanding and engaging with the world – different epistemological (how we find out about the world) and ontological (what we consider to be real) models, in addition to those of the physical sciences. This must include, for example, perspectives from traditional and indigenous knowledge systems, which often begin from very different first principles to those of mainstream materialist physical and social science, including, for example, an emphasis on the animacy of the world, the importance of reciprocity and relationship and the role and value of ceremony as a mode of engagement with the human and non-human world (Kimmerer, 2011; Tuhiwai Smith, 2012; Foster, 2019; Yunkaporta, 2019). This would effectively entail a 'decolonisation' of paranormal research (cf. Glazier, 2021), and a willingness to bring new concepts, perspectives and insights to the field.

With these ideas in mind, an ontologically flooded perspective would seem to be an ideal starting point for making sense of the large "number of information bits […] each of which is difficult to explain in common sense terms" (Hynek, 1979, p. 42), that characterise high strangeness experiences and phenomena, and to provide a framework for approaching mystery from multiple simultaneous points of view.

Conclusion

The term 'High Strangeness' was introduced into the discourse of paranormal research as a scientific term – by a scientist – as a framework for making sense of some of the most complex extraordinary experiences. As a scientific term, High Strangeness may have broader usefulness in the wider study of extraordinary and religious experience. There is a great deal in the approaches of Fortean writers that could help to expand, and breathe new life into the academic study of extraordinary experiences. The high strangeness perspective encourages us to take seriously those elements of extraordinary experience that might seem bizarre or absurd, and to try to understand them in a comparative context – to look for similarities and differences between as wide an array of extraordinary experiences as possible. This may go some way towards helping to bridge the gap between popular Fortean perspectives on the paranormal and academic research on religious and extraordinary experience – revealing not only the threads that link the highly strange to established themes of religious experience research, but also showing how elements of religious experience often tip over into the highly strange. High Strangeness, then, may not simply be a feature of outlying cases, as I suggested at the start of this chapter, but might actually be a fundamental characteristic of extraordinary experiences more generally, and as such deserves wider scholarly attention. Facing up to high strangeness also amounts to an acknowledgement that there is much in our world that our models do not yet accommodate, which is both unsettling for the dominant perspectives and an opportunity to learn.

This Book

The chapter contributors gathered together in this book have been carefully selected so as to give as broad and far-reaching a perspective on the deep weird as possible, as well as to scope out new and innovative directions for researching and theorising extraordinary phenomena and experiences. To this end, the book is split into three interconnected parts.

Part 1: Deep Weird Phenomena

As with some of the other books in the 'varieties' tradition discussed above, each chapter in the first part covers a particular kind of experience, but with an emphasis on those cases that defy neat classification and push boundaries. There are, of course, likely other phenomena that could be discussed as well – diversity, as we have seen, is fundamental in this area – but it would be too large of an undertaking to encapsulate *all* of the varieties and permutations of extraordinary experiences. In the pages that follow, then, we are offered a revealing cross-section of the deep weird – a perspective that encourages us to keep an eye open for intersecting motifs, characteristics and processes across a spectrum of extraordinary experiences and phenomena.

To begin our descent into the depths, philosopher Sharon Hewitt Rawlette's chapter gently allows us to dip our toes into the waters of the weird with a discussion of the experience and implications of synchronicities, which she defines as "any alignment of events that could be mere chance but that nevertheless suggests a possible hidden connection, Jungian or otherwise." But these are *weird* and convoluted synchronicities – cases that cannot be neatly explained in common sense terms. As is likely already clear, synchronicities permeate the deep weird.

Next, in his chapter, cross-cultural researcher Gregory Shushan disentangles the universal, cultural, and individual layers of the enigmatic and widespread near-death experience. As we have been exploring in this introduction, the NDE is shown to be *both* a universal experience *and* an individual psychologically and socio-culturally modulated phenomenon, and cannot be reduced to any one of these factors in isolation from the rest (as is often attempted in studies of NDEs and other extraordinary experiences).

Staying with disembodied states of consciousness, medical anthropologist Samantha Lee Treasure next introduces us to some of the further-out reaches of the out-of-body experience. Treasure charts the hyper-real transformations that are taking place in some contemporary forms of astral projection, with a new generation of 'Shifters' claiming to regularly have very real out-of-body encounters with all manner of fictional characters and worlds. The OBE landscape is changing and the entities encountered in OBE states are becoming increasingly varied.

Michael Grosso's chapter then turns to religious miracles, and considers what such phenomena might tell us about the nature of the imagination and the future direction of human evolution. Extraordinary phenomena documented under well controlled conditions with various religious and spiritual mystics and ascetics are offered as examples of the future physical, biological and psychological evolution of humanity.

Continuing the previous chapter's exploration of the more extraordinary end of the mind-body spectrum, Zofia Weaver next examines one of the strangest reported phenomena to have emerged from the nineteenth century Spiritualist movement – ectoplasmic materialisation. During séances at the turn of the twentieth century many impeccably credentialed scientists claimed to have observed mediums "produce extra limbs, heads, or whole phantoms with an independent life of their own that then fade away" in carefully controlled séance conditions. My own fieldwork with trance and physical mediums in twenty-first century Britain also involved this enigmatic substance, which has done anything but disappear completely (Hunter, 2020b).

Then, Alan Murdie's chapter on the enigmatic poltergeist phenomenon begins by detailing his own involvement in some of the most unusual poltergeist cases of the twentieth century, having had the opportunity to work alongside legendary poltergeist researchers Maurice Grosse and Guy Lyon Playfair. Drawing on his background in law and psychical research, Murdie builds an evidential case for the reality of poltergeist phenomena, including some of their more bizarre manifestations.

Next, David Luke's chapter revolves around his own extraordinary encounter with a terrifying entity that referred to itself as 'Za' during a DMT trip on the banks of the River Ganges. The entity, with a thousand eyes, described as the "ominous luminous voluminous numinous," proceeded to let our intrepid psychonaut know that he "should not be there and that [he] should certainly not be peering into the hallowed space beyond [...] which it clearly guarded." Luke's research takes him on an ontological quest to make sense of his experience, employing the lenses of folklore, mythology and parapsychopharmacology to piece the puzzle together.

Folklorist and fairy investigator Simon Young's chapter then moves to chart the evolution of fairy encounters from traditional interactions (as recorded in folklore) through to contemporary experiences, which have proliferated in some very bizarre directions. As well as surveying the characteristics and behaviours of traditional fairies, Young provides some new categories of fairy entities for the twenty-first century, drawing on data from his excellent work with the *Fairy Census* (Young, 2018), which suggest that "Fairy is a far more chaotic place today than two hundred years ago."

From here we tumble deeper still down the rabbit hole, and further into the varieties of non-human interactions, with Zelia Edgar's discussion of some of the most unusual high strangeness entity encounters and their psychological effects on witnesses. We are presented with a dizzying array of deeply weird interactions with Bigfoot, Mothman, telepathic Dogmen and "unearthly pink, glowing humanoids."

Part 2: Researching the Deep Weird

With the next group of chapters we shift focus slightly – away from the range and variety of extraordinary experiences and phenomena and toward different approaches to researching and making sense of them.

To begin, Leonardo Breno Martins provides an extremely useful overview of methodological and ethical issues that arise specifically in the context of conducting interviews with witnesses of anomalous phenomena. Martins notes that "the analysis of personal first-hand narratives acquires central importance" in the study of extraordinary experiences, and as such "[i]nterviews are one of the most promising methods for collecting" data. It is therefore critical for the purposes of good research to develop qualitative interview skills that are both ethical and methodologically sound, and that elicit high quality data for analysis.

Next, folklorist Peter M. Rojcewicz's chapter elaborates his 'extraordinary encounter continuum hypothesis,' which is an effort geared towards de-compartmentalising the folkloric study of extraordinary entity encounters. Rojcewicz explains: "All the traditions along the Extraordinary Encounter Continuum are discrete but related. They are separate but not separated, like an individual's relationship to a hand. Although the traditions can be distinguished from each other, they nevertheless display similar complex patterns of appearance and activity." The extraordinary encounter continuum hypothesis is a framework to help make sense of the varieties of reported interactions with supernormal beings.

Barbara A. Fisher and Christopher Diltz then go on to outline an innovative project they have undertaken to create a user-friendly searchable database of anomalous humanoid encounters, building on the work of Fortean researcher Albert S. Rosales, who has collected and catalogued thousands of historical and contemporary cases. New developments in computing, specifically involving the implementation of artificial intelligence, have made it possible to realise the dreams of earlier researchers of high strangeness to apply statistical approaches to large datasets of extraordinary entity encounters (cf. Lorenzen, 1977). Fisher, Diltz and their colleagues are doing great work expanding the scope and capability of high strangeness research.

Part 3: Modelling the Deep Weird

In the final part of the book we turn to consider different frameworks, models and ontologies for making sense the deep weird and its place in our conceptualisations of reality.

In his chapter, Joshua Cutchin takes a novel perspective on high strangeness experiences, employing cinematic techniques as a lens on the weird. As already alluded to above, high strangeness experiences often seem to 'play out' in front of witnesses like dreams or surrealist films, and frequently appear to be deliberately orchestrated to induce maximum disorientation in the experiencer. Cutchin explains: "We may never meet the filmmakers, but perhaps understanding cinematic tools will yield new insight" into the nature of high strangeness experiences.

Anthony Peake's chapter is an exploration of the egregorial model proposed in his 2016 book *The Hidden Universe*. Drawing on concepts from the neuropsychology of hallucinations and models from quantum physics Peake seeks to provide a rationally grounded framework for comprehending encounters with what appear to be mind-manifested non-human entities.

Next, psychedelic philosopher of mind Peter Sjöstedt-Hughes presents a philosophical evaluation of panpsychism as a solution to the mind-body problem – the hard problem of consciousness, that is how mind is related to matter. According to panpsychism mind is fundamental to matter, and as such is in fact ubiquitous in nature. Sjöstedt-Hughes explains: "The complexity of the human body is parallel to the complexity of the human mind, the simplicity of a particle being parallel to the simplicity of the mind associated therewith. A human brain and body may be necessary for human consciousness, but not necessary for non-human forms of consciousness." Panpsychism opens up many possibilities for exploring and making sense of deep weird encounters with the non-human.

Cosmic witch Susan Demeter's contribution then outlines an experimental approach to conjuring through ritual magick. She explains how an "experimental conjuring model asks us to see a door where others see a wall. It invites us to cross over the boggle threshold and immerse ourselves in the deep weird. The model I am working towards pushes the boundaries of what is generally accepted as consensus reality."

Finally, Renee E. Mazinegiizhigoo-kwe Bedard's chapter on *Jiisakiiwigaan* – the Anishinaabeg Shaking Tent Ceremony – gives insight into an indigenous cosmological perspective on the deep weird. Here weird entities are welcomed and embraced for their capacity to bring about sacred metamorphosis in those who participate with them. Anishinaabeg metaphysics lacks the "overt fear, disregard, distrust, and horror, which values are so normalised with mainstream western pedagogy related to the deep weird. Instead, Anishinaabeg responses emphasise creativity, wonder, mystery, ethical responsibility, relationality, reciprocity, and learning." As well as providing this counterweight to the dominant 'scientific' mode of discussing the deep weird, this chapter also serves another important function for this book with its final words, which give thanks and acknowledgment to the weird beings and phenomena we have invoked in these pages, and which give us so much entertainment and food for thought.

Acknowledgements

Thanks to Dr Michael Grosso, Prof. Bettina Schmidt, Dr Jake Glazier, Joshua Cutchin and Tony Eccles for their comments on earlier sections of this chapter. Thanks also to Dr Nancy Zingrone for her encouragement in the publication of this volume.

PART 1
DEEP WEIRD PHENOMENA

SYNCHRONICITY

SHARON HEWITT RAWLETTE

In January 2005, I was visiting China for the first time and staying with an American friend outside the city of Chengdu, in Sichuan Province. One day we went into the city to do some shopping, and I found a pair of boots I really liked. I rarely buy clothes or shoes, but these were something special, so I purchased them. When we got back to our house on the outskirts of the city, I opened the box and discovered that both of the boots I had been given were for the same foot. The problem was, neither my friend nor I had any idea how to get back to that shoe store. We had happened upon it while wandering around the vast city and were clueless as to how to retrace our steps. I was really disappointed that my new boots had turned out to be unwearable, but there was nothing I could do. As the Chinese say, "meiyou banfa": there is no solution.

Either that evening or the next, my friend and I were back downtown, and we were following a group of her friends up a street when we noticed a commotion on the sidewalk up ahead. As we got closer, we could see that people were gathered around a huge pile of shoes in the middle of the sidewalk. They were digging through the pile taking whatever they wanted, and, at the same time, more shoes were being thrown out of the store that stood nearby. We were bewildered as to what was happening, but when I looked up at the storefront, I realized that this was the place where I had bought my boots. It also seemed clear that, whatever was going on, this store was not going to be in business tomorrow, so I figured it was now or never. I started digging through the pile on the sidewalk and almost immediately found the boot I needed: right style, right size, right foot.

I walked away with the boot and wore that pair for years afterward, until the sole of one of them wore completely through. They were my favourite boots I have ever owned. But I never did figure out what was going on at that store that night, or what mysterious force had guided our group down the right street at just the right time to catch the entire contents of the store being thrown onto the sidewalk in front of us. Frankly, the whole production seemed like overkill. Would it not have been much easier – and less disturbing to the order of the universe – to make sure I was given the right shoe in the first place? Did an entire place of business need to be pillaged just to get me one little boot?

Unlike many of the other deeply weird experiences examined in this book, deeply weird synchronicities do not involve any obviously paranormal events. The experience I have just recounted did not involve any ghosts or levitation or missing time. And yet, the way in which the events occurred – solving my boot problem in such a ridiculous, improbable way – smacks of purpose and intention. But whose? And what was their ultimate aim? A more usual type of synchronicity would have been one in which I happened upon the shoe store again by chance and was able to go inside and exchange one of my boots for the one that would fit the proper foot. But, instead, my missing boot was delivered to me without my even having to go to the trouble of looking for the store or speaking to a single soul. The missing boot was quite literally thrown into my path, and all I had to do was push a few other shoes out of the way and pick it up. It was, quite frankly, *very weird*.

I have been studying coincidence and synchronicity for a decade now, and there are certain patterns I have seen over and over. I am no longer surprised to see synchronicities deliver to people things they need, though it still delights me to see this process in action. I am, however, still surprised when I see a relatively trivial need met in such an ostentatious way. Generally, I assume that the ostentation is designed to get the experiencer's attention, but it is noteworthy how often it fails at that goal. It is very common for people to have weird experiences like this and then to promptly forget about them, maybe because there is nothing else in their experience with which to connect them. I certainly forgot about this experience. In fact, I did not remember it at any time during the three years I was writing my book *The Source and Significance of Coincidences* (2019). It only came to mind two years later, when I started research for this essay.

Let me give you an even weirder example. This one comes from author Trish MacGregor, whose husband Rob is also a writer. Trish recounted the following in a recent email to me:

> It was 1988. Rob and I travelled to Venezuela with my parents, the first time we'd gone back since my parents, sister, and I left that country and moved to the U.S. Our destination was the Gran Sabana, one of the most fascinating wilderness regions on the planet. Rob hauled around a clunky Radio Shack laptop computer and found time to work on the rewrite of *Indiana Jones and the Last Crusade*, the novel adapted from the script. It was an ideal setting to be working on that novel – soaring buttes, waterfalls, forest, an area steeped in legends and myths.
>
> From Gran Sabana, Rob and I flew on to Merida, an area in the mountains, and my parents returned to Caracas, where Rob and I were to catch our flight to Merida. The synchronicity happened while we waited in line for that flight.
>
> At the time, the Colombian drug cartel had been using Caracas to export cocaine and the government was cracking down. All passengers had to carry their luggage so it could be checked before boarding the flight. Military guys were everywhere, all of them armed with assault rifles, and the atmosphere was tense and uneasy.
>
> The guards were particularly interested in the man in front of us, a tall middle-aged Venezuelan. He wore a dark, three-piece suit and his only luggage was a briefcase. The guards were particularly interested in his briefcase and demanded that he open it. Slowly, the man unlatched it and the guards leaned forward to see what was inside. Since we were directly behind him, we leaned in also.
>
> There was only one item in the briefcase – a paperback copy of one of my novels, *Fevered*, a title that described the environment. I used a pseudonym for the book, Alison Drake, so it wasn't like I could tap the man on the shoulder and tell him the author was right behind him. Even if I'd had proof that I'd written the book, I was too shocked by the synchronicity to say anything.
>
> [...] I couldn't fully understand the clue or where it might lead unless I spoke to the man and asked why he was carrying that book. I never even thought to go after the man and ask. The environment wasn't exactly conducive to it – too many guns – but I could have caught up with him outside or looked for him once we got on the plane. I never saw him again.

The tense military atmosphere, the strangely otherwise empty briefcase carried by a man in a suit, and the fact that Trish never saw this man again, not even on the plane, remind me of the Men in Black – those mysterious men in suits who approach UFO witnesses, generally claiming to be military officers and advising the witnesses to keep quiet about what they have seen. There is often something decidedly "off" about these men, in their appearance or behaviour. For instance, one of these men, who claimed to be an officer in the American Air Force, was offered some Jell-O and attempted to drink it, apparently not knowing that it was supposed to be consumed with a spoon (Keel, 2013, p. 200). These men often disappear mysteriously and have untraceable identities and license plate numbers.

The man in Trish's airport story reminds me of one of these guys, as though he was a character created solely to play this bit part in Trish's life story. I mean, who takes an airplane flight with nothing in their briefcase but a single novel? Was this guy's prop master on a budget? Or was the briefcase left otherwise empty to make sure that Trish would see the book and maximise the drama of the moment?

Recently, Trish has reflected on the possible meaning of this event and wonders if it was connected to some big changes that happened in her life not long after. "Less than a year later our daughter, Megan was born," she says. "Six weeks after that we moved into our first house, Rob's novelisation of *Indiana Jones and the Last Crusade* hit the *NY Times* bestseller list, and he got a contract from LucasFilms to write six prequels to the novelisation. I got another two-book contract from Ballantine." The following year, Trish's editor at Ballantine – the man who had launched her career – died. His death led to her changing publishers and then to her parting from her agent, another person who had been with her since she got started in the profession. And her agent then died less than a year later. So, the few years following this synchronicity involving Trish's novel *Fevered* were clearly transformative, especially with regard to her writing career. Was the novel in the briefcase foretelling or marking these coming events in some symbolic way? It is hard to say for sure. But the event was highly strange, and it begs for an explanation, even if there is no simple one near at hand.

Of course, high strangeness is a relative concept. What seems deeply weird to one individual will make perfect sense to another who has had more experiences of that type. Perhaps some readers will find the synchronicities I have just related to be perfectly explainable, maybe as winks from the custodians of the "matrix." On the other hand, there may be other synchronicities that I take to be easily explainable that others will regard as deeply weird. Their categorisation depends on what a person has previously been exposed to and whether their worldview has already expanded to incorporate synchronicities of that particular type.

Scholarly discussion of synchronicity has so far been largely dominated by the ideas of Carl Jung, according to whom a synchronicity is best explained as an acausal conjunction between an inner (psychological) event and an outer (physical) event, both of which carry a similar meaning, which Jung understood in terms of archetypes. For instance, one might dream about a potent symbol of one's current psychological reality and then the following day encounter this symbol in waking life – just as Jung's patient related a dream of a golden scarab, a symbol of rebirth, and then a golden scarab came knocking at the windowpane (Jung, 2010, pp. 22, 109-110).

Even more simply (and somewhat more mechanistically), many synchronicities can be explained via psychic connections between the human mind and the rest of the world. Once we allow for the reality of psi – telepathy, clairvoyance, precognition, and psychokinesis – we have gone a long way toward explaining many of the everyday synchronicities people experience: thinking of someone right before they call, or dreaming of something that then happens. Katrin Windsor, for instance, told me about a time when she was wondering how an old friend of hers named Gus was doing, only to turn on the television and immediately see an image of Gus being interviewed on the news because he was stuck at an airport.

While these synchronicities can be very striking, and in some cases life-changing, in this chapter I want to focus on synchronicities that resist explanation in terms of straightforward inner/outer correlations, whether understood according to the Jungian archetypal paradigm or as the products of experiencer psi. I want to examine types of synchronicities that have been neglected in the scholarly literature precisely because they do not lend themselves to either of these common modes of explanation. After all, it is the experiences that do not fit into existing categories that offer us the greatest opportunity to expand our understanding of reality!

Before we dive into further examples, however, let me say a brief word about terminology. There is some dispute about the best word to designate an alignment of events that could just be coincidental but that nevertheless suggests a possible hidden connection. In my previous work, I have used the term 'coincidence' to cover all such alignments of events, whether they turn out to be the products of chance or something deeper. I liked this term because it avoided the presupposition that these alignments were meaningful, when that is a question the investigator often wants to leave open. 'Coincidence' also seemed preferable to the term 'synchronicity' because it didn't presuppose a Jungian interpretation of the events in question.

However, in the last few years, I have begun to be persuaded that 'synchronicity' has, in popular usage, become the generic term for coincidences that *suggest a possible hidden connection*. While there are some who still want to restrict its use to events that match Jung's original definition, it is my impression that most people who use the term today are unaware of the precise content of Jung's theory and are using it in a theory-neutral way. 'Synchronicity' has come to mean any intriguing coincidence in much the same way that 'Kleenex' has come to mean any facial tissue. Given that this is how the language is evolving, I have chosen not to hold out against it any longer. Please understand my use of 'synchronicity' in this essay to cover any alignment of events that could be mere chance but that nevertheless suggests a possible hidden connection, Jungian or otherwise.

Synchronicities Related to Survival of Death

The first broad type of deeply weird synchronicity I would like to draw attention to are those synchronicities that strongly suggest the survival of consciousness after bodily death. Ostensible after-death communication is a vein of synchronicity intensively mined by the popular press (Guggenheim & Guggenheim, 1995; Jackson, 2020), but there has been little scholarly discussion of this type of synchronicity (excepting Schwartz, 2011). While there is a large body of scholarly literature on the subject of life after death, this has primarily been focused on blatantly paranormal phenomena like mediumship, apparitions, and poltergeists. This literature, when combined with research on near-death experiences and memories of life before birth, provides cohesive evidence in support of the reality of the survival of human consciousness after death (see Rawlette, 2022), and I believe it also provides strong reason to consider the possibility that, in certain synchronicities, it is not the psi abilities of living people that are at work but the psi abilities of the so-called dead.

Now, I want to acknowledge right off the bat that there are many cases of after-death synchronicity that, while meaningful to those who experience them, are difficult for others to find convincing as messages from the deceased. These synchronicities often involve the unexpected appearance of birds or butterflies, or of small objects like coins, and they often occur on important anniversaries, or in response to specific requests for a sign of the deceased's continuing presence. Such synchronicities are often accompanied by a strong feeling of the presence of the deceased, which can be very convincing to the person experiencing it, but third parties can have an understandably hard time believing that they are truly caused by the dead.

Nevertheless, there are synchronicities in which the connection to a deceased source is suggested in a more objectively convincing way. For one thing, specific synchronicities are often mentioned by mediums who have no normal knowledge of them. Take, for example, the experience of geologist Jim Calzia, who had been with his childhood sweetheart, Kathy, for 45 years when she passed away from the H1N1 virus. After her death, his grief was bottomless; nothing seemed to assuage it. One night, he was driving home from a family reunion when he saw two meteors streak down through the sky. He was sure they were going to hit the ground, and he braced for the shock of impact. But suddenly the meteors were gone. Everything looked as if they had never been there at all. A few hours after this event, unbeknownst to Jim, his daughter-in-law had a reading with medium Laura Lynne Jackson. Jim later saw a video of the reading, during which his daughter-in-law asked Jackson if Jim's wife had tried contacting him after her death. Jackson told her, "Oh, yes. She has tried and tried and tried. But every time she gets close he goes deeper and deeper into the darkness. She doesn't want to hurt him, but she keeps trying. She has tried everything. She says she has even tried meteors!" (Jackson, 2015, p. 150).

While the mere fact that a medium was aware of Jim's meteor experience does not prove that it was a message from the deceased (she could have just been picking up on the meteors clairvoyantly, for example), it is one important type of proof among many others. In other cases of synchronicity, the involvement of a deceased person is indicated by an apparition. Dr Mary Helen Hensley, a chiropractor and metaphysical healer living in Ireland, tells how her daughter Jemma had developed a terrible cough that was frequently so violent it made her start vomiting, but Mary Helen could not seem to find a remedy. One day, in what seemed like an unrelated coincidence, Mary Helen heard two different people, in two different contexts, mention Mount Argus, a location in Ireland that she never remembered hearing about before. The very next morning, her daughter woke her up and said she had something to show her. Jemma told her that "Mr. Burke," a deceased man who used to live in their home and who often appeared to the family, had woken her up to give her a clue about how to fix her cough. She took her mother to a brick wall in their home and pointed to what Mr. Burke had shown her. Engraved in several of the bricks were the words "Mount Argus."

When Mary Helen asked a friend about the significance of this place, she was told that Saint Charles of Mount Argus was known for healing chest ailments. The next day, before she could figure out what to do with this piece of information, an acquaintance of hers who knew nothing about what was going on brought her an unexpected gift. "Something told me you could use this," he said. It was a small card to which was taped a relic of Saint Charles of Mount Argus. Mary Helen decided to put it beneath Jemma's pillow. Jemma not only slept peacefully through that night but never had her violent, chronic cough again (Hensley, 2015, pp. 261-268).

In this next case, the connection to the deceased is confirmed by a dream, as well as by the way in which the events in question reflect unique aspects of his personality. In his book *An Atheist in Heaven* (2016) author and film director Paul Davids relates an unsettling event that occurred a week after he spoke at a tribute honouring his late friend Forrest J Ackerman. Davids was alone in his vacation home in Santa Fe when he printed a log of the previous year's business meetings and phone calls to review in preparation for filing his taxes. He scanned the document quickly and threw it on the bed while he made a trip to the bathroom. When he picked it up again upon coming out of the bathroom, he discovered the document had been altered: a line on the first page had been blacked out with ink, in what appeared to be very careful and deliberate fashion. In fact, unlike the rest of the ink on the page, the ink used to black out this line was still wet and took minutes to fully dry. Again, Davids was alone in the house, and the doors were locked.

Davids went to his computer to verify what words had been in the line that was blacked out. They read, "Spoke to Joe Amodei." Joe Amodei was not someone Davids knew well. He had only spoken to him this one time, on the phone. It was not clear what the significance of blacking out this man's name could be, but Davids suspected his deceased friend Ackerman might have had a hand in the incident. In fact, he had a suspicion that the way in which this line had been struck out matched the way Ackerman used to edit documents.

Davids decided to call Ackerman's assistant to inquire about this possibility, but he did not get a chance to mention what had happened before the assistant immediately launched into a story of his own. During the week between the tribute to Ackerman and the ink incident, the assistant had had an extremely real-seeming dream where Ackerman "walked into his bedroom with a mischievous smile on his face" and they discussed his thoughts on the recent tribute in his honour. The assistant said to Davids, "I'm a skeptic, Paul, you know that, but it was as if Forry [Ackerman] really came and spoke to me."

It was at this point that the significance of the ink obliteration hit Davids. Ackerman's assistant's name was Joe Moe. The phrase "Spoke to Joe Amodei" seemed an awful lot like a stand-in for "Spoke to Joe Moe." What was more, making puns and playing with names inside of names were two things Ackerman had loved to do while alive. And even though Ackerman had been an atheist, he had told Davids that, if he discovered that life indeed went on after death, he would "drop him a line" to let him know. Obliterating a line of Davids' tax records seemed like a pretty literal fulfilment of that promise. Furthermore, when Davids got a chance to examine some of the manuscripts Ackerman had edited during his life, he found clear similarities in style. Photographs of some examples can be found in his book (Davids & Schwartz, 2016, pp. 31-32, 41-58).

Given that there are cases like this in which evidence for the involvement of the deceased is so clearly indicated, it makes sense to consider this possibility in cases where the connection to the deceased is less explicit. And there are a great many deeply weird examples in this category. For example, many more strange synchronicities and paranormal happenings occurred in association with the death of Forrest J Ackerman. I will mention just one other. Besides puns and word games, Ackerman loved "creepy, crawly things." So his friend Sean Fernald thought it would be a good idea to ask Ackerman to demonstrate that he was still alive in the beyond by making a spider bite him. Fernald says he made this choice because he had not had a spider bite in ten years, so he thought it was an improbable enough occurrence to make a good sign. Within a couple of days of the request, he got *two* spider bites. Another interesting fact pointed out by Davids is that, although Fernald was not aware of it when he asked for the sign, Ackerman once wrote a short story called "A Letter to an Angel" that featured "the concept that a spider could serve as a messenger or even harbour the very soul of a human being" (Davids & Schwartz, 2016, pp. 150-151).

This next case does not have any spiders in it, but it is still decidedly creepy. Psychic William Stillman writes about a former neighbour of his who lost her father. Her father had been a major league baseball player and was buried wearing an important baseball ring. On her mother's birthday, this woman got a mysterious package in the mail. The handwriting on the outside looked rather like her father's. When she opened it, she found the baseball ring he had been wearing when he was buried. Stillman reports that "[t]he postmark was indistinct, and neither the post office nor the funeral home had an explanation" (Stillman, 2006, pp. 106-107).

Some of the weirdest cases of after-death synchronicity involve electronic devices. Caroline Flohr was mourning the death of her 16-year-old daughter, Sarah. One day she had just turned off her computer and lain down on the floor with some of her other children when the computer printer started up of its own accord. Out came a sheet of paper with nothing on it but the word F L O W E R B L A C K. When her daughter Sarah had been three years old, she had insisted for months that everyone call her by the invented name "FlowerBlack" (Flohr, 2012, pp. 6-8, 82-3).

There is also a whole genre of after-death contacts that consists of apparent telephone calls from the deceased (Rogo & Bayless, 1979; Cooper, 2012; Kasprowicz, 2018; Rawlette, 2020). I think of these as closer to apparitions than to synchronicities, as some of them are so complex as to involve several-minute conversations and seem more clearly "paranormal." Still in the synchronicity category, however, are certain text messages that appear to convey the thoughts or feelings of the deceased, but could simply be the waylaid messages of some unknown living person.

French sociologist Laurent Kasprowicz presents the case of a man named Didier who lost a friend who went by the initials JP. During the week after JP's death, Didier kept asking him for a sign. Exactly one week after his death, down to the very minute, Didier got a text message reading, "*Surtout ne t'inquiète pas! Je suis bien arrivé, promets-moi de prendre soin de toi. Je t'aime JP.*" This translates to, "Don't worry one bit! I've arrived safely, promise you'll take care of yourself. I love you JP." Didier tried calling the number that the text message came from, but it was out of service (Kasprowicz, 2020, p. 27).

The next case is similar. Medium Laura Lynne Jackson tells how a young man named Jonathan took his own life, throwing his mother, Leslie, into a pit of grief. A year later, Leslie's father got sick and was about to die. Leslie asked him to please find Jonathan on the other side and send her a sign to let her know he was okay. Three days after her father's death, Leslie got a text message that said it came from her father's cell phone, even though it turned out his phone was turned off and stashed beneath a bed. The message was a photo of her father accompanied by the words, "Everything is fine" (Jackson, 2020, pp. 221-222).

Before we leave the topic of messages from the beyond, I should also mention that the category of after-death synchronicities overlaps with another one that I have seen fairly frequently in my research: pre-birth synchronicities. While not all pre-birth synchronicities are reincarnation-related, those who are familiar with the literature on memories of previous lives (see Stevenson, 2001 and Matlock, 2019) will know that it is not unusual for the memory and personality of one person to appear to reincarnate in the body of another, and that it is also not unusual for that person's "soul" to communicate during the intermission period between incarnations, usually to announce their coming rebirth. These communications frequently come in the form of dreams and sometimes as apparitions, but there are also examples of this type of communication occurring through synchronicity.

In a Japanese case investigated by Ohkado Masayuki, a Japanese girl who died of leukaemia at age six appeared to reincarnate in the body of her much younger half-brother, Kanon. Kanon displayed various behaviours, preferences, and memories that reflected those of his deceased sister. Most striking, however, was the fact that his sister, some months before her death, had told their mother, "I have to go back to the Snow World [...] But, mom, I will write a letter saying: 'Are you OK? Aren't you lonely?'" When Kanon was four and a half, on a snowy winter day, he brought his mother a letter he had written to her. He had not written actual Japanese letters on the page, only two horizontal lines, but when his mother asked what it said, he told her it read, "Mom, are you OK? Aren't you lonely?" The next day, she asked him if he would rewrite his message to her using actual letters this time. He did so, and this copy of the letter reads (in Japanese), "Mom, aren't you lonely? Aren't you lonely?"

But that's not the synchronistic communication. The synchronistic communication happened before Kanon was born, even before his mother knew she was pregnant. His mother had a dream in which her favourite band, Mr. Children, was performing a beautiful song. A couple of days later, in waking life, she turned on the television, and there was Mr. Children, about to perform a new song. The name of the song reminded her of her deceased daughter, and the lyrics convinced her that they were a message from her. Ohkado translates them as, "Even if this is goodbye forever,/I can hear you breathing/I just know that in some other form, with that same smile/You'll come to see me again."[11] This event gave the mother a strong conviction that her daughter would come back. Eleven days later, she discovered she was pregnant with Kanon (Masayuki, 2017, pp. 553-558).

Reincarnation-related synchronicities do not always come in the form of intentional communications, however. Sometimes they come in the form of coincidences between names and/or birthdates. In one case I have recently been investigating, the synchronicities themselves are so strong as to suggest a possible case of reincarnation even though memories of a previous life are absent. In this case, two young girls both named Shania became friends in first grade and a couple of years later became stepsisters when the mother of one married the father of the other. The odd thing was that the Shania who was older (by 12 days) had actually been a twin, but her twin sister was stillborn. The deceased twin had been given the name Chyanna Ryan. Twelve days after her birth, in the same hospital, the second Shania was born and given the middle name Riane. Could the first Shania's deceased twin – Chyanna Ryan – have been reincarnated as Shania Riane, and then somehow found a way to bring her former mom together with her current dad so as to be reunited with her former twin sister? The girls have the same colour hair and are within half an inch of each other in height. When they went out places together as children, people often asked if they were twins. Another curious coincidence in this story is the fact that the first Shania was born on Christmas Eve and the second Shania on Old Christmas Eve, January 5. The second Shania, by the way, hates both Christmas and her birthday. These negative feelings may be linked to an unconscious memory of her stillbirth on Christmas Eve, as many children with conscious memories of a previous life retain phobias related to the manner in which their previous lives ended (Stevenson, 2001, p. 116).

---

[11] Ohkado references a fan site from which he drew much of his translation: https://ijahlovesmrchildren.wordpress.com/2008/11/16/mr-children-hana-no-nioi-the-scent-of-flowers/.

Similarities Between People

The case of the two Shanias could also fit into another category of weird synchronicities that involve similarities between people. One commonly noticed version of this is people who look alike having the same name. But I have also run across more than one case in which someone encounters another person who has the same first and last names and then discovers that their namesake also shares their exact birthdate. For instance, chiropractor and author Ken Harris tells how he was reviewing a new patient intake form and thought the patient had mistakenly written the doctor's name and birthdate where the patient information was supposed to go. The patient had to take out his driver's license to prove to Dr Harris that there was no mistake. He had the same name and birthdate as his new chiropractor (Harris, 2019, p. 29).

French philosopher Michel Cazenave tells how he once found a letter that appeared to be inviting his son to take an admissions exam at a university. His son's first and last name and birthdate were clearly displayed on the letter, but it turned out that it had been delivered in error. It was intended for another young man of the same first and last name born on the same day. After investigation, Cazenave discovered that the births of the two young men were only one minute apart (Vézina, 2009, p. 33).

We should, of course, expect a certain number of these coincidences to arise by chance, and a detailed statistical study would be needed to determine whether they occur above this rate (see Rawlette, 2019). Nevertheless, some cases are so clearly improbable as to make chance an obviously unsatisfactory explanation. Psychic Susan Reintjes writes in her 2003 book *Third Eye Open,* about going to a potluck birthday party to which she planned to take her usual artichoke dip. At the last minute, however, she decided to instead buy the ingredients for a fruit salad and assemble it at the site of the party. When she put her dish out on the serving table, she discovered that someone else had brought a fruit salad with the same three fruits in it: watermelon, plums, and blueberries. Later, when everyone at the party was introducing themselves to the other guests by giving their names and birthdates, Susan discovered that there was another Susan at the party, and that they had both been born on July 2nd of the same year. She immediately knew who had brought the other fruit salad. The other Susan later told her that her original plan had been to bring marinated artichoke hearts. She'd only changed for the fruit salad at the last minute (Reintjes, 2003, p. 111).

Part of the weirdness in this case is the fact that these two women did not know each other. If they had, I would suggest that their culinary choices were synchronised by telepathy. And that may still be the right explanation, except that it does not explain their identical names and birthdays. There seems to be something deeper going on here.

Even weirder connections exist between biological twins. A lot of these similarities can be explained via a combination of genetics and telepathy. Telepathy, in conjunction with a strong psychosomatic connection, could even explain those fascinating cases in which twins seem to transfer injuries to one another, going all the way from cases that simply involve bruising (Playfair, 2012, p. 56, 143), to cases that involve identically fractured ribs (Playfair, 2012, pp. 55-56), and, in one case I know of, death. Joyce Crominski reports that her sister Peg was in a car accident that crushed her chest beneath the steering wheel and that she died on the way to the hospital. At the same time, Peg's twin sister, Helen, woke up screaming and with severe chest pain. She also died while being transported to the hospital. Their deaths were apparently only minutes apart (Playfair, 2012, p. 56).

In cases like this, it appears as though the twins' bodies are behaving as a single organism, with impact to one causing injury in them both. This seems related to the more common phenomenon of simulpathity, a variety of telepathy in which one can feel the pain of another at a distance. But telepathy seems a bit of a stretch in the weirdest cases. The highest level of strangeness comes in when the similarities are not just in the twins' bodily reactions but extend to the external circumstances that precipitate identical injuries. In his book *Twin Telepathy*, the late Guy Lyon Playfair gave six examples of this phenomenon, collected from various news sources:

- Four-year-old Jason Floyd fell through a window. Three days later, his twin brother, Jonathan, fell through the same window and had the same number of stitches in the same place.[12]
- Six-year-old twins Liam and Aaron Lynch were both admitted to the hospital with broken collar bones within half an hour of each other. One had been climbing a fence. The other fell while running.[13]

---

[12] Playfair's source was *The Times* (August 5, 1988), p. 11.
[13] Playfair's source was *The Times* (June 4, 1994), p. 2.

- Natalie and Zara Heywood are mirror twins: one is right-handed, the other left-handed, and they display various other matching characteristics on opposite sides of their bodies. When they both had bicycle accidents within minutes of each other, they cut themselves on opposite legs. When they both pulled muscles while swimming together, they pulled them in opposite legs. And when one broke an arm while roller skating, within half an hour, the other had broken the opposite arm, also while roller skating.[14]
- Romanian twins Romulus and Remus Cozma broke their right legs on the same day. Romulus fell while climbing, and soon after, Remus fell down the stairs at home.[15]
- Twins John and Michael Atkins were simultaneously skiing at different locations in the Alps when they both slipped on the ice and broke their legs at the same time: noon.[16]
- Two Finnish twin brothers died on the same road on the same day by the same means. The two incidents happened two hours apart and at one mile's distance from each other. The brothers were individually crossing the road on their bikes and were both hit by trucks they did not see coming.[17]

Even more puzzlingly, not all such matching injuries occur between two people. Here is a case in which the injury connects a person to an artistic representation of that person. French painter Jules Gabriel Dubois-Menant related in a 1906 issue of the *Revue Scientifique et Morale du Spiritisme* an event that he witnessed in March 1904. He was getting ready for a portrait session and decided that he wanted to use an easel that was currently occupied with a pastel portrait he had made of a woman he referred to as Madame V., a portrait that was already framed and under glass. As he prepared to move the framed portrait to another easel, he had the strange intuitive feeling that, no matter how careful he was in moving it, somehow it was going to

---

[14] Playfair's source was *News of the World* (January 30, 2000), p. 27.
[15] Playfair's source was Dan Gardescu, "Doi frati gemeni ucid in aceeasi zi, la aceeasi ora" [Two twin brothers kill on the same day, at the same time], *Dracula* (September 1993). Playfair investigated the reporter and found no reason to doubt the truth of the story.
[16] Playfair's source was *The Times* (January 11, 1988), p. 2.
[17] Playfair's source was *San Jose Mercury News* (March 7, 2002).

end up falling and breaking. He did his very best to be careful and even put extra props to support it in its new position, but as soon as he turned away from it, it fell to the floor, breaking the frame and the glass. As he removed the shattered glass from the portrait, he was relieved to see that the only damage to the canvas itself was a scratch to the paint on the right cheekbone of the lady's face, easily repairable. He then noted that the time was 2:45pm and that the model for his session was arriving.

That evening, Dubois-Menant discovered that the subject of the fallen portrait, Madame V., had been hurt in an accident that afternoon in the Paris subway. The accident had occurred at 2:45pm, and she had received glass shards in the face. The following day, Dubois-Menant went to visit her, and he was astonished to find that her injury was to the right cheekbone, at the same place where her portrait had been damaged. And, as with the portrait, it was fortunately only a superficial scratch (Breton, 1906, pp. 742-744).

What is this odd form of correspondence between an accident that happens to a human being and an accident that happens to her inanimate likeness? Believers in what is called "sympathetic magic" would tell us that an injury done to a representation of a person will cause corresponding injury to the person themselves. While I cannot vouch for the ability to create such correspondences at will, the synchronicities in this section would appear to provide some (limited) support for the efficacy of such practices. They do at least suggest the existence of connections in our world that are based not on spatial proximity but on symbolism and meaning.

Meaningful Mistaken Identity

Sometimes, weird synchronicities between people who look alike or who share the same name or other characteristics provide us with information that we would not otherwise have had. In these next three cases, mistaken identity leads to acquiring meaningful information that turns out not to be a mistake at all.

On a Friday evening in November 2019, my husband and I stopped to eat at the fast-food chain Arby's, a place we had not been to together in years, even though this particular Arby's held an important memory for us from the first week of our dating relationship. When my husband pulled into the parking spot, I asked him if this is where we had parked that other time, when we had just started dating. He said no, that we had parked on the other side of the lot.

As we were walking into the restaurant, I gestured to some cars on the other side of the lot and asked, "You mean over there?" My husband said yes. Then he commented on one of the vehicles that was parked in that location. "That looks like a car Kevin had," he said. Kevin (a pseudonym) was the name of my husband's teenage nephew. We were actually on the way to visit his family after we ate dinner. I said, "Oh, maybe Kevin works here. Maybe we'll see him inside." I seemed to recall hearing recently that Kevin was looking for a job, but I did not recall he had gotten one, or that it was at Arby's.

My husband laughed and said something like, "Yeah, he's traded selling real estate for selling real *steak*." I did not get the reference to real estate, as Kevin had no connection to real estate that I could think of, but I shrugged it off. We went in to get our dinner, and we did not see Kevin inside. After dinner, we went to my husband's parents' house, where his sister and her son Kevin lived at that time. While we were visiting, my mother-in-law said something about how Kevin had gotten called into work that evening at Arby's. "So he *does* work there," I said to my husband.

"I wasn't talking about *this* Kevin," my husband replied. "I meant Kevin _ That's why I made the joke about real estate." The other Kevin he mentioned was an acquaintance of ours who had recently become a real estate agent.

I was now thoroughly confused. My husband had said something at Arby's that led me to believe his nephew Kevin might work there, and then it turned out that, although my husband's comment had been unrelated, his nephew did in fact work there, and had in fact been there that very evening, even though we had not seen him. It was such a strange tangle of events that I had to confirm the facts several times with my husband, his mother, and Kevin's mother, who was also present. Everything they said confirmed what I had just understood: a car that resembled one belonging to another Kevin had, through a misunderstanding, led me to a correct belief about the presence of *this* Kevin at the same location. A physical pun ended up providing me with valid information.[18] The coincidence also involves the fact that my

---

[18] The analytic philosopher in me can't resist pointing out that this is a real-life example of the classic Gettier problem (Gettier, 1963, pp. 121-123).

mother-in-law then mentioned that Kevin had been called into Arby's that evening, as if the universe wanted to make sure that I understood what had just happened.

I have had one other experience I can remember in which mistaken identity led to true knowledge about a person's presence at a particular location. This other experience happened just a few weeks before the above synchronicity. I was shopping at a local grocery store when I caught a glimpse down an aisle of someone who looked like the father of one of my students. However, when I looked more closely, I could see that, although there were similarities between the two of them, this was clearly *not* the student's father. So I continued my shopping. Maybe ten minutes later, I had just finished checking out my groceries and was loading them into my cart when I heard someone call my name. I turned around only to discover that the person speaking was the father that I originally thought I had seen down the aisle. Now let me be clear that this was *not* the same man I had seen in the aisle. I was absolutely sure of that. And yet here was the person I had at first mistakenly *thought* I had seen. And this is the only time in the nine years of knowing this family that I have run into the father out in public. It felt very much to me as though that man in the aisle was a synchronistic version of the Scandinavian *vardøger*, which is a type of precognitive phantom of a living person. The *vardøger* is heard or seen carrying out an activity that the living person will perform in that location in the near future. Here, it was as though this man's synchronistic double was alerting me to his presence in the store several minutes before I would encounter him.

Psychiatrist and intuitive Judith Orloff has actually learned to use experiences of mistaken identity in her medical practice. She describes the following experience in her book *Second Sight*:

> Once when I was driving up Sunset Boulevard to a friend's house in Laurel Canyon, I happened to turn my head and look into the car next to me. Startled, I did a double take: I was sure the woman at the wheel was a patient of mine, Jane. Though I waved at her, however, she sped right by me without response, and I then realized it wasn't Jane at all, just someone who bore a close resemblance. Such cases of mistaken identity, I've learned, especially if my confusion is so marked, often have special significance and are synchronicities. In this incident, my attention was drawn to Jane, so I knew to tune in to her intuitively and find out what was going on. Right away, I sensed her despair. I

tried to reach her that night but she wasn't home. The next day, when Jane came in for her scheduled appointment, she was frantic, having just discovered that she'd been fired from a teaching job she loved (Orloff, 2000, p. 255).

Communication Thanks to Malfunctioning Electronics

The above cases of mistaken identity help to communicate information about a person that can later be followed up by having an actual conversation with them. But what about when two people need to get in touch with one another but cannot, or for some reason refuse to do so? Deep weird synchronicities often happen in these cases, sometimes with the help of a malfunctioning electronic device like a phone or telephone switchboard.

A woman in London, for example, was visiting a friend when the phone rang and the call turned out to be for her. It was her accountant. He had dialled her number but had somehow been connected to her friend's house instead. Their numbers were apparently not similar, though they were on the same exchange (Inglis, 1990, p. 57).

In another English case, a Mrs. Moat answered the phone one morning to discover that, though the caller had the wrong number, it was someone she knew and felt slightly guilty about not having been in touch with recently. To avoid embarrassment, she disguised her voice and got off the phone without telling the caller who she was. Later that same day, Mrs. Moat placed her own call, to an arts centre in another area of the country. It was not clear if she misdialled or the phone misconnected her, but her call was answered by the same acquaintance who had called her on a wrong number that morning. Mrs. Moat did not actually have this woman's number, so she could not have subconsciously dialled it by mistake. And the woman's number turned out not to be at all similar to that of the arts centre, so a misconnection seems to be the most likely explanation – a misconnection apparently guided by Mrs. Moat's guilty conscience! (Vaughan, 1979, pp. 63-64).

Essex police constable Peter Moscardi relates how a friend was trying to reach him at the police station one day but failed because the telephone number for the station had just been changed. When Moscardi saw his friend the next day, he explained the situation and gave his friend the station's new number. But then he realized the following day that he had gotten a repeating digit of the number wrong and had no way to let his friend know about the mistake. While on patrol in the middle of the following night, Moscardi passed a factory that had a door suspiciously ajar and a light on inside. Moscardi and his colleague went into the manager's office to investigate, but there was no one there. The factory office phone rang. Moscardi answered. It was his friend on the line, trying to reach him at the station. The telephone number at the factory turned out to be the number that Moscardi had mistakenly given to his friend (Vaughan, 1979, p. 63).

Another case of being next to the right phone at the right time happened in France. A musician named Maxime was hanging out with his friend Sophie on the Champs-Elysées one night, and they were discussing a piece he was composing. He wanted to add a flute to it and thought of contacting an old flautist friend of his but no longer had the man's number. It started raining, so Maxime and Sophie took refuge in a nightclub stairway. There were some payphones there, and one of them started ringing. Sophie answered. The man on the other end apparently thought he was talking to his insurance agent. Sophie was having a hard time making him understand that he had been connected to a random telephone booth, so she passed the phone to Maxime. Maxime explained the situation again. There was a pause, and then the man said, "Maxime?" That was when Maxime recognised the caller's voice – it was his flautist friend! And, since he was also in Paris, Maxime invited him to come down to the Champs-Elysées and join their night on the town. The icing on the cake was that, when the flautist showed up, he was in the company of a woman who turned out to be Sophie's former piano teacher. Maxime notes, "It was quite a strange night" (Soulières, 2012, pp. 21-3).

To round off this section, let me describe my own experience of a deep weird synchronicity that connected me to another person via a malfunctioning phone. Some years ago, I went through a period of time where I was thinking obsessively about the country of France, where I used to live, and about a Frenchman I had once been engaged to marry but with whom I had been out of touch for a few years. I was wondering very intently about how he was doing and also about whether I would ever end up returning to France, a country I dearly loved.

During this time, I spent a weekend hanging out with some old college friends in the mountains of central Pennsylvania. Odd coincidences seemed to happen whenever I got together with these friends, so I was already anticipating something out of the ordinary. On Saturday afternoon, I rode along with one of my friends as she drove around looking for a place to buy food. She was not having any luck, so she eventually pulled out her smartphone and gave it a voice command to find the nearest grocery stores. Then, because she was driving, she handed her phone to me. When I took the phone from her, it was displaying a list of four or five stores in our vicinity, close to Johnstown, Pennsylvania. I tapped the "MAP" button so I could determine which store would be the easiest for us to get to. But, when the map loaded, it was not showing the stores that had just been on the list. Instead, it showed me several grocery stores named "E. Leclerc," a French supermarket chain, and each of the store names was followed by the name of a French-sounding town. One of them I specifically recognised – Carhaix – although I could not remember exactly where in France it was located.

I was so startled by the phone showing me these French stores that I ended up just handing it back to my friend, saying, "I don't know what to do with this. Your phone thinks we're in France." When she pressed a button on the phone, it immediately went back to working normally and showing us stores in Pennsylvania. And she could not explain why it had acted so strangely. She assured me she had never used her phone to look up anything in France. Yet, while it was in my hand, that is obviously where it thought it was.

When I got home a couple of days later, I decided to Google Carhaix to figure out whether it was indeed in France. I discovered that not only was it in France but it was in the region of Brittany, where my ex lived, and where we had lived together before we separated. As soon as I saw this, I knew that there had to be even more to the coincidence. If the phone had shown me a location in Brittany, it had to be because that was where my ex was on that particular day. On the off chance that there might be some information about his whereabouts on the internet, I tried Googling my ex's name and the date the GPS incident had happened, and I got a page from his blog that listed five events he planned to attend during the course of that year. One of them was on the day of the GPS incident, and the event was in a place called Kergloff. As Google soon revealed, Kergloff was a village just two miles from the centre of Carhaix. So, if my ex had indeed been in Kergloff on that day and asked his phone to show him nearby grocery stores, it would have shown him the same E. Leclerc in Carhaix that my friend's phone showed me in Pennsylvania.[19]

After this incident, I experienced several more weeks of unrelenting synchronicities related to France and to my ex, and this synchronicity storm eventually convinced me that something really important was going on with my ex and that I needed to write to him. When I finally did, I discovered that he had just had his first child, ten days after the GPS incident. I cannot overstate how immensely reassuring it was for me to learn about this joyful event in his life, and also to know that, in a strange, psychic way, I had been alerted to that impending, life-defining moment. The anomalous behaviour of my friend's phone showed me that I was still connected to France and to my ex, but also that both of us were exactly where we needed to be.

One could attempt to understand this incident in purely Jungian terms, as an outer event that acausally reflects an inner state of longing and connection, but it seems to go even deeper and be even weirder than that. For one thing, there appears to be a psychic transfer of information, both about the whereabouts of my ex and about a pivotal event occurring in his life. It is very difficult to get away from a feeling of *causality* in this case, as it is with the anomalous telephone connections in previous examples. The probability of a GPS accidentally locating someone at the location of someone they are thinking about on the other side of the Atlantic is so very small that it is hard not to say that my connection to my ex somehow *caused* this. Perhaps there was even some sort of psychic melding of identity, as it appears that, for a moment, the GPS in my hand was reacting as though it were in Brittany, in the hand of my ex. This goes a lot deeper and has more profound consequences for our understanding of the nature of the universe than does a mere scarab beetle tapping at a window at a particularly propitious moment.

---

[19] I should add that, once I saw the page of my ex's blog listing his travels that year, I realized I had a vague memory of having seen that page at some other time, probably a few months prior to this event. So I may have maintained an unconscious memory of the list's existence and possibly of the dates on it. And I could have employed that memory in psychokinetically influencing the phone's behaviour on the day of the synchronicity. However, I had no conscious memory of the name of the town of Kergloff, and I can think of no normal way in which I could have known Kergloff's location before searching for it online after my experience with the GPS.

Conclusion

So what *do* all these deep weird synchronicities tell us about the nature of reality? While it is difficult to sum up such disparate evidence in a single conclusion, I would say that synchronicities in general – and deep weird synchronicities in particular – show us that thoughts have power and that meaning is an ordering principle in our universe.

Science has proceeded for several hundred years on the assumption that the physical world operates in an entirely mechanistic manner, unaffected by what anyone thinks or feels about it. The phenomenon of synchronicity, however, demonstrates that our thoughts and feelings *do* influence the evolution of the physical world. And, as we have seen, it is not just the minds of living people that are reflected in synchronistic events. The minds of those who have passed on also seem capable of expressing themselves in this way, as do the minds of those who are not yet born.

The deep weird synchronicities described in this essay show that our minds and bodies are more connected to one another and to our environments than we generally realise. We tend to think that we can change one little piece of ourselves or our environment without changing the whole, but when the death of a woman in a car accident immediately provokes the death of her twin sister at a remote location, or when a scratch on a portrait echoes an identical scratch on the portrait's subject, it makes you stop and wonder whether all of our fates may not be more or less inextricable from one another. It gives a whole new gravity to the admonition to "do unto others as you would have them do unto you."

Ultimately, we are not separate beings, and even the so-called inanimate objects around us are not unconnected to our consciousness. Sometimes, things happen precisely *because* they are meaningful – even if this meaning only becomes apparent to us much later, in the light of subsequent events. The evidence suggests that life may resemble nothing so much as a movie or a novel. Symbolism is certainly rife. And convenient accidents happen all the time in service of the plot.

But lest we tie up this weirdness too neatly, I want to close with a final synchronicity that stirs a whole new set of issues into the pot and connects to some of the other types of deep weird experiences described elsewhere in this book. This event happened to author Mike Clelland and was *the* event that launched him into writing his now three books on the intersections between synchronicities, owls, and UFOs.

Mike is an outdoorsman who spends a lot of time sleeping under the stars, and on some occasions, this has led to unusual experiences. For instance, one night he was camping in a tent in Colorado with a close friend named Natascha when they both woke up screaming. Mike says the fear he felt in that moment was more intense than any he had felt in his life. Later that same night, Mike had an experience (whether waking or dreaming, he is not entirely sure) in which he felt he was floating out of the tent roof into a place that was glowing white. He seemed to think he might be on a table of some kind. The next day, he discovered his chest had a long scratch-like rash across it that he could not explain.

On another occasion, Mike was camping alone in Utah when he noticed a large, round structure perched on a nearby hilltop. It had lights all along its circumference and reminded him of a landed flying saucer. When he later checked Google's satellite maps, he found that there was no structure in the area that matched what he had seen. He even went back to the same spot in daylight and confirmed that it was empty of any buildings that could have been the source of the lights he had seen.

A couple of days after observing this inexplicable structure, Mike wrote a blog post documenting the latitude and longitude of his sleeping spot and of the hilltop where he believed the structure should have been located. After posting his description, he was still pondering the strangeness of the experience when he suddenly had a "psychic download" of a map with three markers and a straight yellow line running through them. He knew what the markers at either end stood for: the two odd experiences I have just described. So he immediately sat down at his computer and created a map with a yellow line connecting those two points.

Mike was not sure at first what the middle point in his vision had stood for, but then he remembered another strange event he had experienced while camping with Natascha in that general vicinity on a different occasion. That night, Natascha was jet-lagged and could not sleep, so she had gotten up during the night to take a little walk. While she was gone, Mike lay in his sleeping bag listening to a great horned owl hooting loudly from somewhere in the bushes close to his head. The next thing he knew, Natascha was waking him up in a panic. While on her walk, she had seen a two-foot white orb gliding over the sagebrush, and then it had suddenly flashed and disappeared. She had been overcome with panic and ran back to wake Mike, all the while convinced she was being followed. She insisted they pack up right then and get out of there, which they did.

Mike placed a marker on his map in the exact spot where he had been sleeping the night Natascha had encountered the white orb. He was surprised to see that the marker did not quite fall on the yellow line he had made connecting the other two points. However, he decided to switch the coordinates for the leftmost point (the night he saw the round structure on the hill) from the coordinates for the location of his sleeping bag to the coordinates for the structure itself (coordinates which he had already published on his blog). When he did this, the new yellow line, 231 miles long, passed *precisely* over the spot where he had been sleeping on the night of the white orb. Even when Mike reduced the line to a single pixel wide and zoomed in close enough to see the individual trees surrounding his sleeping spot, the single-pixel line exactly crossed the spot where he had lain in the sand.

Not only did this perfect, psychically foreseen alignment finally convince Mike that "this stuff was real" and that he needed to begin writing about synchronicities and UFOs in a serious way, but he later had an experience under hypnosis that suggested that, on the night he had seen the mysterious round structure, he had actually been taken inside it and had a life-changing exchange with some alien-looking beings he encountered there. This would explain why it was important for the point on his map to be located at the site of the structure itself rather than the site of his sleeping bag. I will also add, as Mike does, that two of the three events that lined up on his map happened in the company of the same woman, Natascha. She was not present for the event with the round structure, but it did happen on her birthday, March 10th (Clelland, 2015, pp. 354-369; Clelland, 2019, pp. 167-74, 312-321).

As Mike pointed out when he interviewed me for his podcast *The Unseen*, it is interesting that in both my GPS incident and his "confirmation event," as he calls it, we each had a conviction about what we would discover ahead of time.[20] That is, we were somehow aware of the nature of the synchronicity before it fully revealed itself, and this is what led us to investigate further. In yet more parallels, both of our synchronicities had to do with points on a digital map, they both involved someone of the opposite sex to whom we were emotionally close, and they both led us to begin writing the books on synchronicity

---

[20] Mike also had this feeling of conviction about a previous map synchronicity he experienced, described in Chapter 6 of his book *Hidden Experience*.

that we are best known for, Mike's being his book *The Messengers* and mine being *The Source and Significance of Coincidences*. Perhaps even weirder than either of our synchronicities alone is the pattern they both display, a pattern that points to a hidden, directing intelligence that has dramatically altered the course of both of our lives. How far does this directing intelligence reach? It is hard to escape the feeling that it is much bigger – and weirder – than we know.

NEAR-DEATH EXPERIENCES
Peeling Back the Universal, Cultural, and Individual Layers[21]

GREGORY SHUSHAN

Near-death experiences (or NDEs) are sometimes reported by individuals who are resuscitated from a period of clinical death or near-death. The experience typically involves a number of sensations, such as consciousness temporarily leaving the body, rising upwards and seeing one's own "corpse" below, entering darkness or a tunnel, emerging in bright light, meeting deceased friends or relatives, encountering a being of light radiating love and acceptance, a panoramic life review with a sense of moral evaluation or self-judgment, reaching a border or limit, and ultimately returning to the body. Other commonly reported features include feelings of peace, joy, unity, universal understanding, heightened senses and clarity, seeing or entering other worlds (usually idealised mirror-images of earth) which are often seen as one's true "home," time and thought accelerating, precognition, telepathic communication with other spirits, loud noises, music, vivid colours, being instructed or deciding to return, and lasting positive effects on the subsequent life of the NDEr. Those who have such experiences usually interpret them in spiritual or religious terms, and the phenomenon has been the subject of much philosophical and religious speculation concerning the possibility of survival beyond

---

[21] This chapter originally appeared in a different form in Shushan (2022).

physical death, mind-body dualism, religious beliefs in an afterlife, and our understanding of the nature of human consciousness.

Because one of the key issues in NDE studies is determining the degree to which it is a universal human occurrence, defining the experience is important. Since death and dying are obviously universal, the nature and meaning of NDEs should be universal as well. If the NDE is not the same for everyone, this requires explanation regardless of whether we believe the experience is simply an epiphenomenal consequence of a compromised brain, or an actual indication of what happens to human beings when (and after) we die. While even the most skeptical researchers generally accept that NDEs occur, there is still no general consensus on which elements actually define the experience. American psychologist and medical doctor Raymond Moody, who coined the term "near-death experience" in his 1975 bestseller *Life After Life*, identified fifteen "stages" which have been used as the basis for nearly all subsequent NDE research, including the development of the widely used "Greyson scale" (Greyson, 1999). In fact, Moody was describing a composite experience, for no single NDE that he recorded included all of the elements, and only a few had as many as twelve.

Rather than a single experience, the NDE is best regarded as a collection of typical sub-experiences: a variable combination of a number of possible elements from an established repertoire, the details of which differ on a case-by-case basis for reasons which remain at least partly obscure. There is some evidence that the manner in which a person almost dies impacts the experience. Those who attempt suicide tend not to have a life review, for example (Ring, 1980, p. 194). The duration of an NDE may also help account for differences (Stevenson & Greyson, 1996). The life review, for example, may come at a later stage in the dying process. This is supported by the findings of some researchers (Sartori, 2008), though it conflicts with those of others (Grey, 1985; van Lommel, *et al.* 2001). There is also a human tendency to elaborate events into sequential narratives, so it is difficult to determine whether or not the order of the various NDE elements is consistent (Grey, 1985).

The same year that Moody's book was published, a German study by Lutheran minister Johann Christophe Hampe (1975) independently identified the NDE and its main elements. Unlike the examples Moody cites, however, Hampe's NDErs returned to the body the same way they left it (i.e., through a tunnel). Hampe also reported only a few encounters with deceased relatives, and none of a loud noise (cf. Fox,

2003, p. 55ff). An even earlier popular book (Delacour, 1973) also independently confirmed NDEs, though uniquely described accounts in which NDErs claimed the ability to control or influence the "afterlife" environment, similar to a lucid dream. These idiosyncrasies suggest that some elements are experienced only in particular cultures (in this case, German and French), an idea that is supported by later studies of historical and non-Western NDEs as we will see.

Some NDEs are distressing, though their phenomenology appears to correspond thematically to the more typical positive examples, in an apparently inverted way. Thus, the individual feels fear and panic during the out-of-body-experience (OBE), is filled with despair, enters darkness and a void, encounters an evil presence, and sees hellish places. It is unclear if there are, in fact, fundamentally different negative and positive NDEs, or if it is simply a matter of individual perception and interpretation of the same kind of experience (Greyson & Bush, 1992; Serdahely, 1995). The theologian Paul Badham (1997) – one of the first to look at the relationships between NDEs and religious beliefs – notes that in contrast to positive NDEs, however, negative examples are more dreamlike, they do not normally hold the same significance for the NDEr, and are not remembered with the same vivid clarity over time.

Like any experience, NDEs are also subject to the vagaries of memory and narrative. An OBE, for example, is not always explicitly reported, though obviously it is a journey of the soul, not the body, which is being claimed. It may thus be presumed that any individual who has had an NDE believes that he or she did, in fact, leave the body. Darkness is another element which might easily go unmentioned, particularly if the more interesting and memorable element of the experience is the contrasting radiant light. It is also true that like any other narrative, NDE and "otherworld journey" accounts are literary artefacts (Zaleski, 1987; Couliano, 1991). Like any literature, they are at least partly products of intertextuality, meaning that they are situated within a narrative genre and thus follow certain literary conventions. Ultimately, the extent to which interpretation and narrative – by both NDErs and researchers – affect conclusions regarding the phenomenology of NDEs is unclear and surely varies from case to case.

Sex, religion, degree of religiosity, and other demographic factors do not seem to have a significant bearing on the occurrence of NDEs (Ring, 1980). Nor is there a correlation between the occurrence of NDEs and resuscitation technique, types of drugs administered during surgery, fear of death, foreknowledge of NDEs, or education (van Lommel *et al.*, 2001). The NDE is by no means a rare phenomenon. Thousands of books and articles have been written on the subject, and tens of thousands of reports have been collected from around the world. It is estimated that they occur in approximately "10% of people who come close to death, or who survive actual clinical death" (Fenwick, 2005, p.2), and in an even higher percentage when looking only at cardiac arrest survivors (12-18%) (van Lommel *et al.*, 2001).

While these estimates are significant, so too is the fact that they leave up to 90% who do not report having had NDEs. It is not clear whether the experience simply does not happen to everyone who nears death or who is clinically dead for a time, or whether some do not remember the experience or do not report it for other reasons (for example, fear of being ridiculed or doubted). Conversely, NDEs (or at least phenomenologically consistent experiences) can occur in individuals who are not actually near death at all but believe themselves to be, such as when falling from a height, or nearly drowning, though without being in any real imminent mortal danger (Stevenson *et al.*, 1990).

NDEs are complex, multi-faceted phenomena which can be approached from various different disciplines and perspectives, using diverse theories and methodologies. It is not simply a question of "are they real or not," but of the various ways in which they can be understood. As Carol Zaleski (1987, p. 181) pointed out in her book comparing modern NDEs with medieval otherworld journey accounts, "a comprehensive theory of near-death experience" would require a synthesis of "all of the medical, psychological, philosophical, historical, social, literary, and logical factors."

Theories integrating a number of such factors while still taking seriously the testimonies of NDErs have been put forth by McClenon (1994), Kellehear (1996), Badham (1997), Paulson (1999), and Shushan (2009; 2018; 2022), among others. In attempting to account for both similarities and differences between accounts, such theories present models which accept the idea of a structurally universal NDE, combined with a number of other considerations such as local cultural contexts and religious beliefs; cognitive, psychological, and neurophysiological findings; and in some cases (e.g., Badham, Shushan) philosophical and metaphysical speculations.

NDEs, Science, and Survival After Death

From the pioneering work of various psychologists and medical researchers (e.g., Ring, 1980; Sabom, 1982; Grey, 1985), the field of near-death studies has evolved to focus on the key areas of obtaining empirical scientific evidence, cross-cultural comparisons, the relevance to philosophy and religion, and the implications for healthcare and psychology. However, for many the issue of whether or not the NDE constitutes evidence for survival after physical death remains paramount. While pro-survival perspectives are often criticised for conflicting with known laws of science and for drawing conclusions from unverifiable accounts of personal experiences, scientific-materialist perspectives are equally criticised for *a priori* reductionism, and for dismissing or ignoring the challenging evidence instead of adequately addressing it.

Various researchers have attempted to explain the NDE in materialist terms, though none appear to have fully succeeded. Some argue that it results from a deprivation of oxygen in the brain (hypoxia or anoxia; Blackmore, 1993; cf. Sabom, 1982). Opponents of the theory, however, counter that oxygen deprivation causes confusional states quite unlike the hyper-lucidity reported by NDErs, and in fact does not produce effects comparable to the NDE at all (Fenwick & Fenwick, 1995). Excessive carbon dioxide in the brain (hypercarbia) is also enlisted as a materialist explanation of NDEs, and actually can produce NDE-like effects (Klemenc-Ketis *et al.*, 2010). There is, however, evidence that carbon dioxide is actually lowered during NDEs (Sabom, 1982). The theory that the experience results from temporal lobe epilepsy is similarly problematic. Proponents of the theory (e.g., Blackmore, 1993) argue that during life-threatening episodes the temporal lobe is stimulated in ways that could cause the typical effects of an NDE (e.g., triggering memories resulting in a life review, releasing endorphins causing feelings of well-being). However, the neuropsychiatrist Peter Fenwick (2005, p. 2) counters that "No epileptic seizure has the clarity and narrative style of an NDE [...] all epilepsy is confusional." Furthermore, in terms of memory and the brain's ability to construct mental models, "it should be quite impossible to have an NDE when brain function is really very seriously disordered, or the brain is seriously damaged" (Fenwick & Fenwick, 1995, p. 205).

Still others have argued that NDEs are caused by anaesthetic drugs, such as ketamine. However, it has been shown conclusively that individuals not under the influence of such drugs still have NDEs (Fenwick, 2005), leading to a general loss of support for this kind of theory. A related idea is that the brain itself produces a ketamine-like substance, causing the effects of NDEs. A leading expert on ketamine, psychiatrist Karl Jansen (2001), pointed out that a similarity between NDEs and ketamine experiences does not indicate that NDEs are not genuinely "spiritual." Rather, the drug may simply enable access to the same spiritual "reality" as the NDE. Though while ketamine experiences can indeed resemble NDEs (particularly in causing out-of-body sensations and impressions of visiting other realms), such drugs are also known to cause feelings of disorientation and fear, the very antithesis of the clarity, peace, and joy reported by most NDErs. Conversely, other NDE features (darkness and light) are seemingly absent from ketamine experiences (Fox, 2003).

Despite decades of theorising, the most comprehensive attempt to explain the NDE in reductionist terms remains that of psychologist Susan Blackmore (1993), who argues that the NDE is the hallucinatory result of a combination of neurophysiological and psychological events occurring in the dying brain. Some of her key claims are that the feelings of joy and peace are the result of natural opiates being released in the brain as it shuts down; the tunnel, light, and sound are a result of anoxia; the life review is due to "seizures in the temporal lobe and limbic system where memories are organised"; and the OBE is the brain's attempt to "model reality." All this is combined with "prior knowledge, fantasy, lucky guesses and the remaining operating senses of hearing and touch." The intense reality of the NDE is allegedly caused by the brain's attempt to retain the disintegrating construct that is individual personality and consciousness. Blackmore subscribes to the notion that the self is an illusion created by the brain, which attempts to maintain that illusion even in the dying process. However, though her theory rests heavily on the brain as a functional instrument, Blackmore does not adequately explain the purpose or function of this protective mechanism. Furthermore, in keeping with her commitments both to Western materialism and Zen Buddhism, she takes for granted that the self *is* illusory. Blackmore also sees the tunnel experience as "neural noise" caused by a malfunctioning visual cortex, resulting in impressions of light growing increasingly larger and the sensation of moving through a dark tunnel towards that light. This is also problematic. As a supposed neurophysiological occurrence, the "tunnel" should be universal, though cross-cultural evidence shows that this is not the case. It is not reported in Indian NDEs or in small-scale societies, and indeed the tunnel *per se* is actually uncommon even in Western cases (Stevenson *et al.*, 1994). Individual and cultural variations between NDEs should not occur if the experience is caused by a neurophysiological process, and this creates a serious problem for "all-in-the-brain" explanations such as Blackmore's (Kellehear, 1996; Serdahely, 1995). Blackmore has also been criticised for "massaging" her data into an erroneous claim that the tunnel is in fact experienced in India, in order to bolster her dying brain hypothesis (Stevenson *et al.*, 1994; Kellehear, 1996).

Another theory suggests that NDEs can be explained by "REM intrusion" – the activation of the dream state in the mind of the NDEr resulting in hallucinatory visions. This notion is easily countered by the fact that REM intrusion experiences and NDEs differ fundamentally (noting particularly that the hallucinatory, dreamlike REM state is inconsistent with NDE states), and that the theory cannot explain "visual" NDEs in the congenitally blind, or in those who have the experience while under the influence of REM-suppressing drugs (Long & Holden, 2007; Greyson *et al.*, 2009). Yet another reductionist explanation for NDEs was proposed by Michael Marsh (2010), a Christian theologian and biomedical researcher. His "reviving brain" theory states that the NDE is a set of illusions caused by the disordered brain reorganising itself upon returning from unconsciousness. His work, however, has been roundly criticised for failing to take into account cases of NDEs in which the brain was not compromised, or which demonstrably did not occur during recovery; for a lack of serious engagement with competing evidence and recent research; for trivialising NDEr testimony; and for his arguments being deeply informed by his own Christian eschatological beliefs in resurrection via divine "re-creation" of the individual (Kelly, 2010; Rousseau, 2011). Opponents of reductionist theories, such as those of Blackmore and Marsh, also argue that they fail to explain NDErs' feelings of unconditional love and cosmic unity, or why the experience would so often lead to positive transformations in the individual's values, a greater spiritual awareness, and a desire to help others (the "fruits" of religious experience in William James's terms) (Greyson, 2006; Noyes *et al.*, 2009).

Nor do reductionist theories explain cases of individuals accurately describing events they claim to have witnessed during OBEs. Fenwick (2005, p. 4) has shown that NDEs can occur in cardiac arrest patients while they are unconscious with a flat EEG reading, when there is "no possibility of the brain creating any images" and "no brain-based memory functioning." This means that "it should be impossible to have clearly structured and lucid experiences." Arguments in favour of the NDE as evidence for dualism and survival after death thus rest largely upon claims of veridical observations during such periods of brain inactivity. Perhaps the most famous such case is that of Pam Reynolds (Sabom, 1998), who reported an OBE she had during brain surgery, while clinically dead, with her body temperature lowered and her head drained of blood for the operation. She claimed to have witnessed medical procedures from a vantage point outside her body, and accurately described them upon resuscitation, including details such as the design of the bone saw which cut into her skull and the pitch of the sound it made.

A recent international experiment led by resuscitation expert Sam Parnia, the AWARE study (AWAreness during REsuscitation) has apparently confirmed that consciousness can persist when no brain activity is detectable, actually during the period of clinical death prior to successful resuscitation. This was widely believed to be medically impossible, and has profound implications for the notion that consciousness can survive physical death. Researchers have also attempted to verify OBE observations by positioning certain images at vantage points visible only from above, that is, by a person who had floated out of their body. While this proved unsuccessful, one individual accurately described his own resuscitation, which he claimed to have witnessed while out-of-body, including the sound of a defibrillator machine, allowing researchers to pinpoint the time of the event as having occurred during the patient's cardiac arrest (Parnia *et al.*, 2014). In a study conducted in a Welsh hospital, intensive care nurse Penny Sartori (2008) found that only those who had OBEs accurately described the resuscitation process (cf. Parnia *et al.*, 2007). Furthermore, OBEs (and indeed NDEs themselves, as mentioned above) have been widely reported in non-crisis contexts during dreams, meditation, shamanic trance, spontaneously, and in laboratory settings via artificial induction (Ehrsson, 2007). Actually being near death is clearly not a prerequisite for such experiences, a fact that makes the "dying brain" hypothesis untenable.

The investigation of NDEs in the blind is another important area of research, for they report visual perception during the experience. Dozens of such cases have been published so far, including from individuals who have been blind since birth. This is significant because people who have never had the resources to "model reality" in the way Blackmore describes, should not be able to do so during an NDE. Rather than simply impressions of light and darkness, the accounts include detailed observations of hospital rooms during OBEs, deceased relatives, and so on. This is in striking contrast to the dreams of the blind, which are not visual (Ring & Cooper, 1997, 1999).

Research into the NDEs of children, as young as three or four, is important in determining the degree to which the experience might be due to expectation, for they would not have prior knowledge or understanding of the experience. There are, in fact, some phenomenological differences between the NDEs of children and adults. For example, children do not commonly report a life review – perhaps unsurprisingly, given their relative lack of extensive memories and experiences (Morse, 1994). There is also a higher incidence of encounters with animals, and even cases in which children report having met living friends, relatives, or teachers (Serdahely, 1990), challenging the notion that the deceased individuals and other beings commonly reported in NDEs are "real." On the other hand, some children report encounters with deceased relatives they never knew, and are able to either accurately describe them or identify them from photographs. Similar cases are also reported by adults who describe encountering the spirit of an individual whose recent death was unknown to them (Greyson, 2010). If confirmed, such cases support the theory that the NDE is evidence of survival, and that at least some of the deceased individuals encountered during the experience must be genuine conscious entities existing in some kind of afterlife accessible to NDErs.

Given the accumulated evidence, NDEs present a challenge to current reductionist models of the relationship between the mind and the brain (Moreira-Almeida, 2013; Holden, 2009). As with any area of scientific research, new explanatory models must be constructed to accommodate new information. In a recent development in the field, some scientists argue that NDEs are consistent with a "nonlocality" model of consciousness derived from quantum physics, meaning that consciousness is neither generated nor limited by the brain, but is a separate phenomenon which can survive the death of the body (van Lommel, 2007).

The more materialist-minded scientists often dismiss the evidence as anecdotal, or explain it away by reference either to poor research protocol (such as leading questions during interviews) or to faulty memory and invention on the part of alleged NDErs. It is significant, however, that many who were initially confirmed sceptics actually altered their stances as a result of their own research, including Fenwick, Parnia, Sabom, and Elizabeth Kübler-Ross. Cardiologist Pim van Lommel also became more open to the possibility of the survival hypothesis following his study of NDEs in ten Dutch hospitals (2006). Ultimately, however, from the perspective of empirical science there has as yet been no watertight, conclusive proof either way. No reductionist theory has been able to adequately explain the NDE in all its forms and occurrences; and no empirical, replicable study has proven beyond doubt that NDEs are evidence of dualism or of life after death.

As important to human ontological thought as such proof would be, it should be pointed out that NDEs could tell us only what the transitional state after dying is like – not what happens after that transition. In other words, even if consciousness does survive death and leaves the body, it is possible that it would not persist beyond the stages that NDErs have experienced.

NDEs, History and Culture

Accounts of NDEs can be found in apparently documentary contexts in narratives from ancient Greece and Rome (Platthy, 1992), medieval to modern Europe (Zaleski, 1987), ancient to modern China and Japan (McClenon, 1994; Campany, 1995), Pre-Columbian Mesoamerica and modern Mexico (Shushan, 2009), eighteenth and nineteenth-century United States (including foundational Mormon literature; Lundhal, 1982), twelfth-century to modern Tibet, modern Thailand and the Philippines (Belanti *et al.*, 2008; Shushan 2009); and in sixteenth through twentieth-century missionary, explorer, and ethnographer accounts of indigenous societies in the Pacific, Asia, the Americas, and Africa (Shushan, 2018; 2022). There are also phenomenologically comparable narratives in mythological, visionary, and other religious texts ranging from the Mesopotamian *Epic of Gilgamesh*, to the Indian *Atharva Veda* (Shushan, 2009), the *New Testament* (Paul's vision in 2 Corinthians, 12:1–4), and the *Tibetan Bardo Thödol* (Book of the Dead) (Badham, 1990; 1997).

Historical and cross-cultural NDEs are important in establishing the universality or otherwise of the phenomenon, a task made particularly complex by the fact that accounts vary not only between cultures, but also between individuals. Making sense of the similarities and differences is thus the key issue in studies of NDE narratives from different times and places.

When Zaleski (1987) compared modern Western NDEs with medieval European "otherworld journey" visionary texts, she found that in the latter the focus was on punishment and the process of judgment, whereas the former are more concerned with education and rehabilitation. Zaleski (1987, p. 190) considered "the otherworld journey story" to be "through and through a work of the socially conditioned religious imagination." However, this conclusion does not explain the parallels Zaleski herself highlighted, for although the similarities are general and thematic, it is significant that the medieval accounts share with modern NDEs numerous familiar elements: OBEs, tunnels and darkness, glimpses of other worlds, encounters with beings of light and other spirits, evaluation of one's earthly life, borders and limits, guides, reluctance to return to the body, and positive spiritual transformation upon revival. While these similarities may not be surprising considering that Zaleski's medieval and modern examples are both firmly rooted in predominantly Christian milieux, the idea that NDEs are entirely culturally/individually fabricated is further challenged by the NDEs of atheists, children, the blind, and in wider cross-cultural contexts. Indeed, Zaleski's conclusion implies the impossibility of cross-cultural consistency, unless we accept that different, culture-specific forms of "socially conditioned religious imagination" somehow lead everywhere to a similar kind of "story." This is not to ignore the numerous differences between accounts (also unsurprising given the cultural, geographic, and temporal distances involved), though difference neither negates nor explains away similarity.

Kellehear (1996, p. 28) stresses the sociological contexts of NDEs, suggesting that the variations between accounts in different cultures can be "accounted for by examining the way certain societies emphasise or downplay certain cultural images and symbols." Thus, while in the West individuals may describe moving through a tunnel, elsewhere people describe more generally moving through darkness. In other words, the key concept is not the tunnel at all, but the themes of transition and moving from a dark place to a bright one. Kellehear also argued that the lack of life reviews in small-scale societies was due to a corresponding lack of distinction between the self and that which is external to the self, and thus between the natural and supernatural. Individuals in such societies have no sense of personal guilt or individual moral responsibility, for correct behaviour is encouraged by laws and fear of consequences within the social group, not by ideas of divine justice. One would therefore not "seek a life-review in evaluative terms or be impressed by a biographical review of their individual deeds" (Kellehear, 1996, p.38). While largely correct (see Shushan, 2018), this suggestion does overlook the fact that NDEs are not sought, but spontaneous, and that individual evaluation and a reckoning of one's earthly life have also been reported in NDEs and religious beliefs of some indigenous societies (Counts, 1983; Wade, 2003; Shushan, 2018).

As Kellehear acknowledges, generalising about NDEs in such societies is highly problematic, particularly as very few examples were known at the time his book was written. My recent research (Shushan, 2018) explores how NDEs are culturally negotiated in the indigenous religions of North America, Africa, and the Pacific, prior to significant missionary influence or conversion. In Native North America, for example, NDEs were commonly valorised, and attempts were made to replicate them in shamanic visionary practices. In Africa, however, NDEs were often considered to be aberrational, viewed through the lens of local possession and sorcery beliefs, and were thus rarely incorporated into accepted afterlife conceptions. Furthermore, despite the cross-cultural similarities of these narratives with those found in other parts of the world, certain NDE elements do seem to correspond to social organisation or scale. Only in small-scale societies, for example, do NDEs commonly feature an afterlife realm located in or accessed via an earthly locale, and which is reached by walking along a path or road.

Some argue that the NDE is not simply a matter of cultural/individual interpretation, but one of cultural/individual perception. In other words, it is actually experienced in unique cultural and individual ways, including the use of local symbols to express ideas, feelings, and events associated with the phenomenon. As Kellehear summarised:

> [...] culture supplies broad values and attitudes to individuals and these provide individual orientation during an experience. In this way, cultural influences provide a basis for interpreting NDE content, and furthermore are crucial to shaping the retelling of the experience to others from one's own culture (2001, p. 34).

The cross-cultural evidence indeed suggests that certain elements of the NDE are thematically analogous cross-culturally, but experienced and interpreted in individual/culture-specific ways.

The reason for returning to the body is one example. In contemporary Western NDEs, the return is generally a matter of choice: either the NDEr does not feel ready to leave family or friends, or has some important unfulfilled goal to pursue. In Chinese and medieval European NDEs, however, the return is generally due to mistaken identity: the wrong "Jane Doe" "died" and was sent back to her body when the error was discovered. This suggests socially and culturally constructed interpretations of a thematic universal "return" element. In other words, the rationale for the NDEr's return to the body is culture-specific, though being instructed to return (for whatever reason) and returning is cross-cultural. Thus, while NDEs are culturally and individually experienced and expressed (or "mediated"), they appear not to be entirely culturally constructed. If they were, accounts from around the world and throughout history would not share such core elements as leaving the body, seeing the body below, darkness, other realms, encountering deceased relatives, a divinity or other supernatural being often radiating light, conduct evaluation or life review, barriers and obstacles, the attainment of divine or universal knowledge or wisdom, and positive after-effects upon return.

Conclusion: Philosophy, Religion, and NDEs

The existence of structurally similar narratives describing contextually stable experiences (that is, they usually occur as a result of being physically near death) from such different times, places, and cultural-linguistic backgrounds points to a pre-cultural origin of the phenomenon. In other words, the experience must originate in something other than the culture-specific images and beliefs provided by any particular society. Scholars such as Zaleski (1987), however, believe that there is no objective status to the phenomenon at all, writing that because experience cannot be divorced from culture, we must "renounce the notion that some original and essential religious experience can be discriminated from subsequent layers of cultural shaping." This argument is rooted in postmodernist-influenced denial of the possibility that there can be any kind of experience regarded as being "religious" cross-culturally. Again, however, cases of NDEs in children, atheists, and anyone whose prior beliefs conflict with their experience demonstrate that NDEs are not a product of expectation (cf. Athappilly *et al.*, 2006). An acknowledgment of "cultural shaping" as proposed by scholars such as Kellehear (1996, 2001) and McClenon (1994) does not indicate that there are no aspects of the NDE which are independent of culture. In other words, the fact that culture influences experiences does not mean that experiences do not also influence culture.

Zaleski also argues that a supposedly neutral term like "being of light" is not only potentially inaccurate in characterising what an NDEr may claim is Jesus or the Buddha, but is itself a culturally constructed term. However, this type of argument side-steps the issue that what is being described cross-culturally is a being that radiates light. Interestingly, this is explicitly supported in the *Bardo Thödol* which states that a "Clear Light" will appear in whatever form is most beneficial to the individual: as the Buddha to a Buddhist, as Vishnu to a Vaishnava Hindu, as Jesus to a Christian, or as Muhammad to a Muslim (Badham, 1997). The description of dying in the *Bardo Thödol*, in fact, so closely corresponds to the NDE that it can effectively be seen as verification that the book genuinely is what it purports to be – a preparation for what happens at death. This is regardless of whether the experience has a biological or spiritual origin (Becker, 1985; Badham, 1990).

This raises the issue of the relationship between NDEs and religious beliefs about the afterlife, which has been explored by scholars such as McClenon (1994), Badham (1997), and myself. The notion that religious beliefs can be rooted in extraordinary experiences has a long pedigree beginning with E.B. Tylor and Andrew Lang in the nineteenth century, though it was fully articulated with David Hufford's (1982) "experiential source hypothesis." In my book *Conceptions of the Afterlife in Early Civilizations* (2009), I compared such beliefs in ancient societies that had little or no cultural contact with each other (Old and Middle Kingdom Egypt, Sumerian and Old Babylonian Mesopotamia, Vedic India, pre-Buddhist China, and pre-Columbian Mesoamerica). As well as expected culture-specific idiosyncrasies, I found cross-cultural elements to these afterlife conceptions which correspond thematically to the NDE – the very elements listed at the end of the previous section, above. It is worth stressing the overall conclusion that the authors of the ancient texts were familiar with the phenomenon of individuals who appear to die, return to life, and subsequently relate having undergone something very much like what we know as a "near-death experience" today. This is reinforced by indigenous cases, such as those in many Native American societies, where NDEs were explicitly said to have formed local afterlife beliefs and even to have been the bases for particular religious movements (Shushan, 2018). These findings support the notion that while the NDE is both experienced and interpreted in culture-specific modes, it nevertheless has universal elements which in turn influence belief. These findings also independently validate the hypotheses of Hufford, Kellehear, and McClenon: that culture-specific beliefs influence the phenomenon, and vice versa.

OUT-OF-BODY EXPERIENCES IN THE SCREEN AGE

SAMANTHA LEE TREASURE

"We are fashioned creatures, but half made up."
MARY SHELLEY, *FRANKENSTEIN* (1818).

After a conference in East London, I headed to a nearby pub with Samuel[22] to interview him about his encounters with entities in out-of-body experiences. Amid the odour of beer-stained carpet and the faint din of TV sports, he tells me about his experiences with shadow figures, and even blue and green humanoids, until opening up about the most alien encounter of all. After coming out of his body, he explains, he was immediately greeted by "strobe lights [...] amazing patterns coming off of the walls [and] some kind of music." In a mirthful northern accent, he describes to me how he looked up to see "Mickey Mouse, raving his tits off" at the foot of his bed.

Out-of-body experiences (OBEs), or the experience of perceiving the world from a point of view outside of the physical body, can happen in both healthy and unhealthy populations, intentionally or unintentionally, and from sleep, dreams, or wakefulness. The psychological explanation is that, while our cognitive system usually excels at creating models of the world, treating the most stable model as 'real,' it can also make mistakes (Blackmore, 1984). This can happen when there is insufficient,

---
[22] Names have been changed to protect identity.

excessive, or contradictory sensory information, which can be caused by a variety of triggers, including deliberate induction (meditation, sensory deprivation), drug use, or trauma (see Blackmore, 1993, p. 175; Palmer, 1978). When this occurs, the system "seeks to re-establish [...] a new model of the surroundings from memory and imagination [...] treating this as 'real'" – hence the out-of-body experience (Blackmore, 1984, p. 1986). The deployment of this new model can be likened to cache files compensating for a live website when one's Internet connection is weak, in stasis until the connection is up and running again. Strikingly, the cache stores that presumably construct both our lived and OBE spaces are increasingly reflecting our cultural shift towards the virtual and fictional.

The OBE is textbook "eerie," to borrow Mark Fisher's (2016) suggestion that "we find the eerie more readily in landscapes partially emptied of the human." The OBE landscape is often – but not always – void of actors in comparison with dreams, making the experience like a solo journey through a ghostly duplicate of the environment (Treasure, 2019). Adding to the realism of this experience is the exceptional wakefulness and clarity of mind usually reported, with most feeling more wide awake than normal (Green, 1968, p. 83). It transforms the experiencer into a spectre:

> Carrie: You feel like a ghost. It's like you're in this weird isolation zone, and there's no 'spark.' It always feels weird going there, it doesn't feel like 'awesome, I'm home now' (Treasure, unpublished transcript).

The OBE is also textbook "weird," often involving the presence of something "which should not belong" (Fisher, 2016). Although the experience often begins in a realistic facsimile of the immediate environment, which philosopher Thomas Metzinger likens to visiting the set of the mental model when not in use (Rothman, 2018), there are often reports of minor discrepancies, such as a misplaced door or a wrongly shaped doorknob. There might also be strange features of light, like in the following report sent in by an out-of-body experiencer (OBEr):

> [...] the night time occurrence revealed the walls and furniture in a blue-purple light and I could see them and see through them at the same time (Green, 1968, p. 79).

Even more bizarre are the accounts of seeing something that they had no knowledge of, but which is later confirmed:

> [...] I saw my entire school from above with the roof off, seeing forbidden parts clearly. Later I found excuses to go to these parts (or stole in to see) and found it just so (ibid.).

While there is a *lot* that could be said about how eerie, weird and exotic OBEs are (as well as how mundane they can sometimes be), this chapter will focus on content relating to a growing trend that I have noticed over the years: the inclusion of fictional, virtual, or technological elements. I will also add that many, if not most, of the OBErs I have spoken to have revealed that they have had an element of clairvoyance or telepathy during an experience, which contributed to their belief that the OBE reflected objective reality in some way. As we will see below, however, it is sometimes difficult to discern what reflects reality and what comes from the imagination, or some other source.

I had come across the odd account of floating spirits or floating heads, but was recently surprised by reports of floating computer screens and cartoon characters in OBEs. A Sweden-based astral projector (a person who deliberately induces OBEs), told me that upon leaving his body, he saw two computer screens floating in front of him, one with the common meadow desktop background, and the other with the Windows icon in the middle. While these things *do* belong to our environment – that we are presumably storing in mental models of – they certainly do not float (at least, not as of 2022). It is almost as though the programming behind the storage and reconstruction of these models does not quite know what to make of these newer elements. A similar change is occurring in dreams. Robin Sheriff, an Associate Professor at the University of New Hampshire, has noticed that our waking arena is being increasingly muted by our mental focus on social media scrolling and similar virtual behaviours. In effect, we are becoming evermore mentally absent from the traditional stock scenes of human life (e.g., the dining table). In tandem, Sheriff has observed a steady increase in screen-mediated content such as cartoons and celebrities in dreams (Sheriff, 2017).

We expect dreams to be weird, but when encounters with fictional and technological elements occur in more realistic out-of-body experiences, it can have interesting implications for cosmologies. As dream characters are speculated to influence beliefs in supernatural agents (McNamara & Bulkeley, 2015), I wondered whether the figures in OBEs would have an even greater impact, and focused my bachelor's thesis on this topic. I was particularly interested in this phenomenon as I had experienced it numerous times, first triggered by a meditation practice and then happening spontaneously. Among the five UK-based OBE practitioners that I spoke to for the study, four of them had also experienced lucid dreams, so we were able to compare figures in both states. First there was the matter of defining the two. While both states involve waking-like cognition, there are a number of neurophysiological and phenomenological differences. For example, lucid dreams involve the realisation that you are dreaming and usually only occur during rapid-eye movement sleep, while, as mentioned above, OBEs can occur from a variety of conditions. It can be difficult to distinguish between the two sometimes, as OBEs can also occur from sleep or dreaming, 'dream-like' OBEs have been reported (Metzinger, 2005, p. 68), and there is evidence of an intermediate state between the two (Green & McCreery, 1994, p. 75).

When asked, my interlocutors said that they mainly distinguished the OBE from dreams by a distinctive set of "transition" or "trance" indicators, such as vibration or electric-like sensations, loud noises, and the realistic sense of separating or floating from the body. Sometimes voices accompanied this transition, for example: "she's going to be here" (Peggy), or "she's asleep, she's useless like that" (Jane), which adds to the theatrics of the phenomenon and the sense that something meaningful is happening. Although there has been a theoretical paper written about the vibrational state (Montenegro, 2020), there is still more research needed on these transition phenomena. On the other hand, in cases when there was no transition, there was a blackout period followed by suddenly finding themselves in a different location. This was in contrast to their lucid dreams in which they were typically already in a dream, and realised it within that environment.

While OBEs tend to begin in one's immediate surroundings, two interviewees also reported having OBEs that began from their childhood bedrooms, suggesting a throwback to an earlier mental model. Accounts from my own study and online commonly also often involve grainy or dark perception if it was night and they were in their sleeping environment (past or present), but this generally cleared or brightened the further away they were from their body, with the environment often becoming more fantastical. For example, they might find themselves in a different country, in daytime scenery when it is night, or in summer when it is winter. If we are to take Blackmore's (1984) approach of understanding the mental model as constructed from memory and imagination, this suggests that – at least some of the time – imagination could play a greater role over time, or at the point of exiting the immediate environment. The entrance into a new environment can occur when leaving the room or building by walking, floating or flying, by fading out of one space and into another, or by means of a portal: usually a wall, door, window, or mirror. Some also enter the OBE from a lucid or vivid dream or from sleep paralysis, sometimes using a similar induction method to their waking practice, and often also involving similar methods of movement from one place to the next.

In the introductory chapter to this volume, Hunter outlines four themes that William James recognised in his studies of religious experience: their ineffable (hard to put into words), noetic (imparts knowledge, of the ultimate reality, God, etc.), transient (short-lived and temporary) and passive (seems to come from an external source) qualities. Two of these characteristics, noetic and passive, were particularly impactful in the development of OBE-related beliefs in my case studies. Whether the experience is spontaneous or deliberately induced, passive elements were common, which contributed to the experience's value as noetic and purposeful. Turning back to manifestations of the eerie, Fisher notes that the question of agency lies at its heart, for instance the possibility of an as-yet unrevealed entity, or finding traces that someone was there before you (2016, pp. 63-64). This includes the dramatic transition, and the occasional inability to direct one's movement, as though they are being guided by a hand or other force, pulling the experient out of their body or to another location. This was also illustrated by discrepancies in my interlocutors' OBE environments, such as foreign items on one's coffee table, or a carved wooden head in the bed with them. Jane, who has been able to have OBEs since childhood, once found indiscernible red writing on her bedroom window but could not read it. She had another OBE immediately after this, and the writing was still there, but its meaning still eluded her.

Encounters with OBE entities nearly always "felt" more real, "as though they are really happening," and were seen as rarer and more meaningful than lucid dream encounters (see also Levitan *et al.*, 1999). When asked how entities compared in lucid dreams and OBEs, Jane said that she could control lucid dream characters to some extent, but not OBE figures. Several interviewees also noted that telepathic communication was more common in OBEs than in lucid dreams. Green & McCreery (1994, p. 115) note that encounters in OBEs can include the perception of people who were present in the physical environment but who were unresponsive to the OBEr, and 'visits' from individuals who were responsive but not actually present in the physical environment. This was the same in my case studies. In addition, unresponsive figures were reported in OBEs but not in lucid dreams. This mainly happened with humans and animals, who could sometimes not see, hear, or feel them, and seemed to be going about their day as normal, giving them the impression that they themselves were the unrevealed entity, able to spy on others. There were also occasions when they *were* seen by humans or animals, who then reacted with fear or surprise. For example, Jane saw a mother and daughter who were running away in terror, so she ran as well, until she realised that they were running away from *her*. Jane too had become a spectre.

In contrast, humans or other-than-humans who behaved as though they were privy to the goings-on of the 'astral plane' were often seen as guides, the deceased, or people from other times or dimensions. If they seemed confused or lost, they were interpreted as dreaming or deceased. When they were able to engage with them, they were felt to either heal or harm (by "charging" or "draining" energy), protect or guide, or to share the space as fellow explorers. Mainly, OBE entities were identified by a sense of knowing or intuition, rather than by appearance, for instance something could *look* human, but feel alien, or look metallic but seem organic. This is not uncommon in dreams – for example, your friend could look radically different, but it still *feels* like them. The transformation of characters in dreams has likely contributed to shape-shifter lore across cultures (Laughlin, 2011, p. 181), and the same can be said for OBEs. In these cases, such entities were usually seen as "masking" themselves, either to deceive or to save the OBEr from being frightened of their true appearance.

During an experiment in a haunted location, Jane had also seen the child ghost from *The Ring*, and believed that it was the resident ghost transforming in order to scare her. This character was also reported by Samuel after the study, but playing a different role, showing that even frightening entities could be seen as teachers or protectors. He explained how the entity:

Looked similar to the child ghost from the horror movie *The Ring*. She had long black greasy, wiry hair and she was looking downwards at all times, keeping her face concealed. She was wearing a kind of long dark cloak. Interestingly, she gave off the most loving energy and although she looked a bit creepy, I felt nothing but safety and security in her presence. My guardian angel perhaps? I'm not sure I believe in angels but she was definitely looking over me and she most certainly had my best interest in mind (personal communication, 2021).

Figures encountered in OBEs could also seem to be living in or exploring the space in much the same way as the experiencer is. This led to speculation that such figures were dreaming or astral projecting, or from a different time or dimension. As mentioned earlier, discrepancies in the environment could be seen as traces of a visitor, but alternatively, they could also be seen as evidence that one is peeking into the past, future, or another dimension. In addition, the entities present in the OBE version of the environment might also reveal information about one's surroundings or the people living there. For example, Carrie noticed that she would only see shadow figures when she was at a certain friend's house but not at her own home, which led her to wonder whether she was seeing manifestations of her friend's problems, or something that lived in his house.

Inhabiting Weird Bodies

Self-identity in OBEs tends to be associated with the mental self rather than the physical body, suggesting that the two are not inherently bound (c.f., Metzinger, 2003; Carruthers, 2015). In Green's (1968, p. 34) study of OBEs in the general UK population, 80% of participants reported that their consciousness was not located in any body or object during their OBEs, while others said that they seemed to be in a near-replica of the physical body. In discussions with astral projectors, I have also heard the second body described as translucent, iridescent, or star-like. This is likely to be highly dependent on one's culture, and in principle one might find themselves in a completely different body (Carruthers, 2015). If there is a mirror nearby, the OBEr might confirm that they look the same as usual, or see that they look slightly different or have no reflection at all (Green, 1968, p. 34, 75). Bizarrely, just as one might 'project' into a childhood bedroom, it seems that one can also revisit previous bodies. I personally had an out-of-body experience in which I looked in the mirror, and was amazed to see my reflection from about fifteen years prior, including my hairstyle and one of my favourite outfits at the time. One of my interlocutors later messaged me with a recent experience of looking in a mirror during an OBE, with an amusing result:

> Jane: I got out of bed (while out of body), and looked at myself in the wardrobe mirror and saw I had three boobs (I was half naked) and no head, although it looked like there was something not very solid where my head should have been, like a faceless ghost head, I guess? Also I think I had wings, but can't remember what they looked like (so probably like the head, not perfectly formed) [...] what I think is that forgotten parts of me tried to come forward (because I'm always trying to remember more about my past life) and got muddled up in the process of projecting (personal communication, 2022).

She quipped that if she regularly appeared this way in OBEs, it was no wonder that the mother and daughter had run away from her in the earlier OBE! These experiences show that there is room for a spectrum between having an "astral body" and experiencing oneself as a disembodied point of awareness, and their effect on cosmologies (e.g., beliefs in reincarnation). Instead of passing it off as dream-like, the imperfectly formed or strange parts can be a muddling of components from bodies across lifetimes. Furthermore, just as fictional and technological elements are cropping up in the OBE environment, so they are also appearing in descriptions of the second body. For my forthcoming book, I spoke with two American astral projectors who looked down to see that their 'astral body' was a cartoon, one in 3D and one in 2D anime style. They reacted to these experiences with surprise and curiosity and did not let on about any deeper effects on their beliefs, although the man who saw himself in anime wondered if this was because he was a huge fan of the genre and had been watching it since childhood.

A couple of years ago during an out-of-body experience of my own, I also experienced an unexpected 'astral body.' Here is my journal entry from that morning:

> I floated above my body and through the wall, expecting to end up in [my flatmate's] room, but instead I floated into a large futuristic bedroom. I saw an android sitting on the floor facing a low table at the

foot of the bed. Then suddenly I seemed to 'toggle' from third person to first person, finding myself now inside of the android body. I played with magnetic popcorn-shaped plastic objects that were in a bowl on the table, and then stood up and walked to the far wall, which was a large window. A sign outside read "Eton Square." It was raining, and the view was of a sterile and dreary square with steel numbers on sticks by the entrance. Meanwhile I noticed a little boy sleeping quietly in his bed and wondered if this android was his nanny.

I posted my android experience on my personal Facebook page, and among the replies there were two that speculated about what it could mean. One of them confidently wrote, "That was a time jump into the future," while another commenter suggested, "AI is consciousness. Jumping timelines?" Anthropologist Miho Ishii (2013) argues that in order to relate to the world in a 'non-delusional' way, a person must overcome their subject-centred perspective, which can be done by imagining the point of view of others. For example, Siberian Yukaghir hunters mimic the animals they hunt, taking on the animals' perspective, but they retain a kind of 'double perspective', careful not to lose their own identity or control (ibid.; see also Willerslev, 2004). In Western therapeutic settings, virtual embodiment has been used for rehabilitation purposes to allow abusers the chance to embody a similar form to their victims, thus increasing their ability to empathise with others (see Seinfeld *et al.*, 2021 for an overview). For some reason, we are experiencing the view from different bodies during out-of-body experiences as well, whether this is due to time jumps or theory of mind processes relating to fictional and technological actors. Considering that our physical bodies are muted in much the same way as a dining room scene, as we begin to manipulate digital avatars in the Metaverse, volumetric capture by companies such as DoubleMe or manufactured exoskeletons, and as our eyes are focused on fictional characters sometimes hours per day, out-of-body experiences promise to only get weirder.

Encountering Weird Entities

The Metallic Tentacle

Carrie is a death doula and dreaming instructor who has experienced over one hundred OBEs. In addition to encountering humans and alien greys, she has also seen numerous shadow figures – entities ubiquitous in supernatural lore that are typically hostile, featureless, and male. She calls these entities "hungry ghosts," as they seem to drain her of energy.

One evening, Carrie woke up in sleep paralysis to the presence of an entirely unique shadow figure. She was phasing in and out of her body when she saw a shadow tentacle emerging from the ceiling above her, metallic yet organic, with a sharp spike on its tip instead of slimy suction cups. Like the hungry ghosts she had grappled with in the past, the tentacle was also violent in its own way, painfully piercing her abdomen with its spike. However, instead of draining her, it began feeding her with energy and an "ancient, yet futuristic code" that transmitted a message: 52.

Years later during an ayahuasca ceremony, she relived this experience again, and realised that the sentience behind the tentacle could interact through other forms depending on which state of consciousness she was in. During the ceremony, it felt like a legion of benevolent aliens was present. They communicated to her telepathically that the message 52 meant that she would die at that age. This naturally spurred a succession of emotions in her, as she felt herself accelerate through layers of her ego, until finally all boundaries disappeared. Then, the being communicated that this had been a cosmic joke – their style of teaching – and that the number was not meant for her but for her friend's sister, who at the time had cancer in the abdomen. The emotions that she had experienced, they explained, reflect what it feels like to die, and that as a death doula this was something that she should know in order to provide better services. They also explained to her that from their perspective the initial visit as a tentacle had only just happened, as time was happening all at once.

Upon returning home, Carrie found out that her friend's sister had passed away at the age of 52, on the very day of her ayahuasca ceremony.

Recently, some of the most bizarre OBE encounters I have come across involve characters from TV. For example, I corresponded with an American astral projector who left her body only to see a strange door in her bedroom, which opened with a button reminiscent of a video game controller. When she pressed it, it revealed a closet with yet another door. Curious, she peeked inside the second door, expecting to see more classical content, such as meadows and ancestors as she had seen in previous experiences. Instead, she was greeted by a "cartoon world," with cartoon characters who stopped what they were doing and stared back at her. This was too weird even for her, and she ended the experience.

On a blog on the Korean platform Naver, a student wrote that they had encountered two entities which left them baffled – one during sleep paralysis, and one during an out-of-body experience. Both of them had been unfamiliar cartoon characters. The sleep paralysis intruder was described as a woman wearing traditional funerary clothing – quite normal in a paranormal context, except that her face was drawn like a manga-style cartoon character. The out-of-body experience also featured a drawn-on face, that looked like it was crafted from white crayon on black paper. Although terrifying at the time, in the clear light of day these entities were recalled with more curiosity than fear, noting, "isn't it funny that it appeared as a cartoon of all things?" (Naver, 2007). The relationship between sleep paralysis and OBE entities are striking and deserve further research. Although the former tend to be overwhelmingly frightening, they normally take place against a backdrop of the immediate environment, even as the figures themselves are sometimes fantastical, similar to many OBE accounts.

Beavis and Butthead

I came across an online post from an American astral projector, and got in touch to ask a few questions about his experiences. Firstly, he described what he considers an OBE to be:

> Chuck: So I can do this thing most mornings after waking up, where I stay still and try to remain aware. I let myself fall into sleep paralysis, then I slowly move my Astral body and I feel for the edge of the bed and slowly drag myself off and on to my feet, then I can move freely like normal. When I do that, I'm almost always in my room which is

upstairs. From there I was regularly using the stairs or the window next to the stairs to get out of the house.

Chuck went on to describe his encounters with fictional entities, including video game characters called "creepers" ("the green guys from *Minecraft* that blow up"), and the main characters from the popular 1990s cartoon *Beavis and Butthead*:

> Chuck: It was during an OBE. The morning I saw Beavis and Butthead I did my normal thing to get out of body but I had the thought to use the window next to my bed instead of the one by the stairs. This window leads to the front of the house where I can see the driveway. So I pop the window out, poke my head out to see what I can see. One side of the driveway there were two normal looking guys working on a car, and standing a few feet away was Beavis just standing there looking exactly like his cartoon self, then I see down the road Butthead riding a bike towards the house delivering newspapers like a paperboy.
>
> I was shocked, I've done this outta body thing a bunch of times, when I leave the house I'm almost always in my neighbourhood, so seeing these two cartoon people, who I haven't even thought about in like ten years, standing in my driveway with regular people and riding a bike down my street, it was crazy. They didn't just appear, as soon as I stuck my head out of the window everyone was just there like they had been there the whole time, and they were to scale with the people working on the car, if I had to guess they were maybe 5'10-6ft tall. Right when I went to fully crawl out of the window and see more, I faded awake, which is like everything fades to black and I'm awake.
>
> I thought it was awesome, and it's amazing how the subconscious just seems to remember everything. I have no idea why they would pop up when they did, like I said it's been so long since I've even thought of them. It makes a little sense though, when I was a kid that was one of my favourite shows, also one of my mom's friends used to call my buddy and I Beavis and Butthead because I'm blonde and he had dark hair [...]

Mickey Mouse and Tadpole Dad

Samuel, the interlocutor who encountered the ghost from *The Ring*, had also seen Mickey Mouse, as recounted above. He had experienced some frightening run-ins with shadow figures before, and set an intention to face his fears in his OBEs. The next time he came out of his body, he found that his room was flashing like a nightclub, with "trippy" imagery projected onto the walls. He could hear music, and at the end of the bed, saw Mickey Mouse dancing to it. When I asked what he made of this event, he said that he liked being in its company, and just enjoyed observing it. I had saved the question on fictional characters for last, after exhausting all other reports of encounters, and it seemed that Mickey Mouse would not have come up otherwise, which makes me think that there are more astral cartoons hiding in the closet than we might expect.

Earlier, Samuel had also described seeing a floating tadpole which had the head of his father. It did not communicate with him, and the strangeness of it confused him, which ended the experience. Besides Carrie's tentacle story, Samuel's experiences were by far the most bizarre among my case studies. He also admitted to having consumed a lot of drugs and alcohol, and to having experienced sleep paralysis multiple times (as had Carrie), and it is possible that these factors may have shaped the nature of his OBE content.

Lego Man

While writing this chapter, I had an out-of-body experience one morning which may have been influenced by these stories, hinting at the power of suggestion.

It started with a buzzing sensation and the sound of a man's voice narrating a TV show beside my bed (there is no TV in the room). As I felt myself float upwards, the voice became nonsensical and faded away. The ceiling had disappeared, and I easily floated past several dark bedrooms with a bird's eye view, not corresponding with my immediate environment. It occurred to me that I would like to encounter someone, and automatically I descended into one of the rooms. I looked around, and one corner of the dark room was lit – to my surprise, it was as though this part of the room was a cartoon. There was a bed, and lying on it was a yellow Lego man. It was human sized in height, but about an inch thick. Unlike its surroundings, the Lego man itself did not look like a cartoon, and I could pick it up (it did not react). I laughed, and the experience ended.

~

The weirdness of the above experiences might relegate them to the 'damned' category of OBE accounts. But to do so could deny us the opportunity of knowing what possibilities lie beyond the categories we are familiar with. Among the astral projection workshops and discussion groups I have attended in person, as well as in some online communities, I noticed that a common reaction to such OBEs was to dismiss it as "just" a dream. One suggestion was that it was the result of watching too much TV, but many of the people I spoke with said that they rarely watched television or cartoons. Also, many had reported the same transition symptoms commonly used in identifying more 'classic' OBEs, such as vibrations and floating sensations. So where are we to draw the line? Despite my annoyance at the dismissiveness in response to these experiences, I also found them difficult to come to terms with at first. Due to the realism I mentioned earlier, when I first began having out-of-body experiences I assumed that I was peeking behind the curtain to see a greater reality, a spirit world. But when I encountered discrepancies, instead of wondering if it was a parallel world or time jump, I thought that I might be seeing thoughtforms, or that the OBE was more dreamlike than we often like to think. But whether I believed that OBEs reflected the spirit world, thoughtforms, or cache files (or a mix of all three), I assumed that none of these had any business containing artefacts from TV or virtual worlds. However, just as there are diverse ways of lucid dreaming depending on the culture and individual, suggesting that they are a "cultural construction of a biological potential" (Lohmann & Dahl, 2014, p. 37), out-of-body experiences are also culturally diverse, perhaps to an even greater degree because they have a variety of causes, including dream, drug, or meditation-induced experiences. When you take into account Blackmore's (1984) suggestion that the OBE is constructed from both memory and *imagination*, there is even more room for diversity as our imaginations are practically limitless. If anything, rather than saying that the OBE is a kind of dream, as some would argue, you could say that the dream is a type of OBE, with the perceptual model at a different point on the spectrum between memory and imagination.

Several alternative perspectives have emerged online in relation to these 'non-standard' OBEs, with some astral projectors speculating that, like dreams, everything they see in the OBE state is from themselves, or that it can include thoughtforms that can be seen by others. These thoughtforms might have manifested from a powerful fandom, for example, or were residue from a film that never found its way to the silver screen. One interesting comment suggests that "they" are trying to "[poison] us with TV even in the astral realm," but it is unclear whether this is tongue-in-cheek or not. Another wondered whether it was the mind's way of attaining peace or joy, like a sort of self-therapy using content reminiscent of childhood. In the next section, we will see how these concepts are becoming increasingly common among younger generations. As for what the experiencers above thought, the tendency was to either enjoy these weird elements as curiosities or comforts. In my study, only Samuel suspected that some OBE figures might be imaginary – but then again, he was also the only one to report seeing a cartoon character. They were also interpreted as the products of shapeshifting; the child ghost from *The Ring* as a protector (to Samuel), and a hostile ghost (to Jane), while Carrie's alien being took different forms according to the state of consciousness. The person who saw the floating screens in his bedroom speculated that this could be a "thought form" or "tulpa," referring to the Tibetan and occult practice of manifesting thoughts into external spaces. He simply observed them in a neutral manner – it is aliens that would scare him, he added, not desktop icons. As for my Lego Man, I am still working out what to think about it!

Many, but not all of the accounts included in this chapter are from astral projectors, that is, people who have deliberately attempted to have an out-of-body experience. It has been shown that deliberate OBEs tend to provide a less accurate reflection of the physical environment (e.g. seeing a chimney that, when checked the next day, is not there) than spontaneous one-off cases, but this can vary between subjects (Green, 1968, p. 75). Discerning whether an OBE is spontaneous or deliberate is not always straightforward, however. It was repeatedly difficult for my interlocutors to answer whether their experiences were one or the other. For example, they may have attempted to have an OBE in the recent past, only to achieve it when they were no longer thinking about it. In this sense it is spontaneous, as it seems to sneak up on them, but at the same time it is pre-programmed in a way, via previous intentions or practices. Further studies could explore the correlation between entities or other features, and the circumstances of the OBE.

Finally, there was evidence of OBEs changing over a person's lifetime in my study, generally becoming increasingly populated by entities as experiencers became more adept. OBEs before adolescence were often described as devoid of visible entities, and involved simply floating around the bedroom. Usually in the late teens, OBEs occurred again, generally stemming from sleep paralysis, meditation or cannabis use. This kindled an interest and further attempts at astral projection using techniques, such as candle meditation or breathing exercises. The places seen, bodies inhabited and entities encountered left rich impressions on them, influencing spiritual beliefs and practical decisions such as where to live and who to share the sleep environment with.

My own out-of-body experiences, on the other hand, seemed largely to develop from my childhood dreams. I had had recurring dreams of a shopping mall with a hotel on top since I was a toddler (according to Sheriff, shopping malls are a common dream template in the modern world). Over the years, my dreams became lucid, and I memorised how to get around in some areas, occasionally seeing (and being) recurring characters. The shopping mall area fleshed out to include the surrounding city – Tokyo, which I assumed was down to my *Sailor Moon*-obsessed tween years. It continued to expand until it encompassed other countries and even a human colony on a pink dusty planet. I had always found these dreams comforting, and I thought that my mind was creating a fun and stable environment for me to explore. But things got weirder when I started to have OBEs in my mid-twenties. They often started with transition sensations in my sleeping environment, but increasingly I would feel a sudden tug from my lower back, accelerating until I reached this Future Tokyo world, although I would occasionally wind up in other locations. In OBEs beginning with a blackout period, I would often simply find myself already there, running track or doing tests on the water.

As I referred to above, OBEs typically feel more realistic or immersive than lucid dreams. Then and there it usually felt as real as walking around while awake – perhaps even more so, without my smartphone muting my surroundings. There were two pivotal moments that made me question reality: (1) Falling into water and being shocked at how realistically cold the water felt as I sank, and (2) waking up in a medical clinic that I had seen in a previous OBE, and panicking until I was given a shot of something which put me to sleep, only to wake up again in the same bed feeling groggy. This 'world' was so real and consistent to me that during these experiences I started to wonder whether it wasn't the real world, with *this* world that I am writing this chapter from only a hallucination (or better yet, some sort of simulation). If this was my imagination, I thought, I am in the wrong line of work and should perhaps turn to sci-fi. If it was a mental model based on an objective reality, then that opens up a new can of worms. A turning point came when I befriended a Romanian woman, who mentioned during lunch one day that she had had recurring dreams of a hotel with a shopping mall underneath it since she was a child. As she described the settings, I absent-mindedly told her that it reminded me of my recurring dreams. A minute or two later, we were finishing each others' sentences and napkin drawings.

After my study, Jane and I spent three hours on her living room floor conducting a thought experiment. Over many crumpled post-its, mugs of tea and plates of haggis, we asked ourselves, "if we were to take our OBEs at face value, what would that say about the nature of reality?" We were left with one simple sentence: *Jane is an alien and Sam is from the future.* This led to the speculation that this was a simulation of some sort, possibly a prison, an immigration test or a witness protection program. We laughed, partly because it was fun and partly because it made us nervous. I was not sure how much of my experience reflected memory and how much reflected imagination, but I was more aware than ever that OBEs can have a huge impact on cosmologies. I felt ill-prepared for the ontological shift that these experiences promised, and decided to try and stay tethered to this reality, while allowing myself to speculate on the possibilities. In the end, I decided to cool it with the OBEs for the time being, and focus solely on the OBEs of others. They still happen occasionally, and even after several years, I am still usually pulled to the same world. I sometimes miss it terribly.

As I tried to wrestle some logic out of my recurring journeys to 'Future Tokyo,' I thought about how OBEs can start in one's childhood bedroom. It occurred to me that since I had moved so much throughout my life, this may have been the most stable (or consistent) model for my mind to choose as the 'real' one, even if it had come from a recurring dream.

Either that, or we are living in a simulation from the year 2450.

Dating Draco Malfoy: Gen Z's Shifting practice

In addition to changes over one's lifetime, out-of-body experiences also seem to be transforming from generation to generation, especially when there are large cultural shifts at hand. This was seen during the recent social distancing periods during COVID-19 (2020). At an age when teens and adolescents are normally extending their social circles beyond the family home, they found themselves isolated indoors for extended periods – and with a wide variety of media to keep them company. During this time, personal screen time (outside of school) more than doubled for American teens (Nagata *et al.*, 2022). In these circumstances, perhaps it is no wonder that the digital natives of Generation Z[23] have curated their own altered states, using meditation, visualisation and scripting techniques to journey to their comfort characters. This has been dubbed 'shifting,' or 'shifting realities,' and although its aim is usually to enter fictional worlds, shifters often target a more attractive, parallel version of their own life, calling to mind the law of attraction and the many-worlds interpretation of quantum mechanics. Some shifters believe that they can 'permashift' (permanently switch to) their chosen destination.

Techniques are introduced, for example, via text instructions on sparkly pastel Instagram backgrounds, in snappy TikTok videos filmed in fairy-lit bedrooms, in longer YouTube videos in bright and welcoming bedrooms, or in anonymous Reddit communities. With every click, like or follow, algorithms discern the content that can hold users' attention for longer, to keep their paying advertisers happy. These algorithms usher the chosen ones onto the feeds of other users, spreading the techniques, stories and ideas that keep them clicking. The content is largely shared and consumed by teenage girls and young women, and overlaps to an extent with astral projection groups, with techniques such as the rope method (visualising oneself climbing a rope), or the use of binaural beats. Instagram user shiftingwith.lilly recommends the practitioner "put on some theta waves"[24] during their meditation,

---

[23] People born after 1996.

[24] Winkelman's integrative mode of consciousness (2013) posits that certain techniques such as drumming and fasting can alter one's brain state towards theta brainwaves (3-6Hz), inducing an experience of ecstasy or trance. Binaural beats which claim to have the same effect are popular with astral projectors, lucid dreamers and shifters. There is a paucity of

which is often associated with astral projection and lucid dreaming, before trying the popular shifting 'Julia Method' summarised below:

> Repeat in your head [...] "I am" "I am" until you get some sort of sign of shifting [she includes vibrations and twitches].
>
> Then start counting from 0-100 very slowly, TAKE YOUR TIME!
>
> [...] After you've counted, start using identity affirmations like "I am in (DR name)", "I love (hobby)" [...] keep on doing this until you feel completely disconnected from your body.
>
> [...] Once you feel your surroundings changed, open your eyes and you should be there (2021).

Accounts of successful shifting describe realistic immersion, although the content is occasionally mixed up, or the characters do not behave in the way they might wish them to. In the early days, one of the most popular goals of shifting was to date Draco Malfoy, the unpleasant Slytherin from the *Harry Potter* series. In spring of 2021, TikTok user strawbrryserena shared her account of meeting Draco Malfoy in her DR (desired reality):

> I was dating Draco. I still am, in my DR, I just haven't shifted since then, obviously [...] Although I am still there in my DR, you know, doing whatever, when you're in your DR in the moment, for me anyways, I don't really change as a person, if that makes sense. Like I still have my feelings, I'm still in my own head from CR [current reality].

Like having another Internet tab running in the background, shifters describe multiple lives that they switch back and forth from. The belief in multiple personal souls is wide-spread cross-culturally, and this is an interesting new take on it, with souls existing in parallel or fictional worlds. While in many cultures it is said that the detachment of one or more souls from the body can cause bodily, mental or spiritual illness (see Tylor, 1871, pp. 6558-6595), shifters tend to approach this split as a

---

scientific research with only small sample sizes to back this up (Abraham, 2021), but there is anecdotal evidence that it does have an effect on some people.

kind of multitasking. A claim that has become popular is that a 'clone,' or "piece of consciousness you leave behind in your CR (current reality)," is holding down the fort while you shift (Reddit). From accounts like the one above, it seems that this goes both ways, with a part of them also 'running in the background' within the DR while they go about their regular waking life. This is hinted at in her video when she mentions that the last time she shifted, Draco was visibly upset and revealed that he felt she was distant and out of it. She finds this interesting as it alludes to her main consciousness being 'away' in her CR in between her shifts. His behaviour, then, tells her something about the effects of returning to the CR on the characters in the DR, e.g. noticing that she is not all there.

The reactions of astral projectors to shifting is similar to reactions to the cartoonified experiences described above, but are even more cynical. One common accusation is that they are lying to get views, which can sometimes be monetised or give them social clout. These criticisms sometimes come from shifters themselves, e.g. Instagram shifters warning followers to ignore the advice of TikTok shifters. In the subreddit r/Witchcraft, a discussion titled "People believing they can astral project into an anime world?" expresses scepticism that fiction can be experienced via spiritual or supernatural avenues. Not everyone is cynical of the abilities of shifters, however; one witch suggests that these characters and fictional worlds may have been birthed in other realms before breaking through into this one. Another points out the hypocrisy of people who believe in luck and money spells but who cannot consider that someone might manifest a space inhabited by anime characters. But there is also a fair amount of ridicule, mainly in YouTube videos stating that shifting is not real (mostly made by guys, one commenter points out). In the witchcraft subreddit, someone argues that the people in question "don't even know the difference between lucid dreaming, astral projection, and quantum shifting so they have no business doing any of these things," adding that it is ridiculous to call it a "spiritual practice."

Lucid dreamers and astral projectors from the older Millennial generation have also questioned whether shifting is just a different name for these experiences, as there is substantial overlap with techniques and characteristics. There are shifters who both agree and disagree with this. There is some degree of control and order in shifting practices, with 'safe words' or phrases that safely return them to their CR, and a 'waiting room' that they first enter before reaching their final destination.

This is extended to their practice known as 'scripting,' involving the writing or typing of affirmations and intentions about how they want the experience to play out. The scripting, or incubation, of the experience is shared with many lucid dreaming practices (and consorting with celebrity crushes is popular in both communities). However, therapist Grace Warwick argues that shifting is not the same as lucid dreaming, calling it instead a transliminal experience (Smith, 2021), referring to the hypothetical tendency of psychological material to cross into and out of consciousness (Thalbourne & Houran, 2000).

While many shifters and lucid dreamers seek to control their experiences, in contrast, many of the astral projectors that I spoke to from my generation have taken a more random approach, waiting until they are out of the body before they shout their intention or aim (which does not always work), or alternatively deferring to the wisdom of the OBE, sometimes allowing themselves to be guided by another being or force. On the other hand, reports of shifting often share the transition sensations associated with out-of-body experiences such as the vibrational state, and phenomenological characteristics like stability in the environment and the realistic feeling of telepresence. Shifting is also similar with deliberate OBEs – and it could be argued that shifting *is* the deliberate induction of an OBE to a degree – in that imagination seems to be reflected more strongly than in spontaneous OBEs. Returning to Blackmore's (1986) paper, she suggests that the skills needed for deliberate OBEs are:

1) The ability to disrupt or ignore sensory input [...] a 'letting go' of the world.
2) The ability to construct a viable alternative model from information in memory (i.e. to imagine it), and
3) The ability to attend to the imagery model rather than the sensory model (1986).

These three points are at the core of shifting practices, which can be achieved through (1) the ability to 'let go' of the world (achievable through meditation and focus), (2) scripting and visualisation – especially from different viewpoints, and (3) the capacity for 'absorption' (Irwin, 1981, 1985, cited in Blackmore, 1986). Blackmore's study, the participants in which were all parapsychologists and psychical researchers, showed that lucid dreams, the ability to choose or stop dreams, concentration, and seeing with the eyes closed were more common in those who could deliberately induce OBEs, whereas day-dreaming, forgetting one's surroundings, and mystical experiences were slightly more associated with those who had spontaneous OBEs (Blackmore, 1986). I would argue that shifting is a new state of consciousness, and possibly an example of the intermediate state between lucid dreams and out-of-body experiences posited by Green and McCreery (1994, p. 75). Keeping in mind "how large a shift in functioning [there] must be to warrant recognition as a different 'state'" (Seligman & Kirmayer, 2008), there seem to be enough divergences from both lucid dreaming and astral projection in terms of both the phenomenology and the social markers to argue for it being a new state of consciousness. It is important to keep in mind, however, that because there are diverse physiological and cultural factors involved, shifting will likely be experienced differently by part of the group, even if they follow the same instructions (see Cassaniti & Luhrmann, 2014). We cannot rule out that some shifters may indeed find themselves in a lucid dream while trying to shift.

By December 2021, while the *Harry Potter* world was still a popular destination, shifters also aimed to connect with anime worlds, K-Pop singers, and TV series like *Glee* and *The Chilling Adventures of Sabrina*. The motives given by shifters themselves range from entertainment to therapy, allowing them to be themselves or feel a sense of belonging which might be missing from their lives while living out fantasies in familiar worlds. One shifter shared that she felt starved of touch, and was seeking to compensate for this in altered states. Although screen-mediated socialising is convenient, we are missing out on an important aspect of interaction – touch and telepresence – which can be fulfilled, at least in part, by out-of-body experiences in particular (Treasure, 2019), as well as similar states. With the rise in media consumption, there has also been an increase in research interest on parasocial relationships, or one-sided relationships with fictional characters or public figures (see Hartmann, 2016). If what shifters say is correct, they have found a way to overcome the screen and make their parasocial relationships a little bit less *para*.

It is not just about who or what they are running *to*, but what they are running from. The practice offers a respite from personal or world problems such as the pandemic, personal illness, climate disaster and political upheaval. One shifter from Turkey told me that it allows her to improve her mental health without burdening her loved ones with her problems, and acts as a free alternative to expensive or inaccessible therapy. Others express comfort in the knowledge that they are not completely stuck in their sick body. An exchange in the comment section of one YouTube video titled *How I shifted to Hogwarts* (Au, 2020) reflects this need for spiritual and emotional freedom during the pandemic:

> Gen z really said "I hate it here <3" and left. [This comment had 11K likes].
>
> The government told us "stay home" and we shifted to another reality.
>
> I mean technically we are [...] home to Hogwarts.

I suggested that we are so steeped in fictional worlds that the media we consume are seeping into the building blocks of our mental models, and that this is reflected in out-of-body experiences. Unexpected encounters with fictional characters in out-of-body experiences were generally seen as curious or amusing without greatly impacting cosmologies, in comparison to encounters with other types of figures such as humans, shadow figures or supernatural-like entities. Overall, their OBEs led to beliefs in time travel, multiple dimensions, and the ability to communicate with the deceased during this state. Once they were able to achieve this state, they usually used it to explore, heal, or to attempt connection with the living and the deceased. Carrie's experience with the tentacle had a deep meaning for her, which made her more empathetic towards those at the end of life, guiding her along her path as a death doula. In Jane's case, *she* seemed to be the supernatural entity striking fear into the figures that saw her.

There seems to be a definite overlap between the fictional content reported by the OBErs in the first part of this chapter and shifters, who are largely digital natives of Generation Z and actively seek this content out. Their proactive attitude towards altered states of consciousness, in comparison with previous generations of astral projectors, is perhaps the result of a life growing up with more control over media, with interactive Internet and streaming services, rather than passive television following a set schedule (I grew up with four channels and three siblings). As noted in Shushan's chapter on near-death experiences, there is evidence for the effect of culture on NDEs, and the same can be said for OBEs, demonstrating the need for caution against forcing definitions and frameworks that limit rather than inform. And even when scientific models may elucidate aspects of this phenomenon, the question of what is coming from one's mind and what might signify contact with another being or world promises to enchant us.

SUPERHUMANITY

An Exercise of Active Imagination

MICHAEL GROSSO

In the flow of ordinary life, things occasionally occur that strike us as strange or weird. The more compelling forms of weirdness force us to face something we do not understand and to question our basic assumptions about what is possible. The weirdness hints at something independent of the known "laws" of nature – *anomalies,* outlaws in the Wild West of the imagination – aka miracles, or paranormal phenomena (psi for short).

When I scan the spectrum of reported extraordinary phenomena, the different parts fall into place to form the image of a possible human. The picture that emerges is a futuristic version of ourselves – a model of our potential superhumanity. I am trying to understand what that would be like, however fantastic and incredible it might seem at first sight. Thanks to some psi experiences of my own, I have a smattering of internal benchmarks to help me in this exercise (Grosso, 2012). So, in this chapter I will attempt to imagine what a more fully evolved paranormal human existence might be like.

What are called "miracles" are closely associated with religion, where they are usually explained by reference to the direct influence in the world of one or another divine agency. That is not how I will use the term here. There are many possible ways we might explain extraordinary phenomena, but there is no consensus. The religious explanation is just one possibility. The aim here is to paint a broad picture and to try to imagine what that picture might mean to us as human beings – perhaps as our remote evolutionary future. Instead of trying to explain extraordinary phenomena, the aim here will be to inhabit the psychic space of what the facts suggest is possible. Nothing more is required than following the images of the conceivable wherever they take us. The exercise is about owning our latent potentials, instead of distancing ourselves from them.

Weirdness has a futuristic overtone I want to underscore, as with the *Weird* Sisters in Shakespeare's play, *Macbeth*. The witches are confusing, ambiguous, but secretly point to *what will be*. So the weirdness of the paranormal may be pointing toward things to come. As with Franz Brentano, consciousness is always *of something*, always intentional, pushing onward.[25]

My aim here is twofold: first, to lay out a selection of extraordinary phenomena; parapsychological, historical, religious, and so forth. Second, we will look at the phenomena in terms of our possible future: give them a voice, unroll a large canvas for their self-expression. The extraordinary data must exist for a reason. Suppose, in fact, that they are signalling to us about the possible future of our species?

We might imagine our futuristic transformation taking place in two ways. In the first, the powers implied by the miracles may represent a more completely evolved human being; today's anomalies would prefigure our future reality as *homo supernormalis*. How long and what sorts of mutations or futuristic experimentation this might entail are unknown, but the case for a next step toward a more evolved human can be made – grounded, as it is, in our super-data bank. The first possibility has appeal in light of the unfortunate downward trend of our species and the climate apocalypse looming before us.

On the other hand, our supernormal powers might be a preview of our postmortem survival. Survival in a mentalist universe may explain why we have extrasensory and psychokinetic abilities, they may represent parts of us that presumably carry on after we shed our physical bodies. There are no physiological organs for the exercise of our psychic abilities and no really reliable use of them in adapting to our earthly environment. Yes, there are occasionally helpful psychic experiences, but on the whole, nothing that could be called reliable.

---

[25] According to German philosopher of mind, Franz Brentano (1838-1917) who influenced Husserl, intentionality is the essence of consciousness.

Their true function may in fact be pre-adaptive to our post-biological existence. The psi data, on this reading, are precognitive signs of our postmortem continuity. It is also possible that we have psi abilities for the purposes of both terrestrial adaptation and evolution *and* as an intimation of our postmortem existence.

Our Extended Self

Whatever words we use to describe our unusual mental abilities – miraculous, paranormal, supernormal – they are extraordinary expressions of mental abilities we all possess to variable degrees. Clairvoyance is an extension of ordinary sight; clairaudience of hearing. Precognition is a shortcut to prediction based on inference; retrocognition an extension of memory. Psychokinesis is kin to the wilfulness of a child, or to the focused will of an ascetic or a worldly entrepreneur – all extensions of common intentionality.

Miracles may come from the unknown depths of our own minds. This is an idea worthy of actively trying to imagine. After all, Jesus did say that the Kingdom of God was within us. The Indian Upanishads tell us that our real self, Atman, is at bottom identical with Brahman, the supreme being. Plato tells us that our souls are cluttered with material we are attached to that needs to be cleared away before full contact with our enlightened self is possible. The problem is that we are unconscious of the transcendent depths of our being. The normal human condition is marked by severe psychical contractedness.

An Outline of Reported Inexplicables

We can distinguish three classes of phenomena that point to our possible futuristic selves. The first includes UAPs – unidentified aerial phenomena (aka UFOs). Since 2017, the US government has finally decided to level with the American people, and admit that there are unknown intelligent entities cavorting in our air space. Their technology far outstrips our own, which is a momentous challenge to science, to say the least. The UAP spectrum of phenomena is also of interest to theorists of religion. There are accounts of religious experiences that include UAP-like phenomena. There are libraries of testimony on these aerial enigmas.

So that is the first class of phenomena that interests us. They are largely about uncanny events that we witness *external* to ourselves, but they can also affect the way that we view ourselves *internally*, especially if contact or abduction are part of the experience. So we find reports of people who are convinced they are in some way biologically linked to extraterrestrials (Hopkins, 1981). UAP data is also connected to the history of religion, and examples frequently pop up in the context of the world religions, from Moses and the burning bush (Exodus, 3) to a UAP staging visions of the Virgin Mary at Fatima, Portugal, in 1917.

The second class of extraordinary phenomena is perhaps the largest, most copious, and covers several types. The two main types are extrasensory perception (ESP) and psychokinesis (PK). ESP has three forms: telepathy, clairvoyance, precognition and retrocognition. Psychokinesis is perhaps the most versatile of these weird phenomena, from providing help in a dice game to causing vast quantities of milk to dematerialise before statues of the Indian god Ganesha.

All of these are termed *psi* phenomena, and cannot be explained with the models and concepts of current physical science. But why do we have these powers? How are they woven into the deep texture of our lives? What is their purpose? They operate outside of our biological organ systems. Nevertheless, they are somehow linked to some highly weird and highly public physical and biological phenomena.

There is a third category of effects that is uniquely strange and transformative, and strange in a deeply positive way – namely, mystical experiences. Some people, as part of their spiritual practice, or as the result of obscure circumstances, undergo an experience of unity, peace, and love that is utterly unique and transcendent. The mystical experience should be key to any new science of evolutionary psychology. Moreover, there is a strong causal connection between mystical and paranormal events, the former being conducive to the latter (see Grosso, 2016).

A Note on 'Obvious Miracles'

Before proceeding, I want to say something about a category of phenomena that we can identify as *obvious miracles*. By an obvious miracle I mean something that is right in front of us 24/7 but is a complete mystery. It is worth noting that our very existence is founded on three obvious miracles: the physical universe, life, and consciousness. All three are astonishing, but radically unexplained by our scientific models. It looks as though the universe, along with space and time, exploded out of a point about 13.7 billion years ago and is still expanding at an accelerating rate. Nobody knows why or how, just as nobody knows how life was created out of nonliving substance. Biological science knows how to describe, analyse, manipulate, kill and replicate existing life forms, but the creation of life *de novo* remains a mystery. Finally, there is the unexplained phenomenon of consciousness – the miracle of miracles, indeed, the entire universe of mind, in which we are all perpetually enclosed. All efforts fail to reduce or explain consciousness and its infinitely varied forms to the physical; there are slippery correlations and causal connections, but never identity, never an exact reduction of one to the other. Reminding ourselves of these three fundamental mysteries ought to keep us humble. We are entitled to ask big questions and speculate on extraordinary possibilities (Kelly *et al.*, 2006).

Supernormal Transformation

So, what are we as humans doing with all these weird, miraculous potentials? One possibility, as mentioned, is that they represent the unacknowledged seeds of human evolution. It is, after all, reasonable enough to say that humans are not a fully evolved species. Moreover, judging our species as a whole, we have mishandled the world around us, and each other, to a point where our collective behaviour has driven us to the threshold of planetary climate chaos.

It might then be useful to actively imagine our possible future in light of the stories and images – the memes of the marvellous – that we gather from historical experience. It can be done from the standpoint of three tiers: physical, biological, and psychological.

Physical

The general drift of transformation is toward a new lightness and elasticity of our physical being. It seems oriented toward evolving what is sometimes called the "subtle body." I can only mention a few examples of this physical lightening up. In the UAP and UFO world, we find reports of people being levitated. Linda Moulton Howe (2002) presents detailed accounts of light beams with stunning counter-gravitational effects. There is an experimental side to this as well: Kenneth Batcheldor

(1984) was able to teach non-psychically endowed subjects to levitate tables into the air without any physical contact. Numerous reports of poltergeists are similarly notable for their apports of rocks and other physical objects passing through solid matter.

Against the background of current modes of transportation and the planet-wrecking over-burning of fossil-fuels, I am drawn to a phantasy of supernormal travel and of landscapes purified of automobiles and airplanes. We can advert to images of aboriginal clever men, ecstatic saints like Joseph of Copertino and Tibetan yogis like Milarepa who were known to levitate, bilocate, teleport, physically elongate, and disappear completely.

Once we realise that we, our inner selves, are not in three-dimensional space as our bodies are, clairvoyant travel becomes possible. Imagining futuristic and surrealistic spaces has been a central theme of modernist art (Nadeau, 1989). Moreover, we have data that subverts our normal idea of time, evidence for pre-cognition and retro-cognition (MacKenzie, 1975). I was convinced of the former in 1981 when I had three dreams showing me the attempted assassination of President Ronald Reagan and his recovery weeks before the event. I shared my dreams with students in a class discussing the mind-body problem; and we were able to confirm them on the day Reagan was shot. Evidence for retrocognition is harder to come by, but real enough. In light of such data, we can imagine ourselves as beings whose consciousness is unbound by time and space (Denton, 1866). Of course, this will not be apparent as long as we psychically dwell on the surface of our mental life.

Who knows how we may evolve new ways of negotiating the constraints of space and time? The eco-pressure against burning fossil fuels might stimulate the psychic mutations needed to develop new forms of communication and new modes of transportation.

Our new supernormal body will not only be highly mobile in space and time, it will also be invulnerable to forces that are normally damaging. We have already seen gravity tamed and the need for nutrition suspended. In fire-walking ceremonies the world over, it has been demonstrated that individuals who enter the right state of mind can render their bodies immune to the effects of fire and extreme heat. Besides the fire-walking ceremonies, so well documented, there are stories of saints, yogis, and physical mediums that handle fire and intense heat in ways that defy normal human expectations.

There are two sets of complementary phenomena that relate to the super-physicality of our future human, and they certainly raise the weirdness quotient: materialisation and dematerialisation. These are effects we instinctively associate with stage magic or superhuman creative power.

Sathya Sai Baba was either the supreme master of legerdemain *or* a mystic with a miraculous ability to create physical objects out of thin air. For starters, two entirely credible persons recounted to me how photographs of Sai Baba in their possession, spontaneously exuded *vibuti,* or sacred ash. For those who want to bear down on the details of Sai Baba's spiritual and miracle-rich career, I recommend two books in particular – Murphet's *Sai Baba: Man of Miracles* (1971) and Haraldsson's *Miracles are My Calling Card* (1987).

Sai Baba's reported phenomena included materialisations in broad daylight of *vibuti* (sacred ash) and things ranging from jewellery and talismans to exotic foods, with an emphasis on delicious sweets. Some will insist that sleight of hand can produce all sorts of illusions, but one thing your best stage magicians cannot do is produce objects *on demand.* For example, on one occasion, Haraldsson could not understand what a "double rudraksha" was and Baba produced one on demand, an acorn-like object, a rare anomaly in nature. Baba once asked Dr Roerichs, "Whom do you worship most?" The doctor replied, "Ganesh," so Baba produced a silver ring with a picture of Ganesh engraved on it. A Mister Krishna out of the blue asked Baba for an apple as they were walking along. Baba walked up to a tamarind tree and picked out an apple. Mrs Radakrishna and her daughter report that Baba once placed leaves in their hands and told them to wish for anything, any fruit or sweet or holy object, which then they found in their hands. Baba often produced on demand fruits out of season and "hot foods, sometimes steaming hot, even after he has been out of his quarters for an hour or longer" (Haraldsson, 1987, p. 25). It is hard to imagine the Swami with steaming hot food up his sleeve.

The intrepid Haraldsson and his research colleague, Karlis Osis, managed to meet Sai Baba face to face, and tried to get him to do a scientific experiment with them. That was not going to happen. But, upon meeting the Western scientists, Sai Baba materialised a big hunk of candy out of nothing for the visitors. Duly impressed, the scientists ask, "How do you do this?" And Baba replies: "Mental creation. I think, imagine, and then it is there." And then he said, "Spiritual love is central, miracles are small items. Love is giving, and forgiving." Haraldsson argues that he and his colleagues, including Doug Henning, a famous stage magician, never detected any sign of prestidigitation. The steady stream of producing all sorts of things on demand hardly supports the magic trick hypothesis.

Just as Sai Baba's photographic images reportedly exude sacred ash, so are there images of Jesus that reportedly bleed or shed tears; so do images of different saints, and of the Virgin Mary, also weep and bleed. By chance I was able to witness a miracle of materialisation on October 27th, 1994, in Astoria, New York City at the St. Irene Chrysovalantou Cathedral. I had heard on NBC News about an icon of Saint Irene – a name that means peace – shedding tears. So I drove to Astoria, got into the line of visitors and observed what looked exactly like large tears roll down from the icon's inanimate eyes. The tears were interpreted as signalling new woes in the Mideast. The icon had a history and was known to shed tears at times of trouble and served to lift the spirit and unite the great body of believers. Some miracles occur in a collective crisis, and are existentially helpful, like the multiplication of food and drink, or the calming of a storm. The Bible is full of miracle stories like that. In other forms of miracle, archetypal symbols like tears and blood materialise on paintings and statues (Grosso, 2020, pp. 1-7). This astonishing power I relate to accounts of supernormal healing.

Materialising something apparently *ex nihilo* ill fits our customary idea of what is possible. Dematerialising a physical object – making it vanish from existence – is not just very weird but also slightly scary. There are true tales of paranormal disappearance. I would rather not try to imagine myself dematerialising, but I have witnessed an instance of dematerialisation, an event that has been called 'the miracle of the millennium' by Hindu writers who witnessed it. India has many gods and one of the most popular is Elephant-Headed Ganesha, the Remover of Obstacles. Statuettes of Ganesha may be found in temples everywhere; they are as popular as crucifixes or plastic Madonnas in Catholic churches.

Lord Ganesha is honoured by feeding him milk. On September 21st, 1995, a man dreamt of Ganesha asking for some milk. The man rushed out to the nearest temple with milk for Ganesha, which to his astonishment was drunk up into empty space as he placed it near the statuette. A crowd gathered around him, and before long everybody was watching milk disappear into nothingness all over the world. By the end of the day there was a milk shortage in India.

By a stroke of luck, I saw on my television screen an amazed BBC reporter lift a small cup of milk to a small statue of Ganesha; the milk slowly and clearly diminished and then *disappeared*. Millions around the world were observing the same phenomenon repeated again and again. Two of my Indian students reported their experience to me in detailed written form; one of them explained that he stood in line twice to experience the phenomenon. The attempts of "scientists" to explain it away were ludicrous. The miracle was global and there were millions of eyewitnesses, but then it stopped, after one full day. If the alleged scientific explanation was true (involving some kind of capillary action), it would happen every time milk was presented to the statue. But it happened for just one day and then abruptly stopped. The phenomenon upends our idea of reality in the same way that materialised food, blood or tears can throw us into a metaphysical tailspin (Grosso, 2020, pp. 104-107).

Where did all that milk go and where did all the blood and tears come from? It is daunting trying to reimagine our physicality along the lines implied by the preceding accounts. It suggests that our four dimensional world is enclosed in some configuration of hyperspace. In sum, data suggests that our common sense, four dimensional world of time and space is *not all there is.* Our weird data allow us to imagine ourselves existing in a spatially and psychically extended world, a world whose boundaries are nowhere to be found, as the Greek philosopher Heraclitus once observed when he remarked: "You would not find out the boundaries of soul, even by traveling along every path: so deep a measure does it have" (Kirk & Raven, 1957, p. 205).

Biological

Now to shift to a biological perspective on our possible psi-based evolution. Begin by imagining yourself enjoying perfect health, but living without need of food or drink. You are endowed with the gift of inedia, of being attuned to a higher form of nutrition. Would you be willing to forego the infinite pleasures of the palate? The conviviality? The phenomenon of inedia involves living without food or drink for months, even years, and without negative effect. People do brief fasts, with physical and mental benefits. Much less widely known is that some people carry the fast to inordinate lengths of time and manage to function quite well.

Modest forms of fasting are used to purify mind and body in most spiritual traditions, and are a normal technique for maintaining and improving health, as you can learn from Dr Alan Cott in his fascinating book, *Fasting: The Ultimate Diet* (1975). In another intriguing book on this underrated topic, the author quotes the anthropologist E.B. Tylor, who suggested that "fasting is among the strongest means of disturbing the functions of the mind so as to produce an ecstatic vision" (Shelton, 1978, p. 68). Tylor is not talking about modest, healthy fasts here, but rather the prolonged fasts of hunger-strikers (such as Gandhi), shamans, yogis, saints and other mystics.

The Bavarian stigmatic and visionary, Therese Neumann (1898-1962), reportedly ate and drank nothing for the last thirty-five years of her life. She claimed to be nourished by the Eucharistic host, a thin wafer devoid of nutrients. A group of scientists and nuns kept her in sight continuously, day and night for two weeks, recording her vitals throughout, and certifying that she took nothing in and eliminated nothing. The rather cheerful, healthy-looking mystic passed her two week test with flying colours (Steiner, 1967, pp. 27-30). Jani the Indian yogi (1929-2020), said to be initiated by his local goddess, is supposed not to have taken any nourishment for most of his long life, and he too was very carefully placed under close observation by scientists. Like Neumann, Jani demonstrated two weeks of perfect abstinence. He too claimed his source of nourishment was sacred power, not ordinary food.[26] Given the versatile nature of telekinesis, why not?

In our world many live on the brink of starvation, with climate change threatening the global food chain, resulting from the alarming insect extinction rates.[27] There is a growing evolutionary pressure for humans to reconfigure the way that we nourish and vitalise our bodies. New modalities of nutrition are part of our futuristic story.

If inedia is a discomfiting idea to muse upon, then the next item of miraculous transformation is much more heartening. For it seems that somewhere in the depths of our archetypal being lie powers of miraculous healing. Stories of such are often linked to religious persons, places, or symbols. So, for example, when we open the first written account of that favourite saint, Francis of Assisi, by Thomas of Celano (1200-1260), we find in Part III, a *"Treatise on the Miracles of the Blessed Francis."* In one story, a man steals water that Francis used to wash himself and sprinkles it upon his oxen to stop the pestilence that was sweeping through his neighbourhood. After that, we are told, there was an end to the pestilence. The belief that anything touched by

---

[26] Prahal Jani was tested and observed 24/7 for 15 days by the Indian DTPAS.

[27] As well as other geopolitical factors.

a person of holiness and spiritual power goes on to retain something of that person's power is widespread and explains the appeal of relics.

In the case of the seventeenth century saint, Joseph of Copertino, I found well-documented accounts of healing as a result of contact with an object that had been in contact with the saint. We know that belief, expectation and an attitude of unclouded confidence are hallmarks of the mind-set that is most conducive to psi events. Feelings of physical contact with the source of the alleged power must increase the feeling of confidence known to facilitate paranormal results.

There are many assertions of *instantaneous* healings in Celano's biography of Francis. For example: "Another citizen of that city had a tumour between his shoulders the size of a large loaf of bread. After he was blessed by St. Francis, he was suddenly so completely healed that no trace of the tumour remained." Reports of such instantaneous healings are found in abundance in the miracle literature, and are bound to strike most uninformed modern readers as incredible. And yet there are modern examples of the phenomenon. The case of Pierre de Rudder is one of the most famous, occurring on April 7th, 1875, at a Lourdes sanctuary in Oostacker, Belgium. For eight years and two months, de Rudder suffered from a broken leg whose suppurating wounds never healed, causing him great pain and forcing him to move around on crutches, in spite of the best doctors' attempts to help him. The bottom broken part of his leg hung freely so that the heel of his foot could be turned so it faced where the toe normally pointed.

On the morning he set out for Oostacker, his family, neighbours, and physician clearly saw his pus-dripping leg, and had little hope for him. Upon arrival at the sanctuary, de Rudder said a short prayer before a statue of the Madonna, and instantly was totally healed. This case became famous and created a controversy that resounded through much of the world, the fanatical anti-clericals refusing to accept the overwhelming scientific evidence for the reality of this particularly shocking miracle (Bertrin, 1908 [2018], pp. 164-184).

Now for another case that involved instantaneous healing, but one that is stashed away very discreetly in the annals of psychosomatic medicine. In this case a man was dying from a cancer-ridden body full of orange-sized tumours. It happened that a story was floating about a cancer cure called Krebiozen, a horse serum derivative. The man (a Mr. Wright, pseudonym) conceived a hope in this experimental drug, was given it by his physician and the patient's cancer promptly disappeared. He walked out of the hospital and returned to enjoying his life for several months, until, that is, he heard that the scientists had serious questions about Krebiozen. The cancer came back with a vengeance the moment his faith was challenged. His doctor then made up a story about a stronger version of the same drug, convinced Mr. Wright to take it, and again the cancer vanished and he returned to normal life, cancer free, again for months. But again Wright read a report confirming the worthlessness of Krebiozen, but this time the cancer came back and promptly killed him. What this astonishing story tells us is something about the incredible power of the mind over the body and the role of belief. It also strongly suggests that what counts as the healing agent is faith, not the object in which one has faith.

Let us now look at one of the weirdest of reported phenomena, featured in a scholarly book by Joan Carroll Cruz, *The Incorruptibles* (1977), a study of what happens to saintly people's bodies after they die – or rather what does not happen. Their bodies, though dead, do not behave as if they were dead – they remain incorrupt, flexible, impossibly warm, fragrant, even mobile, and manage for varying periods of time to look more asleep than like decaying corpses. The phenomenon presents an image that seems like a message. The image of an incorrupt body seems to want to tell us that we do not die, and that a higher form of existence awaits us. The details and exotica of this phenomenon rank very high on the scale of weirdness.

Herbert Thurston's (1856-1939) treatment of the subject begins on a quizzical note. The Catholic Thurston wonders why it is that many of the most striking miracles are produced by persons who are not exactly outstanding in their spiritual reputations, while many of the most notable saints who live more perfectly in line with Catholic doctrine and God's will display none of the strange phenomena. There is one fairly obvious explanation for Thurston's observations: God is not causing these deviations from normal nature. They may have more to do with the believer than what is believed in. We saw that this was the case with Mr. Wright, whose belief in a useless horse serum cured him of a deadly cancer twice.

Thurston provides a nuanced review of the abundant case histories of the weird phenomenon of incorruptible saint, of which he describes six categories. In summary, there is a "preternatural fragrance," which we have already cited, the perfect opposite of what we would expect from nature. Moreover, the fragrance may persist for months or years. Next, the body displays no "cadaveric rigor." "Immunity from natural decay" is a third – again, sometimes lasting hundreds of years. Bleeding that occurs long after the actual death of the body, is another category. When St. Catherine of Bologna was exhumed three months after her death and burial, she bled from her nostrils. Fifth is the persistence of warmth in the body, and sometimes to a shocking degree. The sixth category may well reach some kind of apogee of weirdness: in these admittedly rare cases "the dead saint is alleged to raise his arm in benediction, or lift his foot to be kissed."

Thurston focuses on one particular case in great detail whose supernormality seemed compelling, that of Blessed Maria Anna of Madrid (1565-1624). In 1731, a hundred and seven years after her death, her body was exhumed in response to the cause of her beatification. Thurston writes: "The remains were found soft, supple, flexible and elastic to the touch, and emitting a remarkable perfume, while 'from the whole body there exuded a certain oily fluid, like some fragrant balsam,' quoting from her Vita. Eleven leading medical experts of Madrid examined her body aggressively, making incisions and probing all manner of cavities to make absolutely sure there were no preservatives, or any natural way to explain the incorruption. As they virtually mutilated her body the fragrance only increased; the over-zealous physicians concluded unanimously on the miraculous state of the beatified body" (Thurston, 1925, p. 261). An image to contemplate and inhabit.

Psychological

And now to the psychological category: the ways that extraordinary phenomena force us to wonder about our sense of self and the image of reality we normally inhabit.

We can begin by reminding ourselves of the most obvious miracle of consciousness, that 'no thing' that makes all things possible. Consciousness is radically unlike physical things – it is always of, or about, something. The mental interacts with, but is different from, the physical world. My thoughts, desires, feelings, memories and dreams form a world – a monad – invisible, intangible, and so on, and not in physical space or time.

Our psychological transformation would be based on extrasensory perception (ESP), which has three aspects. Clairvoyance, as noted earlier, is our sight of the external world, but beyond the range of our optic apparatus, in principle, a scanner of all space. The second expands our range in time with precognition, but also bristles with weirdness, for how can you know about something before it exists? Something you had no way of predicting or inferring in the present?

For example, the aforementioned dreams of my own that seemed to precognise the attempt to assassinate Ronald Reagan in 1981 (Grosso, 1997, pp. 130-139). Three dreams all converging on the same future event were no coincidence. How could the future land in my head? How do you turn causation upside down? The effect preceding the cause? Precognition makes my sense of time uneasy, dislocated – where am I? Could it be that deep down we know the future because we have already lived our lives? That would explain precognition, at least. But it would also make things hopelessly weird.

Telepathy is the third branch of extrasensory perception, and perhaps the most important. Telepathy means feeling at a distance, in other words: connecting with another's feelings, directly, mind to mind, apart from space or time. Telepathy raises questions about our self-conception and our boundaries (or their absence). It seems to imply that we are part of a larger network of mental life than one's limited sense of ego. We might now see ourselves as less isolated and perhaps less helpless than otherwise – enmeshed in a greater, transpersonal, mental life, allowing for whole ranges of interaction and conversation. How to inhabit this calls for an active imagination, centred around new ways of being on a living planet.

Telepathy allows us to imagine that we are in principle linked to all beings who, like us, think, sense, and feel. There is a link between telepathy and empathy. Empathy implies becoming one with the subjectivity of the other, in short, telepathic contact. Both terms denote a deepening of the range and depth of what and how we can feel and sense. Of all the various possible changes we have mentioned, telepathy and empathy may be the most practical, and critical.

Imagine if folks at large suddenly acquired a new, entirely natural ability to divine the inner world of all living and even non-living things, stones and seas and clouds, everything other and around them. It would be harder to hate and be violent toward people whose soul and world you could sense and feel. For contrast, we need another word, *psychopathy*: the inability to feel anything except oneself. We know this is a real problem. An increase of empathy would generate more harmony in human affairs. It would be good for all living things and for all of nature. Empathy for nature would characterise the new human. In the slow pace of evolution, there might be movement toward a more pervasive species empathy. Another possibility is that from a violent, global near-death experience, a quantum leap of empathy might spontaneously unfold, a kind of herd reaction.

Postmortem Consciousness

It seems that we are actively imagining our godlikeness, simply by tracing the implications of supernormal experience. But to be godlike requires that we be immortal. Is there a case to be made for postmortem consciousness? The answer is yes. Evidence (not proof) for postmortem continuity is based on various phenomena: hauntings, apparitions, poltergeists, mediumship, death-bed visions, near-death experiences, and reincarnation studies.[28] This is a complex issue with a vast literature. The data, I say, empirically entitles us to imagine that our story has a future that continues on the other side of our mortality.

Now Seal Your Lips

Finally, we have another tier of super data to conjure with – data under the rubric of *mysticism:* think *mystes*, a celebrant of the ancient rites, literally from the Greek verb *muein,* to seal the lips, enter the silence. Scholars of religion and other academic disciplines are acquainted with a class of human experiences of great interest, a type of peak experience, as universal as it is rare and difficult to describe.[29]

The overriding theme of the mystical experience is the rapture of unification. All veils are lifted, all obstacles removed, all blunders absolved and resolved. The literature abounds in stories of super-ordinary moments of bliss, illumination and liberation, and in all manner of circumstances. Mystical encounters are also powerfully

---

[28] There is a vast literature here. Two examples include: Kelly, E. (2015). *Beyond Physicalism: Toward Reconciliation of Science and Spirituality.* This covers much background terrain for this topic. For an overview of the different types of survival evidence, see Grosso, M. (2004). *Experiencing the Next World Now.* Paraview Pocket Books.

[29] In Kelly, E. (2015). *Beyond Physicalism,* see Paul Marshall, 'Mystical Experiences as Windows on Reality,' pp. 39-78, which explores the connections between mystical and paranormal experience.

transformative. The strange journey assumes many forms, an experience of ultimate indelible satisfaction that typically beggars description.

When we combine the whole spectrum of supernormal capacities into one composite picture, it all points to a being as different from us as we differ from the classical Greek deities. We are not perfect gods, but we are immortal and can do all manner of weird magic. With all these amazing potentials in our latent being, it is not hard to see how the cults, movements, and religions of the world arose through the supernormal powers periodically made manifest by certain oddly talented individuals.

Powers that seem to transcend common nature surely exist, but who, what, how, and why remain a mystery. Nonetheless, since time immemorial humanity has been in dialogue with these transcendent powers. Different cultures name and describe their encounters and their history in their own unique way and at different times. I would agree with a statement from the Indian Rig Veda that "Truth is one: people name it differently."

The conclusion of this brief exercise, grounded in matters of extraordinary fact: When the various extended capacities converge and form an image of the "new human," we see a being of godlike quality and dimensions, we see a futuristic version of ourselves. And here is my healing fiction – forming the image, it feels like I am breathing in a new atmosphere, fully alive in every cell of my being, and I feel wide open to an unprecedented radiance.

ECTOPLASM

Where Biology Meets Imagination

ZOFIA WEAVER

> "There is a crack in everything
> That's how the light gets in"
> LEONARD COHEN

Physical Mediumship and the Far-Out Boggle Threshold

In many areas of science, real progress in understanding is driven by anomalies, those little irritants that open up cracks in otherwise coherent worldviews built painstakingly through concerted effort over long periods.

You might apply this metaphor to the whole field of psi research – research into forms of anomalous cognition and extraordinary experience opens up cracks in the mainstream physicalist worldview. However, there are some cracks that even psi researchers prefer to give a wide berth to, and one of them is the extreme end of physical mediumship, namely materialisations and the strange force/substance known as *ectoplasm*.

The continuum of strange physical events reliably observed during mediumistic séances includes a range of phenomena that seem to merge into one another. Most of what might be called "ordinary" successful physical mediumship involves slight noises, breezes, and subtle movements of objects, without going much further. Physical mediumship has much in common with poltergeist phenomena, which these days tend to be associated with suppressed negative emotions often involving a young person and/or dysfunctional relationships. In more spectacular poltergeist cases we also have violent disorder: objects that materialise suddenly out of nowhere (as they also do in mediumistic sittings, where they are referred to as apports), relocate, travel along impossible trajectories, self-destruct, or seem to acquire a will of their own. One of my favourite examples is a teacup full of tea flying at the investigator and emptying itself on him (Bugaj, 1996). These events may be related to tangled human emotions, and may have explanations in terms of familiar energies behaving in unfamiliar ways, but they still represent what might be described as *the extraordinary behaviour of ordinary things*.

It also seems that the ability to produce such effects is shared by a reasonably large section of the population, as witnessed by the 'table-tipping' craze that swept throughout America and Europe in the mid-nineteenth century. There is good evidence to show that anomalous noises and movements, and the ability to control them to some extent, can be brought about by a focused and expectant state of mind, particularly in a group of people sharing the same aim, as shown by experiments conducted in the 1960s and 1970s (see for example Batcheldor, 1984; Owen, 1967).

Materialisations, however, refuse to tag onto any model resembling the world as we know it. They are beyond what might be called the "normal paranormal" – they are a different order of creation. Amongst these phenomena you might find a grotesque hand forming out of nothing and grabbing you by the neck, only to dissolve in the next instant; half-formed heads and torsos, monstrous shapes that respond to suggestions (Bottazzi, 1909 [2011]; Feilding *et al.*, 1909); physical limbs that leave evidence of their momentary physicality in the form of paraffin gloves (Geley, 1924; 1927); entities that interact with the experimenters like living human beings – except when they dematerialise (Okołowicz, 1926) – and, finally, beings that seem to come from another realm altogether (Haraldsson, 2011). Such reports would be easier to dismiss if they came from fanatical spirit believers but, unfortunately for those of us with a boggle threshold based on experience of the normal world, they come from rational people with trustworthy credentials – scientists in a laboratory, experimenters with vast experience, witnesses whose judgment we would trust without hesitation – if only the phenomena were not so outrageously beyond belief!

Physical mediumship has a long history of problems with evidence. Spiritualism – the belief that it is possible to communicate with the spirits of the dead, which became widespread in the English-speaking world in mid-nineteenth century – inevitably attracted a great many bogus claims from fake mediums. Much of the early work of the Society for Psychical Research turned out to involve a great deal of detecting and unmasking of fraudulent psychics and mediums.[30] The ways of cheating are manifold: from manoeuvring out of bonds, escaping hand and foot control by creating distractions, importing hidden objects into the séance room, or regurgitating hidden material, to sophisticated equipment utilising rods to manipulate objects, cutouts of hands, masks and cheesecloth to impersonate materialisations, skilful use of luminous paint and lighting, all aided by the cover of darkness and the protection of a cabinet (often simply a curtained off corner of the room) supposedly protecting the entranced medium. More sophisticated materialisations could involve specially designed premises with in-built gimmicks (such as a removable ceiling panel), and any number of accomplices.

Even without fakery, the phenomena of physical mediumship present real problems of consistency and subjectivity: even if the conditions are deemed satisfactory and the medium has an impeccable record, what may work on one occasion will not necessarily work on another, even with the same set of people and under the same conditions. And, in contrast to mental mediumship, where the medium's statements can be accurately and permanently recorded, the evidence of physical mediumship consists mainly of "one off" subjective observations of transient phenomena.

It is therefore hardly surprising that William James,[31] so enthusiastic about the mediumship of the mental medium Mrs Piper, described

---

[30] But well before then physical mediumship had acquired a negative reputation. Daniel Dunglas Home, perhaps the most famous medium of them all, with a record of apparently genuine phenomena, devoted a chapter to the tricks employed by fake mediums in his *Lights and Shadows* (1877).

[31] William James (1842-1910), a professor at Harvard University, and the most celebrated of American psychologists, perhaps of all psychologists (after Gauld, 2022, p. 5).

physical phenomena as "dark-sitting and rat-hole type," contrasting them with the "calm air of delightful studies" of mental ones in his SPR Presidential Address (James, 1896, p. 6). It was not only James who held this opinion, and it came to be the view of the majority of the SPR leaders (Gauld, 1968, p. 246). Andreas Sommer makes a good argument for the need to keep the boggle threshold low at this time, so as "to bolster the scientific status of psychology" (Sommer, 2012, p. 23), but the problem goes a lot deeper, to the very nature of the phenomena. It is one thing to be uncertain about the extent of our mental powers, but the material world on the whole tends to be predictable. In that world human bodies do not produce extra limbs, heads, or whole phantoms with an independent life of their own that then fade away. In this context, it is not surprising that Frank Podmore, one of the early psychical researchers and co-author with Frederic Myers and Edmund Gurney of the monumental *Phantasms of the Living* (1886), was convinced that the famous mediums D.D. Home and Eusapia Palladino were super-tricksters. And when he could not find any faults in the reports of sittings with Palladino, held in good light with a stenographer by three experienced SPR investigators, in Naples in 1908, he fell back on the suggestion that "the events of the three most important séances can be readily explained if we assume [...] that a single person was hallucinated" (Podmore, 1910, p. 141). Nearly a century later a false door panel and an accomplice are offered as a possible explanation for the same outrageously weird sittings (Wiseman, 1992).

It is easy to feel sympathy toward this resolute stand on the boggle threshold and the rejection of unacceptable experiences, and we find this even among the investigators themselves. Having collectively witnessed the phenomena in person they cannot reject the evidence, but reporting the presence of human hands not belonging to Eusapia nor any of the sitters, "[...] is so utterly at variance with common sense that one finds it next to impossible to believe it" (Feilding *et al.*, 1909, p. 456). Such comments recur in many reports; the desire to reject "the wholly other," therefore, affects psychical researchers as well. Unfortunately, at times this leads to various less than helpful strategies – from the obvious one of avoiding the issue altogether, through ignoring the larger phenomena, to attempts to discredit the mediums or the investigators on the basis of what these days would be described as fake news.

Ectoplasm and the Nature of the Evidence

By now the evidence for materialisations is quite substantial. Alongside accounts of similar phenomena involving macro-pk, such as in poltergeist cases, we now have, with a century-and-a-half history behind the subject, an historical perspective that enables us to look for patterns and consistencies among reports from different cultures and different periods. Outstanding physical mediums are rare in the general population, but there are enough reliable, detailed and consistent reports to suggest that we are dealing with something genuine.

Talking of materialisations invariably involves the concept of ectoplasm. Perhaps unsurprisingly there are problems with defining the term: it usually brings to mind the image of a white substance that looks very much like cheesecloth or cotton wool and exudes from the mouths or other orifices of the medium, such as in the photograph below.

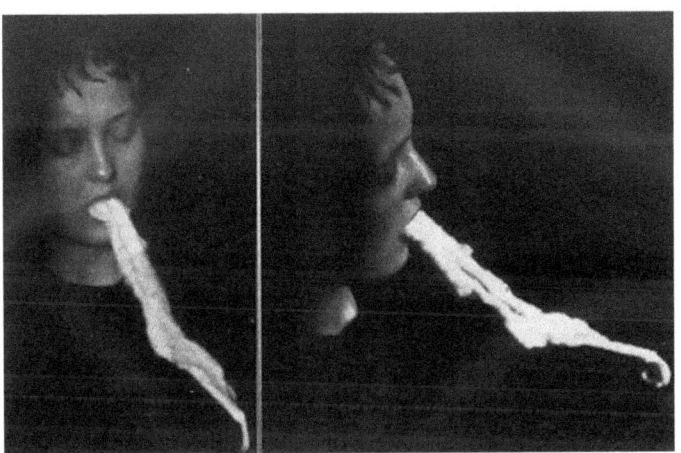

The medium Stanisława Popielska (after Schrenck-Notzing, 1920/23 photo in public domain).

This substance was captured, analysed and found to consist of nothing but unexciting organic matter (Lebiedziński, 1921). Yet if we understand this as referring to a "primary substance" that emanates from the medium and acts as a substrate for the phenomena that can take many forms, there must be a lot more to it than mere physical detritus. According to Gustave Geley (1927, p. 213), whose research involved many mediums, in most cases the "primary substance" is first excreted in gaseous form. The various descriptions of it talk of a force, a vapour, a substance, an externalisation, a channelling of unknown energies that are somehow connected to the medium. It can look like rough wool, cotton wool or towelling, a white napkin, a transparent gaseous pillar, a small white cloud, or a luminous body (see Alvarado, 2019; Feilding *et al.*, 1909). But it need not be visible at all, or may take the form of lights from which shapes are formed, or something like "a psychic waterspout – a whirlpool of invisible energy" (Carrington, 1946, p. 23). None of these descriptions capture adequately what is a *process* – often incomplete – that varies from one individual to another, or in the same individual on different occasions. There is plenty of evidence that the beliefs of sitters in séances affect the messages produced by tipping tables, and that the nature of ectoplasm may well vary depending on the expectations of the researchers or participants, with the "psychic force" sometimes shaping the phenomena accordingly.[32]

While the phenomena are often acknowledged to have some intelligence behind them, discussions of physical mediumship usually focus on the manifestations themselves, their nature and frequency and the conditions under which they take place. There has been very little discussion of the minds involved in the proceedings, even though mediumship is to a large extent a mental, volitional process. Historically speaking, while the beliefs and judgment of the sitters/researchers might sometimes be subject of intense scrutiny, mediums have been regarded instrumentally, as tools for producing effects, and little is known about their feelings and thoughts. Also, in some of the best known cases the quality of the evidence was and remains controversial, thus further restricting opportunities for exploring the threads that link the minds and the physical phenomena in very different personalities in very different situations. Such evidence needs to be plentiful, reliable and to come from various sources, with some information on the material and intellectual background of the people involved, as well as the cultural context in which they operated. These considerations led to the selection of the six individuals whose phenomena are to be discussed in the following pages.

---

[32] There is a wide-ranging chapter on "psychic force" in *Talking about psychical research* (Barrington, 2019, pp. 185-199).

The People Behind the Phenomena

The Mediums

Five of the six mediums I have selected were men. Only two of them were professional mediums, in the sense of charging for séances: Rudi Schneider (1908-1965), who came from Austria, and the Italian Eusapia Palladino (1854-1918). Indridi Indridason (1883-1912), who never left his native Iceland, was paid a small salary by the society set up to investigate him, but you might say that he was owed it, having been "highjacked" into mediumship and prevented from a career in printing (he arrived in Reykjavik as a printing apprentice and, having stumbled into a sitting, demonstrated extraordinary physical phenomena). The most famous medium of them all, Daniel Dunglas Home (1833-1886, Scottish by birth but brought up in the USA), never charged for his services, having from the earliest days of his mediumship been "adopted" as a welcome guest in the homes of Spiritualist friends and sponsors, and both his wives came from wealthy Russian families. The Englishman Stainton Moses (1839-1892) started out as a clergyman, became a teacher, and his mediumship was a private affair on which he built a religion.

The Pole Franek Kluski (1873-1943) was a journalist and a poet who worked in banking and who for a short period accidentally wandered into physical mediumship.

Rudi Schneider became a medium as a boy of eleven, but having an older brother who was already a medium, and growing up within an environment of spiritualist beliefs, he presumably accepted their teachings, so this is hardly a surprising choice of career. Eusapia Palladino was discovered as a medium by spiritualist circles when she was a young girl and introduced her 'control'[33] – "John King" – who came to represent her somewhat confused belief framework. Young Indridi was steered into experimental mediumship in his early twenties and had a difficult time coming to terms with his controls, who could be extremely violent. Daniel Home was thrown out of the home that his aunt had provided for him from childhood when, as a teenager, he had violent poltergeist phenomena forming around him. These phenomena may have been linked to a lack of outlet for his spiritual needs and experiences, which had been apparent from childhood. Stainton Moses

---

[33] The 'controls' which appear in trance states in mediums are usually interpreted as aspects of their personalities.

suffered from poor health from a young age, had a breakdown while a student at Oxford, and his phenomena from the beginning had a distinctly religious aspect. Teofil Modrzejewski (Franek Kluski was a pseudonym), was a sickly child with a vivid imagination and with episodes of clairvoyant premonitions; he also had a bullet pass through his body as a result of a duel in his youth.

The Investigators

The list of distinguished scholars, scientists and reputable researchers who at various times were involved in investigating the above mediums would require a chapter in itself, so it will be easier to do some name-dropping instead. Rudi Schneider was investigated by, among others, Dr Albert von Schrenck-Notzing in Munich at his purpose-built private laboratory, Lord Charles Hope in London, Eugene Osty at his laboratory in Paris, as well as numerous experimenters in Prague and Vienna. Great efforts were undertaken to ensure control, including various technical innovations, such as infrared circuits. Experiments carried out by William Crookes, pioneer of research in chemistry and physics, with Daniel Home, have the status of classic instrumental studies. Many Italian scientists, as well as the famous physicist Oliver Lodge and the Nobel prize winning physiologist Charles Richet, studied Eusapia Palladino, and Richet also took part in experiments with Franek Kluski, the quality of whose sittings may have had something to do with the participants, many of whom were intellectuals and creative artists. The phenomena of Indridi Indridason had a whole experimental society devoted to them, formed by distinguished university professors and scholars (Haraldsson & Gissurarson, 2015). Stainton Moses, while of an impeccable character, is somewhat of an outlier, since what we know about his phenomena comes mainly from his own notebooks and witnesses. On the other hand, this evidence was verified by two of the founders of the SPR, Frederic Myers and Edmund Gurney, and it comes with a great deal of valuable information about the medium's evolving states of mind as the phenomena developed.

The Phenomena and the Minds Behind Them

In much physical mediumship, the initial basic effects tend to be the same and this applies to the protagonists of the story presented here. To start with, there are reports of breezes, raps or knocks, familiar from poltergeist phenomena, and slight movements of objects. In the case of Eusapia Palladino there is also the frequent billowing of her skirt as if by a breeze (there was no apparatus under it, many experimenters checked this obvious source). While the entranced Rudi Schneider is in full view, the curtains of the cabinet are pushed out as if by wind; gusts of wind are reported at sittings with Indridi Indridason. "Cold air" is frequently mentioned during sittings with Stainton Moses, and Kluski's séances feature breezes on a regular basis. None of the mediums discussed here produced any substance from mouths or other orifices, but, with the exception of Rudi, lights of various kind feature largely in the descriptions their phenomena. Little lights are seen around their heads, but some manifestations seem to start with light displays, and go on to form images relating to what goes on in the medium's and the sitters' minds – and sometimes to something beyond it.

Compared to the other five, the materialisations produced by Rudi Schneider (whose career as a medium encompassed the 1920s and 1930s) are the least spectacular, but they provide some of the best, most reliable records in physical mediumship. It seems strange to describe phenomena such as the formation of "thin mist," "snowlike masses" or "pseudopods" (parts of a body resembling limbs), as less than mind-blowing, but the reports read *en masse* can be numbingly boring, with their repetitive minute details of conditions, controls and individual impressions. They are "monotonous in the extreme, and not in any way comparable to conjuring performances" (Gregory, 1985, p. 408). Rudi would be entranced, unconscious and visible, and the proceedings were negotiated with his mediumistic personality known as 'Olga.' Olga's repertoire was very limited: there were never any fully materialised forms; the curtain would move, a toy zither would play, knots would be tied in handkerchiefs, tables would be knocked over, and objects would be pulled about. But sometimes they would appear to be carried about by something like a hand (with three or four fingers), and we have a number of detailed descriptions of the formation process. At a sitting in Paris in 1930 there were "odd movements as if the curtain were being pushed outwards by a rounded object inside the cabinet. Dr Osty and both controllers saw, coming from under the lower edge of the right-hand curtain a thick, greyish mist at least 30cm in extent, which moved in a leisurely fashion towards the upper edge of the table which, as soon as the mist reached it, proceeded to slide more than 20cm in the direction of the sitters. Dr Osty was in a good position to observe the entire process. He particularly noticed that as soon as the fog mass reached the table, it instantly became invisible, and he was not able to spot it returning whence it came" (Gregory, 1985, pp. 178-179).

Gregory attributes the limitations in Rudi's repertoire at least in part to the limited imagination of the experimenters, but perhaps it had even more to do with the medium's imagination, or lack of it. Rudi inherited the ready-made concept of 'Olga' from his brother, and seemed happy to go along with whatever was required by the experimenters without much input or interest from himself.

In contrast, the experiences of a much earlier medium, William Stainton Moses, were, from the beginning, directed by his intellectual and spiritual concerns. He was an outstanding scholar at Oxford University, but his progress was disrupted by illness. Originally hostile to Spiritualism, he began to take interest in it in the late 1860s, and from 1872 started to experience various phenomena himself, which developed over the following ten years. It is significant that his first mediumistic manifestations took the form of a spiritual message provided by meaningful apports. In August 1872 a complete cross gradually formed on his bed out of various articles present in his bedroom after the room had been searched and locked – Moses was staying at a friend's house at the time (Myers, 1893-4, p. 264). For Moses, this constituted "assured intervention" by the agency, whose teachings he came to trust, at the very beginning of his involvement with the phenomena.

Moses himself attached the greatest importance to his automatic writing. His *Spirit Teachings* (published in 1883), an account of the many communications he obtained in this way, and his reflections on them, had a great influence on the subsequent development of the Spiritualist movement. The messages came from his 'controls,' who formed the "Imperator" group (some 84 principal 'spirits' including various philosophers, biblical characters, as well as Benjamin Franklin and Beethoven, and variously regarded as genuine, impostors, or as expressions of the medium's personality). However, our main concern here is with the spectacular physical manifestations he produced and their relation both to his beliefs and to similar phenomena produced by other mediums. Myers obtained confirmation from outside independent witnesses who heard raps, experienced cool breezes, smelled exquisite smells, and saw lights "like the flame of a candle" over Moses's head, as well as listening to elevating lectures (ibid., p. 48). Much of the time Moses was deep in trance and relied on witness reports, but at times he was able to witness the phenomena himself, and sometimes the phenomena carried on after the séance had drawn to a close.

One such account comes from a witness while Moses was entranced: "The first occasion on which we saw the large luminous appearances [...] was on June 7th, 1873. By that time we had become very familiar with the floating masses of luminous vapour [...] on several occasions we had seen these masses condensed [...] until a distinct objective light was formed" (ibid., pp. 273-4). Sometimes there would be a dozen or more cones of soft light, with a nucleus of soft yellow light, surrounded by a haze. Such lights seem to have been carried in materialised hands, the fingers of which could be seen, surrounded by soft drapery, and on at least one occasion Moses himself could feel them: "By request [the light] placed itself, surrounded by its drapery, in my outstretched palm. I could distinctly pinch the drapery" (ibid., p. 319). At another time "the light [...] was a tall column, about half an inch or rather more in width, and six or seven feet high [...] of a bright golden hue [...] and did not illuminate objects in its neighbourhood. For a minute a cross developed at its top, and rays seemed to dart from it."

Materialised forms of members of the Imperator group, dictating the automatic writing, feature in some accounts of the Moses sittings, but materialised hands tend to be reported more frequently. In fact, all the mediums discussed here produce materialised hands, some more spectacular than others. Such were the hands witnessed by sitters with Daniel Home, a contemporary of Moses, whose exploits are too wide-ranging to encompass here, but whose hand manifestations are confirmed by many witnesses. Daniel was intelligent, articulate, artistic, refined (or vain according to some) and socially adept (as evidenced by his books, his dramatic readings and the numbers of people who befriended him). He may also have been one of the greatest mediums of all time judging by the ease with which phenomena formed around him. There are fewer descriptions of full materialisations, but hands are plentiful:

> [...] We all saw a hand descend from the top of the curtain and play the Accordion. It was a large hand, and its reflection on the window blind was strong. After this a head shewed in similar way. When Mrs. Crookes was told to go into the room and occupy the chair marked in the plan, a form was materialised as far as the middle. It floated near

the folding-doors and advanced towards Mrs. Crookes who screamed and it vanished" (Medhurst *et al.*, 1972, pp. 218-219).

We also have "a lady's hand – very thin, very pale, and remarkably attenuated," with extremely long fingers, very pale, that ends at the wrist and writes on a piece of paper in handwriting recognised as that of a deceased relative (Home, 1888 [2006], p. 33).

And just in case the many accounts from those who favoured Home are suspected of bias, we also have reports from hostile witnesses. One of them was Eliza née Branicka, sister of Home's powerful friend in Rome and Paris, Count Alexander Branicki. She initially felt superior to the table-turning craze, but then she encounters Home, and on 22nd March 1857 writes in a letter:

"[...] What do you think of a table in which the boards open up and a pale hand appears in the crack, takes a sheet of paper and a pencil, writes under the table and all this is returned, while the three-branch brass candelabra leaves the mantelpiece, moves through the air and hangs above the participants gathered around the table. On the sheet there are two cabbalistic signs, and then these words:

Be good catholics (!)
Love God
To confession go everyone (!)

What do you say about this orthography, is there not some malicious parody there? ... " (Sudolski, 1996, p. 200, translation by Zofia Weaver).

The content, as well as the strange grammar and spelling seem to reflect the tangled relationship between Home, his spirits, his new religion (at that stage he was a recent convert to Catholicism) and that of his Roman Catholic sitters. Unfortunately for us, Eliza's main concern was to save her family from the influence of Satan's servants (she had masses said with that intention), rather than to objectively describe in detail their various other antics.

Catholics were not the only ones that had a problem with such phenomena. "In Crookes's day those who accepted a spirit world as an actuality seem to have felt that physical phenomena were caused by 'low spirits,' and that for edification or information mental communications were to be preferred. Stainton Moses frequently complained that he dreaded "rough manifestations [...] spirits who rapped on floors and tables, or threw objects around the room, or who chose to float trunklessly over the séance room" (Medhurst, 1972, p. 228). However, rough manifestations are just what you might expect during a séance with Eusapia Palladino.

Eusapia was temperamental, touchy, and prone to cheating. According to the experienced investigator Hereward Carrington, she took "mischievous delight" in seeing how far she could hoodwink her sitters. She was vain and thought of herself as "the great Palladino" (Carrington, 1954). But her mediumship was subjected to the most wide-ranging investigations, and it provided the turning point for many researchers in the late nineteenth and early twentieth centuries.

Her phenomena included the usual movements of furniture, noises and lights. There were also fingers, hands, fists and arms, skin-coloured, translucent or black, smaller or bigger, quick or slow, sometimes isolated, sometime sitting on people's arms or shoulders, sometimes above Eusapia's head. During one of the experiments conducted by Filippo Bottazzi, the father of Italian biochemistry, in his laboratory and in the company of other eminent scientists, all the participants see an enormous black fist come out from behind the cabinet curtain and grab Bottazzi's neck (with Eusapia in full view). As he tries to free himself, freeing his hand held by another observer, the hand vanishes, describing an arc as if re-entering Eusapia's body (Bottazzi, 1909, pp. 59, 90-91, 165). An interesting aspect of the Bottazzi accounts is that such spectacular phenomena were a byproduct of the actual aim of the sittings, which was to get Eusapia to interact with various instruments in a way that could be permanently recorded, and these interactions did take place. However, her most spectacular displays took place at the already mentioned sittings with three experienced SPR investigators in Naples in 1908 (Feilding *et al.*, 1909). Eusapia had already been investigated by the SPR at Cambridge in 1894 who found her demonstrations to be badly wanting,[34] but her continued

---

[34] "Certainly, Eusapia must have been a somewhat trying guest in so distinguished a literary, philosophical and learned milieu as that in which the Sidgwicks and Mr. and Mrs. Myers moved. To speak plainly, Eusapia was vital, vulgar, amorous and a cheat, and this combination must have jarred upon those whose interests in psychical research was rather to find a sure road to immortality than to inquire too closely into the queer phenomena produced by a woman whose behaviour both in and out of the cabinet revealed a femininity which must often have been a little disturbing to the Cambridge philosophers" (Dingwall, 1948, pp. 189-90).

and growing international reputation led the SPR to revise its position on never investigating mediums known to have cheated. Every effort was made to exclude the possibility of cheating during the 1908 sittings, hence three top investigators, a stenographer, and the neutral venue of a hotel room.

The investigators must have been much better at creating an atmosphere congenial to Eusapia than those at Cambridge, because she spontaneously and very quickly produced a range of spectacular phenomena. Our main concern is materialisations, so we cannot dwell on the small table from the cabinet climbing over Eusapia's shoulder (with the little objects still on it), and then retreating (ibid., p. 81). But we have descriptions of phenomena that are very close to those found in the Rudi Schneider sittings, such as the following account relating to some clay being transported from the cabinet to the séance table:

> [...] I saw a white, opaque substance, about two inches broad and six inches long, apparently carrying this clay, which came across the medium's left arm [...] The movement of the clay was peculiar. It travelled slowly as though carried through the air, and was most certainly not *thrown* (ibid., p. 213).

So perhaps invisible hands manoeuvred the table as well. Unlike Rudi, Eusapia produced a number of materialisations that exhibited some responsiveness and aspects of human behaviour, but that were nevertheless totally alien in appearance:

> From the extreme right of the curtain there appeared a thing like a knobbed nine-pin, or like an arm with a closed fist, wrapped up in something black. It came slowly towards me (who was sitting on Eusapia's left) as though pivoted on her right shoulder, made a kind of grotesque reverence, about a foot above the level of my head and retired with deliberation, having been visible at least three seconds [...] I complained that it didn't look in the least like a man, that its head was too small [...] It immediately reappeared, this time larger, but still an outrage on any kind of humanity (ibid., pp. 188-9).

There were other phantoms as well: heads and head-like objects appearing suddenly, looking like two-dimensional faces made of cobwebs; objects that look as if made of cotton wool or white muslin, or white handkerchief rolled up, or a square head at the end of a long stalk-like body that shoots out over the medium's head. But it is interesting to look back to the different atmosphere and the mental aspect of some of the sittings held with the illiterate Eusapia by Julian Ochorowicz in the 1890s:

> When the circle of participants is joined by another medium, John King [Eusapia's control] is suddenly able to write, as happened [...] in Naples, at the home of Countess K., whose daughter is a writing medium. Because the daughter was able to write Russian, John also wrote Russian – and because somewhere in her mind were lodged some Ukrainian legends, John turned into a Cossack [...] and when we sat down in Rome in a purely Polish circle, he [...] began understanding Polish. When asked how he suddenly understood Polish, his answer was that, in the days when he lived on earth, he met some Poles during his wanderings in America (Weaver, 2018, p. 133).

Ochorowicz draws the logical conclusion, that the sitters' thoughts were reflected in Eusapia's mind, so perhaps Eusapia could have produced more imaginative manifestations on other occasions if the investigators acted more like participants than observers.

This idea leads to the next set of phenomena, where the participants and the medium act as a group. Franek Kluski's mediumship has a very different context from the other mediums discussed here. Kluski was a successful writer, poet and journalist, and by the 1920s he was on the board of one of the main banks in Warsaw. A professional man in his forties, he was discovered to be a powerful medium when he attended a séance at a friend's house, and phenomena formed around him while the official medium produced nothing. For six years, from 1919 until about 1925, he acted as a physical medium, under the impression that he was contributing to a new science. His séances were private, more like a home circle, with sitters who were intellectual, artistic and creative, and it is not surprising that many of them became involved in what was then the latest project in modern science, called metapsychics, led by the new International Metapsychic Institute in Paris in 1919, with Gustave Geley in charge.

Kluski was subject to strange happenings throughout his everyday life and not just at séances. Knocks and raps were often heard in his vicinity, lights came out of his mouth and fingers, bulbs flickered when he passed close by, and his body seemed to absorb strong scents that lingered for days. His mediumship started with the usual movement of objects and furniture, but developed into spectacular displays of lights, interactive materialised phantoms and the thing he is best known for – thanks to Geley – the production of paraffin wax moulds of materialised limbs (Okołowicz, 1926; Weaver, 2015). Geley describes the development of the phenomena, with the onset marked by the sudden strong smell of ozone and a mist appearing around the medium, usually above his head, rising like a light cloud. Clusters of lights would appear, of varying size and intensity, sometimes just as lights travelling along various trajectories, and sometimes as the first stage of materialisation, creating the impression of a framework for the emergence of human hands, fingers, and faces. When it comes to hands, Geley's obsession with creating a Permanent Paranormal Object, in the shape of paraffin moulds created by phantom hands, is responsible for the multiplicity of their examples. Hands were seen and touched, and sometimes resemble closely the refined manifestations of Daniel Home. At a séance in his IMI laboratory in Paris Geley reports witnessing:

> [...] a hand at the end of an arm form under my eyes, cross the circle in front of Mr. Kluski and touch Mme. Geley, who was facing me. It was a masculine hand very well formed. The wrist was slender, the forearm and upper arm were enveloped in white tissue with regular longitudinal folds. (The medium was wearing a black coat). Immediately after the contact felt by Mme. Geley the hand disappeared [...] (Geley, 1924/1927, p. 218).

We also have accounts of various occasions (not just those involving Geley) when points of light descend into the paraffin container and are seen rising up, then lowering the mould onto the table, or onto the sitters' hands. In Warsaw, among many perfect as well as defective moulds, Geley also had the experience of a mould gluing itself to his hand.

From the séance on 30 September 1921,
Geley 1924/1927, Fig. 79.

The mould shown in the photograph fell on Geley's hand during the sitting, when it was still very hot and soft. Geley did not move and after the sitting he found that the mould had flattened as it hardened, which means that the anatomical details are a little less clear. The line in the middle which cuts through the hand is the result of an accident with the casting (Okołowicz, 1926).

In Kluski's mediumship there are distinguishable phases, and the participants contribute to their development. Especially during the earlier phases the sitters are often involved in improving the phenomena by observing and commenting if the apparitions seem shapeless, or if they look like carelessly produced cut-outs. When the participants demand a clearer face, it improves as they watch; if it is too much like the medium's face, it changes; if a materialised hand feels unpleasant, complaining makes it become warm and more human. We also have many occasions where the contents of Kluski's mind, his preoccupations, can be seen in the phantoms. When Kluski is translating a historical novel from Italian, a beautiful Italian Renaissance lady starts appearing at the séances, and an essay about an eighteenth century female spy brings along a phantom of an elderly lady in characteristic period costume (who appears both in sittings in Warsaw, and in Geley's laboratory in Paris). As his mediumship develops, so do the phantoms, some of which acquire distinctive personalities and become regular visitors over several séances (Okołowicz, 1926; Weaver, 2015).

However, in the final phase (from mid 1923 to 1925) we have truly magnificent phantoms, symbolic religious and archetypal figures illuminated with their own powerful lights which flood the whole room. There might be parallels here with the various lofty messages that come through Stainton Moses's automatic writing, or it might reflect Kluski's need to align the séance activities with his own religious faith. Kluski's religion was very important to him, and he became increasingly concerned about the direction of the sittings, which seemed to move from a purely scientific endeavour to seeking contact with the dead (strictly speaking a mortal sin). As his main collaborator said, "Kluski, a deeply devout Catholic, tries to limit his séances also because he fears that they may give rise to some religious doctrine" (Okolowicz, 1926, p.582). In fact, the sittings ceased around 1926, coinciding with a political upheaval that caused a split among many of the sitters.

Towards a Conclusion

An aspect of Kluski's mediumship that gets little mention is automatic writing; it weakened the physical phenomena that were a priority for Geley and Richet, and so they discouraged it. It remained private, but started alongside the physical mediumship; apparently there were different handwritings and different languages, some totally unfamiliar to the medium. A variety of communicators came through, much like people popping in for a chat, some of them the very ones who "attended" the physical séances as phantoms. Myers also reports this in the case of Stainton Moses: "As a general rule the same alleged spirits both manifested themselves by raps [...] and also wrote through his hand when he was alone" (Myers, 1893-4, p. 256). Interestingly, the famous mental medium Eileen Garrett was able to produce a "misty, translucent stuff" in which faces formed, but such experiments were stopped by her mentor, Hewat McKenzie as he thought that they would interfere with the finer aspects of her mental mediumship (Garrett, 1939, p. 142).

It seems that this attitude, that mental and physical mediumship are separate – the mental striving towards higher (spiritual) meaning, the physical confined to lower, meaningless spheres – has influenced the development of both branches of mediumship. Yet Frederic Myers could see the connections and hoped that investigations of Eusapia's mediumship would corroborate the phenomena reported by Stainton Moses (Myers, 1896-97). It did not happen in his lifetime, but by now we do have the beginnings of a pattern. For a start, in all the phenomena reported here we find hands, or something approaching hands, that can handle physical objects; it is more than mental reaching out: something pushes, lifts, carries, and that entails a way of physical interaction. Anita Gregory was not the first to suggest, on the basis of the Rudi Schneider investigations:

> [...] that there is a form or phase of matter or a force of which science has, to date, taken no account. The observations point to a tenuous and unstable form of matter directly under the control of whatever mind may be. The phenomena were personal in the sense that there was every appearance of someone, an invisible or barely visible "person" acting upon the everyday world, moving objects, knotting handkerchiefs, patting sitters on the head [...] (Gregory, 1985, p. 412).

But the nature of the phenomena and interactions seems very much tied up with the mind, its creativity, inventiveness and ability to control events. Rudi never tries to go beyond expected simple tasks and neither do the investigators' expectations; the illiterate Eusapia does better when more imaginative minds work with whatever she provides; the highly spiritual intellectual, Stainton Moses, creates a world along the lines of his concerns, while Daniel Home creates phenomena that fit in with the desires of his sitters. Kluski's creativity gets free rein with the help of the participants, with productions like works of art, until it is made uneasy by expectations that conflict with his beliefs.

So, in physical mediumship there is a strong mental element, a striving for meaning. Beyond the boggle threshold we get order from disorder if there is intellect, imagination and creativity. And there we might leave it, ignoring various phantoms of unconfirmed identity in Home's and Kluski phenomena, if it were not for Indridi Indridason, in whose case we get a new perspective on the input of the mind.

Indridi's phenomena started very much like Kluski's, with violent poltergeist phenomena (Haraldsson & Gissurarson, 2015): raps, knocks, gusts of wind, odours, furniture piling up, tongue-shaped lights of various sizes and colours, touches and lights. We also get a variety of conflicted control personalities, luminous hands carrying objects about, automatic writing, trance speech from deceased personalities (some of them famous), mysterious and beautiful singing (ibid., p. 207).

As powerful as these sound, Indridi provides us with a yet bigger puzzle of mediumship, a case that straddles all aspects of psychical research. At a sitting on 24th November 1905 a luminous pillar appeared with a human form within it. It identified itself as 'Mr Jensen' (a common Danish name), spoke in Danish (unknown to Indridi) and described a fire then currently raging in Copenhagen (Haraldsson, 2011, p. 205).[35] Later on 'Jensen' appeared on a number of occasions, and detailed records of his statements were kept in the experimental society's books. However, it was not until 2008-9 that Erlendur Haraldsson, the late well-known investigator, was able to verify all the specific information provided by Jensen (a manufacturer, a native of Copenhagen, first name

---

[35] There was no telephone or telegraph communication with Iceland in 1905, and confirmation of Jensen's specific statements (a fire in a factory in Copenhagen starting around midnight on 24/11/1905 and being brought under control within an hour) arrived in Reykjavik by Christmas time in the form of newspaper reports.

Emil, a bachelor with no children, but with siblings) (ibid., pp.215-216). It turned out that there had been only one manufacturer named Emil Jensen (1848-1898) in Copenhagen. The fire reported by the Jensen entity in 1905 was close to where he had lived, and his siblings were alive at that time. In the words of Haraldsson, the "'hit rate' with respect to the identity of Emil Jensen is 100 per cent, as is the description of the fire in Copenhagen" (ibid., p. 220). The Jensen entity, unknown to anyone present at the time eventually "became an important figure in the séances with frequent appearances [...] usually very briefly but several times during the same séance and at various locations in the hall." The 'pillar of light' was larger than Jensen and emitted light in such a way that Jensen and Indridi could sometimes be seen side by side at the same time" (Haraldsson & Gissurarson, 2015, pp. 71-3).

To sum up, matching the original records of the sittings with archival information confirmed both the entity's claimed identity, and the events it described. The entity was not related to or known to the sitters; it spoke in a language not spoken by the medium; in modern times, a record has been found that such a person did exist; that person died some years before the sittings with Indridason in the 1900s; and the then contemporary events also took place. Haraldsson titled his report: "A perfect case?" (Haraldsson, 2011). So what do we do with a sophisticated, coherent physical manifestation of a classic 'drop-in' communicator, familiar from mental mediumship?

Lawrence LeShan suggested a way of interpreting such phenomena as 'functional entities' – entities that "[...] do not have any length, breadth, or thickness. They cannot be detected by any form of instrumentation, although their effects often can be [...] They do not have continuous existence whether or not they are being mentally conceptualized [...] they exist only when they are held in the mind [...]" (LeShan, 2009, p. 106).

But whose mind?

POLTERGEISTS AND HIGH STRANGENESS

ALAN MURDIE

"I have been studying poltergeists for forty-five years and I am still just as puzzled as to what causes them as I was at the beginning."
So declared veteran psychical research Guy Lyon Playfair just a few months before his death in April 2018. In pursuit of possible explanations, Playfair had recently started corresponding with Dr Jacques Vallée, the pioneering ufologist, arising from the mention of poltergeists in Vallée's published diaries.

It would be a trite remark to challenge why we might need to contemplate the concept of 'high strangeness' in relation to poltergeists when it might be said that the phenomenon is already strange enough. With the poltergeist we are faced with mysterious events reported across the globe and clearly happening in the material world. Occurring predominantly in domestic settings, poltergeists are characterised by strange noises, "thumps, rappings, scraping, ticking noises, self-playing instruments and physiologically impossible vocal utterances" (Crabbe, 2002), and by the physical movement or destruction of objects. Typically, crockery and ornaments may be broken and upset, stones may be thrown and, in some cases, even heavy items such as large furniture may be displaced. Pools of water and outbreaks of fire have also been known, together with a huge collection of other effects (Grosse, 1980; De Aguilar, 1995).

I knew both Guy Playfair and his co-investigator of the famous Enfield Poltergeist of 1977-79 – Maurice Grosse (1919-2006) – for twenty years and had the opportunity of often discussing the phenomenon with them. Between them they had probably seen more poltergeist activity than anyone else living, their experience even exceeding that of parapsychologist William Roll (1923-2012).

The willingness of Playfair to remain open-minded on the question of causation reflected how, after many years of practical investigation and study, he and other researchers had reached the point of a 'high-strangeness' explanation. Most parapsychologists would prefer to attribute poltergeists to an aspect of psychokinesis from the unconscious minds of living persons, if they are prepared to acknowledge such disturbances as involving psi-faculties at all. The fact that poltergeists are capable of leaving material traces opens them up to recording by way of physical instrumentation, which puts them into a different class of psi phenomena, in contrast with events on a purely subjective level, which are clearly in the minds of percipients, such as telepathy, precognitive dreams and clairvoyance. The very physical nature of manifestations comprising a large part of poltergeist activity means that they involve objectively real events, but their causation has been hotly disputed.

The basis for considering poltergeists as a proven phenomenon can be advanced if the evidence for their occurrence is treated in the same fashion, and to the same standards, in which disputed evidence for objective events in the human world are resolved (e.g., crimes, traffic accidents and custody disputes) – using the judicial tests applied in legal proceedings. This point came home to me in a trip to Latin America a quarter of a century ago. When visiting Bogota, the capital of Colombia in October 1997, I decided to undertake some research into local ghost and poltergeist stories in the country using the books and archives housed in the National Library, the Biblioteca Nacional.

Quite possibly, back in 1997 I was the first psychical researcher from the English-speaking world to specifically go looking for accounts of poltergeists in Colombian archives. Colombia is a diverse and colourful nation known for many marvellous things, but poltergeists are not among them, so far as the English speaking-world was concerned. Before leaving Britain, I had already searched in vain for references to Colombian poltergeist cases in English-language sources and found none, the country never having featured in any collections of poltergeist cases compiled by researchers in the past (Carrington & Fodor, 1951).

There is no parapsychological tradition in Colombia and so I was directed to shelves headed 'folclor' (folklore) and 'occultismo' (occultism). On perusing different titles, I soon discovered a wealth of interesting stories of ghosts and phantoms in both old and new Colombian books and periodicals. Amid the mostly folkloric accounts of exotic ghosts – 'fantasmas y appariciones' ('phantoms and apparitions') in particular – I soon located a number of historic accounts which resembled very closely details of the type of poltergeist activity I was seeking. These cases had all originated within Colombia, and were hitherto unknown to anyone outside of the country (Murdie, 1999).

One story I discovered in the Biblioteca struck me as a particularly classic example. It occurred in the year 1837, in the city of Popyan in the south west of the country, and clearly described a poltergeist outbreak, even though at that stage the word had not yet come into the English language and is still absent from Latin American Spanish.

The events at Popyan involved a mysterious rain of stones from the air upon a sizeable house that was occupied by a Dr Ospina, his wife and children. This began without warning, with the property appearing to be under constant bombardment from stones and small pebbles. Members of the household were understandably disturbed and, knowing that stones do not generally fall out of the sky (with the exception of meteorites, which had only been accepted from 1803), they sought a human culprit. Though the origin of these rocky missiles could not be traced, Dr Ospina suspected that a neighbouring family was somehow responsible and playing some kind of malicious prank. The Ospinas were seemingly persons of some influence in their community for they were able to persuade the police to summarily arrest these neighbours and take them all in for questioning. However, their temporary detention failed to halt the mysterious bombardment.

Twelve soldiers were then deployed to watch the Ospina house. The stone throwing continued unabated, with the soldiers failing to detect anyone responsible. It was eventually realised that the rains of stones had a sort of shyness about them – they were never seen to begin moving and their source remained unidentified.

Quickly the pressure of unexplained rocks and gravel raining down on their house took its toll on the nerves of the Ospinas, with the wife being greatly affected. With her family watching, she went out into the walled courtyard surrounding their home and rather melodramatically declared that if the disturbances did not cease, or nothing was done to stop it, she would hang herself to escape the invisible persecutors.

This provoked an instant and highly disturbing reaction from whomever, or whatever, was responsible. Seemingly in response to her words, a length of rope curled into a hangman's noose suddenly fell out of the air, landing in the courtyard. Senora Ospina was deeply distressed by this incident. She collapsed and was taken to her bed, stricken with a severe illness from which she never recovered. She died soon after whereupon the mysterious manifestations waned and then ceased entirely.

This story appeared in a book of Colombian ghosts and hauntings from a region called Antioquia, published in 1950 (Escobar Uribe, 1950). Proffering names, a date and a verifiable location, the strange manifestations proved typical of a number of comparable cases found in the country and Latin America. Such incidents are attributed to 'los duendes,' from the word 'duende' usually translated into English as 'elf,' 'goblin' or 'dwarf.' The term is applied to hauntings that involve strange sounds, the throwing of objects and baffling physical disturbances that suggest an invisible presence prone to playing silly and mindless tricks. In other words, the same phenomenon that would be labelled as a poltergeist in English, or in German (the word for 'rattling or rumbling spirit,' first coined by Martin Luther in Germany in the fifteenth century, Lecouteux, 2012).

What struck me on finding this story is not that it was exceptional (other than the person at the centre of the ordeal dying), but rather it was its sheer familiarity. The story from Popyan in 1837 matched numerous cases in the annals of psychical research. Its significance was in its insignificance and ubiquity. Basically, everything from the manifestations themselves to the social reactions to them made the case indistinguishable from all the other outbreaks of stone throwing recorded in vastly different times and contexts.

Just as striking a similarity between outbreaks was noted by anthropologist and folklorist Andrew Lang (1844-1912) in 1903: "It is the extraordinary uniformity in the reports, from every age, country, and class of society, the uniformity in hallucination, that makes the mystery" (Lang, 1903). Lang argued that these parallels in vastly different settings pointed to an underlying reality. Similarly, in 1953, fifty years later, the parapsychologist Raynor Johnson (1901-1987) wrote:

> The accounts of happenings have their own peculiar features, but in general they show a remarkable similarity: unexplained noises, such as footsteps in empty rooms and corridors, loud bangs upon doors, sounds of furniture being dragged about, blows and raps upon the floors or beds, objects improbably flying about and broken (Johnson, 1953).

In their book *Contagion* (2014), English authors Michael Hallowell and Darren Ritson also drew attention to similar recurring patterns in poltergeist cases, comparing the position of psychical researchers to homicide detectives who find matching forensic traces at different murder scenes.

These widely separated writers confirmed a common pattern in disturbances many miles and many years apart. In doing so they had unwittingly acknowledged and enunciated a key principle enshrined in the law of evidence, as applied in court rooms in the English-speaking world. Known as the 'similar fact evidence principle,' it treats otherwise isolated reports or facts as probative if there are striking similarities between them.

The modern starting point for similar fact evidence is usually treated as the case of '*Makin v Attorney General for New South Wales* [1894],' a case of serial infant murder, with the principle being re-stated and refined many times in different jurisdictions ever since. Utilising the similar fact principle, recurring patterns, facts or features are treated as probative, enabling the standard of 'beyond reasonable doubt.' The mere existence of similarity in itself is not enough; what is required is that the similarity must be striking and that no other explanation is feasible when viewed in terms of the totality of the evidence and testimony available. The rule has been used with some of the most serious offences on the statute book, including homicide and cases of multiple sexual offending.

Where otherwise inexplicable accounts, or similar physical traces can be shown, the isolated cases can be assessed together to identify a linked causation and point to the guilt of a particular person beyond reasonable doubt. If the same similar fact approach and standard is applied to the best attested poltergeist cases gathered by psychical researchers, then poltergeists may be considered proven as an unexplained phenomenon to a standard beyond reasonable doubt.

For instance, writing in *Australian Poltergeists* (2014), two Australian researchers, Paul Cropper and Tony Healy, noted the tendency for "several instances where very odd, seemingly "one-off" effects reported during some of our cases have been found to match incidents recorded during very obscure episodes that occurred in different parts of the country many decades earlier [...] [S]ometimes the match was found in obscure foreign cases." In law these would build up into probative evidence.

Once it has been realised that the similarities and patterns found in poltergeist cases cannot simply be ascribed to chance coincidence, or any other credible explanation, the existence of such patterns becomes proof in itself, at least applying a judicial standard to disputed events outside empirical and clinical settings.

Speaking from a legal perspective, it should also be noted that in a well attested poltergeist case involving multiple incidents – during which researchers may acquire a large volume of testimony and other forms of evidence – what ultimately is accrued may actually exceed what is available in many cases that come before the courts for determination. For instance, with the Enfield Poltergeist alone the volume of material now archived at Cambridge University Library is substantial. During the first nine months Grosse and Playfair visited the troubled family on 180 days and nights between September 5th 1977 and June 1978, including 25 all-night vigils. Over 140 hours of tape recordings were obtained, resulting in initial transcripts running to over 500 pages (a substantial number of original recordings have still to be transcribed). Just a fraction of the details of the case of what came to be known as the Enfield Poltergeist were condensed three years later in Playfair's book, *This House is Haunted* (1980). Much more material remains unpublished. Certain elements in the family house at the centre of the case resembled classic incidents of spirit possession, particularly when eleven year-old Janet Hodgson, then passing through puberty and experiencing her first menstruation, began speaking in a gruff voice like an old man. Researchers considered that much uttered by the voice originated from the unconscious mind of Janet, but there was also verifiable information not apparently known to anyone present. Many hours of audio recordings exist of such material. A subsequent re-investigation reached the conclusion that psychokinetic incidents were occurring in the property. The report runs to nearly 200 pages, arising from an approach of re-interviewing available witnesses (EPIC REPORT, 1982).

Other cases have also yielded substantial volumes of material, including the Battersea poltergeist, active between 1956-1968 (Chibbet, 1965), the Miami Poltergeist of 1967 (Roll, 1972), and the South Shields Poltergeist 2006-2007 (Hallowell & Ritson, 2008; Ritson, 2021). With such cases the sheer scale of the task of analysis is one that justifies engagement by a team of researchers and scholars. Maurice Grosse identified the problem in an article in *Alpha* magazine in the UK in 1980. Grosse stated that "[c]ontrary to popular belief, poltergeist activity does not cover just psychokinetic events but embraces practically the whole spectrum of psychic phenomena." Amongst the phenomena occurring at Enfield were instances of:

[...] apparitions, apparent telepathic communication, shared dreams, innumerable so-called "coincidences," headaches that came and went with the phenomena, appearance of fire and water, trances or altered states of consciousness, interference with electrical and mechanical equipment. Raudive-type voices, doppelgänger effects, etc. All these events and many more besides were often experienced by individuals involved in the case (Grosse, 1980).

Grosse wrote this in the context of an estimated 1500 logged incidents. As with other large scale or lengthy cases, patterns of disturbances seemed to be pointing towards some kind of low-level consciousness seeking attention and communication.

Faced with multiple events, merely logging incidents – and reading about them – may become monotonous and hinder deeper analysis. Grosse cautioned:

We must be careful, therefore, in our analysis of the phenomena, not to concentrate on the most spectacular at the expense of other events more mundane, but nevertheless just as important is the overall picture presented by the case [...] (Grosse, 1980).

Thus, the variety of alleged phenomena in a poltergeist outbreak may include a far greater diversity of incidents than hitherto realised. Facing such a wide-ranging variety of phenomena the formulation of any coherent theory becomes especially difficult.

Poltergeists remain a puzzle because of their complexity and the fact that in many cases it has been suspected that they appear to bear a relationship with the mental states of those amongst whom they occur. Often poltergeists are reported among troubled families in stressful domestic settings, but this is in no way an invariable circumstance. Historically, it has not been possible to develop an all encompassing theoretical basis to account for poltergeist manifestations because of the scale and complexity of incidents and their settings. As Sir Karl Popper put it:

A scientist engaged in a piece of research, say in physics, can attack his problem straight away. He can go at once to the heart of the matter: that is to the heart of an organised structure. For a structure of scientific doctrines is already in existence, and with it, a generally accepted problem situation (Popper, 1959).

This is not the case with poltergeist research.

Compounding the problems yet further is a recognition that spontaneous incidents of isolated psychokinetic phenomena may take place on a fairly regular basis. These are effectively one-off incidents that are never repeated, and may also be more commonplace than realised. These have been labelled 'JOTTs' – 'Just-one of-those things' by Mary Rose Barrington (1926-2020) – odd, one-off physical happenings (Barrington, 2018).

So the challenges of synthesising data and devising theories from them is immense. However, this has not prevented many theories and hypotheses from being advanced over the centuries, including those postulating a paranormal aspect, sometimes in keeping with wider cultural trends and beliefs. A condensed summary of the postulated explanations runs as follows:

> *Pre-1550* – the dead from Purgatory; *1600-1700* – demons and witchcraft; 1840s – 'electric girls' (Crowe, 1848); *1848-present* – spirits; *1896-present* – 'naughty girls' (Podmore, 1896); *1913-present* – unconscious fraud in states of automatism, sleep-walking, epilepsy and hysterical conditions (Hyslop, 1913); *1920s* – unconscious mediumship (Carrington, 1931); *1930s-50s* – PK projection from the (Freudian) unconscious (Fodor, 1953); *1943* – PK projection from a (Jungian) unconscious (Layard, 1943); *1945-present* – PK and 'elementals' (Price, 1945); *1950s-1980s* – geophysical and seismic effects (Lambert, 1957; Persinger, 1986). One of the first and few points of agreement across these perspectives was that poltergeist disturbances often arose in the proximity of an adolescent, usually female.

The major change came between 1957-1970s with the proposal by William Roll that poltergeist incidents involving physical effects might be attributable to instances of 'Recurrent Spontaneous Psychokinesis' (RSPK), an idea derived from studies of psychokinesis in the laboratory (though with effects in poltergeist outbreaks exceeding those recorded in laboratory conditions – see Cornell, 2002).

Throughout the 1960s and 1970s Roll's conception of RSPK became the predominant idea among parapsychologists prepared to countenance a psi factor, particularly attractive because of a presumed connection with much weaker psychokinesis (PK) effects reported in laboratories. In Germany a similar view was taken by Hans Bender. The view of unconscious human causation led to increased studies of the psychopathology of households and the emergence of new therapeutic models. Roll considered that disturbances in the central nervous system might be involved in some way with poltergeist effects.

Yet the explanatory adequacy of the RSPK model has been challenged in actual real-world cases. Significantly, the initial firm boundaries that early psychical researchers drew between cases featuring apparitions and those which did not have come to be questioned, the boundary proving artificial or even non-existent (Myers, 1903; Wilson, 1981; Playfair, 2010; Fraser, 2021).

A problem afflicting any theoretical approach has been the lack of any shared perspective amongst investigators themselves. So many topics in parapsychology may still be described in terms of philosopher Thomas. S. Kuhn's "pre-paradigmatic science," which reflects a long-standing difficulty with spontaneous case research. Whereas experimental work in laboratories allowed some standardisation of paranormal research, testing poltergeists by way of controlled empirical trials is an impossibility. This leaves researchers proceeding on a case-by-case basis, not really knowing where they are heading next – whether geographically, or any other direction. This problem is compounded by poltergeist research being the preserve of a very small number of individual investigators, each with his/her own methods, perspectives and set of findings. In the natural course of things, researchers die leaving no successors, often with decades passing before any researcher returns to their findings, if at all.

Consequently, poltergeists might remain a phenomenon best suited to the eclectic approach advocated by Charles Fort – of gathering 'damned data.' Such is the diversity of phenomena discernible in reported cases that at least one writer surveying the field abandons any hope of an all-encompassing theory ever being possible (Fort, 1931; Tucker, 2021). This will already be clear to serious researchers facing a surfeit of evidence to assess, rather than the reverse.

When no theory yet devised can fully account for all aspects of reported phenomena (certainly not the variety listed by Grosse), then no explanation is potentially off-limits, even if it would be categorised as one involving 'high strangeness,' for example: pointing out the possibility of spirits (human or non-human), or some discarnate force or agency. Leaving aside the purely naturalistic explanations that are monotonously applied (e.g. fraud, hallucination, misperception), because of their explanatory inadequacy in well-evidenced cases, it is clear that an extremely complex phenomenon is being considered with psi-related theories of poltergeist causation broadly divided into those favouring an agency originating *within* a living human consciousness and those postulating an *external* discarnate consciousness or force as responsible.

Two studies of poltergeist activity have potentially pointed in such a high-strangeness direction, in respect of at least some cases. In 1972 Ian Stevenson (1918-2007) wrote an article for the *Journal of the American Society for Psychical Research* titled 'Poltergeists: Are they Living or are they Dead?' Stevenson argued that while psychokinesis from a living agent, such as a troubled adolescent, might explain shorter term cases with relatively simple phenomena, there were others that were much more complex and where a discarnate intelligence was suggested, based upon marked differences within cases.

Stevenson argued that a number of complex and remarkable features in certain historic cases were better explained by presuming a discarnate agency, a survival of consciousness after death, and the traditional idea of a ghost as the returning spirit of a deceased person. Stevenson believed this could be inferred from the type of phenomena recorded during a poltergeist outbreak.

Category	Living Agency	Discarnate Agency
1. Types of objects moved	Mostly light objects.	Heavier objects, e.g. stones, bricks.
2. Range of distance over which objects move	Shorter range (a few inches to 15 feet).	Longer range (average perhaps 30-50 feet).
3. Flight paths	Simple trajectories.	Complicated trajectories with sharp angle turns, deflections and marked changes.
4. Damage to the objects	Breakage common.	Objects rarely or never break.
5. Landing patterns	Objects seem to fall or to be knocked over. They land forcefully.	Objects seem to be carried or deposited gently.
6. Apparent motive	Motiveless movement of objects; objects knocked over in a seemingly random fashion.	Movements suggest purpose, e.g. throwing a brick at someone.

Category	Living Agency	Discarnate Agency
7. Benefit to subject	Subject may express their destructive impulses toward other persons by the effects produced.	Subject may be the object of destructive impulses or exploitation. There is no benefit and actually perhaps some disadvantage or injury.
8. Significance of raps	No meaningful communication.	Meaningful responses obtained from raps.
9. Apparitional and Visual phenomena	Absent or occurring later, and not collective.	Occurring early, abundantly and collectively.
10. Mediumistic trances and auditory communications from apparent discarnate entities	Absent.	Present.
11. Location of phenomena	Localised around a particular person.	May be localised around a person or place.
12. Age of subject	Usually under twenty years old.	No characteristic age.
13. Means of resolution	With psychotherapy of the subject.	Intercession, placation, exorcism, or other activity directed toward the presumed discarnate entity.

Regrettably, Stevenson drew these conclusions from a very small sample of historic cases. A more systematic study in the form of a cluster analysis of 64 characteristics contained in 500 historic cases conducted in 1979 by Alan Gauld did, however, provide a partial statistical confirmation of this broad division of short and long duration cases containing identifiable, separate and distinctive clusters of features (Gauld & Cornell, 1979).

The results demonstrate that poltergeists are not purely random compilations of manifestations but rather are a phenomenon showing identifiable characteristics, with some centring on a living person and other cases that lacked such a focus. Gauld found 76% of poltergeist cases lasted six months or less, with disturbances centring on particular individuals. These suggested human agency with more females than males as the postulated foci. However, 24% of longer term cases (one year or more) seemed unconnected with an individual and appeared to be more place-centred. Occupiers might change (haunted pubs exemplify this). Such longer-term poltergeists displayed noticeable differences from the shorter cases, resembling traditional hauntings, suggesting a purely mental origin or link with a living human, and the longer-term suggesting influence from an external haunting entity or presence engaging in rudimentary communication. Gauld's analysis showed that patterns are discernible within amorphous collections of facts and cases. Gauld's cluster analysis went some way towards confirming William Barrett's (1844-1925) observation of 1911 that 'The disturbances may be centred on persons of either sex, and appear to be attached to a particular place as well as to a particular person; some animate as well as inanimate *point d'appui* seems to be essential' (Barrett, 1911).

A combination of discarnate influence and adolescent psychokinesis was considered in Enfield in North London between 1977-79. Guy Playfair had previously encountered poltergeist activity in Brazil between 1973-75, and was familiar with spiritist explanations but did not consider them sufficient. For his part, Maurice Grosse ultimately eschewed theories altogether emphasising that the primary task was the collection of evidence. In this regard he even viewed theories as a handicap to any assessment, commenting in 2001:

> In the past we have had underground streams, ley lines, absorbent building materials, planetary influences, faulty observation, delusions, over-active imaginations, alien visitors, low and high frequency sound, earth tremors, temperature changes, to name but a few of the reasons to account for PK, haunting and all the other phenomena associated with our subject. I look forward to the next popular and fashionable revelation (Grosse, 2001).

Given that the subject is a graveyard of theories one might caution against extending hypothesising any further. On such a basis one may hesitate to open up poltergeists further and introduce elements of 'high strangeness'; it might be felt by now that the incidents could not be any stranger!

Nevertheless, future researchers should have regard to the approach of Stevenson and Gauld and the patterns illuminated thus far; coupled with the 'similar fact' approach applied to data and evidence (in essence also recognised in the case collection approach to apparitions taken in the late nineteenth century), new insights may emerge. This is where scope exists for open-minded researchers who are not wedded to any particular theories or ideological axioms to consider seriously 'high-strangeness elements.' This is not something researchers should shirk from (though I appreciate that this may be vastly more difficult for those in academia facing institutional pressures and restraints than for independent researchers such as myself).

From what has been accumulated hitherto an evidential case can be made that manifestations may involve the influence or intervention of an external, or discarnate, form of consciousness, either human or non-human. In this regard, let me say that personally speaking I would much prefer poltergeists to be explicable within the framework of the RSPK model – a matter of phenomena originating as an extension of postulated psi abilities generated by or originating within living human minds, rather than a discarnate or external form of consciousness being involved. An RSPK explanation in such terms might well only require an ultimate extension, or revision, of existing materialistic theories of the universe rather than the extensive substitution required if non-human or super-human agencies are involved.

Ideally, investigators should be prepared to follow all possible leads, regardless of perceived absurdity or irrationality in the context of current scientific or philosophical orthodoxy.

A further ground for not disregarding poltergeists with 'high strangeness' elements is that aberrant behaviour may be far more impressive and important than the stereotypical conduct (if such a thing can be countenanced) we think of as comprising normality, even with what might be deemed 'normal' poltergeist activity. It may prove the case that some kind of normal distribution curve applies to poltergeist phenomena, as it does with many phenomena within nature. However, given that experiences are far more widespread than was once thought, the most astonishing or incredible features must not be automatically rejected if we are ever to reach a point where we can plot such a curve with parameters – which would approach infinity at each end, and at a very low level of probability.

However, over years of studying the phenomena, collecting testimonies of those who have directly encountered them, and adding in some personal experiences of my own (to which I am prone giving the least weight, as seeing is not always believing!), I concede the possibility that in a minority of cases some kind of discarnate intelligence must be seriously considered. Some areas of future research also suggest themselves here, applying the case collection and similar fact evidence approaches based upon certain features in cases which have hitherto attracted relatively little attention. Some of these might include:

Contagion and Transmissibility

A feature of certain poltergeists in major cases is that they can seemingly attach themselves to observers. This was proposed by researcher John Spencer, author of *The Poltergeist Experience* (1996). Darren Ritson and Mike Hallowell reported being dogged by strange incidents in the aftermath of the South Shields poltergeist. I interviewed both writers in October 2010 on these incidents ahead of their publication of a book exploring the issue titled *Contagion* (2014, 2022). They recalled how during the South Shields poltergeist investigation both authors discussed the case in a room used as an office at one of their homes. As they walked out of the office they heard a tremendous bang from behind, startling them both. Turning around, a local history book entitled *The Borough of South Shields* by George B. Hodgson weighing almost four pounds had deposited itself on the middle of the office floor. In the 1970s physicist John Hasted reported apparent contagion of PK effects in a domestic context following a visit to his home by the Israeli psychic Uri Geller (Hasted, 1981).

Connections with Spirits as Conceived in Traditional Societies

As noted, some poltergeist outbreaks might potentially be treated as indications of the survival of consciousness beyond death. A similarity with certain manifestations claimed in physical séances and spontaneous poltergeist rooms has long been recognised and is often treated as grounds for suspicion (Podmore, 1902). In some cases, the eruption of PK effects during adolescence is the prelude to the development of enduring mediumistic powers in living persons, a possibility suggested with Daniel Dunglas Hume (1883-1886), Eusapia Palladino (1854-1918), and Matthew Manning (1955-), to name just a few. A number of mediums report this and it would be worth detailed study. However, despite the assertion that 'the poltergeist is the citizen of the world' (Roll,1977), much of the evidence for their occurrence has hitherto been drawn from Western societies; only 8% of Gauld's sample of 500 cases were drawn from outside Europe and North America. Given the diversity of human afterlife beliefs in traditional societies there is clearly much scope for cross-cultural study and comparison if the idea of the spirits is to be explored, Western spiritualism only being one culturally limited perspective. A high strangeness factor has already been acknowledged among some researchers in the field of experiential anthropology where Edith Turner (1921-2016) wrote:

> We may have to come to terms with the fact that we are not the only souls occupying this earth, that there are indeed other entities, and that the sense needed to communicate with them requires a little care to develop [...] (Turner, 1993).

A caveat that such spirits may only come into being when conceptualised should also be factored in to any assessment (LeShan, 2009), as should the influence of the cultural context and the contents of the minds of observers, which affect the behaviour of manifestations – a kind of out-of-lab experimenter/observer effect.

Yet a further complication is that secondary personalities associated with spirit possession and manifestations attributed to discarnate intervention are moulded by the socio-cultural environment in which the phenomenon occurs (Watson, 1986). American psychical researcher D. Scott Rogo stated that:

> All through the study of the poltergeist we have seen how fickle it is. If it is called a demon it readily assumes the role. If it is treated as an intelligent entity, it will rap coherently in answer to questions. Treat it as a witch, and it will give you animal familiars. Apparently, the poltergeist is extremely sensitive to the attitudes and beliefs of those witnessing it (Rogo, 1979).

Traditional Beliefs Concerning Non-Human Entities

Such a connection was aired by Sir William Barrett as long ago as 1911 'that the widespread belief in fairies, pixies, gnomes, brownies, etc, probably rests on the varied manifestations of poltergeists.' In Celtic and traditional British folklore poltergeist activity has resonances with the fickle actions of household spirits known as brownies, by turns helpful or mischievous, a link also made by a handful of parapsychologists such as George Owen and Serena Roney-Dougal (Owen, 1964; Roney Dougal, 2001). Possibly the oldest documented example from England is a twelfth century case from Suffolk which is replete with strange elements. The chronicler, Ralph of Coggeshall recorded how during the reign of King Richard (1189-1199) a 'certain fantastical spirit' troubled the family of Sir Osberni de Bradewelle at Dagworth in mid-Suffolk. This entity was invisible and played silly tricks terrifying the family before they became hardened to its antics. The spirit developed a voice like a child expressing itself in English, the regional dialect and in Latin. It called itself 'Malekin' with the chronicler recording: 'The things which he did and said were both wonderful and very funny, and he often told people's secrets.'

Malekin could be felt physically, but not seen, save on one occasion when he materialised 'as a very small child clothed in a white tunic, in the chamber of a certain maiden.' Claiming to be a human child abducted into fairyland the entity declared he would remain in his present condition for seven years until he would be restored to his human form (from *Chronicum Anglicanum*).

Today Dagworth is a very small community, the type of quiet, rural hamlet where little happens over the centuries. The story was cited by Harry Price in *Poltergeist Over England* (1945). As an example of a historic poltergeist, it contains hallmarks identifiable with parallels in later cases (Price, 1945), including a 'certain maiden' (an adolescent focus?), 'silly actions' (pointless physical disturbances), and complaints of the presumed haunting presence being heard and physically felt but not generally visible.

The present hall at Dagworth dates from the fifteenth century but retains a portion of the earlier manor house occupied by Sir Osbert and his family. It was therefore most interesting to receive a letter in spring 2000 from the late Major Patrick de Vere Patey recalling how a school inspector of the 1960s had moved into 'the old part of the former Dagworth Hall' only to 'leave pretty sharply due to what must have been the action of a Poltergeist behaving in the traditional manner' (De Patey, 2000). Regrettably the details of this tantalising incident went otherwise unrecorded. It is also, of course, just hearsay. However, in the course of producing a book on Suffolk fairly lore, historian Dr Francis Young spoke to the current owner of Dagworth Hall in 2016 who told him about the reactions of his young son who seems to interact and talk with an apparently childish invisible presence, a most intriguing parallel given the context.

Notably, there are widely separated cases of child-like apparitions, usually of a little boy. For example, in the Cardiff poltergeist in 1988-89 a form like a school boy was seen once amid poltergeist disturbances; likewise the apparition of a boy was once seen in the Hannath Hall, Cambridgeshire case in 1959 (Cornell & Gauld, 1979). An earlier example comes from Texas in 1881 (Lawson & Porter, 1951). Just as I was completing this chapter, I came across a press cutting from 1977 concerning disruptive poltergeist phenomena at a butcher's shop and domestic flat in Torbay, Devon. An apparition was witnessed by a Jacqueline Harding, who is quoted as saying: "He was a boy aged about 12 and dressed in a sailor suit." She had never seen him before and says that he vanished into thin air as she watched. The figure appeared only once ('Hubby quits home over a spook,' *Sunday Mirror* of 22nd May 1977). When Luther first used the word poltergeist in the sixteenth century many other popular terms were already in use for a large class of traditional domestic spirits. According to ethnologist Dagmar Linhart, these include many superhuman or demonic beings which may be invisible or manifest in diverse forms, as human beings or animals, and attract attention through noises and strange actions (Linhart, 1995). Across Spain and Latin America, as mentioned above, manifestations are attributed to 'los duendes,' typically conceived as invisible diminutive humanoid entities resembling traditional images of gnomes or dwarves. Clearly there is scope for specialists in ethnology, folklore and anthropology to examine the cross-cultural data.

The Appearance of Animal Apparitions

Noted among the forms that traditional poltergeists take are appearances of animals. Here we have a further high-strangeness feature recurring in widely separated locations. In the classic Wesley poltergeist case at Epworth Rectory, over the winter of 1716-1717, in the family home of John and Samuel Wesley, the founders of Methodism, Mrs Wesley recorded: 'Upon my looking under the bed something ran out pretty like a badger and seemed to run directly under Emily's petticoats' (Southey, 1846). At Willington Mill on Tyneside witnesses saw a mysterious white cat with a long snout and another creature resembling a monkey. A poltergeist recorded at Durweston, Dorset between 1894-1895 involved unexplained responsive noises, mysterious writing and objects being displaced in the vicinity of two orphan girls who lived with their adopted family in an isolated cottage: 'Annie [...] saw a queer animal with green head and green eyes, and a big bushy tail, sitting up and pulling her doll to pieces with its paws. Gertie, the younger girl, she added, saw the same apparition when Annie called to her' (Podmore, 1896). At Cashen's Gap on the Isle of Man between 1931-1936 it was claimed that a poltergeist voice was the work of a supernatural mongoose calling itself 'Gef' (Josiffe, 2017). Links between such stories and the tradition of witches possessing animal familiars have previously been made by individual scholars (Sitwell, 1940). This list could be extended.

Coincidences, Synchronicity and a Cosmic Dimension

Ultimately, the limitations of a similar fact approach – or any other paradigm – may be reached in poltergeist cases in which seemingly meaningful coincidences occur, in particular strange and striking coincidences (Chibbet, 1965). This may lead investigators to think that some external or higher force or power is working in poltergeist outbreaks. Such an outlook was characteristic of seventeenth century Protestant thinking, with theologians such as Martin Luther and writers such as Ludwig Lavater attributing poltergeists to tricks of the devil, a view still promoted by certain religious fundamentalists today. The notion of cosmic dimensions orchestrating matters was contemplated by Sir William Barrett in 1911, who stated that:

> We ourselves and the whole world may be but nucleated cells in a vaster living organism, of which we can form no conception. Some incomprehensible intelligence is certainly at work in the congeries of cells and in the galaxy of suns and stars. But evolution in animate and inanimate nature is unlikely to be confined to the *visible* universe. Living creatures of different types and varied intelligence may exist in the unseen as in the seen. Possibly these poltergeist phenomena may be due to some of these (Barrett, 1911).

Following her experiences in PK testing with one-time poltergeist agent and psychic Matthew Manning (who believed he channelled spirit communicators), psychologist Anita Gregory wrote:

> Coincidences have always intrigued and, latterly, amused me. The occasions upon which an electrical apparatus designed to test has malfunctioned are too numerous to recall. It is almost as if there is a cosmic joker whose sole job it is to incapacitate researchers' machinery [...] At some level we are all part of one another, linked through our unconscious minds. We are all part of every living organism, no matter how small. We are cogs in a cosmic system (Gregory, 1982).

This higher intelligence is not necessarily benign according to some. The theme of a higher intelligence manipulating things for its own purposes was taken up by Peter McCue in his book *Zones of Strangeness: An Examination of Paranormal and UFO Hot Spots* (2012). In *Contagion* (2014) Ritson and Hallowell proposed an 'Arch Poltergeist' hypothesis – a single discarnate entity responsible for orchestrating manifestations to account for similarities between otherwise isolated outbreaks around the world.

Whilst many researchers may feel like they have special coincidences from time to time, any statistician or student of coincidences and synchronicity will grasp it is a subject containing enormous difficulties of assessment, calculation, subjectivity, interpretation and proof.

Obviously, postulated cosmic agencies are currently very difficult to encompass in an empirical scientific framework. In the case of the poltergeist, striking similarities between manifestations suggest an underlying pattern but one must caution as a matter of logic the conclusion that there must automatically be a single entity behind all of them. To give an analogy from the history of astronomy, observations over centuries showed the brightness of certain stars changed (so-called variable stars) with widely separated observations indicating patterns not attributable to observational error by individual astronomers. Whilst demonstrating to Arabic and later astronomers that the heavens were not unchanging, it did not follow that ancient observers of the variable star Algol in the constellation of Perseus were correct in ascribing these variations to a mocking demon. Later, and better equipped, observers would go on to establish the presence of an eclipsing darker companion star as astronomical science advanced.

Whatever the case, it is a sound bet that somewhere in the world poltergeist activity is believed to be taking place at this very moment. It is necessary to combine the strictest scientific rigour possible in poltergeist investigations with the greatest liberality of explanatory hypotheses. Academic resistance, whether rooted in mainstream materialist theories or post-modern philosophies should not impede research or be allowed to act as a new form totemic taboo to prevent fresh explorations of this most enduring of mysteries.

DISEMBODIED EYES REVISITED

An Investigation into the Ontology of Entheogenic Entity Encounters[36]

DAVID LUKE

> And all should cry, Beware! Beware!
> His flashing eyes, his floating hair!
> Weave a circle round him thrice,
> And close your eyes with holy dread,
> For he on honey-dew hath fed,
> And drunk the milk of Paradise.
> SAMUEL TAYLOR COLERIDGE, *KUBLA KHAN* (1797).

All that glitters is not gold. Such a maxim might well serve any psychic voyager on a journey into the weirder realms of psychedelics. After all, out here on the edges there is seldom any firm evidence that the beatific or hellish visions beheld whilst chemically neurohacking your wetware have any basis in consensus reality. Indeed, these visions are often so extravagantly strange and terrifyingly ineffable that reminding yourself that they are not real can serve to keep one's sanity on a short leash when madness looms.

Nevertheless, as John Lilly put it, how does one recognise one's insanity from one's out-sanity? And in any case how would anyone even

---

[36] A version of this chapter was first published in *The Entheogen Review*, Vol. 17, No. 1 (2008).

begin to try and prove the ontological credibility of the psychedelic experience if they were to visit some other world or meet some alien entity? No one has yet put forward a solid method for testing these supposed realities within the domain of science, despite some admirable but flawed attempts recently (e.g., Rodriguez, 2007), so all we have left to rely on is anecdote and phenomenology. This story lies somewhere between the two, but also takes on a new dimension that has urged me to depart momentarily from the fruits of science into the "foamy custard" of folklore, myth, cultural studies and related disciplines. What I have uncovered in this adventure seemingly has enough semblance of objectivity to warrant a whisper of truth – whatever that may be.

A Brief Glance at the Truly Forbidden

I had taken a full dose of DMT (~ 50mg smoked) about forty or fifty times, but always with some trepidation and reverence for its power. True to form I met a variety of extraordinary entities on these excursions (as Terrence McKenna once said, "you get elves, everybody does") – sometimes unknown God-like beings, sometimes shape-shifting mischievous imps – but increasingly I kept getting the feeling I was intruding upon a cosmic gathering I was not invited to. Sometimes, the effects failed to go any further than an ego-dissolution and a wild swim through a fractal geometry of pulsing light with all the usual wild array of colours. Yet, I often felt as though I was being blocked from accessing whatever lurked beyond these multiple geometrical dimensions, as well as from the places I had been to previously. A couple of times I had felt so uninvited and intimidated by the entities I encountered that I did not wish to return, regardless of my curiosity.

On my last DMT session I had been determined to return to the mystic bliss I had once known and I took myself off to a secluded beach on the banks of the River Ganges. I prepared myself with an improvised ritual, hoping to gird myself against whatever lay beyond, and inhaled a pipe full of the foul plastic-tasting resin. Sucked into the space between the pipe and my brain I found myself breaking through the veil like a gatecrasher at a party of swirling smiling eyeballs all attached to snake bodies, which were as startled to see me as I was to be there. The whole ordered assortment of eyes and snakes acted as one being and in the brief moment before it reacted to my arrival I managed to catch a glimpse over what might loosely be described as the shoulder of this strange entity and instantly realised that I had seen something I should not have – a brief glance at the truly forbidden.

Afterwards I could not recall what this was exactly, having somehow blocked it out, but could only remember that it was a scene that seemed both ineffable and highly illegal for mortal minds. Then the multitudinous eyes of the being before me quite suddenly and quite deliberately blocked my curious consciousness explorations any further by mesmerising me with its squirming rhythmic geometrical eyeball hypnosis. I mean, this thing really scared me! It had acted with utter surprise at my being there and then, alarmed, the ominous luminous voluminous numinous had proceeded to let me know that I *should not be there* and that I should certainly not be peering into the hallowed space beyond it, which it clearly guarded. I opted not to defy this terrifying entity and attempted to remain as passive as possible while it pulsed and gyrated intimidatingly at me for the next ten minutes, though it seemed like an eon.

I finally came out of it all a bit shell-shocked and decided that this would be my last DMT experience, for a long time at least. [This event actually happened something like fourteen years ago and I ventured into my first full DMT voyage since then only last month, as a volunteer subject in a DMT brain imaging study with some colleagues. I lived to tell the tale, but that is another story].

Like many of my psychedelic encounters with seemingly discarnate beings I did not know quite what to make of this experience, but it had rocked me to the core. It was not until a few years later that I began to piece it together with some other visionary fragments. In a dream once I, quite naïvely, had a mind-blowing encounter with Azrael, the Islamic angel of death. The angel had told me its name, though I had not heard it before. Unfortunately, it never showed itself because among Muslims the archangel Azrael is considered to have ten thousand eyes, and is the holy psychopomp responsible for ushering souls into the realm of the dead.

A similar character, Azrail the god of death, belongs to the Hausa people of western Africa (Besmer, 1983). I also later stumbled across Ezekiel's vision of the cherubim in the Bible (Ezekiel 10: 12). Guarding the ark in the temple of Solomon, they too were covered in a multitude of eyes, all over their hands, back, wings, etc., much like the multi-eyed beasts guarding the throne of god in heaven (Revelations, 4:6) and this struck a chord of recognition, although the being I had met on DMT had not seemed quite so angelic.

It was not until several years after this last DMT event that I made a surprising discovery when I accidentally came across a reference in a book on Tibetan magic and ritual to an ancient deity by the name of Za [gZa' in Tibetan]. Za is known to appear with half the body of a snake, no less, and is covered in a thousand eyes. Interestingly, like the cherubim guarding the ark, the Tibetan Za functions as a "protector of the law" and is a guardian deity belonging to a class of demon-gods called Lu or Lhamayin (associated with the Indian nāgas), who appear with snake bodies. The author Beyer wrote, "These Lu are undisputedly spirits of the underworld, found in places where their realm impinges upon ours, such as in springs, wells, and rivers" (1974, p. 295). This struck an even greater chord when I realised that on that last occasion I had smoked DMT on the banks of the River Ganges near the Tibetan border, which in retrospect would seem like a sure way to meet this Tibetan deity.

The idea that I had been interloping into the sacred realm of the dead, the underworld, and was blocked by a powerful guardian spirit, sat well with my experience, which had me wishing I had not turned up uninvited, as I was obviously not on the guest list. Knowing that I should not be there, I clearly recall spending the duration of the trip trying to keep my tryptamined mind inconspicuous. To do this, I focused on the mesmeric rhythmic eyes and nothing more, realising that I had stolen a glance at some holy grail when I burst through the veil. The entity there responded quickly and I could not have been more compelled *not* to mess with it. This feeling was further corroborated by Beyer who wrote, in relation to Za and the other fierce protector deities, that they:

> [...] are powerful deities who symbolise currents of cosmic force to be tampered with only at one's peril. They constitute the monastic cult [of the Nyingma yogin – the oldest Tibetan sect] because they are best left to the ritual experts. It is not that their cult is particularly secret, just as there is nothing esoteric about the workings of a television set; but in both instances the forces involved are too potent to be played with by a layman, and in both instances the same warning applies (1974, p. 54).

The same sentiment was echoed by the noted scholar of Tibetan demons, Nebesky-Wojkowitz (1956) who offered that the Nyingmapa consider the planetary god Za (Rahu) to belong in the highest trinity of deities and that he "guards the religious teachings, and his thousand eyes watch the happenings in the three worlds" (p. 260).

Worryingly, Nebesky-Wojkowitz indicates that the elaborate propitiatory dough cake (*gtor ma*) made to honour Rahu (Za) is shaped like a large red serpentine pyramid dotted geometrically with numerous eyes and bearing stakes "arranged around the base of the '*gtor ma*' on which dough effigies of men and animals have been impaled as offerings" (p. 353). (Somewhat weirdly this multi-eyed-pyramid bears a resemblance to the be-tentacled pyramidal monster of Robert Anton Wilson and Robert Shea's *Illuminatus* trilogy, the Leviathan). Beyer (1974) even submits that a lama led him to believe that Nebesky-Wojkowitz died accidentally before his time because of his careless interest in these fierce protector deities.

Reading Beyer's account made me feel particularly alarmed that there might been some objective reality to my encounter and that I had, seemingly, really run into this Tibetan underworld guardian. But these few coincidences barely constitute enough to convince most folk about the objective reality of DMT entities or Tibetan deities, and nor should they, particularly those folk, like James Kent (2004), who argue that these entities are merely the imaginary output of our neurochemical meddlings. Others have suggested that these entities cannot be considered either real or fictitious, but might be better thought of as just another part of ourselves (e.g. Turner, 1995). It might have ended here, but soon after I discovered that the experience I thought was unique to me was not so unique after all. Alarmingly, this discovery threatened to bolster the tentative argument that should our particular DMT entity – who we could call Za – have some objective reality, then so too might all those other beings we encounter along the way to Chapel Perilous, be they mischievous dwarves, machine elves, ancient gods or praying mantis aliens.

Snake Eyes

Only a few days after reading about Za I chanced across an article by Meyer (1994) on *Apparent Communication with Discarnate Entities Induced by DMT* in which was included the following account:

I noticed what seemed to be an opening into a larger space, like looking through a cave opening to a starry sky. As I approached this I saw that resting in the opening was a large creature, with many arms, somewhat *like an octopus, and all over the arms were eyes,* mostly closed, as if the creature were asleep or slumbering. As I approached it the eyes opened, and it/they became aware of me. It did not seem especially well-disposed toward me, as if it did not wish to be bothered by a mere human, and I had the impression I wasn't going to get past it, so I did not try [my emphasis].

The fact that this creature was quite intimidating, and appeared to be guarding the way to something beyond, matched my own experience, but it does not end here. I was conducting a web-survey of paranormal psychedelic experiences at the time (Luke & Kittenis, 2005) and found that one of my respondents had also had a similar experience, but with psilocybin rather than DMT:

I was convinced I was dying, I saw another dimension, one filled with eyes in a fibonacci vortex/dome [...] I've explained this to so many people and regardless of how many things I see, be it in art or biblical references, they all say I'm nuts.

Encouraged by finding these chance reports I then began searching through psychedelic journals and on the internet for similar stories and found a few more corresponding accounts. This first one occurred with psilocybin-containing mushrooms and is from the journal *Entheogen Review*:

I began seeing a peculiar phenomenon during low dose mushroom sessions: a pattern of threatening eyeballs. I intuited that the mushroom was trying to scare me, and I marvelled at the workings of the mind, feeling humoured rather than frightened [...] In spite of my scientifically orientated worldview, I was being visited by a spirit which seemed to be anticipating a deeper encounter.

[...] I took about five grams [...] This is when I felt the strange spirit enter me: the many eyed apparition that had already been haunting my consciousness. The difference was that this time the "creature" seemed to be inside of me [...] I immediately began questioning its intentions – who was it, what did it want, and was it a demon? I received no answer, and so, not being certain that it belonged in my head, forcefully commanded it to leave, which it apparently did [...] I had the creepy feeling that I was either going crazy or was infected with a spooky denizen of hyperspace [...] Perhaps like an insect under a magnifying lens, I have difficulty fathoming this mysterious being of a thousand eyes. Interestingly enough, one of my companions later commented that at one point he perceived my forehead to be covered with eyes (Owl, 1995).

This next one, from the web-based *Vaults of Erowid* – an immense collection of psychedelic trip reports – actually occurred under the influence of LSD:

Countless numbers of eyeballs were looking at me. They were the most evil things I have ever seen. They were all on these snakelike bodies that were weaving back and forth. I reopened my eyes and saw the eyes and the worms all over me and on the ground (Trip333, 2007).

Although I only found these three isolated reports associated with LSD and psilocybin, I was able to find numerous DMT trip accounts that mentioned eyeball-riddled snake entities in variously weird or disturbing sequences. I need not quote them all as this last one offers some kind of "radical empirical" (James, 2003) mystical triangulation of my own experience, as well as providing a tentative interpretation of it:

I remember the veil, like rubber, or the surface of jelly stretched in front of me [...] I leaned forward to touch the surface of the membrane and then what happened next I swear nearly killed me from its sheer bizzarity [...] A creature emerged. It was not a happy, smiley elf [...] It had innumerable tentacles, like a cross between some weird octopus or jellyfish [...] and the EYES! OH MY GOD THE EYES!!!

I froze on the spot thinking 'shit that's it. I've gone and done it now. I'm fucking toast.' I never believed. I should have believed. And now. Now I am at the mercy of something much, much, bigger and complex, and clever and definitely malevolent than myself. I asked it its name. I wish I had not asked. It's voice utterly destroyed me. It was like being caught in a storm of psychic noise – a whirlwind of deadly electrical shrapnel [...] With its innumerable eyes, It gazed at me steady and extended a tendril. At the same moment it fired a beam of light directly between and above my eyes. The alien laser was pinkish-green. It hurt. I begged it to stop. I whimpered 'please stop. You're hurting me. I'm fragile. Please be careful – I am sentient and mean you no harm [...]'

It seemed to consider this; the laser was withdrawn but the tendrils (there were more now) still held me in place. I was trying to make out details of its shape or structure but the closer I looked, the more it slipped away from me. It seemed to tell me in some weird non-verbal fashion not to struggle and to stop making noise with my eyes. I took this to mean 'Be calm, do not struggle. Clear your head. See but don't look.'

Then it became a little clearer. It seemed to be cloaked in some way – some sort of organic hood and covering was wrapped around it – some sort of armour or protection. The tentacles had no substance as we know it and the eyes were the most awe-inspiring/terrifying thing I have ever beheld. They defied counting. They defied reason. The whole thing was too much and I felt myself losing my mind.

I...JUST...LOST...IT...gooooooooooonnnnnne (Pup, 2006).

I guess this account really did it for me. There actually seemed to be some degree of objective reality to all these experiences, including my own, because they had historical precedent, shared experience and, perhaps most importantly, some apparent meaning. On a level-playing field of explanation, where all theoretical perspectives hold equally convincing – or perhaps equally unconvincing – positions, the notion of *meaning* can provide the greatest intuitive appeal to one's understanding. For instance, a physiological, or neurotheological explanation might suggest that the highly similar visions reported between individuals are due to similar neurochemical reactions, but this devalues the complexity and cultural significance of the experience and also extends itself much further than the current explanatory power of neuroscience. Alternatively, a parapsychological explanation might suggest that these similar visions all belong to a particular morphogenic field (a field of consciousness that contains imprints of past experiences that can be experienced by others), which is activated by chemically-induced near-death-type experiences. Yet there is little understanding, or evidence, for morphogenic fields of this kind, even though they may be possible in principle (Sheldrake, 1988; Sheldrake, 2018 also explores this notion in more detail).

Any number of other theories might be put forward but, with all such explanations appearing equally un-compelling. The possibility of this entity somehow being real as an independently sentient discarnate being – whatever that may be – has comparable explanatory power. However, beyond other ontological speculations, this level of explanation – an acceptance of the experience at face value – also has esoteric and cultural *meaning* because it fits within a mystical understanding of the universe in which the existence of supernatural beings is accepted.

Sentient Entities

That said, I have little problem assuming that entities – be they dream angels, DMT elves, or mythical beings – have at least the *possibility* of independent sentience, or some kind of objective reality, because I do not confine myself ultimately to any one ontological perspective. So, as clearly as I can make sense of it, it seems that smoking DMT can lead temporarily to some kind of death realm – an idea championed by Rick Strassman (2001) and supported by shamanic concepts arising from ayahuasca states – and in such a place the traveller might encounter one of the (we could say 'archetypal') guardian deities of the underworld. One such guardian is the angel of death, who appears with thousands of eyes. Yet it seems that sometimes this multi-eyed being also assumes the tentacled or snake-bodied appearance of Za. And like a guardian of the underworld no doubt should be, this being is not to be trifled with and holds whoever encounters it in the grip of utter fear and the urge to obey its hypnotic glare – to just "see but don't look" – because it seemingly guards the sacred way on after death.

On reflection, my encounters with both Za and Azrael have resonance with each other and possibly represent the same psychic atavism or Jungian archetype, albeit an archetype which may have independent sentience, that may become activated by tryptamines, such as DMT, or by dreaming or other altered states. This entity is the archetype of the guardian of the realm of death and the doorway to occult knowledge. Thankfully, I was lucky enough to find a book by two occultists that made some sense of this (Jackson & Howard, 2000). In the book the authors offer the argument that the Islamic Azrael, the angel of death, is synonymous with the Hebrew Azazel, the fallen angel of light and the serpent of the Tree of Knowledge who, as the Promethean prototype, stole the gnostic fire from God and gave it to man – in much the same way that psychedelics can. They also associate the Persian fallen angel Azza, or Shemyaza, with the Luciferian Azazel, who in similar Promethean style swapped the name of God for sexual favours with the mortal Ishtahar making her immortal.

Jackson and Howard likewise associate Azazel, the great watcher, with the Persian dragon serpent Azhadaha, the black serpent of light and leader of the Inri, the fallen angels – known appropriately as the watchers. Interestingly, they connect the etymology of the common root *az* with the Hebrew letters *ayin* (or *ain* in Arabic) meaning eye, and *zayin* (*zain* in Arabic) meaning sword, which represent the all-seeing eye and the flaming sword of initiation, the guardian of the garden of Eden in biblical and kabalistic tradition. Jackson and Howard note that "The secret significance of the Zayin Sword is typified by Azazel as Master of Metals and Lord of the Forge" (p. 92), because smith-craft and fireworking were the crafts first taught to humans by the watchers, much as in the myth of Prometheus. They note that:

> The Hebrew letter-form of Zayin, ז, the sword blade, is the supracosmic fire that, like a shining lightning flash or thunderbolt, 'cuts' through the veil of material nescience (Jackson & Howard, 2000, p. 92).

Assembling all these links it did not take a huge cognitive leap to also associate the Tibetan eyeballed serpent of my own DMT encounter – Za – with these anarchic archangels of other cultures. Without making any great claims to the exclusive resemblance of any of these myths to each other – for the different legends feature both similarities *and* differences – further comparisons to Za and Azrael from elsewhere can also be made. Such as the Persian Zahhāk, also known in Iranian mythology as Aži Dahāka the serpent, or dragon, who was struck down by the divine Frēdōn, after which snakes issued forth from the wounds (Boyce, 1975). Like Prometheus he was condemned to be chained to the side of a mountain for all eternity. The likely etymological link here between the interchanged ayin (a) and zayin (z) of *za* and *az* is itself compelling, especially in the case of the Zahhāk/Aži Dahāka, but the myth story of Za himself has further resonance with the other fallen archangel and Promethean myths.

In Tibetan mythology, Za (known as Rahu in the Indian tradition) features in the *Dri Med Zhel Phreng* version of the Buddhist "churning of the oceans" story about the origins of the original entheogenic ambrosia par-excellence – amrita, or soma (Crowley, 1996). Having been left in charge of the Buddhas' newly made water of life – the amrita – before its supposed dissemination to humanity, Vajrapani (associated with the great soma-fiend Indra), carelessly left the sacred amrita unguarded and returned to find that the demon Za – the Lhamayin – had drunk it. In further offence to the gods, Za proceeded to urinate what remained of the processed amrita back into the vessel, and as penance Vajrapani was made to drink what had now become poisonous liquid and so turned permanently blue as a consequence. The similarities here between the methods of enjoying amrit and psychedelic *Amanita* mushrooms have not gone unnoticed (Crowley, 1996), and furthermore the apparent link here between the psychedelic and Promethean features of the myth is clear.

As just punishment Varjapani finally caught up with Za, wounded him many times and then sliced him in two with his vajra, the lightning bolt. But, because Za had drunk the amrita, the water of life, he survived the attack. Amrita translates literally from Sanskrit as "deathlessness" and it seems appropriate that this guardian of the underworld himself should become "deathless." But as further punishment the Buddhas replaced Za's severed legs with the tail of a serpent or dragon (much like the Iranian Aži Dahāka mentioned above) and fixed eyeballs upon his numerous wounds giving him his unique appearance.

It is here that I saw a further transcultural myth-story emerging with the legend of the Greek Lamia, the serpentine daimon and prophetess. Lamia is somewhat similar in name and character to the Lhamayin, the class of Tibetan serpent spirits to which Za belongs. However, there is some contention, not least from the Tibetan scholar, psychedelicist, and etymologist Mike Crowley (personal communication, Dec 2005), that the Tibetan language has no roots in Middle-Eastern and Mediterranean languages because it is uniquely related to Mongolian. Nevertheless, in the same vein with which Robert Graves (whom we can credit for tipping off Wasson's re-discovery of psychedelic mushrooms) makes more poetic than precise associations between cultural myths, we can say that there is a resonance between the legend of Za – the Tibetan serpentine Lhamayin – and the Greek serpentine Lamia, whom we may also associate with Python, the serpentine prophetess of Delphi.

Accordingly, Python was responsible for maintaining the secret of prophecy, the wisdom of the underworld and, similar to Za, was struck down by the sun-god Apollo, thereby heralding what Graves (1961) describes as the usurpation of the Goddess for the rights over divinatory power, and henceforth recasting Python in the role of demon. Something similar also resounds in the Greek myth of Perseus and Medusa the Gorgon, and perhaps also with the Norse Loki and the Assyrian-Babylonian Zu (or Azu) – who was struck down by a lightning bolt for stealing the tablets of destiny from Tiamat the dragon queen.

With the dawning of the age of patriarchal theism two to three thousand years ago the Promethean-type tale of the Python retells the same story of the divine maverick: a chthonic being existing betwixt this world and the underworld – the all-seeing serpent divinity holding the key to man's enlightenment, who steals that wisdom or shares it with mankind and then becomes re-branded as a demon, a fallen angel, a trickster or a deceiver, much like Za, Azazel, and the rest. The Aryan demon Rahu (Za) had once been a Dravidian god and it is clear that an old culture's gods often become a dominating culture's demons, and that the archaic tools with which the old culture accessed their divine – be they psychedelic or otherwise – are branded heretical.

Subsequently, the old chthonic sacramentals, such as amrit, or henbane – called "pythonian" by the ancient Greeks in honour of Python (Rudgley, 2000) – fell out of grace as easily as Lucifer fell from heaven, or Adam and Eve fell from the Garden of Eden. But like poor old Frank Olsen, did they fall, or were they pushed?[37] The identity of amrit was almost completely lost, and remains a matter of debate, and although few soma hunters have proposed tryptamines as the culprit (save perhaps McKenna, 1992, who championed psilocybin-containing champignons, and Matthew Clark, 2017, who argues for an ayahuasca analogue), what the Tibetan lama Chogyom Trungpa says about it fits happily with the various tryptamine visions mentioned above:

> [...] amrita is the principle of intoxicating extreme beliefs, belief in ego, and dissolving the boundary between confusion and sanity so that co-emergence can be realized (1982, p. 236).

Perhaps a report of a multi-eyeballed Za-like entity being induced by *Amanitas* might say something more for the usual favoured identity of amrit, and yet, even though there is some certainty that the ancients of the East never smoked DMT, perhaps any old entheogen will do (though see Clark, 2017).

But is there anything that can be found in this wayward meandering through myth and vision that offers a case for the genuine reification of 'the other' encountered in that psychedelic space on the far side of the psyche? Knowing that speculation is the vice of the precise and yet the virtue of the poetic, I am in no doubt that those wearing their right brain today will already have departed company with me somewhere along the line here. As a scientist myself I have deeply questioned

---

[37] Frank Olsen was supposedly the first LSD user to try to fly from an upstairs window, but years later was discovered to have been murdered by the CIA.

this temporary departure from so-called rational thought, but as an explorer of the weirder realms of the mind I have also been forced occasionally to leap the fence at the edge of my field of expertise and traverse unknown territory. I do not offer any of this as 'fact' beyond the phenomenological, but merely as 'possibility' in a psychic landscape as 'off the map' as that provided by DMT. Here be dragons indeed, and, yes, beware that among the dragon's treasure all that glitters is not gold. Yet who can resist inspecting a few gems occasionally in case they are of any real value?

Postscript: More Fishy Than the Greenwich Pie'n Eel Shop

Things started to get much weirder when I began studying the shape of pinecones and noticed their resemblance to the reported shape of the multi-eyed beings. I soon discovered that the end of the pinecone forms a Fibonacci spiral. Indeed the entire pattern of the scales on a pinecone forms a Fibonacci sequence, much like the structure of DNA. The most curious part about this, however, is that the pineal gland is named as such precisely because of its resemblance to a pinecone, and furthermore endogenous DMT is speculated to be produced in the human pineal. It is also speculated that this supposedly nocturnally produced pineal DMT might be responsible for dreams – the other altered state in which I had an encounter experience with the (this time unseen) multi-eyed empyrean entity Azrael.

Upon realising this I found myself engaged in a mind-boggling mental bootstrapping exercise and pondered the possibility that myself and other psychonauts were somehow perceiving our own (DMT-producing?) pineal glands in such states, which was somehow given sentience and perceived as the guardian on the threshold. A threshold to what though? Insanity perhaps, following such lines of thought – ending up as a psycho-nut rather than a psychonaut (Salway, 2015). Nevertheless, the aim here is to be agnostic about even the most strange of propositions.

The plot got even more esoteric after discovering that the pinecone was a sacred object to many ancient deities, and is seen in ancient artwork being held prominently by gods from numerous ancient cultures, such as in ancient Sumerian, Egyptian, Mithraic, Roman, Mayan and Greek traditions, to name just a few. Significantly, the pinecone often forms the tip of the staff held by certain deities, such as with the thyrsus, the staff of the ancient Egyptian deity Osiris (the lord of the underworld no less), which is entwined by two serpents, much like the staff – called the caduceus – of Hermes the psychopomp who conducts the souls of the dead through into the afterlife. Osiris' thyrsus also appears somewhat transformed with a pinecone on top, but only one snake around the staff for the Greek god Asclepius. Also a psychopomp, Asclepius is god of dreaming and healing, and his temples were the antecedent institutions for medical colleges, hence Asclepius' staff is still used as the symbol for medicine (Luke, 2012a).

Is it possible that the ancients knew about the function of the pineal, considering it important for dreams and other altered states, especially those giving rise to psychopompic and underworld experiences. Like Osiris' thyrsus, on the Indian subcontinent the concept of one's kundalini energy is also depicted as a central column (approximate with the spine) entwined by two serpents rising up. The central shaft of this kundalini ends at the ajna chakra, which is the etheric counterpart of the pineal gland, and is considered the power source for psychic abilities (siddhis) (Satyananda, 1972, 1996). It seems apparent that both the tantric system of South Asia and the mythology of the ancient Mediterranean cultures seem to point to the importance of the pineal gland, the pinecone and serpents in embracing all things post-mortem and otherworldly.

Since beginning this research I also keep coming across psychedelically inspired artwork that depicts multitudinous eyes, often in a Fibonacci sequence. It is as though no psychedelic visionary artist is bona fide these days without such a piece in their portfolio. They are so numerous, in fact, that without searching for them I have now amassed several dozen such art pieces, some of which were made before my article was published, and some since. It is debatable as to whether or not the later ones have been made naïvely through the artist's direct experience, or have been influenced by the publication of an earlier version of this chapter in 2008 (Luke, 2008). It is not that I hope to claim any credit for the inspiration, rather, it is impossible to really know which art made post-2008 has been culturally mediated, consciously or unconsciously, now that I have set loose the psychedelic multi-eyed serpent beasty meme. One possible insight comes from some research that was conducted in Brazil by the Hungarian psychiatrist, psychopharmacologist and DMT researcher, Ede Frecska. I met Ede in Brazil whilst visiting Luis Eduardo Luna's home, Wasiwaska, where he runs the Research Centre for the Study of Psychointegrator Plants, Visionary Art and Consciousness. Ede had just finished collecting data from ayahuasca participants who had been given several creativity tasks before and after drinking the psychedelic jungle decoction (the main active ingredient of which is DMT). One of the tasks was to merely draw whatever they felt inspired to draw inside a number of presented circles.

Discussing the experiences described in this chapter with Ede he announced that he had expected people to draw more classic entoptics immediately after drinking ayahuasca, but that he was surprised to find that a large number of his participants spontaneously drew eyes, so much so that he created a new category for them when coding the data. However, he had not yet analysed their frequency so we sat down together and did the analysis there and then and found that, despite his small sample, there was a significant increase in the number of circles depicting eyes after drinking ayahuasca than before.

Unfortunately, when the final paper was published it only discussed the spontaneous generation of entoptic art among participants, and not the prevalence of eyes (Frecska, Móré, Vargha & Luna, 2012). In any case, the widespread reporting of multi-eyed, multi-serpent/worm/tentacle beasties – akin to the entity encountered in my own experience – prior to the first publishing of the article re-worked in this chapter seems to suggest that these experiences are relatively common with psychedelic users, especially with DMT and related compounds. What the nature of these visions is, however, remains a mystery.

A few final notes probably also deserve adding here, although from this point onwards things really start to get deeply weird.

Near the start of a talk on entoptics I was giving at a festival a few years ago I was holding up an entoptic-rich ayhuasuca-inspired Shipibo yarn picture to the audience when a small boy interjected. I recognised him to be the 5-year old son of a friend of mine. He said that he had seen a similar pattern as he was going off to sleep and that he saw the same but inverted pattern when he wakes up. I was not surprised at the phenomenon occurring, having recently just read about entoptics appearing during hypnogogia (Mavromatis, 1987), which is how I responded, although I *was* surprised that a boy so young would interrupt my adult lecture with such an intelligent comment.

I sought him out afterwards to talk to him some more and he soon began to blow my mind. He told me that once every eight days as he was going to sleep he would see these geometric designs and would enter into a 'special world,' where he would meet the same character each time. Later he would re-emerge through the inverse of the pattern again, at the end of his nocturnal adventure. It was when he started describing the character encountered that I became astonished, because he described exactly a multi-serpent being covered all over in eyes. He said he met him a lot! Well, every eight days anyway. And he would hang out with him all night. I listened intently, intrigued, suspicious (in case I was being duped), amazed and baffled, and I asked him very clearly several non-leading questions to see where it would go.

He said that the multi-eyeball multi-serpent being would sometimes appear as one creature and sometimes it would send its wiggly snakes out in different directions to do things. Mostly what they did was usher round spirits of the dead, according to the boy, and he said that 'the man' was very busy – although he was able occasionally to stop to make the boy laugh with a joke or silly multi-eyed multi-serpent daft pose – and that sometimes he would get the boy to help him.

Mr Za, as we proceeded to call him (my suggestion), was a very busy man indeed, and the boy said in describing him how "he has a near-infinite number of eyes, because he has a near-infinite number of souls to look after!" I practically fell off my chair at this point. How many five year olds know what infinity is let alone near-infinity, and then I thought: if this hypothetical lord of the underworld did look after all the souls that had ever lived then that would approximate nicely to a near-infinite number, one presumes.

All this could have been made up of course (though why he would do this, and how so convincingly, boggles the mind), perhaps as some kind of elaborate set up by someone (an adult presumably) who knows me and my writing – although that seems too paranoid. But what he said next took it to the next level. He told me how when he was helping Mr Za round up the lost souls, they were quite scary and he did not like them getting too close to him. Mr Za had given him some special silver 'ghost string,' as he called it, to lasso the souls with and lead them off. What he said stopped me in my tracks because the boy was describing the very same thing that happened to me in my extremely intense dream of many years ago. A dream I had told but only a handful of people close to me. This following direct unedited excerpt is taken from a private journal I wrote in 2004:

> *I am in some old derelict Tudor monastery-type building, there are a number of lost dead spirits present that appear as people, but either with highly distorted and deformed faces, or with no face at all. I am trying to move the six of them on through into the next world, but one in particular is causing a lot of difficulty*

and is being very stubborn. I understand from this spirit that he was previously a murderer when alive (a long time ago), but is unwilling to depart this plane of existence. It takes all my effort just to stop this spirit from attacking me. Suddenly the space is filled with an immense, intense, and huge presence, I do not see a form or a face, and it does not speak, but telepathically I am told the great being's name. The form gives me a set of angelic wings, feathered and white like that of some huge bird, but big enough to lift me easily into the air. With this new advantage I am able to take to the air and subdue the troublesome spirit, entwining it in some ethereal binding, I lash it to the rafters and fly around effortlessly rounding up the rest of the spirits to be ushered through into the next plane.

I awoke suddenly with the name Azrael on my lips. I found the whole experience completely amazing and wrote it down. I was quite surprised to have been given the name of the angelic being. Numinous dreams, although uncommon, are one thing, but being given something tangible like a name is another. I was astounded. Once again, I consulted my good friend and mystic advisor and described the dream to him. At first, I did not give him the name. He asked me if the name was one of the four archangels; Gabriel, Ariel, Michael, Raphael. But no! So he suggested it was one of the ten holy angels of the Qabalah, which, although I knew very little of the Qabalah at this point, was a proposition that intuitively appealed. Checking the names with the ten angels of the Qabalah, which includes Gabriel and two of the other three archangels, there was no Azrael amongst them.

I was a bit perplexed, and thought maybe I had got the name wrong, though really I knew it was this name that was inked indelibly on my mind (and my dream notes). The experience stayed with me, but it was not until about two weeks later that I found an explanation, despite not looking for the answer. Casually browsing through someone's bookshelf I came across a book called *The Little Book of Angels*, and flicking through it, to my complete astonishment, I found a couple of pages referring to Azrael, as the Angel of Death! I was quite amazed. That seemed like quite a hefty title, but I was more amazed when I read that the angel of death, called the archangel Azrael by Muslims – but not Christians – has a thousand eyes and a thousand wings and would occasionally employ people in the enormous task of gathering in all the souls of the departed. Holy shit! I had been given a job working for the

Angel of Death. That was going to look a little bit deranged on my CV!

I think the thing that really struck me during this event, though, was that I had no knowledge of this angel, or its name, before the dream. Nor would I have had much likelihood of coming into contact with this divine character, who was only known to Muslims, because I had very little knowledge of Islam and did not even have any Muslim friends (such was provincial life!). Yet, my dream experience, which had been incredibly vivid, numinous, and powerful, had perfectly matched the habits and activities of this divine being.

Perplexity took another step towards the incredible. In such cases, where something seemingly unknown is revealed to the conscious mind there is always the possibility that the information was already lurking hidden and unremembered in the subconscious. Is it possible that I already knew about Azrael, the angel of death, his many wings (spares, perhaps?), and his employment of earthly characters for gathering souls? This would be known as 'cryptamnesia,' or hidden memory, and although it has been shown by psychologists that people may be able to process information without consciously remembering it, this explanation is all too often wheeled out by sceptics as a frail old argument to account for spontaneous psychic experiences involving clairvoyant information.

And so it was that the young boy spoke of being employed as a psychopomp, seemingly by the lord or guardian of the underworld, and in his fear of the old lost souls he had been given some ghost string to help bind them and move them on. And when he said it I knew exactly what he was talking about and could not have found a better phrase to use than ghost string to describe my own 'ethereal binding.'

It is at this point that I thought he must have been bluffing or cold reading – extremely hard to have come up with that – despite my non-leading questioning and retention of my own information. In all my readings of Azrael, and the other seemingly mythical incarnations of 'him,' I had never come across this reference to psychopompic ghost string for 'his' assistants. It was then that I began to seriously doubt that he was taking me for a ride, which could leave two plausible explanations. Either he was extremely telepathic and was just extracting my deepest secrets from me, or he really was having these experiences, with such striking resonances with my own.

And yet, I had this psychopompic experience in a one-off dream (an extremely powerful dream nonetheless), and had pieced all the other fragments together over the period of some decade or so of mystical jigsaw puzzling, whereas this boy said he had these experiences all night, every eight nights. That dream – and the later discovery of Azrael as the 'hand of God' – had been one of my most profound life experiences, and yet here was a five-year old boy who fused all the disparate pieces of my jigsaw together, and some, in just 10 minutes. The boy was virtually an apprentice to the Angel of Death, cracks jokes with him, and says things like "he has a near-infinite number of eyes, because he has a near-infinite number of souls to look after." Well it is one eye for every soul I suppose, but that must take a strain, so even the angel of death needs a hand now and then.

Heading back on the train home from the festival I remember my journey there. On the way to the festival the train had been packed and I was having to stand and was leaning over a young boy who happened to be reading a Terry Pratchett book. I had looked on fondly recalling my own joy at reading Pratchett in my youth. But it was the book he was reading that then came back to me, a book called *Mort*, about an ordinary young boy, Mortimer, who becomes an apprentice to Death! Some synchronicities are just too uncanny.

So what to do with all that information? I decided to mine it further and resolved that I must go and visit the boy and his mother, who I knew only by association. I had never been to visit them at their home, and it was a couple of hours drive away, but I would have travelled any distance to find out more. I arranged to go to their house and immediately the boy got me to work 'playing.' This was no ordinary play though (for me at least), he said he was a black belt Jedi and that he would train me if I was worthy, so we spent the next two or three hours with him and I running around fighting kung fu style and performing feats of derring-do.

Luckily I was quite athletic and acrobatic at the time and was able to impress him with my finest moves, and now and then he would upgrade me to the next level belt. My disappearing trick (using misdirection and then diving over a low wall) had impressed him enough for him to make me red belt, one below him, and I felt I had now won his trust enough to finally begin the conversation I wanted to have, which he had seemed unmotivated to give me. A natural pause came in our game and, with my dictaphone ready in my pocket, I looked to him and asked him directly to tell me some more about Mr Za, the many-eyed multi-serpent. He stood motionless and said nothing, his face screwing up with disappointment. Then, from out of nowhere, he swiftly kung fu punched me with all his might straight in my groin and I doubled up in agony on the floor, incapacitated. It was certainly one way to tell me that he would say no more on the subject. And he wouldn't. Not one peep.

This (serpent's) tale could probably end here, but recently, a few weeks either side of the 2016 Autumn equinox, two friends, independently of each other, and without knowing each other told me that they too had had a terrifying encounter with a multi-eyed, multi-serpent being on their last toke of DMT. One knew my story, the other did not. Both had had the prior experience with DMT of being told by the entities that they encountered that there was nothing more for them to learn from going to the DMT 'world' and they should not return. Both had nonetheless returned and met with our ostensible Mr Za. For both of them, this had also been the last time they smoked DMT, as it had been for me. At least it was for about fourteen years until I was a subject in a DMT brain imaging study. I was injected with DMT rather than smoking it, but it was still my first full hit since my seeming Za encounter. One day I will tell the story of what happened when I did return to the DMT realm, but for now, well, I am not actually allowed to say publicly until the research has been published by my colleagues. I guess there has to be some mystery left with this myth-story: my story.

> The night has a thousand eyes,
> And the day but one;
> Yet the light of the bright world dies
> With the dying sun.
>
> The mind has a thousand eyes,
> And the heart but one;
> Yet the light of a whole life dies
> When love is done.

Francis William Bourdillon, *Light* (1873).

FAIRY AIN'T WHAT IT USED TO BE

Traditional vs Contemporary Fairies

SIMON YOUNG

A 'fairy,' it is well known, is a magical humanoid. But 'Fairy' is also in the longer *Oxford English Dictionary* – indeed this is its first meaning there – a *place*: 'the land or home of the fays; fairyland.' There are many supernatural realms: the plains of the dead, the forests of the sasquatch, the planets of alien visitors, and so on. But Fairy is the most openly paradoxical: its reality is unreality. In the moonlight the pedestrian becomes the extraordinary: a breath of wind carries a fairy host; a bleak uninhabited moorland is filled with impossible music. Conversely, in the light of day fairy money becomes crisp autumn leaves, fairy cattle and sheep become insects, and a fairy castle reveals itself to be a mean hovel. If the deep weird has a home, it is in Fairy.

However, even in the apparently timeless lands of Fairy there is change. In the following pages I want to consider how British and Irish fairy ideas and fairy experiences have evolved through the last five hundred years, by looking at differences between the 'traditional fairy' and the 'contemporary fairy.'[38] I will start by giving an overview of

---

[38] The British supernatural sees, I have come to suspect, an important shift in the period of the early Reformation: the traditional fairy was never an unchanging form. I have avoided, then, medieval references here to keep to a period where there is (in my view) *relatively* little change in traditional fairylore. For other opinions see Harte 1998 and Hutton 2014. In relation to their arguments I would point to: i) assumptions built around gaps in

the characteristics of the traditional Fairy. I will then outline the main types of fairies that appear in the *Fairy Census* (2014-2017), including such marvels as the SWFs, the *dwomes*, and the *tresps*. I will point to the manifest differences between the traditional fairy and its twentieth and twenty-first century successors. I will ask, finally, how something as constant in human experience as the supernatural can change so dramatically.

Traditional Fairies: An Overview

'Prior folklore' refers to the beliefs of the agricultural communities that dominated, in many European countries, up until the inter-war period. Within their supernatural folklore systems there were witch beliefs, ghost beliefs and, in most countries, fairy beliefs. This was certainly true of Britain and Ireland. In those two islands fairy beliefs first emerge into writing in the early Middle Ages: though there are hints in archaeology and in some antique images that fairy belief is older still (see Young, 2019, pp. 19-23). Fairy references then build in Britain and Ireland through the Middle Ages to become strikingly common in writing in the late 1500s and the 1600s. Fairies turn up, in that period, in legal cases, theological tracts, songs, plays, poems and ritual magic.

What were these fairies like? The most important point to make about Tudor and later traditional fairies is their social nature (Latham, 1930; Thomas, 1973, pp. 724-734; Hutton, 2014). Fairies were often met individually by humans wandering over obscure parts of the countryside, but these individual fairies were, it is made clear, part of a wider society. We are constantly reminded in our sources that fairies were like humans. Traditional fairies had clothes. They had weapons. They had tools. They then used these objects to create and to cooperate in common fairy ventures. Traditional fairies cooked, they hunted,

---

our evidence; ii) the demonstrable presence of a British social supernatural being from Anglo-Saxon times onwards, by whichever name we wish to call it. It should also be noted that in all periods there will have been competing views of these social supernatural beings (much as I suggest for the contemporary period below, see figure 1): e.g. the cleric's vs the philosopher's vs the magical practitioner's fairy. Prior to 1800 we have just too little evidence to tease out those differences, but we should assume that they were there. Thanks to Chris Woodyard for help with this article.
something that they coveted

they made love, they bore children, they marched, they fought, they had funerals and they washed their clothes. They were ruled and they had rulers. Traditional fairy aped humanity with a frenetic soap opera of tension, conflict and resolution.[39]

These traditional fairy communities were to be found in the wilderness (or what passes for the wilderness in Britain and Ireland), across the river, in the next valley over, where the silver birches grow. They were a distorting fairground mirror held up by and to human neighbours. Britain has (in English, Gaelic and Welsh) hundreds of place-names that mark fairy homes and amenities in the wilds: a Fairy Seat here, a Fairy Church there, a set of Fairy Steps on the side of this mountain and a Fairy Kettle on that river. Generally speaking, fairy communities were associated with large boulders, caves and bodies of water, often in high points on or near fairy hills, or *sídhe*. In England and in Lowland Scotland some of the fairy sites that come closest to human communities, and which are in a sense shared, are a number of Fairy Wells (Harte, 2019).

Although traditional fairies lived out in the wilds, they were not described as nature spirits in our sources. There was no sense that these fairies were the spirits of trees or flowers. If they were spirits of anything they were the spirits of places, and if the fairies 'represented' something it was a life-giving but implacable countryside. Traditional

---

[39] It is interesting to note here the similarity between traditional ideas about fairies and fairy society with what anthropologist Eduardo Viveiros de Castro has called 'perspectivism' in the context of Amerindian cosmologies. He explains that in many Amerindian cosmologies:

"[...] the world is inhabited by different sorts of subjects or persons, human and non-human, which apprehend reality from distinct points of view [...] Typically [...] humans see humans as humans, animals as animals and spirits (if they see them) as spirits; however animals (predators) and spirits see humans as animals (as prey) to the same extent that animals (as prey) see humans as spirits or as animals (predators) [...] By the same token animals and spirits see themselves as humans: they perceive themselves as (or become) anthropomorphic beings when they are in their own houses or villages and they experience their own habits and characteristics as a form of culture [...] they see their food as human food [...] they see their bodily attributes as body decorations or cultural instruments, they see their social system as organised in the same way as human institutions are [...]" (Viveiros de Castro, 1998, in Lambek, 2006, pp. 307-308).

fairies were sometimes connected to general fertility. Oberon, in *Midsummer Night's Dream* blames rotting crops and unseasonable weather on his argument with Titania: 'And this same progeny of evils comes/From our debate, from our dissension' (II, 1). Irish fairies, meanwhile, were held responsible for the potato famine (Wentz, 1911, p. 43). Traditional fairies were also connected with general misfortunes in the nineteenth century including everything from the collapse of railway works to storms.

Traditional Fairies: Appearance

What did these traditional fairies look like? A useful text here is Shakespeare's *Merry Wives of Windsor*. In that sex-romp comedy Mrs Page decides to trick Falstaff by dressing up local children as fairies, with an eighteen-year-old Anne (Mrs Page's daughter), as the fairy queen. They will, Mrs Page determines, ambush Falstaff at a saw-pit near a fairy oak in the woods of Windsor:

> Nan Page my daughter, and my little son,
> And three or four more of their growth, we'll dress
> Like urchins, ouphs, and fairies, green and white,
> With rounds of waxen tapers on their heads,
> And rattles in their hands [...]
> Let them from forth a sawpit rush at once
> With some diffused song; upon their sight [...]
> And fairy-like, to pinch the unclean knight; [...]
> My Nan shall be the Queen of all the Fairies,
> Finely attired in a robe of white (IV, 4)

To which Mrs Ford adds: 'Let the supposed fairies pinch him sound,/ And burn him with their tapers' (IV, 4). In a later scene we learn that the fairies will be 'mask'd and vizarded,' and that Nan 'shall be loose enrob'd,/With ribbands pendant, flaring, 'bout her head' (IV, 6).

The very fact that Mrs Page decides to use her adolescent daughter and 'little' children for her gag suggests that fairies were imagined as being smaller than adults. This is confirmed by many other Tudor sources that talk of child-sized fairies: and this is true of accounts of traditional fairies going forward into Victorian and Edwardian Britain too; Ireland and Highland Scotland seems to have been somewhat different in this respect. When we think of traditional fairies we would do well to imagine humanoids between three and five feet tall. The insect-sized fairies of Shakespeare and his seventeenth-century successors were a literary conceit, though one that was to prove durable (Latham, 1930, pp. 67-80).

The Windsor fairies are dressed in green and white clothes. In Elizabethan texts fairies were associated with a number of colours: In the *Merry Wives of Windsor* reference is made to 'Fairies, black, grey, green, and white' (V, 5); a fairy-witch; John Walsh told the court that 'ther be .iii. kindes of Feries, white, greene, and black' (Anon 1566, unnumbered). The exact meaning of this fairy spectrum is unclear: are these references to the skin, to dress or to personality? As to their clothes, fairies were associated with elegant (often silk) apparel (Latham, 1930, pp. 86-91). They also tended to be dressed in a similar style: fairies may not have had uniforms, but they were generally uniform in terms of their apparel, with the same colours. It should also be mentioned that Mrs Page does not give her fairies wings: fairy wings are unheard of in traditional sources (Young, 2019).

The tapers on the head point to another important aspect of fairies: their luminosity. Fairies are frequently, in Tudor and later traditional sources, associated with lights: they "can light candles in the night, and vanish like a sparke" (Nichols, 1788, II, p. 85). Encounters with fairies often began with a light being seen: "at ane hill he saw a light not knowing quhair he was [...] he entered having many candles lighted, and [...] saw them all dancing about the lights" (MacPhail, 1914, III, p. 87 for 1676). Fairy disorientation (pixy-leading), likewise, kicked off with a benighted traveller deciding to follow a light in the dark and said traveller then getting led into the ditch or a pond (Young, 2016).

Traditional Fairies: Sports and Hurts

Traditional fairies were frequently associated with music and dancing. We see that Mrs Page's 'fairies' were to carry rattles and that they would rush out of the pit with 'some diffused song' (an excellent description of fairy music). Fairy music was heard by night travellers and what music! "[S]uch musicke [...] that Orpheus, that famous Greeke fidler (had hee beene alive), compared to one of these had beene as infamous as a Welch-harper that playes for cheese and onions" (Collier, 1841, p. 9). Music was often used, in fairy productions and masques, to bring fairies onto the stage: "after that the musicke plaies & ther Enters 3 antique faires dancynge" (Collier, 1881, III, p. 402).

Dancing comes back again and again in accounts of fairies from the sixteenth to the eighteenth centuries in Britain and in Ireland: in Britain particularly it was their most common pursuit. Fairies danced "in rounds in pleasant launds, and greene medowes" (Nashe, 1883-1885, II, p. 117); fairies "are they that dance on heaths and greens" (Burton, 1881, p. 124); and "generally they dance in Moon-Light, when Mortals are asleep, and not capable of seeing them" (Bourne, 1725, p. 83). Shakespeare implies in *The Merry Wives* that there was an oak where fairies danced in Windsor wood: fairy dancing left circles of mushrooms or burnt discoloured grass in the fields, "green sour ringlets" (*Tempest*, V, 1). Samuel Johnson in his dictionary, meanwhile, wrote that fairies: were small; that they "rewarded cleanliness"; and that they danced in meadows (Johnson, 1834, p. 438).

For all their elegance, the Windsor fairies were quite ready to hurt: those fairies that "rewarded cleanliness" also punished slatternly households with nips and scratches. Fairies, in fact, like Longfellow's girl with a curl, went easily to extremities: "when she was good, she was very, very good [...] when she was bad she was horrid." Mrs Page wanted the children "fairy-like" to pinch Falstaff, and Mrs Ford says that they should "burn him with their tapers." Traditional fairies were famous for their vindictiveness against humans who broke their bewildering laws or who had something that fairies coveted or who were a potential source of amusement. Fairies in no way limited themselves to lazy maids. They killed livestock, stole children and food, misled night-time walkers and brought misfortune down on those they resented.

A Traditional Encounter: The Elf Dancers of Cae Caled

Seeing is perhaps believing. An encounter is offered here as a sampler of the traditional fairy. In or about 1757, four Welsh children ran into a group of fairies in a field on the border of Denbighshire and Flintshire. The incident was termed by Welsh folklorist Elias Owen (1833-1899) "the Elf Dancers of Cae Caled," after the field where the children came face to face with the impossible:

> In a summer's day about noon, I with three others [...] We were playing in a field called Kae-Kalad [...] where we perceived a company of

dancers in the middle of the field, about seventy yards from us. We could not tell their numbers, because of the swiftness of their motions, which seemed to be after the manner of Morris-dancers (something uncommonly wild in their motions) but after looking some time we came to guess that their number might be about fifteen or sixteen. They were clothed in red like soldiers, with red handkerchiefs spotted with yellow about their heads. They seemed to be a little bigger than we, but of a dwarfish appearance. Upon this we reasoned together what they might be, whence they came, and what they were about. Presently we saw one of them coming away from the company in a running pace; upon seeing this we began to be afraid and ran to the stile. Barbara Jones went over the stile first, next her sister, next to that my sister, and last of all myself: while I was creeping up the stile, my sister staying to help me, I looked back and saw him just by me; upon which I cried out, my sister also cried out, and took hold of me under her arm to draw me over; and when my feet had just come over, I still crying and looking back, we saw him reaching after me, leaning on the stile; but did not come over [...] He who came near us had a grim countenance, a wild and somewhat fierce look. He came towards us in a slow running pace, but with long steps for a little one. His complexion was copper-coloured, which might be significative of his disposition and condition; for they were not good, but therefore bad Spirits. The red, of their cruelty, the black, of their sin and misery; and he looked rather old than young ([Jones], 1780, pp. 47-49).[40]

The experience conforms to traditional fairylore. The fairies are of smaller than adult size. Their clothes are identical: see the 'uniform but not uniforms' rule above. They are associated with dancing and by implication music. They are clearly part of a social unit: they are dancing a series of complex moves together. There is something magical in the way that they suddenly appear; perhaps also in the nature of their dancing – where the children have problems counting them – and in the way that they suddenly disappear when adults came out to see what the

---

[40] This account was written by the youngest of the four children there that day: Edward Williams. Edward, who went on to become a famous Methodist preacher, wrote these words in his early twenties: it was put in a letter in 1772 and published a decade later. He wrote a second (very similar) account as an autobiographical reflection towards the end of his life. This was only published posthumously in 1896 (Owen, pp. 97-99).

children's terrified shouting was about. The fairy chasing the children suggests malevolence: he had "a wild and somewhat fierce look." He stops at the stile: a supernatural boundary in British folklore (Spooner, 1968). A fairy experience of this kind would be almost unimaginable in twenty-first-century Britain.

The Road to Contemporary Fairy

Traditional lore tells us (and has been telling us for centuries) that the fairies long since left Britain: Irish tradition has less to say about a fairy exodus. The traditional fairies were driven away by Protestantism, by gun-powder, by factories, by railways and by the school teacher: different generations blamed, according to their prejudices, the destruction of fairy on different agents of modernity. In some cases, the fairies rode out in a glorious procession to happier realms (Miller, 1859, p. 207 in a note). In other cases, they took more unconventional routes out of the human world: some Cumbrian fairies, for instance, climbed up a ladder and into a cloud (Sullivan, 1857, p. 137). On the basis of this and other similar accounts Katherine Briggs called fairies "the Vanishing People" (1978).

Fairies, then, had gone from Britain by the time of Victoria's death. Or had they? A young spiritually-inclined American Walter Evans Wentz (1878-1965) thought not and went to look for them in some of the most isolated parts of the island. Indeed, Wentz was able, between 1907-1911, to gather many fairy accounts from traditional agricultural communities in Britain (and Ireland, Man and Brittany). He wrote a doctorate at Oxford proving (at least to his own satisfaction) that fairies existed (for what is effectively an earlier version of this thesis see Wentz, 1909). This must surely be numbered among the most eccentric British doctorates ever defended. Oxford University Press published Wentz's research as a volume, *The Fairy Faith in Celtic Lands* (1911). At first, it sold poorly, but has since become a classic, above all, for the scores of memorates that Evans Wentz brought together in the first part of the book.

Evans Wentz was able to visit traditional communities where older ideas had persisted and the fairies with them. The fairies that he learnt about (and vainly tried to encounter (1911, p. 108), were clearly very similar to the traditional fairies described previously. But there was also something new in Fairy. In Cornwall, for instance, the reader learns of pixies drinking 'astral' milk from a contact versed in occult terminology (Wentz, 1911, p. 164). In Ireland Wentz met a university-educated mystic who divided fairies into "opalescent" and "shining" categories (Wentz, 1911, p. 60, the mystic was A.E.). An Irish friend in Oxford, who also dabbled in mysticism and saw fairies of a distinctly non-traditional type, told Wentz: "Through meditation and psychical training one can come to see the spiritual world and its beings" (Wentz, 1911, p. 84).

Wentz eventually got bored of fairies and moved on, first to Egypt and then to the Himalayas to search for new supernatural challenges: he eventually helped to translate the *Tibetan Book of the Dead* (Winkler, 1982, pp. 49-62). But the new interpretations of fairies that he had encountered persisted, as the traditional fairy withered. Since the 1880s some spiritualists had been including fairies in their universe by explaining them as "nature spirits." The "nature fairy" became far more important under theosophy and Steinerism. Here screeds were written on the crucial role that fairies played in natural processes. As spiritualism and theosophy grew in strength after the Great War so did the nature fairy. Fairies were no longer spirits of place – that hill or this dale. They were the souls of individual plants and trees, spiritualised sap.[41]

A competing version of the fairy had also emerged out of nineteenth-century popular culture. What we might call the Victorian popular culture fairy, which appeared on everything from magazine covers to soap boxes, was feminine, petite, usually winged and often very small. The small size of these fairies had been inherited from Shakespeare and his successors, Drayton and Herrick. The wings were borrowed from innovations in late eighteenth-century British art. This cutesy fairy also frequently starred in children's stories, in newspapers and books and on the stage in fairy choruses. If a child in London or Dublin had been asked, in around 1900, to draw a fairy, they would have given us the classic modern Tinkerbell look.

---

[41] There is perhaps no area of contemporary fairy-lore that more badly needs study than the rise of the spiritualist-theosophic fairy. Gardner (1951) is a useful primary source, but rather late. The process begins in the 1870s and 1880s.

The Cottingley Revolution

These two fairy currents – the spiritualist nature fairy and the popular culture fairy – united in a bizarre set of events that played out between 1917-1921, and that have come to be remembered as the Cottingley Fairy Photographs (Cooper, 1990). In 1917, two young English girls, Elsie Wright and Frances Griffiths, claimed that they had seen fairies around a stream near their home at Cottingley in Yorkshire. Frustrated by the refusal of adults to believe them, they set out to photograph the fairies: actually some paper fairies that the girls had artfully positioned on the edge of Cottingley Beck. These photographs were, in 1921, widely publicised in *The Strand* magazine by Arthur Conan Doyle, who subsequently wrote a book about the latest revelation from fairy (1922).

The Cottingley farrago mattered because the children had borrowed their cut and paste fairies from the traditions of Victorian and pre-war popular art: some of the dancing fairies had been copied, line for line, from a 1914 children's book (Anon, 1914, p. 104; they even added wings!). But Doyle and others who publicised the fairies belonged or sympathised with the broader spiritualist movement. The talk and writing around the photographs situated these Victorian popular culture fairies in a tradition of nature spirits and natural processes (Doyle, 1922). The girls' fakes became, in fact, a respectable version of what spiritualist and theosophist nature spirits should look like. Cottingley is sometimes used by writers to symbolise the death of the British fairy (see Purkiss, 2000, p. 284). It was nothing of the kind. It marked the beginning of an exciting new chapter.

Fairies were still – as Cottingley had shown – seen and discussed in Britain and Ireland during and after the Great War. There were even attempts to catalogue experiences. Arthur Conan Doyle and Edward Gardner published works around about the Cottingley photographs, which included many other modern fairy sightings by way of context (Doyle, 1922; Gardner, 1951). In the 1930s the *John O' London* Magazine ran a line on fairy experiences and received a score of letters from Britain and Ireland.[42] In 1959 Dermot Mac Manus published *Irish Earth Folk*: the last substantial collection of traditional Irish fairylore with

---

[42] The originals were published in Spring of 1936, beginning 7th March. They are published in an edited form by Johnson (2014, pp. 235-243): Johnson had come to know many of the correspondents and so her 'edits' are often well-informed.

an emphasis on practice (memorates) not theory (fairy encyclopaedia guff) (1959; republished 1973). The most impressive work was *Seeing Fairies*, a book with some four hundred fairy experiences collected from the 1930s to the 1990s by Marjorie Johnson, a Nottingham fairy seer. *Seeing Fairies* was finally published in 2014 by Anomalist Books, two years after the author's death.

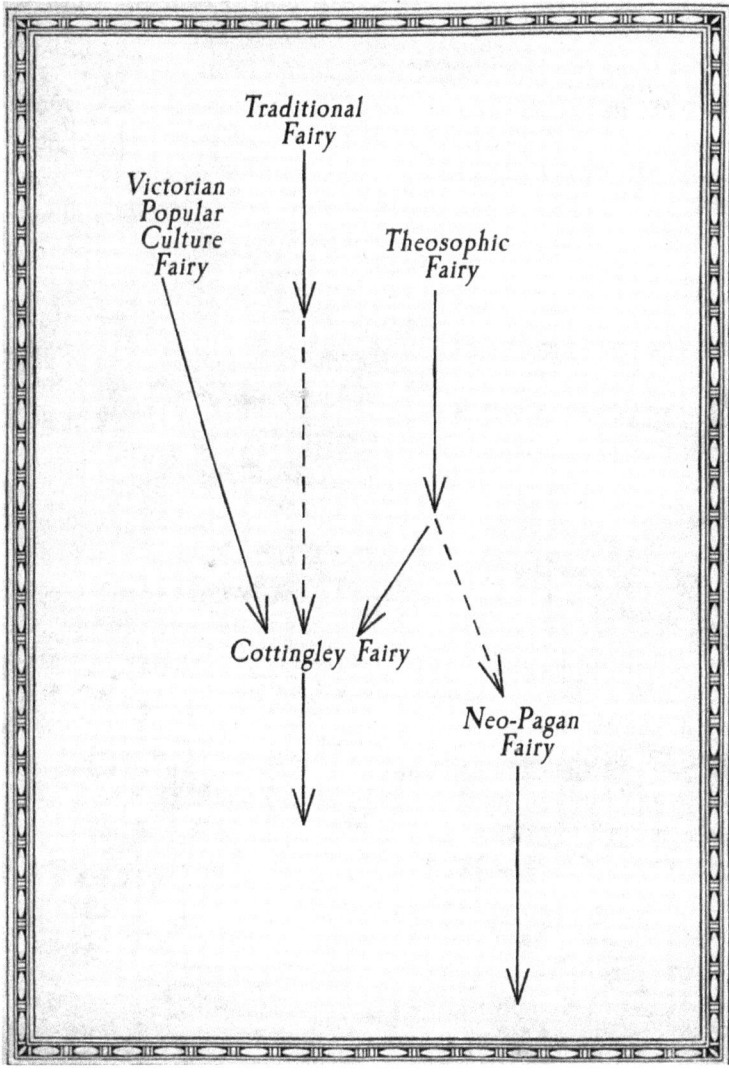

Figure One: The Contemporary Fairy.

Can we talk of new trends in fairy sightings since the Second World War or are we still in the grip of the hybrid Cottingley fairy? One new development that has come through in more recent years might be called the 'neo-pagan fairy,' for '[n]owhere is interest in fairies more intense than among practitioners of modern Paganisms' (Magliocco, 2018, p. 326). Neo-pagans, in connecting to the natural world, have fully embraced the theosophist and spiritualist idea of the fairy nature spirit. Fairies are the spirits of plant and tree and flower growth. However, neo-pagan visions tend to be more gritty and less twee (see Letcher, 2001). Glitzy tutus and pink ballroom dresses are out, as are wings: wings, many neo-pagans will tell you, are not traditional. We have gone from a dreamy technicolour to a stitched patchwork of natural shades. One contemporary survey of fairy experiences focuses in particular on neo-pagan fairy encounters (Magliocco, 2018).

Enter the Fairy Census

With traditional fairies it made sense to offer a single case study: fairy-lore suggests a relatively small range of variation. The Elf Dancers of Cae Caled conformed usefully to that ideal. There were, among traditional fairies, doubtless regional and national variations – I alluded above to some differences between traditional British and Irish fairies, for example. Perhaps also many of the more eccentric accounts were edited out of our much sparser written records. But even taking these points into consideration, Fairy is a far more chaotic place today than it was two hundred years ago. The uneasy cohabitation of the Spiritualist Fairy, the Victorian Popular Culture Fairy and, in the last decades, the Neo-Pagan Fairy has created competing ideals of what fairies should look like. These different trends in contemporary fairylore knock sparks off each other in fairy art and in fantasy writing. They also, naturally enough, have consequences for fairy experiences.

The present author has attempted to gather a large sample of contemporary fairy experiences with the *Fairy Census*. The *Census* was inaugurated as an online survey in late 2014, as a successor to *Seeing Fairies*: indeed, it is dedicated to Marjorie Johnson. The first five hundred accounts (overwhelmingly first person) were published in 2017 as a free PDF. I will publish a further selection (I hope) in 2023. My aim is to eventually get to 2000 experiences. In the questionnaire used for the *Fairy Census* the respondent is asked a great deal of information not just about the fairy experience, but also about the conditions under which they saw or heard or felt a fairy and their more general views about fairies and the supernatural. This is to facilitate work with the data (for studies see Smith, 2019 and Dickson, 2021). Fairy experiences were remembered as far back as the 1930s: with most dating from the 1980s onwards.

In the *Fairy Census* 191 experiences relate to England, Ireland, the Isle of Man, Scotland and Wales: the vast majority of the others related to other parts of the English-speaking world and particularly to the United States. I used these 191 as the basis for a survey of contemporary British, Irish and Manx fairies. Of the 191 I ignored 33, either because they lacked details or because they had no visual cues; they were based on noises or feelings. There are, then, 158 references. This is not to say that the excluded entries are inauthentic or that they are uninteresting: they would prove instructive in other contexts. In comparison with traditional fairy experiences – where such indirect experiences are less commonly recorded – we are obliged to look, first and foremost, at what is seen.

Fairy Types: The SWFs and the Dwomes

So what is seen? The difficulty with any survey of the 158 British, Irish and Manx visual experiences is that there is such a bewildering range of different fairy types presented. However, two important categories stand out: what I call here, for convenience, the SWFs and the Dwomes.

SWFs, 37%:

> Small-winged fairies; hand-size or smaller; often feminine; beautiful; dress tends to be natural (leaf hat, etc.) or luxurious (ball gowns, etc.); frequently connected to nature; sometimes in groups; benevolent and happy contacts with humanity; seen in homes and outside.

> Example: *'I was sick in bed with swollen glands in my throat. I was six years old and the fairy came to me. She was beautiful dressed*

in yellow her wings were also yellow I will never forget my time with her' (§60).

Dwomes, 27%:

> Dwarf-gnomes; anything from six inches to five feet; no wings; often masculine; rarely in groups; natural colours and rough clothes; not conventionally beautiful; usually seen outside, not indoors; awkward, reluctant contacts with humanity; occasionally angry; frequently connected to nature.

> Example: *'I saw a brown leathery-skinned, very angry looking old man, standing about two and a half feet high, completely naked apart from a loin cloth type clothing. He was pointing right at me with his index finger'* (§27).

How can we explain the difference between the fairies created by Mrs Page in Shakespeare's play, or those encountered at Cae Caled, and the SWFs and Dwomes glimpsed today? Do we have the evolution of two divergent species? They would be Eloi and Morlocks, in science fiction terms. The elegant and generous side of fairy has evolved into wee females and sprouted wings (the SWFs). The dwomes, instead, inherited the old physical form and some of the less attractive parts of the traditional fairy's character. But they also dropped a couple of notches on the supernatural social scale. Most strikingly, they stopped buying their clothes at fairy Harrods.

Fairy Types: The Minor Contemporary Fairies

There is also a third "miscellaneous" category with a series of sub-categories. These are looser and messier than the SWFs and dwomes. There is more bleed between types.

BOLs, 11%:

> Balls of Light ranging from multiple tiny lights, to (usually single) larger lights; seen outside; often connected to trees or plants.

> Example: 'I was in a field not far from my grandma's house [...] Saw several lights in and about a hedge. I walked up to the

hedge and the lights started to fade, I also thought I could hear tinkling sounds [...] definitely something wanted to attract me to them/it' (S30).

Tinies, 8%:

Humanoids; under six inches, often smaller; not winged; indoors and outdoors; usually seen (unlike Dwomes) in large groups; sometimes connected to nature.

Example: 'A large tree stump was near the field gate [...] I recall at times going there to look at little figures living in the stump and moving around the outside edges as if busy at their business. I could only see them when alone and it was special and magical [...] I can only say that they were very small and pale' (S125).

Tresps, 7%:

Tree spirits; usually tall and thin; sometimes tree-shaped or with tree appendages (branches, etc.); sometimes awkward movements; emphatically connected to nature alone (see Dickson, 2021, pp. 57-58).

Example: 'The figure was approximately seven-foot tall, slim, [...] a trunk like body from the waist up, branch-like arms and a quite haggard face with short branches coming from the top of the head and sides, but not like a true tree, they didn't seem to taper to twigs [...] walked [...] as though putting one foot down and then making effort to pull forward, arms swinging' (S39).

There are, then, a number of less numerous types, namely: adult-sized fairies (4%); fairy animals (3%); shadows or fuzzy forms (3%); a face glimpsed in a pagan bookshop in Cambridge (S10); and walking fluorescent cards from the Isle of Man (S160, more of which below).

Traditional vs Contemporary Fairy

In 1930, fairyist Minor White Latham offered an interesting thought experiment. What, she wondered, would someone born in the 1500s have made of the Cottingley Fairy photographs: the most important SWFs in history. "Had these photographs been shown to an inhabitant of sixteenth century England, he would have had to inquire who the very diminutive beings with wings were, and he would have repudiated with scorn, the contention that these pictures were pictures of the fairies" (1930, p. 66). Latham was right. There is nothing in Tudor experience to explain the SWFs recorded in the *Fairy Census* and elsewhere. Perhaps, if pushed, the Tudor would have talked of a demon or a new bird from the Indies. These were not fairies.

The SWF is different from the Tudor fairy. But what of the dwome? What would a Tudor have made of, say, a three-foot man in a loin cloth? Here surely there would have been something much closer to sixteenth-century expectations. Certainly, in terms of size the dwome conforms. The dwomes seem also to be wary of humans and to avoid human contact in a way that recalls early modern fairies. The dwomes tend to vanish when seen. They also have a temper: something much rarer with SWFs. That temper does though recall the anger of traditional fairies: think of the fairy at the stile at Cae Caled. But anger is rarer and never ends tragically in *Fairy Census* accounts.

There are also important differences between the traditional fairy and the dwomes. Traditional fairies were dressed in fancy uniform clothes, often with bright colours. There was something self-assured and elegant in their mien and dress. Dwomes are almost always described as being dressed in dismal colours, old clothes or natural clothes (leaves, twigs, and so on). Dwomes are more likely to be male than to be female, a bias which is not there in traditional accounts: or at least that is not as pronounced. Dwomes are also described as being nature spirits; or the same is implied. Traditional fairies were, *genii loci*: place spirits.

However, the most important difference between traditional and contemporary fairies is the lack of a human-like social existence: at least fairy society is rarely seen. Traditional fairies are inherently social. They have their own community. They are governed by hierarchies, and they carry out social activities. This element of Fairy seems to have disappeared in contemporary accounts. SWFs and dwomes are normally seen alone. Dwomes are sometimes seen in pairs or threes or fours, but very rarely in larger groups. SWFs at least occasionally keep up the tradition of dancing. When SWFs are seen in larger groups there is something hive-like about their social interactions. They resemble not so much humans but social insects.[43]

Category Changes

How can we explain this shift in fairy visions over three or four centuries? Some changes can be explained by moving categories. In the last two hundred years the meaning of 'a fairy' has slowly expanded. This happened, in the later nineteenth century, largely in the writing of folklorists. Fairies went from being socially-inclined humanoids to encompassing much of the British and Irish supernatural, minus the undead and the diabolical. Folklorists retrenched this expansion of 'fairy' by making a distinction between 'social fairies' (sometimes 'the trooping fairies') and the so-called 'solitary fairies.' Solitary fairies could be anything, note, from a bogie hiding under a bridge, to a Will o' the Wisp, to Jenny Greenteeth intent on drowning children in her pool, to a house hob or a leprechaun.[44]

Let us say that 158 individuals in the eighteenth-century had the same experience as those reported above. Many, perhaps most would not, in the 1700s, have thought of their 'vision' as a fairy experience. For instance, 'will o' the wisp' (one of a score of traditional designations for BOLs) was a common supernatural experience in Britain (and indeed over much of the rest of the world, see Hand, 1977). In some cases

---

[43] Characteristic, for instance, is the work of Hodson (2010). Take his sighting at Cottingley with dancing fairies, 'They are under the control of a superior fairy who is very autocratic and definite in her orders, holding unquestioned command [...] Each member of this fairy band is connected to the directing fairy, who is in the centre and slightly above them, by a stream of light' (p. 79).

[44] The division between solitary and social fairies seems to originate, in British and Irish folklore, with Leinster writer, John O'Hanlon (1870, p. 237) in a chapter entitled 'solitary fairy': 'By many writers on Irish superstitions, the following individuals of our elfin tribes have been confounded. All of them, indeed, belong to the solitaire species of sprites, but they have distinct peculiarities and callings. In the traditions and ideas of our peasantry, they are likewise constantly distinguished. How nearly or distantly they claim relationship with the social denizens of the raths may admit of various explanations.'

BOLs were associated with fairies: this is particularly so in south-west England and Wales (Young, 2016). But, in other cases, BOLs were said to be the spirit of the dead or were simply a malicious or playful spirit.

Folklorists began to include BOLs in the newly expanded world of fairy in the later nineteenth-century as examples of solitary fairies. This process of calling BOLs 'fairies' has then been reinforced at the popular level by the widespread, but little studied, BOL fairy photographs. These are photos, frequently referenced in the *Fairy Census*, taken at fairy or uncanny sites: the photographs are developed and show BOLs, which are interpreted as being fairies (e.g. §372; inside BOL photos are usually interpreted as the dead). BOLs have become fairies in part thanks to pre-existing folk traditions, in part because of the changing terminology of folklorists, and in part because of new trends in photography.

Deep Weird Fairies

The expansion of fairies depends partially on shifting categories. But there is also another factor, the way that deep weird experiences gravitate towards Fairy. Let me give an example from the Isle of Man in the 1970s:

> I was in a taxi driving from a farm back to my hotel in Castletown [...] A few minutes later I saw in the headlights and several feet ahead of the car three strange forms going across the road. They were not humanoid in shape but looked as though they were flat rather than 3D and had a jagged outline about eight inches or so high. Strangely they appeared in the headlights to be bright pink! The driver saw this too but couldn't explain it [...] (§160)

Why should the respondent have thought that this was a fairy experience? In part it was perhaps because the taxi had crossed, some minutes before a fairy bridge. But also I suspect it was because there was no other box to slot the experience into. Aliens, ghosts, mermaids, Sasquatch... Everything else breaks down when faced with the walking pink cards: Fairy to its credit can just about stretch its arms around them.

I offer next an example of a fairy experience that will appear in the second round of the *Fairy Census*. Two young men are on an Irish road after a night out:

> The road was illuminated by orange street lights on either side of the road [...] I thought I saw a thin gossamer spider thread connecting street lamps opposite one another on either side of the road, then thinking that couldn't be right because that was a hell of a distance for a spider thread to connect. As I focused on the filament that was connecting the street lights the thread narrowed in width/length and got thicker in girth, so it started to resemble this orange golden rectangular thing. The rectangular golden thing then started to hover over us [...] I recall the golden orange thing landing behind the wall that the bus stop was on, and I can remember being able to put my hands into this golden gossamer stuff that was sort of spread out in the shrubbery behind the bus stop (as yet unnumbered).

Again one could reasonably ask why the respondent thought that this had anything to do with fairies? Fairy, I suspect, was the best worst fit. A final example is this case from 1950s London:

> I was in the back garden. My mother was hanging clothes on the washing line, and a sort of wicker-basket affair with a balloon on top came down by my side, but not landing on the garden path. I was rather frightened but stood there with one eye on my mother, who had not seen it. Inside were some small people, but one older man dressed in grey trousers, I remember, a grey top hat and black jacket. He had silver hair and it was curly and long, and the gist of it was that I was to 'go away with them.' I refused of course, but gosh, he was so persistent (§80).

Hold All Fairies

If we go back to the 1700s these experiences would never have been interpreted as fairylore. Either they would not have been offered as such by the one who had the experience; or fairy editors – an Enlightenment Walter Evans Wentz, say – would have rejected them from the much narrower fairy profile of that time. Most likely they would have been understood as a diabolical encounter (the closest there was to an eighteenth century hold all category) or as something to do with witchcraft. One of the reasons that fairy has become a hold all is because these two categories have evaporated since the Great War. Alternatively, the experiences would simply have fallen between the cracks: the person who had the experience would have had little success in telling the tale to others because it was difficult to give the experience a name.

These rules of selection are still true today for many parts of the supernatural. The Sasquatch author rejects wild man accounts that do not conform with his hairy primate thesis. Take, for instance, the many (ignored) nineteenth-century news stories of American wild men with Sasquatch-like characteristics who are, it is revealed, actual human beings who have left society (Arment 2013; Young, 2022b, pp. 181-184 for the North American wild man). As to UFO enthusiasts, how would a UFO editor deal with the wicker-basket and balloon account given above? My suspicion is that they would treat it as a practical joke. A *Fairy Census* editor has necessarily a much higher boggle threshold (Hunter, 2021a). The 2014-2017 *Fairy Census* includes: a person who communicates with the fairy spirit of Whitney Houston in the shower (§241A); a lemon-headed monster in a bedroom (§315); and 'erotic' night fliers from New York State (§338).

These deep weird experiences would have been lost in earlier times. We are most likely to come across them, if at all, in compendiums of strange experiences, which do not concern themselves overly with categorisation, but are more concerned in demonstrating the existence of the supernatural. Take, for instance, the many peculiar experiences gathered together by Baxter in *The Certainty of the World of Spirits* (1691). I remember the wife who begins to be haunted by a spirit resembling her husband, who was alive and well in Ireland. Are we dealing with a ghost, a demon or an astral double (Pearson, 2016)? A successor to Baxter was Edmund Jones, whose *A Relation of Apparitions of Spirits in the Principality of Wales* includes many raw and deeply weird experiences (1780). Think here of the giant woman 'prodigiously tall,' half as high as a beech tree, who one poor Welshman met at night (Jones, 1780, p. 3). Ghost? Fairy? Demon? Jones did not care.

Conclusions

I have offered above an overview of traditional fairies from Britain and Ireland, comparing them with accounts of contemporary fairies. It is fair to say, I hope the reader will agree, that there are dramatic differences. Some of these come down to the way that the word 'fairy' has changed in meaning over the centuries. Some of them come down to the way that fairy has – with the collapse of the diabolical – become a hold all category for supernatural experiences that do not fit elsewhere. But playing with definitions and categories cannot explain away the contrast between the fairies imagined by Mrs Page or those seen at Cae Caled with the SWFs and dwomes spied today.

How can we explain this revolution in fairy sightings? A fairy believer could argue that the connection with nature or the social dimension might ultimately be a problem of perception. Perhaps fairy-seeing Tudors did not have the necessary ecological consciousness to understand the plant nature of fairies; or possibly modern fairy-seers are less likely to be invited to meet the queen of the fairies. A fantasy writer would be able to have fun with the shift. But the arrival of the SWF and the dwome more generally cannot just be explained away by limited points of view: the blind men are touching different parts of the elephant, and so on. Here we have a revolution in how the supernatural has been perceived through time.

Of course, fairies are not alone in this. Take another area of the supernatural where we have centuries of records: ghosts. Every documented society in the history of the world has believed in the undead: it is perhaps the 'original' belief (Steadman *et al.*, 1996; Oesterdiekhoff, 2015). Death is the end of the human condition and mourning is, as such, a human universal. Even a ferocious sceptic would admit that if ghosts did not exist then they would have to be invented by credulous humans. Ghosts change from society to society and from age to age. In Western ghostlore chains were a part of the ghost kit: they can be found from ancient Greece to Dickens. But ghosts had stopped using them by time of the Great War. The dead are seen with shrouds in the seventeenth and eighteenth centuries. These survive as sheets in modern cos-play. Ghosts used to shape-change: in Britain, at least, they no longer do so (see Finucane, 1996, for the shifting image of ghosts).

Why should something as constant as the soul of the undead or a fairy suffer such time-and-place changes? A Richard-Dawkins-style materialist could argue that supernatural experiences are entirely socially determined: the winged fairy has become part of the supernatural model labelled 'fairy' and so we start to see winged fairies. A wimpy agnostic might wonder whether we don't see the supernatural through socially-coloured spectacles: we graft wings onto a fairy after 'secondary elaboration.' A fairy seer could argue that entities deliberately take on forms that we can process and understand: 'If you want wings,' the entity hisses, 'you are going to get them!' There is a great deal of difference between these three positions. But, whichever option you plump for, social templates of the supernatural are vital for understanding impossible experiences.

ANYTHING-BUT-STANDARD

High Strangeness Entity Encounters

ZELIA EDGAR

In November of 1977, an interior decorator from Sandusky, Ohio, by the name of Millard Faber was walking near the west branch of the Huron River when he encountered what *Awareness Magazine* referred to as "the now standard Sasquatch or Bigfoot creature." Faber claimed to come upon a bipedal, hair-covered being that stood around eight feet tall with a slight stoop. The creature had a hairless face and glowing eyes. Upon noticing Faber, the creature jumped into the water and vanished, leaving behind a huge footprint, a broken tree limb, and a hideous stench. Faber reported his encounter to the sheriff's department of two adjacent counties, as well as to two local papers.

However, if this portion of the encounter was "standard," what occurred to Faber three days later was anything but. As he retired to bed for the evening, Faber became aware of a presence. He looked to the doorway and saw five pink, glowing humanoids with bulbous heads and luminous eyes, clothed in tight-fitting skin-diving suits, gliding through the air. He claimed that these beings, though hovering several inches above the floor, still made the motion of walking, and that each one was around five feet tall, again with a slight stoop. They settled at his bedside and radiated a feeling of rage at him which he believed was directly connected with his reporting of the Bigfoot sighting. He also claimed to be impressed with the notion that the beings intended to take him with them. Eventually, as so many anomalous entities do, the beings vanished, leaving Faber alone to the mystery of his experience, and open to a further occurrence where he believed he was being watched by something unseen (Perry, 1978, pp. 5-17).

What do we make of such a bizarre encounter? Into what field of paranormal research does it fall? The 'now standard Sasquatch,' complete with trace evidence, can easily be claimed by cryptozoology – but what of the distinctly unearthly pink, glowing humanoids? The Sandusky area was beset by UFO activity at the time of this report, and the humanoids' appearance certainly corresponds with many accounts of so-called UFO occupants. However, as in this case, countless encounters with anomalous humanoids are chalked up as UFO occupants, whether the entity in question is seen to occupy a UFO or not. By that merit, what exactly is a UFO, which, in its very name, insists upon its un-identification? In this case, the description of beings walking several inches above the floor calls to mind spectral encounters where, it is claimed, ghosts walk several inches above or below the surface of the floor due to historical changes in ground levels, or walk through walls where doorways once stood.

But who ever heard of glowing pink spirits in skin diving suits?

Possibly the peskiest notion of all is that Faber believed that the encounters were directly connected. His description of the humanoids' anger and intent implies a telepathic bond, further strengthened by the later experience of feeling watched. And how did the beings know, in the first place, that he had come forward with the sighting? How did they know about the sighting at all?

It is second nature for the human mind to categorise, and the unexplained is no exception to this obsession. However, anomalous entities of every conventional categorisation all share marked similarities, none quite so marked as attendant high strangeness phenomena. Effects on witnesses, apparent electromagnetic interference, light phenomena; these sorts of disturbances are rampant throughout entity encounters, not to mention those experiences with entities that defy any sort of conventional description. Many accounts appear nonsensical or whimsical at first, while at second glance are shown to exhibit folkloric, occult, or religious patterns.

The dogmatic skeptic doubts the witness' whole encounter, the dogmatic believer doubts only that which does not suit their preferred paradigm. Uncovering the truths lurking beneath anomalous encounters requires that they be considered in their entirety, regardless of convention.

Ghoul-Haunted Lives: Witness Effects

Effects on witnesses of strange entities are varied and encompass all the same effects affiliated with other types of paranormal phenomena. However, one of the most prominent is for the witness to go through life with an increased likelihood of encountering other strange phenomena, and not restricted to whatever the initial event was – in other words, a UFO witness will often not just see more UFOs throughout their life following their first experience, but may also develop a propensity to witness ghostly phenomena, cryptids, and so on.

One of the strongest cases in this regard involves a key witness to the Mothman of Point Pleasant – Linda Scarberry. Of course, she was one of the four witnesses in the vehicle during the infamous Scarberry/Mallette encounter in the famed TNT area. On the night of November 15th 1966, two couples, Linda and her then-husband Roger Scarberry and Mary and Steve Mallette, had driven out to the TNT area, an abandoned munitions dump outside of Point Pleasant, West Virginia. After spotting a winged, man-like figure with hypnotic red eyes, the two couples sped out of the area. The creature, which would later come to be called Mothman, easily kept pace with their speeding vehicle.

However, while this is likely the most infamous of Scarberry's encounters, after this initial sighting she not only had a later encounter with the creature, but other types of paranormal activity began to plague her as well. About a month after her first encounter, she claimed to see the same creature outside of her bedroom window. Scarberry said that it was sitting on the roof near the second-storey window, wrapping its arms and wings around itself as though 'it was trying to keep warm.' She claimed that she knew it intended no harm and felt that it looked lonely (Sergent & Wamsley, 2002, pp. 18-22).

Scarberry would also go on to witness multiple UFOs and anomalous lights. Poltergeist phenomena soon invaded her home as well, so she and her husband moved into the basement apartment in her parents' house. The phenomena followed and intensified, including strange lights appearing in the home, the scent of cigar smoke, and objects moving by themselves (Keel, 2002, p. 253). Eventually, the apparition of a man in a checkered shirt walked into her bedroom and stood above her baby's bed before vanishing (Sergent & Wamsley, 2002, p. 30).

Harkening back to the fact that Linda Scarberry did not believe that the Mothman intended any harm, many entity encounters detail the singular concept that the witness somehow has a bond, or some sort of telepathic connection or exchange, with the entity they are observing. Sometimes, as in the Millard Faber encounter, this is as simple as 'knowing' that the entity is angry at being observed. Other times, as in the next case, it seems to be a form of manipulation.

Throughout her impressive series of works, Linda Godfrey has detailed many accounts of telepathic exchanges between witnesses and strange canine creatures, though perhaps none so chilling as an encounter in Oklahoma in March of 2009. This particular encounter was only one of many experiences claimed by a single family. It occurred on the same traffic ramp near Muskogee, Oklahoma where the reporting witness claimed that he and his fiancée had each had an earlier sighting of a strange canine. On this particular evening, the reporting witness' mother-in-law was riding with a friend when they saw a large, dark wolf with glowing red eyes. The friend, who was driving, proceeded to slow down. The mother-in-law began screaming for her to lock the doors and keep driving, which finally snapped the driver out of her strange state. She later claimed that the beast was "in her head", saying that it was "a nice dog and she should stop to rescue it" (Godfrey, 2010, pp. 51-52). This seems to tie into another concept, mentioned later in this chapter under the section titled 'Wonderland Logic,' about the folkloric motif of assistance in modern entity encounters.

Possession states are highly debated in the fields of psychology, parapsychology, anthropology and spectrology (see Hunter, 2020b), though they also have a mooring in the field of cryptozoology. No other experience details this more clearly than a particular account from Stan Gordon's *Silent Invasion: The Pennsylvania UFO-Bigfoot Casebook* (2010). Not only does this case sit at a phenomenological crossroads, but it is also just one of dozens of equally strange cases which occurred in Pennsylvania in the years of 1973-74.

On October 25th of 1973, George Kowalczyk – referred to pseudonymously as Steve Palmer in *Silent Invasion* – in the company of his wife, drove out to his father's farm when they saw a large, round, red object hovering low in the sky. When they arrived at the farm, their family members were already watching the strange object. Kowalczyk and two boys from neighbouring households decided to drive out to the spot where the light appeared to descend, noticing that all the dogs in the area seemed upset. They heard odd whirring noises, accompanied by the sound of a baby crying (two of the most prevalent sounds in cases of poltergeist phenomena, hauntings and, incidentally, cryptid encounters). As they neared the area, the headlights of their truck dimmed as though the battery was being drained. Up ahead, they saw a bright white, domed structure on, or immediately above, the ground.

However, their attention was soon attracted to the wailing, baby-cry sounds which came from a nearby fence line. They saw two dark figures moving towards them. The figures were covered in brown-grey hair, stood about eight feet tall, and had bright, glowing green eyes described by Kowalczyk as 'cat-like.' Kowalczyk fired a tracer shot over the two creatures, and a second tracer shot at them. The larger of the two creatures whined and moved to grab the tracer, at which point the large, domed object vanished, leaving behind a strange, glowing area. The two beings turned and began to move in the direction of the woods. Kowalczyk shot three rounds at the beast, but there was no indication that the creatures were harmed in any way. They merely turned to look back at the frightened witnesses before continuing on.

While this particular case details many high strangeness aspects, one of the most frightening occurred several hours later, after an investigation by the state police, during which the glowing area that had been left behind was still visible. At around 2:00 in the morning, Gordon and investigator George Lutz were on site when Kowalczyk's dog began acting up. While describing the events, Kowalczyk began rubbing his face, then moved back and forth like he was going to faint. He began to breathe deeply, then growled loudly and threw his father and Lutz to the ground. Kowalczyk's dog then began barking as though it was going to attack, when Kowalczyk himself moved to go after it. The dog ran away whimpering as Kowalczyk continued screaming and growling. Two other investigators claimed they also began to feel faint. Kowalczyk abruptly collapsed, and the field filled with the stench of sulphur. Kowalczyk later claimed that, although he could not remember what had physically happened to him during this period of time, he did recall seeing a man-like figure in a black robe and black hat carrying a sickle, conveying – as so many cases of extraterrestrial, demonic, or angelic contact do – apocalyptic messages (Gordon, 2010, pp. 227-238).

Shock and Circumstance: Apparent EM Effects

Electromagnetic effects, such as electronic interference or vehicular failure, are accepted – and very nearly expected – effects in the fields of spectrology and ufology. It is a commonly held belief among paranormal investigators that batteries drain in the presence of spirits, or EMF spikes can point to possible haunting-type occurrences. UFOs have consistently been held responsible for car stoppages and electronic interference of all sorts.

As in the previous Kowalczyk encounter, many times this occurs in the presence of both a UFO and a strange entity. In that case, the vehicle's headlights dimmed as they approached the luminous aerial anomaly, which was accompanied by the two fur-covered bipedal entities. In the case of the infamous Flatwoods or Braxton County Monster of West Virginia, spotted by a group of five people the evening of September 12th, 1952, there was a following claim of vehicular failure in conjunction with a sighting of the bizarre entity – described as a floating, metallic, spade-shaped being with a bright red helmet-like head – and an anomalous light.

On the same night of the encounter at Flatwoods, George and Edith Snitowsky were driving with their baby between Gassaway and Frametown when their vehicle, complete with a new battery, stalled. A smell, compared to ether mixed with sulfur, suddenly assailed them and their baby began gagging. George left the vehicle to see if he could identify where the smell was coming from and saw a large globe of light hovering near the ground. He felt a prickling sensation upon drawing closer to it before becoming ill. As he retreated to the car, Edith yelled that something was behind him. An eight-to-nine-foot-tall creature with a large head and spindly arms glided towards the vehicle, which the couple promptly locked. It then waved its hand over the windshield, reportedly leaving a V-shaped burn mark on the hood of their vehicle (Coleman, 2002, pp. 24-25).

During the events recounted in John Keel's *The Mothman Prophecies*, multiple residents of the Point Pleasant area were beset by odd interference with their televisions and radios. None stands out more, however, than the account of Merle Partridge, one of the first experiencers of odd phenomena during this fantastic series of events. On the evening of November 14th, 1966, Partridge and his wife were watching television when the set began making a high-pitched, whining, generator noise. Partridge's German Shepherd, Bandit, began howling from the front porch. Suddenly, the picture tube in the set blew out, splintering glass everywhere.

Partridge went to check on Bandit, who began running off into the field. Partridge saw red lights going around, and called Bandit back, but the dog did not return. He would later see the dog's trackway, which terminated in a large circle of smashed-down grass, but Bandit was never found. The lights disappeared after a few minutes, followed shortly after by the strange noise (Wamsley, 2005, pp. 49-50). While the spinning lights of the Partridge encounter are not an entity per se, this case is so inexorably tied to the broader Mothman case, and contains such a profound account of electronic interference, that it warrants inclusion here.

However, the same effects can also occur in the presence of strange entities *sans* haunted house or flying saucer, as detailed in the following case.

In October of 1960, a man by the name of W.C. 'Doc' Priestley was following two of his friends through the Monongahela National Forest near Marlinton, West Virginia to do some turkey hunting. Priestley later told newspapers that his car, which had been "purring like a kitten," began sputtering before stopping completely. He looked to the roadside and saw a bipedal, Sasquatch-like creature with its long hair bristled straight up. Priestley claimed to be so scared that he could not move. Eventually, his friends realised that he was no longer following them, and backtracked to his location. At the approach of the camping bus, the monster seemed afraid, dropped its hair, and disappeared into the foliage.

The car started up again immediately, and Priestley continued following his friends. Some miles down the road, however, the car started acting up once again, only this time worse than before. Sparks flew from under the hood as though it had a bad short, and it came to a sputtering halt. As before, Priestley saw the creature standing by the roadside, hair raised and, as before, his friends came to find him. However, this time, after the creature ran off, the car refused to start again. The points were completely burned out (Keel, 2002, p. 130).

Attendant Light Phenomena

One of the most prominent aspects of high strangeness in entity encounters are attendant light phenomena. Light phenomena are of interest because, like possession states and EM effects, they are conventionally tied to both spectrology and ufology, only recently achieving some notoriety in entity encounters despite being classically tied to strange beings. In *The Complete Guide to Mysterious Beings*, Keel even postulated the idea that the inclusion of anomalous lights in entity encounters may be the giveaway that one is dealing with something paranormal, as opposed to a flesh-and-blood creature, especially in those numerous cases of entities with self-luminous eyes (Keel, 2002, pp. 140-143).

Stan Gordon's *Silent Invasion* details many cases of cross-boundary paranormal encounters, including this singularly excellent account of an unusual light phenomenon in the presence of a strange entity.

On September 27th of 1973, two teenaged girls were standing outside of one of their homes near Beaver, Pennsylvania when they saw a seven-to-eight-foot-tall Sasquatch-like creature covered in white hair. In one hand the creature held a luminous sphere. The landowner, and father of one of the girls, went into the woods shortly after the creature had been spotted, staying in the area for around an hour. While he was in the woods, his daughter saw an unidentified object fly overhead, projecting a beam of light down at the ground.

Oddly enough, considering Kowalczyk's earlier experience, this man apparently began discussing apocalyptic prophecies after his hour in the woods. Gordon leaves open the possibility that the man may have actually lost an hour at that time, in line with the iconic 'missing time' experience usually associated with UFO contact accounts, but the witness refused to discuss it with anyone (Gordon, 2010, pp. 196-198).

However odd the case of the orb-carrying Sasquatch is, it is by no means odder than this next case.

In October of 1966 in Nottinghamshire, a group of three teenaged boys with an interest in UFOs formed their very own 'contact group.' They regularly met to look out for UFOs, and on this particular evening decided to walk near to a disused canal. As the afternoon became late twilight, they began to walk back, when the ground mist of the canal seemingly gathered into a distinct cloud about four feet off the ground and began moving at an independent rate. It formed into a glowing, 'doughnut-shaped' disc of mist that moved forward and onto their path before stopping.

As the trio continued on their way, keeping a watchful eye on the disc, they realised that it was following them, and soon two white spheres could be seen materialising in the cloud. It continued following them, gaining distance, when the boys decided to run for safety.

However, one of the boys pointed back at the object, and the reporting witness claimed that in front of the cloud was a flat, dark figure. He claimed that it appeared almost as a cut-out, but still with the distinct impression of being covered in hair. Much like classic Sasquatch reports, it had no neck, its head set deep in its shoulders, and its arms hung low. The witness claimed that it had no legs from the knee down – they seemed to fade out of existence. Each arm ended in a single curved hook-like finger and, in each of these appendages, the creature held a red, glowing rod.

The reporting witness and one of his friends began running away, however, the strangest aspect of this encounter is that the third boy did not immediately join them. He called after them for a moment, then followed them, claiming that he could not see any sort of creature – all he had seen was the strange cloud and the unusual lights (Devereux, 1982, pp. 221-225).

On January 19th of 1972, four teenagers drove to the Battle Creek Bridge near Anderson, California, to do some night fishing. As they were driving, they saw a bright, glowing, blue-white object cross the road in front of, and above, them. It was near enough and bright enough to light up the surrounding countryside and the interior of the car. They parked near the bridge when they heard a blood-curdling scream come from the nearby bushes.

Upon shining their flashlights in the direction of the noise, they saw a strange, hunched, drab-green entity, covered in lumps described by one witness as "like pouches in a flight suit." The entity ran from the four teens, who, likewise, retreated to their vehicle and sped off. However, as they fled the scene, the countryside was barraged by light anomalies. Soundless 'firecrackers' appeared to be going off near ground level, as the fields played host to erratic orbs in both blue-white colour and an orange-red. One of these objects appeared to morph into a human-like figure (APRO, 2006, pp. 1, 5).

In this case, it is intriguing to note that not only do we have a highly strange entity in and of itself, observed in conjunction with anomalous lights, but also that one of these lights seemed to transform itself into a humanoid shape.

Wonderland Logic: Nonsense and Sense

One of the predominant themes across high strangeness entity encounters is a certain quality of nonsense. Often, witnesses to long-lasting encounters with a high degree of exchange are baffled at what, on the surface, appears to be pure absurdity. Often, what seems absurd in fact belies strong ties to old mythology or folklore. No other case so clearly exemplifies this notion than the infamous Simonton Encounter of 1961, or, as J. Allen Hynek remembered it in *The Edge of Reality: A progress report on Unidentified Flying Objects*, "the man in Wisconsin with the pancakes" (Hynek & Vallée, 1975, p. 152).

Joe Simonton, a plumber and chicken farmer from Eagle River, Wisconsin, was eating his breakfast at around 11:00 in the morning when he heard a strange noise, described as like "knobby tires on wet pavement," coming from outside his home. Looking outside, he saw a shiny silver object, about twelve feet tall and thirty feet in diameter, hovering above his lawn. It was shaped like two bowls put together with exhaust pipes spaced around its edge. He walked up to the object when a hatch opened in the side.

Inside of the craft were three short men, each wearing two-piece black turtleneck suits and knit helmets. Simonton said that they looked "like Italians," and the one closest to the hatch appeared to be the leader, denoted by a red track stripe down the side of his pant-leg. He gave Simonton a jug that was comprised of the same material as the saucer, which Simonton took to mean that he needed water.

After giving the man water, Simonton noticed that one of the beings was cooking something on a flameless grill. The track-striped being, apparently noticing Simonton's interest, then gave him three small objects – what would come to be known as the "alien pancakes" – and attached a belt to a hook on his clothes before the hatch closed and the saucer took off.

The 'pancakes' – flat, perforated, disk-shaped things – were analysed by the Food and Drug Administration where it was uncovered that they were comprised out of "hydrogenated fat, starch, buckwheat hulls, soya bean hulls, wheat bran." No trace of alien, or otherwise anomalous, ingredients was found, which is good for Simonton, who had tasted one of the cakes and determined it tasted "like cardboard." The Air Force signed off on this case as "psychological" in nature, stating that Simonton, a stable and respected member of his community, had a sudden dream which he enacted out by making terrible, cardboard-like pancakes. The cause of this dream remains unknown.

While the nonsensical nature of this story made the overall encounter unappealing to conventional ufology, Jacques Vallée in his classic book, *Passport to Magonia: From Folklore to Flying Saucers*, points out the age-old motif at work in this case: the exchange of assistance or items between humans and the Good Folk, gods, or, in this case, spacemen. However, in this particular case, the fact that the object traded was a flat bread or cake ties it clearly to the Fairy Faith of Europe, where many accounts link that particular food to the Good Folk, right down to the buckwheat hulls (Vallée, 2014, pp. 35-37).

A very different sort of exchange, albeit unsuccessful, occurred to one John Trasco of Everittstown, New Jersey, on November 6th of 1957. He had just returned home and went outside to feed his ill-tempered dog, King, when he came upon a luminous, egg-shaped object accompanied by a 'little man,' about two-and-a-half feet high, with a face described by Trasco as putty-coloured with large, frog-like eyes. Perhaps oddest of all, the being was dressed in a green suit with shiny buttons, green gloves, and a green tam o' shanter style hat. Trasco referred to the strange entity as looking "like a leprechaun." The being spoke to Trasco, stating: "We are a peaceful people. We don't want no trouble. We just want your dog."

Trasco yelled at the creature to get lost, which is exactly what it did. It marched into the object through no visible entry point, and then the object took off into the sky. At some point through this exchange, Trasco got a strange, green powder on his wrist, which came off when washed only to reappear the next day (Vallée, 2014, p. 53).

But what of the powdery substance in each case? Incidentally, powdery, ash-like substances show up in conjunction with all manner of spectral manifestations and throughout the lore of UFO artefacts and contact. Various cultural beliefs tie supernatural entities to dust-like substances, whether the belief that occult beings travel in dust-devils, or the association of dust with fairies, who have been said to vanish in a hail of dust, or to cast dust into the eyes of their witnesses (Rhys, 1901, pp. 111, 191).

One of the most striking examples of folkloric patterning occurred during a wave of extraordinary activity in November of 1980, in the Pennines region of England. On November 28th of that year, Todmorden police officer Alan Godfrey was nearly finished with his shift, at around 5:00 in the morning. An earlier call had relayed that some cows had escaped their enclosure, and Godfrey decided to take one final look for the animals. It is intriguing to note that, when they were eventually discovered, there was no trackway in the muddy field between where they had been and where they were found.

As he was driving, Godfrey saw what he took to be a well-lit bus, but, for some reason, was strangely attracted to investigating the object. As he came upon it, he realised it was not a bus, but a dome-shaped, luminous, hovering object complete with dark windows. He attempted to call the strange sight into base, but both his radio and handheld walky-talky were non-responsive. Eventually, he began to sketch the object, when, a moment later in his estimation, he was suddenly a hundred yards down the road, leaving him with a roughly 20–30-minute segment of missing time.

Under regressive hypnosis, Godfrey recalled leaving his vehicle and being carried, then floated, into "the room" – by all accounts a classic moment in the annals of alien abduction. However, the experience was rife with religious and folkloric elements. Godfrey described a tall, bearded man wearing a white sheet and a white skullcap he referred to as Joseph (in a later review of the hypnotic transcripts, Godfrey would say that the real name was Yosef), accompanied by about eight small, hideous, robotic beings. This pattern, of a taller, usually benign entity, in command of smaller, usually horrifying beings, is a common motif in UFO contact literature as well as in the iconography of the fairy faith, where smaller beings assist the stately fairy queen.

However, the strangest aspect of this encounter was the appearance of a large, black dog just sitting in the room with him. The dog is a powerful archetype across cultures worldwide, especially tied to ideas about traversing from this world to the underworld. Of note here is its strong connection to the folklore of the British Isles, specifically in the figure of the infamous Black Shuck (Randles, 1983, pp. 122-168).

"The Incomprehensibles"

Of course, sometimes the most highly strange aspect of an encounter is the entity itself. Not every sighting can be rightfully pinned to such neat and tidy drawers as 'Sasquatch' or 'Dogman.' Some must simply be labeled, as in Keel's *The Complete Guide to Mysterious Beings*, as "The Incomprehensibles" (Keel, 2002, p. 37). The problem with many of these beings is that they appear once, or perhaps several times in short order, before never being seen again. Conventional, flesh-and-blood cryptozoology dictates that such creatures need a breeding population. If this was the case, there should have been a whole brood of Horrors leaping about Enfield, Illinois in the spring of 1973.

On April 25th, 1973, Mr. and Mrs. McDaniel returned home to find their two children terrified. They claimed that something had attempted to enter the home, first scratching at the door, then at the window air-conditioning unit. As the parents attempted to calm their children, the scratching noise resumed at the door. Mr. McDaniel assumed that he would be greeting a teenage hoaxer when he answered the door. Instead, a three-legged, five-feet-tall grayish creature, with large pink eyes and short, taloned arms, stood on his porch. McDaniel slammed the door, grabbed his pistol, kicked the door open again and fired. Instead of succumbing to its injuries, the creature hissed and bounced off into the night, covering about fifty feet in three jumps.

There had been a sighting of the same strange being about half an hour previously. Ten-year-old Greg Garrett had been playing in his backyard, located right behind the McDaniel household, when the same creature appeared suddenly and bounced on his foot, leaving him screaming and with a shredded tennis shoe. Although McDaniel would have one more sighting of the creature, and odd screams continued to plague the area, whatever the 'Enfield Horror' was, it bounced away as suddenly as it had come (Coleman, 1983, pp. 156-157).

In September of 1968, a man pseudonymously referred to as 'Ken' was serving in the British barracks on the island of Cyprus. Responsible for looking after the upper floor of the building's left wing, Ken had a private billet which faced the stairwell. One night, his guard dog awakened him just after 3:00 in the morning. The dog, which was 'afraid of nothing,' did not respond to Ken's calls and retreated under his bed, whimpering and shaking with fear. Ken became aware of a faint, high-pitched noise and opened his door to see where it was emanating from.

Floating up the stairway was a truly bizarre being. It had a flat, orange face with large red eyes and rough red hair. As it came up the staircase, its head began rotating in an unnatural manner to face Ken, coming all the way over its left shoulder. It was right as Ken realised that this thing was wearing a light blue jumpsuit that he panicked, retreated into his room, shut the door behind him, and loaded his underwater spear gun. Still in a state of panic, Ken also grabbed his diver's knife and sat waiting, facing the door. He heard the high-pitched noise heighten, as well as a strange 'sliding' noise. Eventually, the sliding noises moved past, and the high-pitched noise diminished as well. Ken collapsed where he sat and woke the next morning with his weapons still beside him. Although the creature would not reappear, and it is not stated whether Ken had any lasting effects, his guard dog never recovered, becoming completely submissive at the first sign of any danger (Randles, 1990, pp. 75-78).

In March of 1966, a fifteen-year-old girl by the name of Kathy Reeves was returning to her home in Pioneer Mountain, Oregon, with a friend of hers. They were walking up Pioneer Road when they saw a 'ruddy glow' in the distance which they assumed was a fire. However, when they approached it, they saw that it was actually a burning, dome-shaped object and decided to continue on to Kathy's home. Then, they saw another light which appeared like a flashlight with a cover over the end so that no beam would project from it. Kathy thought someone was playing a trick, so she threw a rock in the direction of the light. Immediately, a series of big lights came on all around the small flashlight-like light. The two girls, frightened, ran the rest of the way back to Kathy's home.

Unfortunately, the Reeves family was soon beset by a range of unsettling anomalous phenomena. Pulsating lights they referred to as 'wall donuts' for their pastry-like shape reappeared nightly, 'crawling' across both the interior and exterior walls of the home. Two blue spots of light appeared to pierce the residence, though no beam was visible. Glowing objects performed manoeuvres in the sky above them. Kathy's mother claimed that her bedroom was often flooded with magenta light, and that she had her doorway blocked by a "watermelon-coloured cloud." One family member actually went for their gun after seeing 'something' through the living room window. Multiple members of the Reeves family and a deputy sheriff also heard a strange, high-pitched noise, like a high-speed saw, which continually haunted the residence (Lloyd, 1967, pp. 29-30).

The whole affair also took place at a time of high UFO activity in the Pioneer Mountain area. However, the entities, if indeed they may be referred to as such, observed at one point in this case certainly fit the incomprehensible bill. Amid all the activity, Kathy claimed to witness little multi-coloured stumps walking through a nearby pasture. While the Reeves family's experiences were investigated from both a ufological and parapsychological angle, unfortunately the stumps were seemingly not of interest to either party, garnering little by way of interest at the time of the initial investigation (Keel, 2002, p. 123).

Conclusions

Regardless of the particular field of paranormal research, patterns exist between accounts and experiences. Strange lights are seen in haunted houses – they have frequently been observed literally hand-in-hand with a Sasquatch. Accounts of centuries past have fairies casting dust in the eyes of their witnesses – a midcentury case leaves a normal paper mill worker confounded, his wrist covered in a green powder. And between conventional descriptors, the tidy boxes set around like discrete things, lurk true monsters – creatures which cannot be, yet somehow are.

Anomalous experiences are so defined by that – their anomaly. Yet, in the field of paranormal research, the all-too human desire to categorise and define often excludes the true scope of strangeness that many of these experiences possess. It is in this extra-anomaly, this high strangeness, that the true possibility of these experiences lies, and in no way excludes or diminishes a more conventional explanation to any given type of entity. It simply points out that, for every flesh-and-blood Sasquatch account, there is an equally viable case of a bullet-proof, translucent Sasquatch lurking in the nearest chicken coop (Coleman & Clark, 2006, part 1, pp. 14-19).

These cases of beings at once material and immaterial – impossible yet somehow observed – tap into the deepest questions of the human condition. They seem tied to us, in equal parts confirming and challenging our beliefs in masquerades both whimsical and terrifying.

PART 2
RESEARCHING THE DEEP WEIRD

STRANGE TALK

Epistemological, Methodological and Ethical Aspects of Conducting Interviews about Anomalous Experiences[45]

LEONARDO BRENO MARTINS

Extraordinary experiences have been reported throughout human history, and across cultures. Narratives often include personal encounters with the 'supernatural' in its various forms, as well as many kinds of altered states of consciousness and events described as 'paranormal' in nature. In recent years the term 'anomalous experiences' has been coined to designate experiences that are somehow divergent from everyday experience, and/or the usual consensus reality, without any mandatory relationship with pathology or abnormality (Cardeña, Lynn & Krippner, 2000). Among the most investigated categories of experiences are altered states of consciousness, hallucinations in non-clinical populations, near-death experiences, mediumship, memories of 'past lives,' psi-related experiences (e.g., psychokinesis, precognition), lucid dreams, and visions of 'supernatural' entities (e.g., saints, angels, demons, aliens, folkloric characters and so on).

---

[45] A version of this chapter was first published in *Paranthropology*, Vol. 4 No. 1 (2013).

The relevance of the study of anomalous experiences can be recognised in three major areas. First, the experiences, narratives and related belief systems have relevance in the individual, social and historical domains, because they are part of everyday life for many people, play an important role in cultural and religious contexts, and in the social construction of reality, among many other possibilities (Cardeña, Lynn & Krippner, 2000). As an example of their high prevalence in many contexts, 82.7% of a sample of 306 Brazilian students and workers reported experiencing at least one type of psi-related experience throughout their life (Machado, 2010). Similar surveys conducted in other countries also showed significant results (e.g., Blackmore, 1984; Haraldsson, 1985; Ross & Joshi, 1992), suggesting that many people have anomalous experiences in different contexts. Thus, the multiple psychosocial, symbolic, mythological, religious and mystical dimensions of anomalous experiences become objects of interest for the social sciences, sciences of religion, psychology and related fields. Second, anomalous experiences may signal gaps in knowledge about the relationship between individual and cultural dimensions in everyday experience, for example, in the emergence of hallucinations among people who do not have psychiatric or psychological disorders (Cardeña, Lynn & Krippner, 2000). Thirdly, there is the relevance to clinical psychology and psychiatry, because experiencers can receive misdiagnoses by professionals unprepared to deal with such experiences. The simple mention of unusual personal events has historically been considered as a strong indicator of underlying pathology (Almeida & Lotufo, 2003; Cardeña, Lynn & Krippner, 2000).

Such diverse relevances invite social scientists to the study of anomalous experiences, but there are multiple methodological approaches available for this kind of research. The copious narrative records – from historical documents to contemporary media – provide research possibilities increasingly utilised in the social sciences, sciences of religion, history and psychology. However, the analysis of personal first-hand narratives acquires central importance amongst the various possible forms of research. Such research might, for example, consider the stages of the experiences (Zangari, 2005), the cultural meanings of the episodes (Marçolla & Mahfoud, 2002), the social roles of experiencers (Zangari, 2005), the adherence to paranormal beliefs (Pereira Silva & Silva, 2006), or the study of spontaneous cases (Alvarado, 2002), among many other possibilities. Interviews are one of the most promising methods for collecting first-hand narratives.

However, anomalous experiences have potentially distinct connotations that make them different to other subjects that the social sciences and psychology are accustomed to investigating. Considering that the general literature on anomalous experiences is still growing, there is an even greater gap in the literature about the specificity of the interview technique in the context of anomalies. Moreover, even with regard to more traditional subjects, little has been published concerning the more subtle aspects of the interview technique. Thus, this chapter discusses some subtleties of interview techniques and their relevance to the field of anomalous experience research.

The Bias of Irreducible Alterity

According to Giesler (1984), scientific research into anomalous experiences can be divided into two major groups, each one rooted in a specific epistemological model. On the one hand, phenomenological research focuses on uses and meanings of experiences and related belief systems as socially, historically and psychologically constructed. Thus, the meanings of the episodes are established by experiencers and their cultural background, their functions are collectively established and their alterity can be recognised (Irwin 1994). The various types of phenomenological research on anomalous experiences are usually present in social scientific and social psychological research. On the other hand, ontological research focuses on processes involved in the underlying causes of anomalous experiences (Palmer, 1978, 1982; Schmeidler, 1994), such as cultural and/or individual factors, physiological and psychological factors, and so on.

Although the social sciences are not accustomed to ontological research and its naturalist epistemological inheritance, it is important to remember that these are two distinct epistemological models, each one representing a particular 'cut of reality' with specific strengths and limitations. Considering just one of these epistemological models as valid (as often occurs with phenomenological research in social sciences), is the equivalent of absolutising a research model, considering the symbolic boundary of alterity as insurmountable and overlooking profitable opportunities for interdisciplinary research. For example, although anomalous experiences are culturally shaped by social pressures, belief systems and other collective forces (e.g., Zangari, 2005; Maraldi & Zangari, 2009), the operationalisation of these psychosocial influences (i.e., the connection between the major cultural influences and the occasional subjective experiences/behaviours of experiencers), involves little known concrete mechanisms, such as dissociation and hallucination in psychologically healthy people, neuropsychological potentialities and limits, the actual effects of psychoactive substances used in rituals, and so on. Therefore, the understanding of the 'whole picture' and the overcoming of the gaps in knowledge about anomalous experiences (as well as other difficult and related topics, such as the nature and functioning of consciousness), are only possible through interdisciplinary research, which neither underestimates different epistemological models, nor ignores researchers technically equipped to formulate and analyse ontological and phenomenological questions during interviews. The following items favour both approaches.

The Biases of Pathologisation, Prejudice and Emphasis on the Intrapsychic

As a complementary opposite of the previous criticism of the exclusivity of phenomenological approaches, many authors still consider anomalous experiences as both rare and as traces of a primitive or pathological mentality (Freud, 1930; Munro & Persinger, 1992; Lukoff, Lu & Tuner, 1992). However, in spite of the high prevalence of experiences in the populations of different cultural contexts, there are significant distinctions between anomalous and psychopathological experiences, so that, mostly, there are no significant correlations with classical disorders (Cardeña, Lynn & Krippner, 2000; Menezes Junior & Moreira-Almeida, 2009). These findings problematise the common automatic pathologisation and 'dogmatic prejudice' towards anomalous experiences (Almeida & Lotufo, 2003).

Similarly, there is an historical tendency to focus on the experiences as intra-psychic constructions (i.e., contained purely within the subjectivity of the experiencer), rather than taking a more productive psychosocial approach consistent with recent findings (Zangari & Maraldi, 2009). Accompanied by automatic pathologisation and 'dogmatic prejudice,' the exclusivism of the intra-psychic may persist in the conceptions of the interviewer (as well as the bias of irreducible alterity), which may have an impact on the questions asked, interpretations of responses, attitudes towards the interviewee, resistances and other counterproductive biases that ignore a number of critical variables and promising research points.

Recognising Alterity and Other Challenges to the Subjectivity of the Researcher

The humanities have the peculiarity of having as their object of study the same subjectivity that produces their knowledge. Depending on the epistemological model, the subject-object relationship – sometimes axiomatised, sometimes problematised throughout the history of science – earns even more obscure contours and deserves more attention. Considering most common objects of study, the literature discusses broad guidelines, including notions of: research as a dynamic process, the active roles performed by researcher and researched, the interview as a negotiation, the mismatches and conformities between the planned and the effective in everyday research, the inescapable biases of the researcher, and the socially constructed relevance of the study, among others (e.g., Bosi, 2003). However, research about anomalous experiences tends to exacerbate the implicit and explicit challenges of the investigation of such subjective questions because of the initial phase of reflections about the matter and some crucial aspects of the subjectivity of the researcher, such as possible religious beliefs.

Thus, the interviewer needs to recognise the alterity represented by anomalous experiences, this alterity emerges from the dialogue between subjectivities and from the common mismatch between the perspectives of the experiencer and those of the researcher. In fact, many anomalous experiences show features that are highly outrageous to most people – researchers or not – such as the complex and standardised alien abduction experience, for example (Appelle, Lynn & Newman, 2000). The classical research of Festinger, Riecken & Schachter (1956) on contacts with supposed aliens, and the resultant theory of cognitive dissonance, warns of the risk that the human anguish arising from mismatches between prior beliefs and actual data motivates the abandonment of provocative findings in favour of prior and comfortable perspectives. Such pressures can also arise from the scientific mainstream, which decides what is or is not publishable. Given the predominantly involuntary aspect of this abandonment of data and the provocative dimensions of anomalous experiences, a more rigorous than usual self-policing is required of the interviewer.

Attitude During the Interview

In direct proportion to the outrageous appearance of the episode, experiencers tend to be afraid to share their experiences with professionals, strangers, close persons and especially with people who may be judged as too critical, such as scientists. On the other hand, an enthusiastic and credulous attitude can also cause effects that compromise the interests of the research, because data can be 'enhanced' to gratify or impress the interviewer (Almeida & Lotufo, 2003; Mack, 1994). Thus, the attitude of the interviewer may be decisive in the quantity and quality of collected data, in addition to causing potentially beneficial or harmful aftereffects for experiencers (Almeida & Lotufo, 2003), such as the strengthening of a positive or negative self-image, and strengthening constructive or destructive beliefs about the experiences, among many other possibilities.

Thus, it is recommended that a neutral but empathetic attitude (Almeida & Lotufo, 2003), cautious of stereotypes and other socio-historical variables potentially involved in the interview (Bosi, 2003; Bourdieu, 1993), and that promotes a 'disarmed conversation' that favours lasting bonds and mutual gratitude (Bosi, 2003), be employed. The gratitude resulting from the interaction tends to occur because there are benefits for all involved. Researchers can obtain information of great relevance given in a friendly, unselfish and sometimes brave way, considering the common concerns of the experiences in relation to the misuse of information, public exposure and other possibilities. In turn, experiencers can obtain the rare opportunity to talk about personal experiences that are 'unbelievable,' sometimes even in their own social context (but are full of emotional significance), with people (the researchers). With this in mind, the interviewer should ideally adopt an amicable, attentive and respectful attitudes and an unwillingness to make pejorative judgements. Moreover, researchers can provide an opportunity for experiencers to obtain scientific information and opinions about their experiences.

Chataway (2001) explains that, unlike the historical subject-object relation – in which the researcher is the active subject of the research, while the volunteer is a passive object – fieldwork is based on a dialectical process of negotiation between two subjects: interviewer and interviewee. All persons involved are active in the process, so that not only the demands of the investigator, but also the motivations and benefits of the deponent should be taken into account. One consequence of ignoring the active role of all those subjects is the occurrence of inadvertent subjective processes that are crucial to the interests of the research, including loss of data, artificiality, barriers of communication, or voluntary and/or involuntary 'sabotage' by the respondent, among many other possibilities. Thus, the planning and implementation of the research must consider: what the participants want (as a group and as individuals), and what the ethical implications of the research are *from the perspective of the participants*. The optimum approach, therefore, is to combine the interests of the researcher and the participants, which includes a flexible research design that encompasses situational changes during the interview.

One example with ethical and methodological value is the subsequent submission of transcriptions to the respondents, for their own interest and possible revision (Bosi, 2003). If the researchers can thoroughly review their work, change and optimise it, or omit sections, why should the respondents, as active subjects in the process, not also have the same right? Similarly, sometimes it is possible to allow a group discussion about the information gathered during the fieldwork because it can also have a collective belonging, and might be significantly improved by input from other community members (Bosi, 2003), all depending on the objectives of the research. If the review and subsequent change of data by the respondent is not detrimental to the overall aims of the study, or if the submission of the material to the social group is a possibility, then these aspects should be considered as part of the negotiation with participants.

The Social Voices

Also, in relation to the attitude of the interviewer, the collected data (narratives and other responses), may be engaged with deeply in order to give voice to socially differentiated circumstances, such as disadvantaged and dominant social groups (Bosi, 2003). The research itself is a social relation as a dialectical encounter between historically situated subjectivities, under the aegis of sociological, anthropological and psychological factors and processes, such as belonging, conflict, domination, subservience, and rebellion, among others (Bourdieu, 1993).

The historical relationship between scientists and protagonists of anomalous experiences can be understood as a relation between distinctive social groups. Since the nineteenth century, anomalous experiences have been considered indicators of pathology, primitivism, fraud, and as functional methods for gaining social compensation (Freud, 1930; Munro & Persinger, 1992; Lukoff, Lu & Tuner, 1992). Only in recent years have psychosocial perspectives emerged, which adopt a more nuanced perspectives (e.g., Zangari & Maraldi, 2009). However, there still remains a general impression among many experiencers that scientists are particularly averse to taking extraordinary experiences seriously, and many scientists and health professionals also have pejorative beliefs about the episodes reported by experiencers (Almeida & Lotufo, 2003).

If interviewer and interviewee represent social voices, Bourdieu (1993) explains that the interview can assume the dimensions of a symbolic violence because of the risk posed by games of domination. So, it is not the intention to annul socio-historical differences, instead an effort should be made to approximate the horizons and reduce the potential symbolic violence of the interview. In fact, many respondents consider research an opportunity to overcome domination and expose their perspective, which has been increasingly frequent trend in the study of anomalous experiences. Thus, everyone involved can take ownership of the research, through respect for alterity and effort by approximation.

Practical Preparation for the Interview

Testimony is a shared work, an active product of the interaction of the subjectivity of the interviewer and interviewee (Bosi, 2003; Bourdieu, 1993). Each participant plays a role. So, the researcher must exercise their subjectivity from the critical and reflective positioning of their own perspective and possible theoretical references, the prior collection of key topics to feed the interview and an exhaustive review of the extant literature (Bosi, 2003). An example of an 'obvious' specificity in the anomalistic field – easily ignored due to its added pejorative value – is the study of not only the scientific literature related to anomalous experiences, but also the material produced by experiencers and non-academic authors, because it often reveals the perspectives of people directly involved in the episodes (Almeida & Lotufo, 2003), including: social representations, hierarchies of belief, mental images, emotional contents, promising themes to be developed during the interview, and other relevant aspects of first-hand testimonies and opinion-makers' discourses.

Contrary to the position of many enthusiasts of anomalous experiences, reports do not provide an immaculate portrait of the related episode. Like the famous 'aphorism' of Henri Poincaré presented in *La science et l'hypotése* (1902), 'science is built of facts the way a house is built of bricks; but an accumulation of facts is no more science than a pile of bricks is a house.' So, it is imperative to use theories or, at least, a general paradigm to guide the research planning process, justify the inclusion of the interview in that planning, organise data, interpret the interview and formulate conclusions (Almeida & Lotufo, 2003). The choice of theories has direct relation to the worldview of the researcher, the research objectives and the desired reach of the results. However, the specific or increased difficulties in the study of anomalous experiences include the un-critical tendency to forcibly adapt findings to fit with favourite theories, the insufficiency of linear criteria of psychopathology, the tendency towards hasty generalisations, the absence of reflections about the epistemological implications of anomalous experiences (such as about the mind-brain relationship; cf. Moreira-Almeida & Santos, 2012), and the deficits of everyday vocabulary for dealing with various subtleties of such experiences (Almeida & Lotufo 2003).

It can be decisive for some informal investigations – such as pilot studies – in contexts where the interviews will take place, to search for clues about the vocabulary usually employed to describe anomalous experiences, as well as other unsuspected situational variables. The language and imagery prevalent in smaller groups exemplify this issue. In several field investigations Martins (2011) tried to find people who claimed first-hand experiences related to unidentified flying objects (UFOs) and aliens. But, in many Brazilian rural contexts, such experiencers were not easy to come by. However, after considering the local folklore and everyday language use, the experiencers began to be discovered in large numbers, and quickly. Instead of asking for UFOs, flying saucers, aliens or related terms – based on a naïve assumption of a notorious terminology – it proved more fruitful to talk about encounters with Mãe do Ouro (Mother of the Gold), Mãe D'Água (Mother of the Water), Carro Fantasma (Ghost Car), Boitatá (Fire Snake), Luz Fantasma (Ghost Light), among many other names, each one familiar in a particular context and strange in others. Performing a phenomenological reduction, defined as the understanding of the experience on some essential perceptual aspects (Forghieri, 1993), many of these narratives were revealed to be related to anomalous lights in the sky that are similar to each other and to what urban people often call 'UFOs,' serving the interests of the research.

The Dynamic and Presentified Memory

Unlike the common-sense view, memory is not a static picture of the past. In fact, memory is a heterogeneous set of dynamic and creative processes of reconstruction and presentification of the past (Bosi, 2003). The sincerity, clarity and vividness of a reported memory do not ensure the accuracy of its content about past experiences, because mnemonic processes include prior beliefs, expectation, suggestibility, fantasies, and cultural, perceptual and cognitive biases (French, 2003). Memories and related narratives are permeated and totalised by intentions and meanings, constituting a 'subjective culture' (Bosi, 2003) that emerges from the encounter between socio-historical and individual dimensions. Thus, although the accuracy of memory is questionable on several grounds, it does not denigrate the common conviction of the witness about its subjective experiential content, even in the case of anomalous experiences, while it certainly is not extended to the interpretations and experiences of others (Bullard, 1989; Marçolla & Mahfoud, 2002). Thus, memory allows research on subjective, rather than objective, truths, and present rather than past experience (Bosi, 2003).

During the interview, one way to optimise research on memories is to seek, through subsequent exploratory questions, the 'constants of memory' (Bosi, 2003), understood as tension points between social signs and individual memory. These points are located in the border areas between stereotypical representations, presented as automated and straight speeches, and subjective processes that require from the individual an effort of elaboration – expressing its idiosyncrasies, doubts, hesitations and silences (see also Bourdieu, 1993). Often, the constants of memory have significant emotional contents and there may even be distress by attrition between social stereotypes and their personal appropriation. Thus, gaps and uncertainties are often subjective seals of authenticity, because they are beyond the stereotyped speech conditioned by culture (Bosi, 2003; Bourdieu, 1993).

Significant Places

Despite the relative lack of studies on spontaneous anomalous experiences, they nevertheless have great elucidative potential for science because of their 'naturalism,' which tends to compensate for the weaknesses of artificial laboratory studies of psi (Alvarado, Machado

& Zingrone, 1998; Alvarado 2002). Thus, research on experiences that occur outside the laboratory finds in the interview procedure a tool with superlative importance, because of the value of testimony about episodes that are rare and/or have uncertain predictability. We must consider that the spontaneity of such anomalous experiences invites fieldwork in search of contextual nuances present only, or prominently, in *places* where the episodes have occurred. Thus, the lack of literature on spontaneous anomalous experiences has as a corollary a lack of specific discussions about research in relevant places for the experiencers.

When conducting interviews about any kind of experience, Bosi (2003) recommends that the interviews take place in significant locations, which may help in the contextualisation and evocation of memories, complementing lack of content and eliciting emotions. While an overlapping of past and present, memory can be stimulated when the experiencer returns to places directly related to the topic of the interview, even if they are modified by the effects of time and cultural change, and if the respondent has also changed in many respects. The famous aphorism of Heraclitus of Ephesus, 'no man ever steps in the same river twice,' is appropriate for the witness who returns to the place of the alleged facts, and refers to the emphasis on the emerged contents of memory as a subjective composition of a whole and presentified person.

Thus, a practice usually tainted as pseudoscientific can regain value and importance, although it does require some resetting. Returning to the places where experiences have occurred is a common practice among enthusiasts of certain anomalies, such as ghost hunters and ufologists, who intend to implement reconstitutions in a tenuous manner (e.g., Reis & Rodrigues, 2009). One of the elements delegitimising this practice is the nescience about the above-mentioned dynamics of memory, so that its contents are un-critically considered to represent accurate pictures of the past. Therefore, although there is a strong possibility that such places may help the interviewee to recall specific details, they can also fuel the dynamism of memory. In summary, the return to significant places needs to be contextualised in the research planning with realistic expectations, and should be used in all its fertility as a trigger for eliciting data.

Dealing With Difficulties and Contretemps

In addition to the usual information, it is recommended that the daily nuances of the research also be published. Such issues of a practical nature are rarely commented on in methodological texts, but they can be important for subsequent inquiries and fellow researchers. The study of anomalous experiences is a field under construction and so is full of inherent difficulties. In addition to the prior example of the difficulty in locating UFO experiences because of the unsuspected terms used to name them in rural areas, the same fieldwork has also benefited from the negative impression that experiencers of unusual events often have about scientists (Almeida & Lotufo, 2003; Mack, 1994). Although the presence of the academic researcher (Martins, 2011) has resulted in an initial resistance among many experiencers, his sincere opinion on the academic neglect of anomalous experiences and the importance of interviews in changing such historic tendencies reversed the resistance of virtually all reluctant experiencers. Thus, it is recommended that future researchers thoroughly publish their difficulties in the field, contretemps and the ways in which they were resolved (or not). Thereby, field diaries can be of great importance, and their use is highly recommended.

Conclusion

Anomalous experiences constitute a relevant topic for the social sciences, psychology, the sciences of religion and related areas because of their subjective impact, prevalence in different contexts and challenges to clinical and scientific knowledge. Experiencer testimony is the primary means to access many of these experiences due to the inherent difficulties in predicting and/or monitoring their occurrence.

However, there is a gap in the literature on epistemological, methodological and ethical aspects of interviews applied in the context of anomalous experiences, and even on some specific nuances of the general use of such techniques. In discussing the biases of irreducible alterity, pathologisation, emphasis on the intra-psychic, challenges to the subjectivity of the researcher, the appropriate recognition of alterity, the interviewer's attitude during the interview, the dynamic aspects of memory, the return to significant places, and the consideration of difficulties and contretemps, it is concluded that the interview should not be treated as a mechanical and un-critical practice. The interview, in the context of extraordinary experiences, deals with sociological phenomena and the subjectivities of both researchers and experiencers at high levels because of the intense cultural and personal implications of the topic. Essential beliefs, important ethical risks, social stigmatisation and experiences on the frontier of knowledge compose a challenging and promising amalgam for science, and the practice of the interview must adjust to the complexities of the issue at hand.

THE EXTRAORDINARY ENCOUNTER CONTINUUM HYPOTHESIS AND ITS IMPLICATIONS FOR THE STUDY OF BELIEF MATERIALS[46]

PETER M. ROJCEWICZ

Most studies of UFOs have confused their structural and phenomenological natures due to inadequacies inherent in both the definition and classification of the subject matter. The acronym "UFO" in popular usage means "flying saucer," that is, a hardware product of an extraterrestrial technology. This reduction of the UFO question to the study of only "flying saucers" has negative effects upon the study of belief materials with regards to 1) definition, which determines our academic levels of involvement and the formulation of research priorities; 2) taxonomy, since our classification systems define the anatomy of the subject matter at hand; 3) epistemology, because encounters with non-ordinary entities raise the issue of the nature and means of knowledge and "knowability"; and 4) ontology, around which revolves the question of socially discovering alternate realities through various cultural experiences and modes of being.

Current definitions and taxonomies do not display an appreciation for the complex interrelatedness of "flying saucers" with numerous

---
[46] This chapter was first published in *Folklore Forum*, Vol. 19, No. 2 (1986).

folk belief traditions. A hypothesis that sees "flying saucers" on a continuum with numerous other cultural manifestations is offered here as an alternative to the conventional exclusionist's argument that "flying saucers" are completely discrete and self-contained. The continuum hypothesis provides a viable explanation of the occurrence of a specified group of human encounters with the extraordinary. This proposition, based on substantial ethnographic data, is asserted as a provisional conjecture (i.e., working hypothesis) to guide investigations in the area of folk beliefs.

The Problem of Definition and Taxonomy

The term "flying saucer" did not come to hold its present position in popular usage until after the June 24, 1947, sighting of nine discs over Mt. Rainier, Washington, by pilot Kenneth Arnold of Boise, Idaho. A problem of terminology developed when numerous reports of other-than-disc-shaped phenomena were likewise termed "flying saucers." The military preferred the term "Unidentified Flying Object," UFO (pronounced Yoo-foe) to distinguish reports that sounded to them more like fairy tales from those reports which they believed to be reliable. Thus the key terms used to distinguish among uncertain aerial phenomena possessed an evaluative and qualitative nature rather than serving an accurate taxonomic function.

A major obstacle involved in securing adequate definitions of unorthodox phenomena like UFOs stems from the failure of the present terms to discriminate between descriptions and interpretations of events. For example, each word of the term "Unidentified Flying Object" contains an inherent confusion. "Unidentified" simply contains too broad a spectrum of possible phenomena, and thus it is too vague. "Flying" is also problematic because of its mechanistic connotation. We do not describe all aerial phenomena as "flying"; clouds and stars are not rightly said to "fly." "Object" begs the question, assuming what needs verification from case to case. Douglas Price-Williams (1974, p. 224) maintains that in the term "Unidentified Flying Object" we find an assumption disguised as a description. In the case of the equally unsatisfying term "flying saucer" we have an explanation disguised as a description.

In addition to the confusion of terms discussed above there is an even greater challenge to accurate definition and taxonomy. A formal

THE EXTRAORDINARY ENCOUNTER CONTINUUM HYPOTHESIS

morphology indicating the primary, invariable features of the UFO experience eludes us at this time. As a result, there exists no precise definition that absolutely distinguishes UFOs from other phenomena and which assures the credibility of data embraced within the conceptual boundaries of the term. This imprecision undermines the effectiveness of our taxonomies which seek to establish order among the data by grouping together features shared by members of the same class of experience.

J. Allen Hynek created the most influential and most widely utilised classification system for UFOs (1974, pp. 31-32, 98-99). Hynek's typology includes:

1) nocturnal lights in the sky;
2) daytime discs;
3) radar visual reports;
4) Close Encounters with space-craft or their occupants.[47]

This schema has worked well for the obvious physical manifestations of UFOs, but it does not address the important issue of psychological and paranormal features (Schwarz, 1980, pp. 184-286, 400; Vallée, 1975, p. 6), nor the complex and plentiful descriptive and phenomenological connections among the above mentioned categories and related folklore traditions (Vallée, 1969; Rojcewicz, 1984), a weakness that the continuum hypothesis is intended to correct. Although people have different things in mind when they use the terms "Unidentified Flying Object" or "flying saucer," we can nevertheless assume that these terms do communicate something significant. This same problem of definition can be observed in other disciplines with reference to their major subject matter. Physicists have not defined the elusive properties of the atom, yet few deny its descriptive validity. Biologists have not defined the cell nor geneticists the gene. Anthropology has never agreed upon a definition of "primitive" (Diamond, 1974, p. 118).

---

[47] Hynek's UFO typology includes three kinds of "Close Encounters." A Close Encounter of the First Kind (CE I) is a "close-at-hand experience without tangible physical effects." In a CE II "measurable physical effects on the land and on animate and inanimate objects are reported." In a CE III "animated entities (often called 'humanoids,' 'occupants,' or sometimes 'Ufonauts') have been reported." Although it was not a part of Hynek's original typology, the UFO abduction experience has come to be referred to as the CE IV.

This same difficulty finds another analogue in folklore itself, wherein neither the discipline as a whole nor a single one of its genres have yet to be satisfactorily defined (Dundes, 1980, p. 21; Degh, 1983, pp. 38-39). This is not to say that some invariable features do not exist, but only that Ufologists and folklorists alike have yet to discover them. It may be that in the case of UFOs the definitive components of the phenomena lie not in their perceivable anatomy, but in what they express, or *how* and *why* they occur.[48]

Description of the Extraordinary Encounter Continuum

In order to more fully understand the nature of the full spectrum of human confrontation with anomalous entities, the operative term "Extraordinary Encounter Continuum" is offered here. These entities can be referred to as "non-ordinary," "unorthodox," "nonconventional," or "supernatural" insofar as they:

5) demonstrate spontaneous activity;
6) demonstrate the ability to produce images independent of sense perception;
7) demonstrate complete control over these images (Jung, 1958, pp. 66-67);
8) represent an actual order qualitatively different from our everyday world;
9) which interacts with our material world in complex ways.
10) Belief in such entities is cross-cultural.

Enumeratively defined, the Extraordinary Encounter Continuum refers to human confrontation with the anomalous, whether in the form of "beings" (e.g. extraterrestrials, fairies, monsters, etc.), "entities" (e.g. apparitions, energy forms, tulpas, etc.), "objects" (e.g. spacecraft, vimanas, fiery shields and crosses, etc.), or unusual light(s). The term

---

[48] John F. Szwed, writing specifically about folksong, has conjectured that "It may be that the irreducible minimum in folklore is social structure, where the roles and statuses of a community are restated in one or another form as a basis for comment, whether humorous, tragic, or ironic. The community, after all, is the setting in which a song emerges, in which it is performed, and in which its meaning unfolds" (1970).

THE EXTRAORDINARY ENCOUNTER CONTINUUM HYPOTHESIS

"flying saucers" is but one descriptive and interpretive frame people employ after confrontations with a particular kind of non-ordinary entity along the Extraordinary Encounter Continuum of experience. Encounters with the anomalous can occur in the context of an abduction, out-of-body travel (OBE), near-death experience (NDE), shamanic journey, or combination of two or more of these forms. No individual encounter category is more important in itself than another. The predominance of attention given in this chapter to UFOs is arbitrary and could easily be focused upon another category of the continuum.

All the traditions along the Extraordinary Encounter Continuum are discrete but related. They are separate but not separated, like an individual's relationship to a hand. Although the traditions can be distinguished from each other, they nevertheless display similar complex patterns of appearance and activity. The continuum hypothesis maintains that to more fully understand the complex nature of non-ordinary events, one must see them in relation to the larger context of human encounters with unorthodox entities. All phenomena along the encounter continuum share at least a borderline, as do a ship's bottom with the water, the ocean with the waves, and the waves with the sky overhead. This hypothesis argues that some belief traditions are so closely related phenomenologically as to warrant inclusion under the umbrella term "Extraordinary Encounter Continuum."

Goals of the Continuum Hypothesis

The continuum hypothesis is intended to accomplish the following: 1) account for the cross-cultural distribution of extraordinary beliefs, especially in modern times when official agencies debunk UFOs,[49] spiritual entities, and non-ordinary realms, predict their demise, and relegate such beliefs to the arena of pseudoscience; 2) allow comparison of a great variety of apparently diverse and unrelated local belief systems in order to permit meaningful generalisations and syntheses; 3) predict and explain the nature of unorthodox belief in ways that are empirically confirmable, logically consistent and pertinent to other fields of scholarly inquiry; and 4) produce an operative definition that more accurately reflects the nature of non-ordinary experiences. This proposition is offered here since no hypothesis

---

[49] A trend that has more recently shifted with the official acknowledgement of UAPs (unidentified aerial phenomena) by the US government.

currently accomplishes all four of these functions simultaneously, although some accomplish one or two (Keel, 1976; Vallée, 1969; Steiger,1976).

Relationship of Definition to Tradition and Experience

The encounter with nonconventional beings often involves phenomena, experiences, motifs, and beliefs which are thought in tradition to belong in separate categories but which sometimes occur together simultaneously in actual experiences. This conjunction of anomalous factors can take the form of a "spirit guide" or "etheric master" possessing an extraterrestrial connection (Rojcewicz, 1985), an encounter with a mysterious globe of light during a supernatural assault of the classic nightmare (Hufford, 1982, p. 49, 217), or a UFO abduction during an out-of-body experience (Clark, 1980, p. 199). Reasons for the belief in the confluence of two or more belief traditions may include:

1) They are related in the culture's body of traditional belief.
2) They are so similar phenomenologically that they are connected by the percipients' interpretations of their experience, even though this connection does not occur simultaneously in the same experience or in tradition.
3) They occur together simultaneously in the same event independent of tradition, or close enough in time and space from the percipients' point of view as to constitute the same event.

An example of the first case listed above can be seen in the Middle Ages when a number of late medieval writers fuelled the belief that fairies and elves were "either devils or diabolical illusions." This hostility toward the fairies was supported by the Reformation, whose writers argued that fairies could only be good or evil, with the latter the more likely possibility. The official doctrine of most Protestant teachers of the time was that it was useless to attempt to distinguish good fairies from bad since the Devil was behind them all (Thomas, 1971, p. 610).

The usual academic response to accounts that link the fairies to the devil is: "Those events took place – or seemed to take place – because you hold that belief." Similarly, it has been argued that UFO legends display a continuity of described features because "the narrators are drawing from a common language" and otherwise "share a frame of reference which enables them to appropriately set up similar narrative structures combining similar contents" (Lowe, 1979, p. 69, 71). David Hufford refers to this conventional academic position as the "cultural source hypothesis" (1985, p. 119). This perspective maintains that descriptive continuities among accounts of extraordinary encounters are always generated from a common tradition rather than a formally consistent experience.

An incident from the UFO abduction experience of Betty Andreasson indicates how one's interpretation of an event can lead to the apparent involvement of two or more belief traditions. Under hypnosis Betty described and drew pictures of her alien captors. These creatures had large pear-shaped heads, grey clay-like skin, and hands with three thick fingers. Their asian-looking faces had large wraparound catlike eyes, holes for noses and ears, and fixed scar-like mouths. Despite the fact that Betty verbally described and drew pictures of entities that are clearly consistent with the appearance of alleged extraterrestrial beings as found in numerous UFO accounts, her interpretation of her experience led her to believe that her abductors were "angels" (Fowler, 1980, p. 13). We can clearly see here the fusion between experience and belief, description and interpretation. Betty's Christian beliefs colour her interpretation of the appearance of her abductors, calling them "angels," despite her verbal and pictorial descriptions to the contrary. This is most likely an example of the "reflective principle" in operation, although it is possible that description of appearance alone is a necessary but not sufficient factor in determining whether any two or more belief traditions intersect in the same experience.

The Reflective Principle: Symbiosis and Short-Circuit

Proponents of the "reflective principle" argue that a percipient's personal and culture-bound values significantly shape their non-ordinary experiences. The colouring of experience by a percipient's psychology or cultural beliefs does not invalidate the potential reality of the event; it merely complicates it. A familiarity with the generic conventions of accounts of human encounters with the supernatural in general, and the specific folk belief tradition in particular, should reveal pressure points, as well as values, within the generic frame. A psychological profile of the informants should indicate how much of their community's belief traditions are mirrored in their individual accounts. Cognisant of the framing structure and conventions of the witnesses and, if the account has made its way into print, the conventions of thought and style of the popular or academic author(s), we can measure the potential for individual variation and elaboration. Measuring personal or cultural reflectivity allows the phenomenology to come through.

The reflective principle often plays a role in how a witness identifies and interprets a nonconventional experience, but it does not always do so. Some good data now exist indicating that people completely unaware of a traditional body of beliefs can still undergo recognisable anomalous experiences (Hufford, 1982, p. 15; Moody, 1976, pp. 123-124). Michael Elliot, conducting initial research on "flying saucers" in 1980, had never heard or read about the esoteric UFO tradition of the "Men in Black" (MIB) when he had his own encounter with a Man in Black in a library in Philadelphia (Rojcewicz, 1987). Encounters with manifestations of the Virgin Mary are not limited to Roman Catholics, Greek Orthodox, or Coptics. J. Gordon Melton, a Methodist minister and now Distinguished Professor of American Religious History at Baylor University, admits to having had a Marian sighting (1980, p. 316). Ramakrishna, founder of the Vedanta Society, has likewise testified to having had a similar vision. Witnesses to anomalies like UFOs often find that their experiences contradict rather than mirror their values and beliefs, and yet they still insist upon the validity of the events (Hall, 1974, pp. 215-216).

Just as traditional understandings can influence descriptions and interpretations of one's experience, so also repeated encounters with non-ordinary entities can influence a body of traditional beliefs. From this perspective, people hold particular beliefs because certain extraordinary events take place. Proposing that experience influences tradition at least as often as tradition influences people's interpretations of their experiences, the continuum hypothesis can account for and predict belief in the presence of two or more folk belief traditions in the same experience. Most present belief-related definitions and classification systems have not led investigators to appreciate the complex connections among folk traditions. Before examining some of these important continuities, a statement about methodology is needed.

Methodology

The Extraordinary Encounter Continuum represents the full spectrum of human interactions with anomalous phenomena through time and space. It is, first, a descriptive phenomenology which systematically organises parallels between human encounters with non-ordinary beings including such features as their appearance, powers, and effects;

and second, a hermeneutical method drawing upon salient ideas from several disciplines and relying primarily on cultural and historical data, proposing specific patterns to better explain the nature of inexplicable encounters. Neither method, it must be stressed, necessitates the researchers' acceptance of all informants' accounts as true, but it does presuppose a refusal to reject *a priori* their potential validity.

An important theoretical assumption of the continuum hypothesis, inherent in both the phenomenological and hermeneutical methods, is that not all reports of anomalous encounters are the products of hysterics, hoaxes, or perceptual and mental impairment. UFO abductees, for example, attend school to some degree (Lorenzen, 1977, p. 155). These abductees tend to be policemen, businessmen, schoolteachers, and other respectable citizens (Hynek, 1974, p. 34). Studies of unorthodox phenomena such as supernatural assaults of the classic nightmare (Hufford, 1982) and near-death experiences (Moody, 1976; Greely, 1975) indicate that a significant percentage of traditional supernatural belief is associated with accurate observation analysed rationally.

Frequently Recurring Traits in The Encounter Experience

An examination of the Betty Andreasson UFO abduction experience reveals significant connections among several folk belief traditions. The Andreasson affair displays continuities among "flying saucers," near-death experiences, out-of-body experiences, and shamanic journeys. This case offers good evidence that two or more traditional systems of unorthodox belief occur simultaneously in experience. The key feature of the Andreasson experience from the continuum perspective is her confrontation with extraordinary beings. It is this encounter with the anomalous, whether in the form of beings, entities, objects, or unusual lights that is the invariable feature inherent in all the discrete belief traditions of the past and present comprising the Extraordinary Encounter Continuum.

Despite wide variation in the circumstances surrounding a person's encounter with the extraordinary, as well as in the kinds of people undergoing them, there are nevertheless striking similarities among the reports of the experiences themselves (Lowe, 1979, pp. 67-79). These continuities are so significant that one can easily pick out ten elements which appear again and again in published and unpublished accounts of encounters with "flying saucers" and their occupants, near-death and out-of-body experiences, and shamanic journeys. They include:

1) Feelings of friendliness, love, fearlessness.
2) Being chosen: "mission" motif.
3) Instruction/Enlightenment.
4) Passing through material objects.
5) Beings of light/Unusual lights.
6) Journeys to non-ordinary realms.
7) Tunnels/Enclosures/Paths and Borders/Limits.
8) (Nearly) Ineffable.
9) Revelatory moments.
10) Psychic manifestations.

For brevity only four of the above listed traits will be explored in this chapter.

Bright or Unusual Lights and Borders and Limits

Like many UFO witnesses, Betty Andreasson, her father Waino Aho, and her daughter, Becky, saw a peculiar pulsating light shine through their kitchen window immediately before the aliens walked literally through the kitchen door. Transcripts of the hypnosis session indicate that Betty said:

> I can see a light, sort of pink now. And now the Light is getting brighter. It's reddish orange, and it's pulsating [...] (Fowler, 1980, p. 3).

The single feature that Betty recalls most vividly about her abduction experience is light. Betty associated the aliens and their spacecraft with a luminescent light, a common descriptive motif not only of "flying saucers," but also of fairies and fairy boats, the aerial cars of the Mahabarata called "vimanas," and numerous other entities in folk belief traditions (Rojcewicz, 1984, pp. 421-39). Betty also experienced light in a more mystical manner. While she underwent physical examination at the hands of her captors – a common feature of UFO accounts – Betty was told:

> We are going to measure you for light [...] You have not understood the word you have [...] You are not completely filled with light (Fowler, 1980, p. 44).

Betty interpreted "light" to mean the light of spiritual grace and faith, that is, the presence of God within her: "I believe I am filled with the light! I believe – I believe that I'm filled with the light" (Fowler, 1980, p. 44). The light motif is ever present in accounts of out-of-body travel, near-death encounters, and shamanism.

During an out-of-body experience, Robert Monroe reported that he witnessed a "ring of sparks about two feet in diameter," with the axis of his body as the centre of the ring (1977, p. 24). On another occasion, as Monroe prepared to induce "astral travel" a "beam or ray seemed to come out of the sky" and struck him, a motif not uncommon to UFO accounts (1977, p. 23). This warm light caused Monroe to vibrate violently. He became "utterly powerless to move" as if "being held in a vice." It is interesting that Kenneth Ring (1980) has found "Seeing the Light" and "Entering the Light" to be two of the five fundamental elements of a close encounter with death. The Ojibway shaman called the *tcisaki* hears voices of the *manitou* spirit and sees light sparks within the ceremonial shaking tent. "Hearing voices and seeing bright lights are traditional signs of a visionary experience among the Ojibway" (Grim, 1983, p. 155; see also Bedard in this volume). Light is a key element of religious and mystical experiences in general.

Journeys to Non-Ordinary Realms

Humans abducted or invited by extraterrestrials to visit distant planets usually travel by "flying saucer." However, when Betty Andreasson obeyed a command to stand directly behind one of the entities, she found herself "floating" several inches above the ground with a "rolling motion" that matched the movements of her captors as they traveled in a single file. As she approached the spacecraft, Betty noticed odd sensations throughout her body:

> My hands and my legs are asleep or something [...] I feel weightless. Oh my feet are pins and needles or something – even my arms and my hands (Fowler, 1980, p. 27).

This "pins and needles" sensation has often been described by mystics, mediums, and visionaries. Betty spoke of a force that held her body rigidly in check: "They seem to have controlled my body somehow so I'm fixed in place" (Fowler, 1980, p. 30). Robert Monroe has published personal accounts of this same catalepsy with its accompanying vibrations (1977, p. 24). It seems reasonable to claim that Betty Andreasson traveled out of her physical body, an experience sometimes referred to as "astral travel." Betty constantly complained that her body was "weightless," but "rigid," pulsing with "vibrations." Betty Andreasson, it seems likely, described two bodies: her physical and her astral.

Sylvan Muldoon and Hereward Carrington (1970, pp. 50-51) have described in full detail the characteristics of the corporeal and etheric bodies, and their findings support the claim that Betty left her physical body. The rigidness of Betty's physical body finds a parallel in the following statement from a case reported by Celia Green in *Out of the Body Experiences*:

> [...] then I was back in bed, but I couldn't move hand or foot, my scalp prickled, starting at the top of the head and the prickling sensation spread all over me [...] (1968, p. 61)

The words "enstatic" and "ecstatic" are helpful in describing the cognitive condition of the Ojibway shaman, which facilitates his dangerous soul journey to the ghostly underworld, according to John A. Grim:

> Ecstatic describes that type of trance in which the shaman's consciousness is said to leave the body. Enstatic applies to that inspired state in which the contact with the sacred is decidedly interior and meditative (1983, p. 144).

The continual beating of the shaman's drum affects the shaman's passage to the numinous world (see Hunter, 2015b). Peculiar noises and the sensation of floating have been otherwise noted by Raymond A. Moody (1976, pp. 37-38). People who have "died" report having traveled through a tunnel, enclosure, void, or cylinder before contacting souls of the dead. Betty Andreasson herself floated through a cylinder or tube:

> It looks like a silvery tube [...] slowly lowering down. We are going down [...] we are going down (Fowler, 1980, p. 34).

Moody found that people who have "died" have described what could be called a border or limit in the form of a body of water, a grey mist, a door, a fence across a field, or simply a line (1976, p. 70). Similarly, Betty Andreasson told Raymond Fowler how UFO occupants took her to the

"Green Realm," a sunless land or island of fog and mist. This place was inhabited by lemur-like creatures (i.e. the living dead) and contained a pyramid with crystal walkways and bridges over water. When Fowler asked Betty if she had actually left the Earth, Betty replied: "I believe we were in space, and somehow we were in the centre of the earth. Now how can that be?" (1980, p. 80). Betty's account of her journey to the mysterious "Green Realm" touches upon several traditional folklore motifs such as "Wonder Voyages" (F 101.1) and "Rivers in the Otherworld" (F 161.2).

Could Betty Andreasson have undergone a near-death experience while being abducted by extraterrestrials, despite not having "died"? Moody acquired two accounts of near-death experiences in which no clinical death actually took place but real psychological stress or injury existed (1976, pp. 67-69). Betty had been under severe stress for several years. Her marriage to James was problematic from the start and eventually ended in divorce. James' severe car crash and subsequent hospitalisation forced Betty into the demanding role of breadwinner while she cared for her elderly father and six children. Despite being physically worn, Betty travelled several hours to hypnosis sessions that she hoped would unlock the mystery of the UFO encounter. Faced with cases as complex as the Andreasson affair it seems likely that no absolute criteria exist by which one can precisely classify every experience as OBE, NDE, or UFO abduction. There will always be borderline cases. This is the *raison d'etre* of the continuum hypothesis.

Revelatory Experience

To conclude the discussion of the four selected features that appear with great frequency among accounts of "flying saucers," OBEs, NDEs, and shamanic journeys, let us now turn to an examination of the lasting life impression that such encounters have upon many percipients. Betty Andreasson believed that her abductors "awakened" something in her when they touched her forehead during the physical examination they conducted upon her. Like the shamans of many cultures, Betty had her own revelatory visions:

> It was as if the infinite opened up on me [...] I was seeing inventions so far advanced – thousands of years advanced – and yet it seemed just a scratch in the infinite (Fowler, 1980, p. 186).

Betty Andreasson's confrontation with the aliens, particularly her interaction with her two "teachers," "Quazgaa" and "Joohop," seemed to have a stabilising effect upon her volatile emotional condition. It has been argued elsewhere that Betty's abduction experience served as a useful "tool," facilitating her mental and emotional competency (Rojcewicz, 1984, pp. 640-670). Shamans also undergo personality adjustment or re-organisation resulting from their encounters with guardian spirits and animal powers of a transcendent reality. Both the shaman and the patient receive a new identity through the healing process. Sometimes this experience occurs to non-shamans after undergoing a visionary quest for the purpose of receiving a guardian spirit power, or it may occur after a serious illness as among the North and South American Indians, as well as the indigenous peoples of Siberia. "Such a radically profound and revelatory experience often encourages the individual to take up the way of the shaman" themselves (Harner, 1982, p. 63). People who have lived through close encounters with death have stated that they subsequently feel their lives deepened, their perspectives expanded. They are more reflective and interested in issues of a philosophical nature. Life contains much for them to learn. One informant told Moody: "I felt like I aged overnight after this happened, because it opened up a whole new world for me that I never knew could possibly exist" (1976, p. 83). The most common characteristics of revelatory experiences are a sudden transformation of the percipients' personality and experience-ordering systems (Hufford, 1983, p. 311; Steiger, 1982, p. 148). While many of these personality and life transformations are positive, many are not. John A. Keel observed from his fieldwork that:

> The Illumination experience changes their lives, but it has no effect on this world. In many instances people are changed for the worse instead of the better, just as the majority of all supernatural manifestations are harmful or at least senseless (Keel, 1975, p. 20).

Whether we can agree or not with Keel that a majority of all supernatural manifestations are harmful or senseless to the percipient, he has nevertheless documented cases of emotional collapse and mental disorder as a consequence of such experiences (1976, p. 229). According to mystical tradition, whether a confrontation with non-ordinary realities is harmful or not depends largely upon skilled guidance and appropriate preparations (Hufford, 1985, p. 109).

Future Research

Alvin Lawson believes that "It is likely that dreams, hallucinations, death experiences and a variety of other phenomena are related to UFO experiences" (1980, pp. 230-31). He employs the term "encounter matrix" to refer to the "extensive similarities between UFO encounters and religious and metaphysical mysticism, folklore, shamans' trances, migraine attacks, and even the operation of creative imagination." Berthold E. Schwarz, M.D., (1983) has conducted pioneer work exploring the extraordinary ability of Stella Lancing of Massachusetts to take random photos wherein unidentified globes, and rays of light can be seen, as well as the whole spectrum of psychiatric and psychic UFO-related conditions and events. David Hufford has pointed out continuities between UFOs and accounts of vampirism, witchcraft, and the classic nightmare (1982, p. 234). Keel (1975, p. 60) and Steiger (1976, p. 39) have suggested that the same unknown mechanism behind UFOs gives rise to all manner of mystical and religious experiences. Robert S. Ellwood sees a very close connection between UFO cults and American Spiritualism (1973, p. 131). J. Gordon Melton has argued that strong continuities exist between UFO experiences and encounters with apparitions of the Virgin Mary (1980, p. 314).

Future studies examining the links between "flying saucers" and their occupants with apparitions, spiritualist and theosophical claims, mystical and ecstatic occurrences, shamanism, the classic nightmare (Old Hag), OBEs, NDEs, and other anomalies would be a tremendous help in further understanding the varied unorthodox ways people gain knowledge about and access to alternate realities. There is good evidence to suggest that encounter experiences between human and nonhuman entities are fundamentally cognitive (Hufford, 1985, p. 94), or "noetic" to use William James' term, and not simply or always an emotional or "oceanic feeling" (Freud, 1961, p. 11).

Conclusion

Arguing here for the relatedness among various folk traditions that compose the Extraordinary Encounter Continuum should not be interpreted merely as a search for functional equivalents. It would be unsupportable to claim, for example, that an OBE is simply a UFO abduction of another name. Such a conclusion would be dangerous since the important differences between the two phenomena would be unjustifiably lost. In addition, it has not been argued here that because these folk traditions are related they are indicators of an objectively real order that can only be extraterrestrial. It should be quite clear, however, that extraordinary encounter reports are significant, not only for the study of folk belief, but also for studies of the acquisition of knowledge and the delimitation of realities.

This chapter is part of an ongoing attempt to develop a coherent hypothesis of folk belief that neither rejects *a priori* reports of anomalous experiences simply because they lack strict scientific verification, nor embellishes them in order to prove that the supernatural realm exists. The continuum hypothesis insists that investigation of the alleged objective reality behind beliefs in non-ordinary events is an important function of the belief-oriented folklorist, despite some scholarly opinion to the contrary (Degh, 1977, p. 244; Ward, 1977, pp. 216, 218). It may well prove that phenomena along the Extraordinary Encounter Continuum are not scientific problems but authentic experiential manifestations. This fact would not necessarily invalidate the significance of these extraordinary events and may instead point to the boundaries of orthodox scientific procedure and scope.[50]

In either case, a general consideration of the overall encounter continuum should prove the best approach to date for defining accurately the anatomy of various as yet inexplicable phenomena like UFOs, as well as for the construction of reliable belief taxonomies. It must be understood, however, that the operative term "Extraordinary Encounter Continuum" serves primarily as an explanatory context for investigation and not yet as the definitive description of confrontations with the unknown.

---

[50] The Society for Scientific Exploration was formed in April, 1982, with 100 founding members drawn primarily from university faculties in the United States. The purpose of the society is to provide a context for intelligent examination of anomalous phenomena and related topics. The society defines "anomalous" as any phenomenon which appears to violate existing scientific understanding or is generally regarded by the scientific community as lying outside their established parameters of investigation. For more information see: https://www.scientificexploration.org

CREATING PROJECT HERA

Application of Deep Neural Networks and Database Architectures to Albert Rosales' Humanoid Encounter Datasets

CHRISTOPHER DILTZ

BARBARA FISHER

In late 2019, while reading Albert Rosales' sixteen volume series entitled *Humanoid Encounters: The Others Among Us*, it became apparent to paranormal researcher Barbara Fisher that the amount of data presented across the series was overwhelming. The encounters were compiled by Mr. Rosales over several decades, beginning in 1993. Collected from a variety of sources – including literature reviews, witness accounts from antiquity, historical newspaper and magazine indexes and personal communications between Mr. Rosales, witnesses and fellow researchers – altogether the books include thousands of individual encounters. Even so, the books do not encompass the entirety of the data Mr. Rosales has amassed. To the present day, he continues to gather reports of encounters with non-human entities from around the world, thus the books, while representing an incredible body of information, are continually outdated.

The amassed encounters range in date from 4780 BCE to 2009 CE and are organised into volumes by decade from 1900 CE to 2009 CE. The first volume is an exception; it includes all of the encounters from 1 CE to 1899 CE. Though strictly organised by date, and mostly categorised by a classification system of nine encounter types devised by Mr. Rosales,[51] there is no simple way for a researcher to statistically analyse the dataset represented by these books by location, time of day, season, or witness demographics. Each encounter includes a relatively brief description of the witness testimony as reported by the source; within each encounter there are myriad details that could provide important clues to researchers wishing to compare or contrast a discrete grouping of these encounters.

For example, a researcher might wish to compare all encounters from the state of Ohio in the United States through history. The only way in which to accomplish this with the books is to carefully read through each of the sixteen volumes, making note of each encounter that includes Ohio in its description, and then taking physical note of any details from each encounter relevant to that research. This is unnecessarily time consuming and tedious and, through human error, could easily lead to missed individual encounters, and thus the loss of relevant data.

While scholars have conducted research this way for centuries, it is not the most efficient means by which to sift through massive amounts of information for small details that show relational patterns in the data. These books represent a wealth of interesting and statistically significant information relating to human interactions with what appear to be non-human entities, but it is frustratingly difficult to analyse effectively.

---

[51] Albert Rosales' Humanoid Encounter Classifications – Type A: When an entity or humanoid is seen inside or on top of an object or unidentified aircraft. Type B: When an entity or humanoid is seen entering or exiting a UFO. Type C: When an entity or humanoid is seen in the immediate vicinity of a UFO. Type D: When an entity or humanoid is seen in the same area where UFOs or unknown objects have been reported. Type E: When an entity or humanoid is seen alone without related UFO activity. Type F: When there is a "psychic contact" between entities or humanoids but an entity or humanoid is not necessarily seen. Type G: When there is direct contact or interaction between a witness and a humanoid or entity; either involuntary, as a result of a forced abduction, or as a voluntary contact. Type H: When there is a report of an alleged crash or forced landing of a UFO with recovery of its occupants or when an anomalous entity is captured or killed either by a witness or military personnel. Type X: When the situation is so uncanny that it does not fit any previous classifications. A new classification, there are several such cases in the files already. I would call these cases, "extremely high strangeness events" (Rosales, 2017, p. 44).

Without the ability to easily compare the individual encounters in this dataset by different metrics, efficient analysis is nearly impossible. Without analysis, data provides information without knowledge. It was determined that the huge amount of information represented in these books would be more useful if one could sift through the individual encounters using a searchable database. In this way, researchers could readily seek patterns of commonality between reports, such as geographic coordinates, time of day, day of the week, types of humanoids sighted, and whether communication between witness and humanoid occurred.

In addition, by using such a database, one would be able to take the data and plot the locations of sightings on a map over periods of time. This would allow a researcher to determine if there are discrete geographic areas that, over long spans of time, are locales that have repeated sightings of humanoid beings, and if there is a predictable periodic rhythm to these encounters – what John Keel called 'window areas' (Keel, 1970, p. 8).[52]

One could also overlay the humanoid sighting map with existing publicly available maps created by NOAA and the United States Geological Service to determine if there are lightning strikes, magnetic anomalies, carbon deposits, unusual ground conductivity, quartz or granite deposits, iron or underground water sources that are found in common with areas that show repeated humanoid encounters.

This database is not meant to replace the books Mr. Rosales has written and published, but instead, to supplement them. The books are invaluable; there will always be readers who will notice time based patterns in the individual books representing single decades of encounters reported worldwide. The books give a valuable snapshot of historical data on human encounters with humanoids and other paranormal phenomena, each presented in a discrete period of time. However, unlike printed books which are relatively static, the database can be continually updated as Mr. Rosales and other researchers find new encounters and upload them, thus deepening the pool of available data.

---

[52] In his writings, John A. Keel claimed that there are areas of the world where paranormal activity occurs cyclically over time, cropping up and dying back rhythmically. "We have a theory. It is not very scientific, but it is based upon known facts. These creatures and strange events tend to recur in the same areas year after year , even century after century. This in itself, indicates that the creatures somehow live in those areas, which we call 'windows'" (Keel, 1970, p. 8).

In the spring of 2020, the authors contacted Mr. Rosales, who graciously not only gave us permission to use his data, but also provided our team with all of his files in word document form that went beyond 2009 to 2019. In return, we promised not only to share with him the database that we would create from the files, but also our findings after we began our own data analysis. At this point, Dr Christopher Diltz began the work of transforming thousands of pages of word documents into a searchable database.

Preliminary Analysis

Mr. Rosales' humanoid encounters collection consists of 85 different word documents that contained approximately 22,178 different encounters from 4780 BCE to 2019 CE. Each humanoid encounter contains the following features: ID, location, date, time, description, source, type and any added comments from Mr. Rosales. The word documents also contain several different features, such as quotes, illustrations and depictions of the humanoids, and comments from Mr. Rosales on specific encounters.

Our analysis began by developing a suitable data template for each of the humanoid encounters. This template consisted of a collection of data types for the different features that made up the individual humanoid encounters contained in Mr. Rosales' data. The collection consisted of an integer type for the ID, string type for the location, date type for the date, time type for the time, string type for the description of the humanoid encounter, string type for the source, and character type for the type category of the humanoid encounter. Each humanoid encounter would be collected in a list where each element in the list would be made up of a collection of each of these different encounters. The next step in our analysis consisted of developing word document parsers to read the different word documents that made up Mr. Rosales humanoid encounters and parse them, removing figures, white space, tabs, and comments tied to the encounter and converting the humanoid encounters, based on the template developed, into a JSON data type.

JSON data types constitute an open standard file format, widely used in the data science industry, for performing data analysis and descriptive and inferential analytics on large data sets. JSON file formats will allow researchers to select different fields for the humanoid encounters and perform descriptive and inferential statistics on the selected feature, such as dates, times, locations, including latitude and longitudes and type categories. This data type is also ideally suited for different database architectures, such as Mongo and SQL. Our parser programs were able to successfully convert the word documents provided by Mr. Rosales and create a single JSON file that contains all 22,178 humanoid encounters that make up the target data.

Database Architecture

Using the single JSON file generated from the application of our word document parser programs to Mr. Rosales' humanoid encounter datasets, our team has created a database that stores and displays the contents of all the different encounters that make up the target dataset. The database applies a unique ID stamp to each encounter and lists out the different features, including the date, time, description and the other features captured. The database system allows the user to look at the different features in the documents and display the results in different histograms and bar charts, such as word counts, frequency plots and more. Our database system allows users to query humanoid encounters, based on features derived from a user defined, custom search query. This makes the database system ideally suited for researchers, both for retrieving data and performing data analysis based on selected search queries, such as specific locations in a country, times of the year, selected time periods and type categories. The search queries are often very fast, making this solution more efficient and user friendly for specific research foci.

Database Analytics

The large, detailed collection of humanoid encounters compiled by Mr. Rosales presents many opportunities to perform customised analytics to identify key patterns and trends. These patterns can either validate or refute hypotheses that have been posited by past researchers, as well as revealing new and interesting patterns that have not been found before.

Our project involves using a myriad of descriptive and inferential statistical tools to perform a number of different analyses, including but not limited to computing sample descriptive statistics, application of directional statistics for humanoid encounters based on latitude and longitude coordinates, inferential statistics to estimate parent population distributions of the sample statistics collected, statistical hypothesis testing using T-test, F-test, Chi Squared tests for model fits and more. The temporal features of the data set allow our team to perform time series statistical analyses, such as computing auto-correlation between time series, partial auto-correlation, moving average, exponential moving average, auto-regressive, auto-regressive moving average, seasonal auto-regressive moving averages, auto-regressive moving average with exogenous input models and transfer entropy estimations between time series to investigate cause-effect relationships between time series.

The large collection of available data also permits the use of deep learning[53] neural networks[54] to perform different inferential tasks, such as classification, regression and prediction. With the application of machine learning[55] and deep learning neural networks, our team can investigate significantly more features in the data that would otherwise be difficult to deduce using traditional statistical techniques. Our team's current focus relies on the application of natural language processing[56] to look at the descriptions of each humanoid encounter and to place them into different categories based on humanoid type, whether the humanoid was in the presence of an unidentified flying object, if the human observer was paralysed during the encounter and more.

The results of the analysis would be contained in a cluster diagram which could then be compared with Mr. Rosales' nine type categories. The natural language processing programs can also be used to focus

---

[53] Deep learning constitutes a class of machine learning processes and algorithms that utilise artificial neural networks to perform certain inference tasks, such as classification, prediction and regression.

[54] Artificial neural networks (ANNs) constitute a class of machine learning algorithms that use collected layers of weighted nodes called artificial neurons to extract features from data for data classification, prediction and data regression.

[55] Machine learning is the branch of computer science and Artificial Intelligence (AI) that involves studying algorithms that can learn and improve performance of certain tasks, such as classification and prediction based on sample data sets.

[56] Natural language processing is a subfield of computational linguistics and Artificial Intelligence (AI) concerned with programming computers and developing algorithms to process and analyse large amounts of natural language data.

on other targeted features and cluster the results together based on key words and phrases provided by a user. These analytic capabilities allow researchers to apply much more robust statistical analyses with higher confidence in a seamless end-to-end workflow using the analytic tools available and the database system that houses all the humanoid encounters provided by Mr. Rosales. Our database architecture and analytics capabilities will help lower the barrier of entry for paranormal researchers to apply some of the latest, state of the art machine learning tools to the available data sets in our database, leading to innovative discoveries not found using alternative approaches.

Display and Visualisation

The results of the data analytics need to be displayed in a readily usable format. These formats can include time series graphs, scatter plots to highlight clusters of data and geographic maps that will highlight the latitudes and longitudes for given humanoid encounters. These maps will also be colour coded to highlight the different type categories of the humanoid encounters based on Mr. Rosales' classifications. Our database architecture and analytics library will contain a broad suite of different visual display capabilities, including 2-dimensional scatter plots, time series graphs, bar charts, feature lists and geographic maps to highlight and display the results of custom analytics to researchers. The visuals and displays will give researchers the ability to find key relationships between different categories of humanoid encounters, observe different humanoid encounter waves through history and identify geo-temporal correlations between humanoid encounter sightings and other geographic phenomena, such as geomagnetic storms, adverse weather conditions or other seasonal trends.

Preliminary Results

With the development of our database architecture and the analytics libraries available to our team, we have performed several different statistical tests and developed a series of different deep learning neural network libraries to achieve a select number of different tasks. These tasks first focus on identifying simple patterns and trends within the data. The tasks then move up to apply much more sophisticated deep learning objectives, such as classification using natural language processing.

To begin, our team performed simple number counts of the different humanoid encounters per year and noted any anomalous spikes of humanoid encounters relative to normal background number of encounters. Our results showed that there were abnormally large numbers of humanoid encounters in the following years: 1897, 1909, 1954, 1967, 1968, 1973-1980 (peaking in 1978), 1989, 1990, 1995, 1996. These windows for increased number of humanoid encounters have been shown to coincide closely with predominant UFO waves that have taken place over the last hundred years. However, tests have not been conducted at this time to show a strong auto-correlation between these anomalous peaks in humanoid encounters and prominent UFO waves.

Other noted features in the results of the data analysis showed that the United States, England, Russia, Spain and Argentina had the highest number of humanoid encounters in descending order, and that California, New York, Puerto Rico, Texas and Florida had the highest number of humanoid encounters in the United States in descending order. Another unique finding from our results also showed that the summertime had the highest frequency of humanoid encounters, peaking in August, and that the winter had the lowest frequency of encounters, reaching a bottom in the month of February. From the different humanoid encounter waves highlighted above, several different countries showed drastic increases in encounters. These countries include France, England and the U.S. in 1954, Argentina in 1968, England and Spain in the 1970s, the Soviet Union in 1989 and 1990 and the U.S. territory of Puerto Rico in the mid-1990s.

Following the completion of our simple statistical analysis on identifying trends and patterns in the datasets, our next objective was to focus on the subset of humanoid encounters and perform natural language processing on the encounter descriptions. For our target data set, we chose to focus on all the humanoid encounters in the United States, consisting of around 8,000 different entries. Contained within this dataset are around 145 descriptions that have no classification type. Our objective was to use supervised learning to take the dataset with known types, train a deep learning neural network using training and validation datasets and work to successfully classify the humanoid encounters with unknown types. Our deep learning neural network model was able to successfully read in the humanoid encounters with known types, train using the training dataset and compare the model against the validation dataset. Our model was able to achieve a validation accuracy of 86.7%. This implies that our model can successfully classify 86.7% of the validation data based on the training dataset applied to the neural network. Our trained model can then be applied to the dataset without known types to provide labels based on the encounter descriptions with an accuracy of 86.7%. More sophisticated neural network architectures with hyperparameter optimisation search heuristics are being applied to increase validation accuracy further.

Conclusion

As the database project came closer to fruition through the diligent work of Dr Diltz, in October of 2021 we added a new member to our team. Taylor Bell, a web-designer and computer programmer, contacted us in June of that year, after hearing the authors discuss the Humanoid Encounter Database Project on our podcast, *6 Degrees of John Keel*.[57] He offered to help us, and after meeting with him, and seeing the quality of his work, Mr. Bell is now designing a public website which will house the user interface of the database. Mr. Bell, Kendra Maurer, Dr Diltz and Ms. Fisher also devised a memorable acronymic title for our project: *Project HERA: Humanoid Encounter Research and Analytics*. Website and logo design development are now ongoing, as is the continued creation of the database itself.

Eventually, after the database and website user interfaces have been thoroughly beta-tested by our team and carefully selected outside researchers, including Mr. Rosales, the database will go live to be used by the public. The plethora of information that is present in Mr. Rosales' monumental work will be presented in an easily accessible, searchable and, most importantly, updatable way that will make it useful to the paranormal research community.

Users will also be able to submit their own experiences for review by Mr. Rosales and our team to be added to the database after verification of details. It is important to keep the data in Project HERA carefully curated to protect the integrity of the extensive work Mr. Rosales has done for decades, and to keep the data as untainted by misinformation and fictitious reports as possible. Analysis of tainted data is essentially worthless, thus we cannot allow unexamined reports to enter the database.

---

[57] https://6degreesofjohnkeel.com

Our team's plan for the future is to take Project HERA beyond Mr. Rosales' dataset. Once we have shown proof of concept by having a functioning, user-friendly database, we will query other researchers, authors and organisations in order to add their datasets to the existing database. We intend to add UFO/UAP sightings, hairy hominid encounters, anomalous light phenomena, historical hauntings, sightings of religious figures such as the Blessed Virgin Mary, and cryptid sightings to the database.

In this way, we hope to determine whether or not there are commonalities and cyclic rhythms to all of these myriad paranormal phenomena by plotting them geographically and over time across the globe. Mapped paranormal phenomena on the continental United States could also be overlaid upon existing United States Geological Service maps outlining areas of geomagnetic anomalies, thus showing whether or not there is some correlation between unusual electromagnetic energy and high strangeness events (Schroll, 2019).

What good are such geographic and time-based mapping projects? They could be used to re-examine older but possibly still valid ideas such as John Keel's "window areas" and Aime Michel's *orthoteny* or "straight-line theory"[58] of UFO encounters. This sort of data analysis could more accurately corroborate or falsify these interesting ideas in ways that were not possible before; in the case of the idea of *orthoteny*; it may show that it is not only UFO sightings which appear to occur in straight lines, but other phenomena as well. It may even be possible to predict times and places of probable future paranormal activity based on analysis of historical data. The applications of such a large database utilising sophisticated deep neural networks is nearly endless.

For thousands of years, humanity has been collecting reports of unusual phenomena and carefully preserving the accounts of witnesses and experiencers. Generally, however, researchers have been unable or unwilling to combine the reports of different phenomena and compare them all together. Most UFO/UAP researchers keep their study to UFOs and possible UFO occupants, ghost hunters

---

[58] In the 1950s, Aime Michel noticed that UFO sightings tended to occur along straight lines geographically, at least in Europe. He wrote a book entitled *Flying Saucers and the Straight-Line Mystery* in 1958 which outlined his idea thoroughly. In the May, 1963 edition of *Flying Saucer Review* magazine, he refined his hypothesis in response to critique from other researchers. It would be interesting to see if similar patterns occur with non-UFO/UAP paranormal phenomena (Michel, 1963).

stick with ghosts and ghost lights, while cryptozoologists chase after Bigfoot, and so on.

In the past century alone, millions of reports of a variety of strange encounters of many types have been duly investigated and recorded by researchers, scientists, journalists and authors. There exists in our libraries, newspapers, bookshelves, filing cabinets and online databases an incredibly gigantic and untapped resource of largely un-analysed data, just begging to be combined and scrutinised, but there has been little effort to build a research database that allows such data comparison.

There is now a growing willingness in the paranormal research community to examine the connections between these seemingly disparate phenomena; a desire to determine if psychic manifestations, ghosts, humanoids, UFOs/UAP, Bigfoot and the Blessed Virgin are all somehow interrelated, or perhaps even variations of the same phenomenon. The team creating Project HERA will enable this process of pan-paranormal data aggregation and meta-analysis in order to push the boundaries of research on the deep weird into areas thus far unrealised. Our work will empower researchers to delve more easily into the realms of comparative paranormal research than ever before.

PART 3
MODELLING THE DEEP WEIRD

"THE PROJECTIONIST'S BOOTH"

Ufological High Strangeness Viewed Through the Lens of Cinema

JOSHUA CUTCHIN

"You are going to know the world!" the sunken-eyed, semi-transparent pair telepathically declared. It was June 14th, 1968. Young Oscar Iriart had been checking a fence line on his family's Sierra Chica, Argentina farm when he spotted the figures by a pond. He approached on horseback to greet what he believed to be hunters – but they were far stranger.

"Yes, of course," Oscar managed. "Someday when I have saved much money, I will travel."

"No!" they exclaimed, "We will take you now!" Pausing briefly, they immediately rescinded their invitation. "No, we cannot take you now after all." At this, they gestured to an object half-buried in a muddy ditch, ostensibly their spacecraft. "We have too much cargo. But we will come back for you."

Instead, the beings handed Oscar an envelope and instructed him to submerse it in the pond. To Oscar's surprise, both his hands and the envelope remained dry. This pleased the beings, for whatever reason, and they climbed into their craft and ascended to the sky, leaving behind triangular indentations in the soil.

Oscar ran back to his horse – who stood paralysed until the craft's departure – feeling "as if in a dream." He immediately raced home to share the envelope and its contents with his parents. His eyes gleamed with a "hypnotic" sheen as he opened the note. Inside was written in crude block letters:

> "YOU WILL KNOW THE WORLD. [signed] FLYING SAUCER"
> (Steiger, 1988).

High Strangeness is here to stay in UFO encounters. Much to the chagrin of orthodox Ufologists, bizarre details not only refute theories that UFOs represent "nuts-and-bolts" spacecraft piloted by extraterrestrials, but pepper the most mundane sightings with reality-breaking aspects. Erratic lights in the sky sometimes respond to witnesses' thoughts, and experiencers' lives are often plagued long afterward by poltergeist phenomena, profound synchronicities, psi phenomena, even visits from the dead. Dismissing these oddities as lies or madness because they fail to conform to one's biases is intellectually dishonest: they must be confronted and integrated into a holistic interpretation of the UFO mystery.

High Strangeness directly confronts one of our most basic human compulsions: the need for overarching narratives. Parsing the meaning of the dream logic embedded in truly bizarre paranormal encounters is an exercise in frustration. Preeminent French Ufologist Jacques Vallée compared flying saucer sightings to our most popular modern storytelling medium, cinema. In his 1990 book *Confrontations*, Vallée wrote:

> UFO encounters are complete frameworks into which the personality of the witness becomes projected. Like a movie that terrifies you, makes you cry, laugh, or perspire in anguish, the experience becomes part of the witness's reality. The ufologists behave like social researchers who, trying to understand the phenomenon of the cinema, would randomly interview people coming out of theatres and take their testimony at face value; like the UFO witnesses, these people are not lying. Some of them have seen Godzilla, others have seen Bambi. The experience, in every case, was real to them.
>
> But the reality we should inquire about, the reality UFO researchers are often ignoring, is the movie projector high up in a small, dark, locked room near the ceiling. In that room is the technology that will give you both *Bambi* and *Godzilla*, *Star Wars* and, yes, even *Close Encounters* [...] While our fellow ufologists are clustering on the sidewalk interviewing

moviegoers, I think the real questions are elsewhere. My own research takes me up the back stairs where nobody goes. My goal is to pick the lock of the projectionist's secret little booth, to discover at last what makes the reels turn and the machine tick (Vallée, 1990).

How far can we carry Vallée's metaphor? Could it shed light on the significance of High Strangeness? If any "projectionist" exists, and there is indeed a meta-narrative at play, perhaps High Strangeness places witnesses into more receptive or vulnerable states via disorientation and confusion. A survey of High Strangeness cases reveals loose comparisons to camerawork, editing, sound design, screenwriting, and techniques of disorientation long-employed to deceive audiences. We may never meet the filmmakers, but perhaps understanding cinematic tools will yield new insight.

Why Cinema?

Aside from virtual reality, which remains in its infancy, the art of live theatre most closely resembles lived experience. Yet even theatre presents limitations. Short of dosing them with psychedelics (wouldn't that be fun?), presenting truly inexplicable imagery to live audiences remains difficult, with wandering eyes easily revealing the practical methods behind stage-bound illusions; creatures, for example, are always puppets, projections, or thespians in a suit, and we reflexively search for seams, no matter how much disbelief we are able to suspend.

Cinema instead exerts nigh-complete control over viewers' attention, choosing *precisely* what is seen, guiding eyes to crucial details. Computer-generated visual effects have begun to bridge the uncanny valley, their photorealism eliding fantasy and reality (future readers, forgive our naïveté – these illusions look spectacular in 2022!). Since the mid-twentieth century, filmmakers have sought to further close the sensory gap between movies and audiences, employing fads like 3-D, Smell-O-Vision, and even tactile stimulation. Gimmicks are unnecessary, as carefully selected visual and auditory cues alone induce manifold effects. Films "live and die in the editing room," the Hollywood adage goes, and many techniques influence perception without viewers' knowledge. Obviously bouncy, lighthearted soundtracks can transform horror scenes from terrifying to laughable, but more subtle tricks manipulate emotions as well, the pace and tenor of edits conveying unspoken subtext.

In doing so, reality and fiction blur. For example, we may intellectually realise the people falling out-of-love onscreen are not real, but the heartbreak felt for these characters can be undeniably authentic. Film lies in our *imagination*, but its impact is *imaginal*: it is *from* your head but not *in* your head. We may perceive within a tension approaching the work of Carl Jung, or French philosopher Étienne Souriau. Isabelle Stengers and Bruno Latour commented of Souriau's perspective:

> Do we finally have the right to grant existence to beings hitherto dismissed as belonging to the 'purely subjective,' for example, to the beings of fiction? To those phantoms, chimeras and imaginaries that are sometimes so inconsistent that we have great difficulty recalling or reconstructing the experience, and yet which sometimes seem endowed with such an insistence that they seem more 'real' than the [humans] with whom we are summoned to coexist? (Souriau, 2015).

This perspective is more aligned with indigenous thinking. "In the Kichagga language [...] there is no word for 'fiction,' because there is no sharp distinction between imagination and reality," wrote R. Sambuli Mosha of Tanzania's Chagga people, though the concept is equally applicable to many native cultures worldwide. "Thought and reality are closely related because imagination has the potential of bringing the imagined phenomenon into being" (Mosha, 2000).

As in music theory, nothing is intrinsically "wrong" with certain compositional techniques in cinema, but they nonetheless impart predictable effects upon audiences. Artistic best practices evolve because certain techniques elicit specific sensations, and should otherwise be avoided. You can use parallel fifths in your symphony, but they may rob separate lines of individuality and leave the music "hollow"; similarly, "jump cuts" in film – sequential shots where the camera does not move but the subject does, giving the impression of abrupt, instantaneous movement – are not bad *per se*, but typically signify forward motion through time. If used otherwise, they may disorient viewers.

High Strangeness narratives indicate mastery over reality and witness perception. Could a meta-positioned intelligence employ similar "cinematic best practices" to manipulate witnesses? For instance, the importance of sudden shifts in perspective – "Next thing I knew, I was aboard a spaceship," a first-person jump cut, if you will – may not lie in physical transportation to other realms, *but in the very act of discontinuity itself*. It is abrupt because the phenomenon wishes to disorient witnesses. We are reminded of Marshall McLuhan's credo: "The medium is the message." This essentially becomes subliminal messaging or, more sinisterly, mind control. As YouTube's popular Red Letter Media film critics fondly quip, "You didn't notice, but your brain did."

Writing in 2020's *The Cinema of Disorientation* on bewildering film scenes, Dominic Lash notes, "we are likely to notice 'something wrong' but unlikely to be very clear as to why we feel this way. Whether the disorientation has been produced by disrupting the connection between [...] we notice that our expectations – or, perhaps better, our *assumptions* – have been subverted, but doing so takes precedence over noticing *how*, or even noticing *what*, those expectations or assumptions were" (Lash, 2020).

Could flying saucers represent "cosmic art projects"? A 2007 essay by author and researcher Greg Bishop played with the idea:

> When a witness sees something flitting through the sky (or perhaps closer) s/he is often forced to at least temporarily suspend what they think about "reality." Some cases (like certain great artworks) achieve a permanent shift in the witness's worldview [UFO intelligences] might be trying to teach us a few things about how we look at our reality by screwing around with it [...] In a way, many UFO encounters cause an effect that any artist would love to have over his/her audience (Bishop, 2016).

Alongside confusion, disorientation is a hallmark of High Strangeness. Before engaging more abstract concepts like surrealism, disbelief-breaking screenwriting, and metalepsis, I first want to consider some of the more practical aspects of filmmaking.

Camerawork, Editing and Sound Design

In early 1993, Mike Clelland awoke to bright illumination flooding his bedroom window. Peering outside, he saw "five spindly grey aliens" approaching his house, backlit by a small light. Despite the horrifying image, Clelland thought, "Now is the time to put your head on the pillow and black out," which he did. Upon reflection, he noted not only his peculiar reaction, but also a hyper-lucid, dreamlike quality. It was "weirdly quiet," he wrote, "sort of a pressurised fish bowl" (Clelland, 2015).

Given their undeniable resemblance to Ufonauts, a similar perception noted in a May 1983 English encounter with the Little People seems only natural. Unsuccessfully hitchhiking and wracked by exhaustion, the witness and his friend experienced shared hallucinations before spying a faerie-elf party feasting just above the waterline below a bridge. He recalled an "obvious difference between the hallucinations and the fairy party. The hallucinations seemed like a mind trick but the fairies seemed an otherworldly or extra dimensional experience almost seen through a fish eye lens as the sizes of things could not be well discerned" (Young, 2018).

Ultra-wide angle lenses instil disorientation in audiences, usually reflecting characters' states-of-mind – consider their early use in 1965's *Easy Rider*, where a 35mm fisheye signified LSD intoxication (Newman, 2006). "Aesthetically, extreme wide angle lenses can suggest fear, panic, illness, drunkenness, a drugged stupor, or nausea," wrote film festival organiser Thomas M. Sipos. "Because these conditions are subjective, the wide angle lens is often used together with POV framing" (Sipos, 2010).

Filmmakers also utilise dolly zooms for disorientation, famously seen in Alfred Hitchcock's *Vertigo* (1958) and Steven Spielberg's *Jaws* (1975). By zooming in while simultaneously pulling the camera towards or away from a subject, a perspective distortion causes the background to shrink or grow in relation.

A French High Strangeness case collected by Denys Breysse featured a similar effect. While sky watching in 1980 just before bedtime, a Vacqueyras woman felt "the celestial vault descend upon her." The sensation, resembling vertigo, was impossible to describe: either the stars descended to her, or her consciousness ascended to the stars. Messages from extrasolar entities followed, their avian features topped by "Egyptian headdresses." Before breaking communication, they claimed to have long meddled in human affairs. Her following years included amnesia, missing time, and psychic phenomena (Breysse, 1994).

Dolly zooms are effective because subjects appear divorced from their surroundings, fixed while everything around changes. This could be seen as a visual representation of dissociative states commonly reported in various encounters, from alien abductions to Near-Death Experiences (NDEs). (While many perceive important connections between the two, dissociation's role as a prerequisite for paranormal experiences, perhaps brought about by childhood trauma, falls outside of the scope of this discussion). Similar dissociative sensations are achieved through the SnorriCam, a camera rigged to an actor's chest in extreme closeup, which, as they move about, shows the subject remaining stationary while their surroundings change.

Sensations of stability while one's surroundings alter are not uncommon in numinous experiences. Following a failed attempt to contact his Visitors, Whitley Strieber – the world's most celebrated alien abductee – tumbled into bed. He awoke around 3:00 a.m., in an altered state of consciousness, an almost electric vibration coursing through his body. "Almost flying" downstairs he saw, perched on his deck, a car-sized object – "Given the strength of the deck's structure, a car would certainly have crashed through" – attended by "indifferent" women who gently nudged him inside.

"There was as yet no sense of motion at all, and I was confused when lights began flying past us," he wrote. "Until then, it had appeared to me that we were in a room with only the small slits as windows. Because of the total lack of movement, my assumption was that we were still on the deck." Strieber was informed the lights represented a city, but he suspected they came from souls, not any Earthly skyline. "A moment later a change came, sudden and silent. As in a dream, the surroundings arbitrarily transformed to address the needs of the moment," and he found himself in a suburb at the foot of the Rocky Mountains (Strieber, 1995).

As mentioned previously, this immediate change resembles a jump cut. Abrupt shifts in perspective figure commonly not only in alien abductions, but also in dreams, psychedelic trips, and NDEs. Researcher Kenneth Ring perceived such "discontinuities" strongly across different contact modalities:

> In reviewing many close-encounter and UFO-sighting cases [...] one soon notices evidence of peculiar discontinuities. These are indicated by such expressions as "the next thing I knew," or "what I remember next," [and so on]. The use of such bridging phrases is of course open to several interpretations, but one of them would be that these experiences may be *inherently discontinuous* rather than linearly unfolding events [...] the very structure of these UFO stories is itself reminiscent of other narrative forms [such as NDEs] (Ring, 1992).

Filmmakers also disorient audiences through nonlinear storytelling, jumping across timelines as in the European cut of Sergio Leone's *Once Upon a Time in America* (1984) or the Wachowski sisters' *Cloud Atlas* (2012). Alien abductions and the like typically feature temporal anomalies, perhaps reflecting the intelligences' perception: explained Betty Luca (née Andreasson) of her alien contacts: "Time to them is not like our time." Bob, her husband, reiterated this, claiming: "There's no time up there [...] nothing changes" (Fowler, 2020).

Cinematic jump cuts suggest temporal lapses without intervening content, similar to the "missing time" phenomenon reported across paranormal experiences. Jump cuts also create montages in films, an editing technique compressing the passage of time. While not disorienting by nature, montages resemble "life reviews" reported by some NDErs ("My life flashed before my eyes!"). Arguably, extraterrestrial warnings of impending cataclysms reported during many abductions – presented as montages on viewscreens, or beamed directly into the mind of the abductee – constitute Gaian life reviews in reverse, depicting the Earth's future apocalypses should humans continue their destructive ways.

Spatial awareness is essential to audiences' understanding. Poor fight geography in action films – characters' spatial relationships, how actions impact the scene between shots, for instance – can render dramatic conflicts an incoherent mess. Filmmakers can also use this knowledge to subversively undermine the layout of locations, subtly imparting a sense of uneasiness. Film critic Rob Ager compellingly argues that the Overlook Hotel's floor-plan in Stanley Kubrick's *The Shining* (1980) is physically impossible. Colorado's Stanley Hotel, which hosted on-location filming, was supplemented by sets contorted into hallways doubling back on themselves and doors to nowhere.

"The Overlook is not just a place of isolation," Ager emphasised. "It is a symbolic maze – a vast labyrinth of winding corridors, mysterious open doorways and disorientating design" (Ager, 2008). Compare this to a statement from transpersonal psychologist Jon Klimo on alien abductions:

> Often, spatial or dimensional changes were experienced. For example, once inside a craft, the interior space becomes much larger than could have been the case when experienced from the outside (Klimo, 2018, pp. 121-287).

The "Oz Factor," as coined by British researcher Jenny Randles, also manifests in extraordinary encounters. Paranormal witnesses, especially of UFOs, sometimes recall complete silence during sightings: no birdsong, no wind, no ambient noise whatsoever, almost as if witnesses are enveloped in "cocoons" where they alone experience anomalies, separated from the rest of the world around them (Randles, nd.).

This mirrors another filmmaking practice, wherein audio is completely dropped from a scene, often underscoring physical trauma or shocking revelations (perhaps another artistic representation of dissociation). Whenever a "soundtrack is abruptly silenced or interrupted [...] the immersive properties of sound are not simply undermined," Lash wrote, they "are also emphasised, because the sudden change makes strikingly evident the disappearance of that in which we were previously immersed." In other words, abruptly removing audio breaks immersion, signifying departures from one reality into another – in cinema, a traditional soundscape into silence, in paranormal experiences, our waking state into whatever High Strangeness represents.

Granted, these comparisons are sparse, incomplete, and imperfect. Such failings may evaporate, however, if investigators actively seek similar experiences when interviewing witnesses. Future analysis may reveal states of consciousness during High Strangeness experiences that resemble disorienting camerawork, editing, and sound design more often than currently appreciated.

Surrealism

In 1952, a driver spotted a flying saucer over the Peruvian desert. Approaching it, he met three naked, "mummy-like" monopods covered in "towely" skin, their faces nothing but transparent jelly with a bubble in the centre. After learning where they landed, the creatures changed their questions from English to Spanish, informing the witness they reproduced asexually – which they demonstrated. Stereotypically enough, the mystery entities asked to be "taken to his chief" and warned against atomic energy. The witness allegedly joined the beings for a joyride down the coast (Greenwell, Lorenzen & Lorenzen, 1968).

Ufologists regularly use the term "surreal" to describe High Strangeness experiences. In many ways, this is appropriate. Surrealist artists display an abiding affection for the occult, particularly post-World War II, in particular because of its potential to empower the unconscious (Noheden, 2017). Art scholar Michael Richardson even compared early surrealist filmmaker Jean Painlevé to the Patron Saint of the Unexplained himself: "[Painlevé]'s quest had certain resemblance to that of Charles Fort: he wished to reveal the gaps in our knowledge, and that these were gaps we should never be able to overcome because they were integral to our relationship with the world," Richardson noted in 2006's *Surrealism and Cinema*. "To believe that we are able to explain the world is nothing but a sign of human arrogance (Richardson, 2006).

Circuitously, surrealism doubled back to influence Fortean perspectives. French authors Louis Pauwels and Jacques Bergier, for example, who coined the term "fantastic realism" in 1960s *Le Matin des Magiciens*, described a newfound mystical perspective emerging from physics and science. The authors not only drew inspiration from UFO enthusiast Aimé Michel, but also from the ideas of the surrealists and Charles Fort. Writes Rice University professor Jeffrey Kripal:

> [...] the phrase itself, fantastic realism, was indebted to both [surrealism founder] André Breton, whom Pauwels describes as "a very great friend," and the general methods of Charles Fort, whom the authors openly acknowledge as "one of our most cherished idols," who "before the first manifestations of Dadaism and Surrealism [...] introduced into science what Tzara, Breton and their disciples were going to introduce into art and literature." Indeed, it was at Pauwels's instigation that [Fort's] *The Book of the Damned* first appeared in France, in 1955 (Kripal, 2010).

However, "surreal" does not simply equate with "bizarre," as surrealist imagery is specifically deployed to particular artistic ends. It is not simply bizarre for bizarre's sake. In Breton's words, surrealism seeks to "resolve the previously contradictory conditions of dream and reality into an absolute super-reality," ergo "surreality" (Chilver, 2009). Surrealism is preoccupied with visually (and, with cinema, also aurally) activating the unconscious mind, ripping constructs like language free from their artificial moorings.

Examples like the Peruvian case above, however, may only use surrealist *imagery*, while not being *fully surrealist*. Encounters affecting witnesses' subsequent understanding of reality, recall Bishop's speculation about the nature of the UFO experience, and represent better candidates for authentically surreal narratives. (Unfortunately, there exists little follow-up on the aforementioned example; investigations of other paranormal experiences, however, suggest profound changes occur regularly among witnesses).

Crossovers between surrealism and High Strangeness further justify examining the latter from a cinematic standpoint, as surrealists held the medium in great esteem as a quintessential means of capturing the movement's goals, "to disclose what lies dormant within the collective consciousness, making manifest what is latent without destroying the mystery of its latency" (Richardson, 2006). In addition to visionary films from artists like Luis Buñuel and Salvador Dalí, surrealists would also go on to embrace the opportunities afforded by Hollywood's genre filmmaking, particularly comedy and horror – High Strangeness is almost definitionally a mixture of absurdist humour and existential terror (Ibid.).

Though surrealism can be, as Richardson puts it, many things but not *anything* (Ibid.), art scholar Jackie Craven breaks its characteristics into several categories reading like a High Strangeness laundry list: "dream-like scenes, symbolic images" and "unexpected, illogical juxtapositions"; "bizarre assemblages of ordinary objects," seen in poltergeist cases; "games and techniques to create random effects," resembling magical practices like sigils; "personal iconography," speaking to the tailor-made intimacy of NDEs, abductions, etc.; "distorted figures and biomorphic shapes" akin to all manner of aliens, spirits, and crypto-creatures; and "uninhibited sexuality and taboo subjects," embedded across time from *incubi* and *succubi* narratives through to the modern alien abduction mythos (Craven, 2019).

Surrealists' interest in "automatism and a spirit of spontaneity," as Craven puts it (Ibid.), parallels Spiritualist traditions like automatic writing, channeling, psychic downloads, and so on; indeed, some surrealists like Benjamin Péret dabbled in automatic writing (Noheden, 2017), and others adopted "automatic filmmaking" as it were – their films emerging from impulse or from esoterically higher powers (Richardson, 2006).

Surrealism also favours "visual puns," rife in High Strangeness (Craven, 2019). For instance, a woman driving through a Navajo reservation saw two orbs of light following her car, hovering alongside before overtaking her and disappearing. Upon returning home, the witness found a large rabbit – over three feet tall – blocking her garage door. It reportedly sported *plaid fur*, a design described as incongruous if not wholly unnatural. She ran into the house and reported her entire experience to the Mutual UFO Network, whose investigators displayed interest solely in the UFOs (Gulyas, 2018). The incident occurred near Leupp, Arizona – Greg Bishop noted the phonetic similarity to *lepus*, Latin for "hare" (Bishop, 2021, personal communication).

Finally, Craven notes surrealism's affinity for "primitive or child-like designs." While many describe reptilians, insectoids, Space Brothers, and ubiquitous Greys, no shortage of alien abductees report clowns, pirates, cartoon characters, and manifold other absurd kidnappers. Equally pernicious are reports of beings appearing as drawings come-to-life, or stick figures.

Surrealism seeks to "reestablish the 'enchanted' dimensions at the core of human existence – poetry, passion, mad love, imagination, magic, myth, the marvellous, dreams, revolt, utopian ideals – which have been eradicated by this civilisation and its values," Michael Löwy (2009) wrote. Surrealists are not fantasists; they do not "create imagined worlds," as Richardson puts it, but instead focus on "transforming *this* world" (Richardson, 2006). Surrealists, in short, seek to re-enchant our waking lives by comparing their overlooked incongruities and arbitrary nature to dream logic and the unconscious.

We have our first inkling of one possible meaning underlying High Strangeness. If comparable to surrealism, High Strangeness may seek to similarly re-enchant the mundane.

Double Mumbo Jumbo

In his 2005 screenwriting book *Save the Cat!*, Blake Snyder introduced the term "Double Mumbo Jumbo" (DMJ) to describe the detrimental effects multiple fantastic plot points exert on an audience's capacity to suspend disbelief: "For some reason, audiences will only accept one piece of magic per movie," he asserted. "You cannot see aliens from outer space land in a UFO and then be bitten by a Vampire and now be both aliens and undead" (Snyder, 2005). Despite inventing the term, Snyder more poorly explains DMJ than screenwriter Erik Bork. (Snyder's criticism of DMJ in M. Night Shyamalan's 2002 movie *Signs* raises the hackles of any unorthodox Ufologist – "I'd say proof of an alien intelligence outside our solar system sorta trumps all discussion about faith in God, don't you think?") On his blog, Bork wrote:

> You're allowed one big leap of faith on the part of the audience. Everything else must seem like completely believable human behaviour [...] once you've got [audiences] accepting your outrageous premise, you don't want to "test" them like that again. They will leave you, if you don't "keep it real." Or if they don't understand what is going on. Audiences enjoy watching outrageous situations, up to a point (Bork, 2016).

Even those lacking a screenwriting pedigree understand this rule. Films about the supernatural are criticised if they fail to establish and follow "rules" – a spirit possessing a person cannot, for example, also possess a toaster. Screenwriters even go out of their way to disingenuously simplify the subject matter their scripts are based upon – for instance, the introductory speech of J.K. Simmons's Ufologist in the 2013 alien abduction film *Dark Skies* entirely dismisses the phenomenon's complexity:

> There are three generally-accepted kinds of aliens: the Greys, insectoids, and the reptilians – but nine-times-out-of-ten what people report seeing are the Greys. In fact I'm dubious about the other two altogether, especially the reptilians. I don't think those accounts are credible.

Granted, mixing fantastical elements – like Nazis riding dinosaurs on the moon – has grown more palatable in recent films, but audiences invariably consume such pulp frivolities ironically. Most such affairs are irreverent comedy-horror pictures.

DMJ primarily remains a cinematic pitfall. *Seeing* the fantastic on film is quite different to *reading* it. Readers' imaginations excel at reconciling literary absurdity, trusting either the narrator's omniscience or the character's perspective. We unquestionably accept Gregor Samsa's transformation into a gigantic insect when reading Kafka's *The Metamorphosis*, but beholding a human cockroach on celluloid is an altogether different experience. Absurd visuals invite inadvertent laughter, easily shattering disbelief; as Harrison Ford ribbed George Lucas on the set of *Star Wars*, "You can type this shit, but you sure can't say it!" (O'Connell, 2017).

Yet High Strangeness *embraces* DMJ. Bigfoot appear in conjunction with – sometimes even inside – UFOs. Abductees meet Jesus aboard spaceships. NDEs include encounters with aliens or interstellar travel, and the dead haunt UFO witnesses' homes. The broader disciplines of cryptozoology, Ufology, and, to a lesser degree, parapsychology mostly toss aside such reports. The net effect is identical to DMJ: doubt and dismissal.

A fine example of High Strangeness DMJ (or perhaps even Triple Mumbo Jumbo!) is an October 25th, 1973 case from the files of researcher Stan Gordon. To quickly summarise the complex events, fifteen people watched a red, barn-sized UFO fly above Fayette County, Pennsylvania before it alit on a farm. George Kowalczyk and his sons investigated, encountering – and firing upon, to no effect – two apparent bigfoot entities with glowing green eyes. The creatures shuffled into the forest as the UFO vanished. Kowalczyk contacted Gordon and they met that evening. During their interrogation, Kowalczyk suffered a fit and, upon recovery, described a vision of a robed, scythe-wielding figure warning of the world's end. After that night, Kowalczyk experienced psi phenomena, including low-level precognition and visitations from the dead. A pair of men in military garb – akin to Men-in-Black – eventually visited his home and shared photographs of bigfoot and UFOs before hypnotising Kowalczyk, assuring him they would be in touch. They never contacted him again (Cutchin & Renner, 2020).

If screenwriters risk disbelief with DMJ, what does that say about its appearance in High Strangeness? It seems reasonable to assume similar sentiments arise in witnesses faced with incongruous apparitions. In short, the orchestrating force behind paranormal experiences may *deliberately seek* to engender disbelief. This confirms the suspicions of parapsychologist George P. Hansen, who argued in *The Trickster and the Paranormal* that supernatural phenomena naturally self-negate, allowing them to reside in a realm of disrepute and unbelievability to all but direct witnesses (Hansen, 2001).

Metalepses

Artistic metalepsis represents a subject's shift from one narrative level to another. These may feature as "stories within stories," or constitute "breaking the fourth wall," where characters acknowledge the presence of the viewing audience.

Metalepsis commonly features in literature, yet rarely interrupts the fictional world's logic. Lash provides a useful example, where a Balzac narrator uses an in-novel time lapse to indulge a digression: *"while* the venerable churchman climbs the ramps of Angoulême, it won't be useless to explain, etc." More disruptive are instances where fictional characters interact with storytelling devices – consider a cartoon character climbing a question mark above their head – or when "in-universe" fantasies, dreams, and stories bleed into the real world of the book or film, as in *The NeverEnding Story* (1984) or *Adaptation* (2002).

A further metaleptic degree facilitates jumps from the fictional realm into our world, more common in cinema. In the 1937 cartoon *Daffy Duck & Egghead*, "Egghead implores an audience member to sit down," shooting him when he refuses" (Lash, 2020). By establishing audience interaction, metalepsis can push beyond simply breaking the fourth wall. Metalepsis even allows transmission of our reality into fiction. A good example from contemporary literature is horror author Stephen King's *The Dark Tower* series, which not only includes references to his unrelated novels, but features King *himself* as a character in the eponymous final entry.

High Strangeness, however, reifies metalepsis on a *literal* level. Whitley Strieber's work can be distinctly broken into pre and post-*Communion* periods, the former exclusively fictional, the latter a mix of non-fiction and fiction largely focused on exploring humankind's relationship with the Visitors first chronicled in 1987. Yet even Strieber's pre-*Communion* output foreshadows his UFO revelation, perhaps unconsciously expressing long-forgotten contact since childhood.

"People can follow [your conversation with the phenomena] even pre-*Communion*," paranormal scholar David Metcalfe observed in a 2021 interview with Strieber. "They can follow that conversation that's been happening as this presence has interacted with you through fiction, through *Wolfen* and *The Hunger*, and the books prior to *Communion* [...] and then after that, that quest for trying to figure out questions" (Strieber, 2021).

Strieber agreed that the werewolves of *Wolfen* prefigured his Grey Visitors, the vampire in *The Hunger*, the beautiful "blond" aliens. "As it seems the phenomenon is kind of circling me and getting closer and closer to my conscious awareness, I then write a book about the dangers of nuclear war, which turns out to be a huge issue in the phenomenon," he reflected, "Then a book about the environment, which is another other huge issue in this thing." Strieber's final pre-*Communion* work, *Cat Magic*, was "about Wicca and the faerie-faith."

In short, Strieber wrote about "aliens" long before consciously realising his apparent ongoing relationship with them. Though his detractors cite this as evidence of a fantasy-prone mind, perhaps "the phenomenon" utilised a metaleptic process to subsume Strieber within its narrative. With *Communion*, he became a character in his own work, the grand paranormal myth itself. This happens time-and-again to authors of paranormal non-fiction: *you start looking at the phenomena, and the phenomena look back*. High Strangeness regularly drags researchers into the paranormal as their interest grows, exemplified in the career of Fortean investigator John Keel. Synchronicities multiply, peculiar telephone calls interrupt sleep, sightings of UFOs and anomalies intrude unbidden.

Metalepsis also manifests in High Strangeness as autoscopy, seeing oneself from a third-person perspective. This is the defining aspect of doppelgänger sightings, NDEs, out-of-body-experiences (OBEs), and a great many alien abduction experiences, which often contain OBE components. In addition to some abductions unfolding in disembodied astral states, some experiencers also report seeing themselves from the aliens' point-of-view (Mack, 1999). This may in turn speak to themes of dissociation.

Filmmakers use characters' autoscopy to disorient audiences both explicitly and through "projection sequences." "A character is shown looking towards something; a reverse shot indicates that what they are looking at is themselves, at another point in space and time; finally, another shot shows that one of the two versions of the character has disappeared," Lash wrote, citing Kubrick's *2001: A Space Odyssey* (1968) and David Lynch's *INLAND EMPIRE* (2006), the latter of which involves childhood trauma.

Metaleptic autoscopy also occurs inadvertently when subjects see themselves onscreen – in a disturbingly dramatic 1910 example, Germany and Austria's Kaisers were watching footage of themselves when the film ripped. Remarked audience member Berthold Viertel: "At that very moment, shivers went down my spine [...] Did that tear also go through the real people? Horrified, I asked myself, who here is the real one?" (Lash, 2020).

Sit Back, Relax, and Enjoy the Show

If cinematic perspectives on High Strangeness are valid, why would a meta-positioned intelligence adopt such techniques? It may seek to disorient; to incorporate us within a greater surreality; to engender disbelief; or invite us towards it via metalepsis. These aims are not mutually exclusive. By undermining distinctions between reality and fiction, the objective and subjective, High Strangeness strikes a balance between hierarchies of significance.

Perhaps the best approach we can adopt is to allow High Strangeness to unfold on a level other than our everyday, conscious, waking thought. We close with observations from cinema theorist Vivian Sobchack, who wrote that initial viewings of disorienting films "compelled our attention to their every frame and gesture, and yet, even after multiple viewings [...] also continued to refuse us." She continues:

How does one resolve the paradox of an experience that was both immersive and alienating? [...] Instead of cognitive, reflective, and after-the-fact sense-making, they make sense – if we let them – in the phenomenological 'now' of seeing, hearing, and touching (if always also at a distance) (Sobchack, 2014).

AN INTRODUCTION TO THE EGREGORIAL

ANTHONY PEAKE

Seven years ago I was involved in research for a book I was writing on the British playwright and author J.B. Priestley. I was advised by Priestley's son, Tom, that it would be useful if I made contact with the hugely influential theatre producer, Braham Murray. Murray had worked with J.B. Priestley in the 1970s and had produced a number of his plays. Imagine my surprise to discover that, on contacting him, Murray had read a number of my books. Not only that, but as he was subsequently to explain to me, my writings had helped him put into focus a curious experience he had way back in 1969, something that completely changed his understanding of the true nature of perceptual reality.

Braham explained that one day in December of that year he had a phone call from one of his theatre associates, Casper Wrede, a Finnish baron who had worked with Murray in setting up the Royal Exchange Theatre in Manchester. Wrede told him that the next day, his mentor, the Norwegian aristocrat Armund Hohningstadt, was flying into London from Oslo, and he asked if Braham could kindly pick him up from the airport. Although Braham had never met this mysterious person, he knew a great deal about him by reputation. Hohningstadt was known to have a formidable intellect and a keen interest in folklore and the occult. After a chance introduction to Jung's writings that afternoon, Murray felt this imminent meeting was portentous!

Over the next few days, Hohningstadt put Braham Murray through an intellectual journey. They discussed all manner of subjects, but mostly revolving around myths and legends. Then one evening Braham asked Hohningstadt about the symbolism of *Beauty and the Beast* and whether the story could be traced back to the ancient Greek myth of Cupid and Psyche. They then discussed the archetype of the beast in man. They agreed that this was rampant during the Nazi period in Germany and that the German people had collectively created a monster, whose character was manifest in the atrocities of the Third Reich. Braham then asked Hohningstadt, "What was the nature of this mind-created beast?"

When he told me what happened next, Braham sent a shiver up my spine. This is how he tells the story in his autobiography, *The Worst It Can Be Is A Disaster*:

> We were sitting at a table which was against the wall of the kitchen. He was at one end, I was in the middle facing him, the chair at the end was empty. His reply to my question was, "It's over there." The empty chair was now occupied by a creature which was constantly metamorphosing between an ancient woman with Medusa-like snakes for hair and a wizened old man. The other world was in my kitchen, as real as anybody I had ever met (Murray, 2007, pp. 101-02).

Braham then explained to me that what he had seen that evening was real, but that it had also been created out of thin air by Hohningstadt. He added that from that moment his understanding of what was real and what was not had been totally shattered.

The term that Hohningstadt used to describe this entity, and, indeed the collectively created "beast" that was Naziism, was an "egregore," or an egregorial manifestation.

This story really intrigued me. What was taking place that evening half a century ago? Was it a form of hypnotism whereby Wrede visualised the creature in his mind and then projected it into Murray's mind by some form of telepathy? If so then Murray himself would have had to subsequently project Wrede's image into his external visual field. The world-model of modern science has no mechanism that allows telepathy to exist. So any mind-to-mind manipulation – whereby an image is sent from one mind to another – must be considered impossible.

So is it possible that the human mind can, in some yet unknown way, create a thought-form that can subsequently become an independent, self-motivated intelligence? My investigations suggest that yes, this may be the case.

It is important at this point to define what is meant by the term "egregorial." It is the adjective of the noun "egregore," which has its roots in the Greek word *égrégoros,* meaning "wakeful" or "watcher." It first appeared in its Greek form in the non-canonical Biblical Book of Enoch. One particular section of this text, known as the Book of the Watchers, is thought to have been written around 3,000 BCE. Although originally written in Hebrew or Aramaic the only full text now available is written in an ancient Ethiopian/Somalian language known as Ge'ez. According to the Book of Enoch, these "watchers" were non-human entities that entered this world from the sky, or from underground. I would like to suggest in this chapter that these beings use human consciousness to manifest themselves in our reality. Indeed, central to the "Enochian" magic used by historical magicians such as Dr John Dee (1527-1608), Edward Kelley (1555-1597) and Aleister Crowley (1875-1947) – as well as in some of ritual magic's modern incarnations, such as Chaos Magick – is the belief that the human mind, using various ceremonies and incantations, can call forth such egregorial entities into our universe.

This is not an idea restricted to Western magical beliefs. For example, in Tibet there is a long tradition regarding the existence of beings popularly known today as *tulpas.* The concept of the tulpa was brought to the Western world by Alexandra David-Néel (1868-1969), a fascinating French-Belgian woman who travelled extensively in India, Nepal, Bhutan, China and Japan between 1910 and 1924. In a fascinating life, she converted to Buddhism at the age of 21. In 1895 she was lead singer (*première cantatrice*) at the Hanoi Opera House in French Indochina. In 1904 she married a French-born engineer, Philip Néel, who in 1910 agreed to her taking a "long voyage" of personal discovery. This odysscy lasted 14 years, including a period in the then forbidden kingdom of Tibet.

In her book *Magic and Mystery in Tibet,* David-Néel describes how she embarked on trying to create her own tulpa, in the guise of a kind, rotund medieval monk. Over a period of months, she imagined this character, giving it a history, a personality and motivations. It initially appeared in her mind's eye and then in her peripheral vision as an element of the world outside her immediate control. At first, there was nothing problematic about this:

> I shut myself in tsams [seclusion] and proceeded to perform the prescribed concentration of thought and other rites. After a few months the phantom monk was formed. He became a kind of guest, living in my apartment. I then broke my seclusion and started for a tour, with my servants and tents. The monk included himself in the party. Though I lived in the open, riding on horseback for miles each day, the illusion persisted. It was not necessary for me to think of him to make him appear. The phantom performed various actions of the kind that are natural to travellers and that I had not commanded. For instance, he walked, stopped, looked around him. The illusion was mostly visual, but sometimes I felt as if a robe was lightly rubbing against me, and once a hand seemed to touch my shoulder (David-Neel, 2007).

But then things began to change. The figure became leaner and more malevolent. It also began to show a greater degree of independence from her. She realised that she had created something dangerous. It took her more than six months to reabsorb the entity back into her imagination.

Of course, the experiences of David-Néel took place many years ago and in a distant land. We now inhabit a modern, globalised world, where such things simply cannot happen. Or can they? Well, Braham Murray's experience in 1969 suggests otherwise.

So what is going on here?

The Metachoric Hypothesis

If you discuss such experiences with somebody deeply embedded in the modern scientific worldview known as materialist-reductionism, they will quickly dismiss such experiences as simply being hallucinations. But there lies the problem; hallucinations are not "simple." They are one of the greatest mysteries of cognitive science and their existence (if they can be said to exist at all), presents profound problems for those who argue that the physical universe is all there is.

The conventional belief regarding hallucinations is that they are very different to "normal" perceptions. Normal perceptions present to consciousness an image of external reality that is an absolute and accurate depiction of what is "out there." Hallucinations on the other hand are totally brain generated. According to the *Oxford Companion to the Mind*, a hallucination is defined as being a "sensory perception in the absence of external stimuli" (Gregory, 1998, p. 299). This idea that hallucinations and normal perception are totally different perceptual experiences is known as the *Dual Process Model*.

But there is a growing opinion in certain scientific fields that this Dual Process Model is in error. Psychologists Celia Green and Charles McCreery, for example, argue that it is important to realise that although the hallucination itself is an unreal image created by the brain it is nonetheless seen as an object in consensual space. This is a very important point. For example, you will recall how Braham Murray stated that he could see a Medusa-like creature sitting on a chair in front of him and that the image was extremely vivid and real. Braham insisted to me that the creature looked totally solid. As such he could not see the parts of the chair that were obscured by the hallucinatory entity. So, in order for this to be perceived, there must be two types of hallucination being created by the brain; one of addition (the entity) and one of subtraction (the loss of visual stimulus from the chair). The latter is technically known as a *negative hallucination,* a failure to perceive something that exists in consensual space. However, it is clear from Braham's description that the medusa-creature was animated and moving around. As such the area of consensual space negated by the hallucinatory process needed to change to reflect the differing areas occluded by the entity's movements. Indeed, there had to be a one-to-one relationship between the areas excluded and the hallucinated movements of the entity. This mystery happens with all hallucinations involving solid objects in consensual space.

In 1975 Green and McCreery proposed a solution to this problem. The image of consensual reality that is presented to consciousness is also a brain-generated hallucination in the same way that a regular hallucination is. All of what is perceived through our senses is technically a hallucination. As such Green and McCreery proposed that all perceptions are hallucinations and consequently one sort of hallucination can overlap with another. They called the hallucinatory spectrum the *Metachoric Model of Hallucinations* (Green & McCreery, 1975).

They argued that the brain can, based upon the percepts processed from data gleaned from consensual reality, create a facsimile environment identical to that of consensual reality. It is this facsimile that a person enters when they lucid dream or have an out-of-body experience. They suggest evidence for this with regards to apparitions seen on awaking, usually at night. This phenomenon is regularly reported. It usually involves the subject waking up and noticing a spectral form in the bedroom. This is usually accompanied by a total paralysis of the body.

Modern neurology and psychology have an explanation for these experiences. The process by which a dream overlaps with what seems like consensual reality is known as REM Intrusion. This is where the person is actually asleep and dreaming but a part of the brain is still awake and processing the sights and sounds of the external world. Any dream-images are then projected into the external world and seem to be part of that world. In this way, a dream can seem to be "real." These images are usually accompanied by a bodily paralysis, not surprisingly known as "sleep paralysis" for obvious reasons. When we sleep the body protects itself from dream-induced bodily damage by stopping the dreamer from acting out any physical actions they may wish to perform in the dream state. For example, hitting out at a dream-attacker. If they mirrored this hitting out by moving their arms they may damage themselves in the physical world, or injure somebody in the bed with them. This paralysis is achieved by a release of the neurotransmitter acetylcholine, which suppresses muscle tone. By paralysing the body in this way the brain stops such motive actions from being carried out. However if one happens to become semi-conscious in such a state the sensation of paralysis can be very frightening.

Green and McCreery argue that such "visitations" provide evidence for their Metachoric model. People regularly report that during some REM Intrusion states, and regularly in general apparition encounters, the spectral figures give off a form of light. This light illuminates the environment around the figure. Now if the figure is a brain-projection into a genuine consensual environment how can its "light" illuminate objects in the real world. Indeed, in some cases, the person describes how the whole bedroom was lit up by the spectral light. This is impossible in the Dual Process Model, but is entirely feasible in the context of the Metachoric model. If all the scene, background environment and spectre are part of the same "hallucination" then such illumination is perfectly possible.

So, if all our perceptions are "brain generated" then beings encountered in hallucinatory states, be they created "naturally" through dreams or "artificially" through psychedelics, such as LSD and Dimethyltryptamine – substances that are sometimes also referred to as entheogens for their capacity to induce apparent experiences of the divine – have exactly the same level of ontological reality as any other beings encountered in waking life, and we rarely doubt the independent existence of these entities. Could it be that Braham Murray's "medusa" and Alexandra David-Néel's monk had, and possibly continue to have, independence of their respective "creators"?

The Philip Experiment

In 1972 one of the most fascinating parapsychological experiments ever conducted took place. The idea was to create a mind-manifested entity that owed its existence to nothing other than the human imagination. Members of the Toronto Society for Psychical Research, under the leadership of Iris Owen (1916-2009), had long been intrigued by how ouija sessions work. They wondered if in some way the participants were unconsciously creating their own self-generated narratives together as the glass moves from letter to letter. To test this possibility, they decided to agree collectively on the life story of a totally fictional historical character and to try to make contact with this figment of the imagination (Owen & Sparrow, 1976).

Owen's group called the entity Philip Aylesford. They gave Philip a whole biography. He was a rich, powerful man who lived in Diddington Manor in England. He had committed suicide in 1654 after an affair with a gipsy girl. Initially, the group was not successful in making contact with this fictitious figure. For more than a year the group meditated on him in vain. Then they decided on a different approach. Instead of serious meditation in atmospheric lighting, they sat around the table in bright light in a deliberately frivolous mood. This, curiously, seemed to work. Much to the group's surprise, the table began to vibrate. Then there was a loud rap. One of the group asked if this was Philip, and a single loud rap gave them an answer. Contact had been made. In the time-tested code of one rap for yes and two raps for no, a rudimentary form of communication was facilitated. Things then took a turn toward the seriously strange. At one point, the table began to move when no one was touching it. It is important to stress that the group were not spiritualists, but objectively minded researchers. Indeed, when the table first moved, they believed that one or more of their number was playing around. In a TV interview the group leader, Iris Owen, stated afterwards that so great was the suspicion of cheating that the group had watched each other "like hawks."

Owen explained that repetitive singing seemed to facilitate the effects. In the studio the group was able to recreate the rappings, even though it was clear no one was directly responsible for making these noises.

The experiment, devised by Iris Owen's husband, mathematician A.R.G. Owen (1919-2003), Director of the Toronto Society for Psychical Research, was overseen by psychologist Dr Joel Whitton. On TV Whitton argued that the group had attained a "child-like creativity," facilitated by playfulness, repetitive singing and humour. The orthodox adult mindset, the idea that "this cannot be done," had been set aside. For me this is of great significance.

Of course, this gesture toward an explanation really explains nothing. How can a collective mindset – embodying an egregorial – create physical effects in the external world, such as rappings and table-turning? In the TV programme, Whitton's expert opinion is conveyed with an air of authority that lends him scientific credibility. However, what exactly does he mean when he suggests that the participants regressed into a childlike state as a form of "subconscious defence mechanism"? A defence mechanism against what? They were not under any form of psychological attack. In fact, they were, by their own admission, feeling very relaxed, telling jokes, singing songs and feeling quite happy.

The "table-turning" is particularly intriguing. When the team initially failed to manifest anything of interest, British parapsychologist Kenneth J. Batcheldor (1921-1988) suggested that they try to reproduce the "table-turning" techniques of nineteenth-century spiritualists. He felt this approach might overcome any residual scepticism in the team, something he suspected was hindering the development of the "entity." In a later interview Joel Whitton explained that in order to see if any of the group was actually pushing or pulling the table in some way, the organisers placed paper "doilies" under the hands of the participants. If they then attempted to push the table, the doilies would simply slide across the surface. This proved that the table movements "were not caused by anybody pushing it." It was also clear from videotapes taken at the time that the group were not using their knees to raise the table. In any case, why would they? They were objective experimenters, not mediums or other occult practitioners trying to prove that they had psychic skills or an ability to communicate with the deceased.

But the question then must be asked: if there was no physical involvement of the participants in the movement of the table (either conscious or subconscious), then how could the group be in any way responsible for the table tipping? (It responded in time when the group sang songs together, for instance).

The whole concept of mind-created entities is far more complex than any simple explanation involving a materialist-reductionist dismissal or a spiritualist's blind belief. Philip seems actually to have come to life – or life-after-death – in a way that our rational minds cannot fully comprehend.

A paper published in April 2019 suggested that the actual location of this kind of super-creative ability may be in a part of the brain known as the "dorsomedial default network." This consists of a group of interconnected brain regions, including the medial prefrontal cortex, the posterior cingulate cortex, the angular gyrus and the hippocampus. This area of the brain is particularly powerful when it comes to visualisation. The team, led by Meghan Meyer, Assistant Professor of Psychological and Brain Science at Dartmouth College, New Hampshire, set out to discover whether creative people have stronger "imagination muscles" than non-creative people.

To see these imagination muscles in action, they asked 27 creative types and 26 control participants to go through simulation tasks while lying in a functional magnetic resonance imaging (fMRI) scanner. Brain activity of the creative adepts and controls was similar when imagining future events over the next 24 hours; however, to the researchers' surprise, the creative group alone engaged the dorsomedial default network when imagining events further into the future. The dorsomedial default network was not active at all among the control group; and yet, even at rest, this area of the brain was active for the creative group.

I cannot help wondering if it is this creative facility that was accessed by the Toronto team, and which assisted in the creation of Philip.[59]

A Type of Group-Think

It seems that human consciousness, specifically when acting collectively, as a group-consciousness, can create something both greater than, and external to, the individuals involved. There is evidence that the entity Philip "created" by the Toronto group showed knowledge and skills beyond those available to the group members, either individually or collectively. In relation to this idea, parapsychologist D. Scott Rogo has suggested that groups can bring into existence something greater than their individual members:

> There is another psychological factor which comes into play during group-PK practices [...] group-PK effects are often directed by a collective mind created by the sitters. By joining forces, several people may actually form some sort of semiautonomous will or mind that directs the PK. Now this "entity" is not "owned" by or dependent upon

---

[59] For more on the Philip Experiment see Susan Demeter's chapter in this volume.

any single group member. It is, on the contrary, semi-independent of all of them. A PK group, therefore, can overcome ownership inhibition because the PK is really being architectured by an ego-alien personality (Rogo, 1978, p. 197).

What Rogo means by PK is a phenomenon known as "psychokinesis." This is an ability that certain people allegedly exhibit whereby they can move objects or influence physical systems without direct contact. Rogo, who built a reputation on evaluating the claims of PK, until his death in 1990, was convinced that such an ability was innate in all human beings. In the passage quoted above, he argues for a form of "collective-PK" in which a group of like-minded individuals can focus their intention to create an alien and non-human intelligence that has a form of independence from its creators. However, this independence comes at a cost: in order to continue to exist, the entity needs sustenance in the same way a living animal needs food and water to stay alive. For such beings, sustenance comes from the energy generated by powerful human emotions such as fear, hate and love.

One of the most intriguing applications of this hypothesis is presented by American parapsychology researcher Paul Eno. In his book *Turning Home: God, Ghosts and Human Destiny*, former Roman Catholic priest Eno argues that many of the "entities" encountered during altered states of consciousness, hauntings and associated experiences are actually psychic vampires that feed on strong emotions (Eno, 2006).

Eno's argument is a particularly elegant one, and worth serious consideration. He observes that the oldest tales of vampires found in various cultural and folk traditions from around the world describe not blood-suckers but ghosts who suck the life out of the living. He then goes on to argue that these entities may masquerade as demons or the ghosts of those once alive, but this is not their true identity. They have the ability to manipulate the perceptions of human beings to appear in whatever guise is acceptable to a particular culture or set of circumstances. This is similar to my own concept of an egregore as a created entity that seems to exist in the three-dimensional space surrounding us, but is, in fact, an elemental creation of the mind – though one with true existence, a reality that is more than illusory.

Eno argues that many of these egregores are parasites that feed on life energy, generated by extreme human emotions, such as fear or hate. These parasites, he believes, occur in a number of different species and all have subtly different motivations. What they have in common is the need to generate emotions in their human prey to provide them with sustenance. To differentiate Eno's entities I will, from now on, use the term Parasite with a capital initial, as he does.

Eno points out that, although human beings are carbon-based life forms, his experiences with these parasitic entities (and he has had many of them) suggest that their existence may be based on plasma. He writes:

> Most Parasites even look like plasma in one form or another, both in photographs and on the rare occasions I see them with the naked eye. Some species appear smoky, either light or dark. Others look very bright, almost like bolts of lightning. Still other kinds appear as shadowy figures, some nearly solid. Some can be quite disconcertingly solid, though this is rare (Eno, 2006, p. 107).

Eno observes that when a Parasite manages to take over the thought processes of a large number of people, it can generate huge amounts of "food" for the entity. He suggests that this may be what takes place when nations are taken over by extremist political philosophies such as National Socialism. The amount of terror and fear that such regimes can generate is incalculable.

This is all well and good, but where is the science to support such an idea. We have touched upon some of the possible neurological elements, but now we need to move to the physics.

The Physics

In my books – specifically *The Hidden Universe* (2019) and *Opening the Doors of Perception* (2016) – I have proposed that the universe consists of two "realities." Although my scientific explanation of these "realities" is unique it must be stated that ancient traditions have had very similar models. Indeed, these models are suggestive that the actual science I am about to propose has been known for millennia, but over the centuries this understanding has been lost, maintained only within the coded myths of religious models. I will therefore use the ancient terminology and explain how these models can be reflected in our modern understanding of the nature of matter and fields.

I call the wider universe (that is the one that contains everything, including the universe of "matter" that we perceive with our ordinary senses – otherwise known as "consensual reality" – *The Pleroma*. This is a word I have used in a number of my books. Although it is usually associated with the Gnostics, its antecedents go right back to the pre-Socratics. The word is from ancient Greek πλήρωμα and means "fullness." I feel this is the perfect term because it is that which contains everything else. It also suggests that although it may seem empty, the vacuum of space is actually a seething sea of virtual particles coming in and out of existence. These particles enter our consensual reality. The linguistic/semantic background is of huge significance here. Pleroma has as its root in the Greek verb *pleroun*, which literally means "to fill up an empty thing." Conversely, the restricted reality that is presented to us via our senses is what I refer to using another Gnostic term, the *Kenoma*. This is the lower world of phenomena, the word coming from the Greek for "emptiness," κένωμα.

It was not just the ancient Greeks that had such a model. In the Kabbalah, it is described how God created the Jewish equivalent of The Pleroma, the *tzimtzum*. In Hebrew this is םוצמצ *ṣimṣūm* which translates as "contraction" or, even more relevant to my model, "condensation" in that the tzimtzum was condensed by God out of something known as the *Ohr Ein Sof* (the "infinite light"). The idea that space was "condensed" out of something else is intriguing. As we shall discover later, central to my model will be the role of plasma as an element of the Pleroma that impinges into our reality.

So, if the Pleroma/Tzimtzum is a process that is continually filling something, what is that "something" that is, by implication, empty? This is the Kenoma, the void that is William Blake's "Mind Forg'd Manacles" and Philip K. Dick's "Black-Iron Prison." It is the empty illusion contained in the shadows flickering on the cave wall in Plato's allegory. In my forthcoming book, *Cheating The Ferryman* (2022), I will suggest that the Kenoma is actually a simulation, or, more accurately, an "instantiation." According to Indian-American researcher Jay Alfred, the void that we perceive as empty space is, in fact, a literal "pleroma" in that it is a *plenum*, something that is completely full. He calls this substance "dark plasma" and suggests that this substance is the source of consciousness.

It is important to understand exactly what plasma is. It is created when a gas is super-heated, which literally tears the electrons from their orbits (shells) around the atom. This creates a free-floating swarm of electrons. The gas then becomes ionised. All electrons are negatively charged. When an atom loses or gains one or more electrons it has a net electric charge and becomes an ion. This is because in its normal state an atom will be neutrally charged because of the balance between the protons (+) and the electrons (-). Of course, in the nucleus the neutron has no charge. If the ion is positively charged it is called a cation ("cata" alongside plus "ion") and if it is negatively charged it is an anion (from "ana" and "ion"). As an example, a completely ionised hydrogen plasma will consist solely of electrons and protons (which are, in effect, hydrogen nuclei). This makes this the simplest aggregation of matter known. It is also important to note that with the exception of solid-state plasmas, such as those within metallic crystals, plasmas do not usually occur naturally on the surface of the Earth.

In 2003 minimal plasma cell systems with life-like qualities were produced by researchers Lozneanu and Sanduloviciu. From this discovery, Alfred proposes that if such cell systems evolved in the early Dark Earth (Pleroma) then they would have evolved in a similar way to how carbon-based life forms evolved on the Visible Earth (Kenoma). As such, they will have evolved intelligent entities with their own technologies, including communication technologies. He argues that this is evidenced by the plasma-like behaviours of UFOs. I would argue that this is too restrictive and that this model can also be used to explain so much more. For example, communications involving mediumship, EVP, and the creation of "egregores."

Alfred is preoccupied with the notion that UFOs are living dark-plasma entities. I would also like to take a much broader sweep on this and suggest that all "egregores" are created out of dark plasma, and that the act of observation, under certain neurological circumstances, can collapse the wave function of these "thought-forms." He mentions that plasma bodies have a "plasma frequency" and when dark matter interacts with ordinary matter electrons can be displaced creating electricity facilitating the emission of photons. This, in turn, creates light of different colours, as well as other forms of electromagnetic radiation, including heat. Of great significance here is that the generation of microwaves heats up the soft tissue in the head which, in turn, via bone conduction to the inner ear, can bring about buzzing, vibratory sensations and other somatic effects. Could this explain the buzzing felt during Out-of-Body Experiences (OBEs) and other related sensations? Are these being generated by dark energy as part of the manifestation process of an egregore? Indeed, could these not also be generated as radio waves? This could explain Electronic Voice Phenomenon (EVP). Further, could this also be the source of the "inner light" perceived during OBE states?

Hallucinations and Plasma

In 2008 in an obscure academic journal called *The Open Atmosphere Science Journal,* a possibly paradigm-changing article was published. Written by Swedish neurophysiologists Gerald and Vernon Cooray of the Karolinska Institute, the paper suggested that a mysterious phenomenon called ball lightning, luminous spheres of energy created out of plasma with quantities of silicon, iron, nitrogen, oxygen and carbon, may create "hallucinations" when human brains are exposed to them. Here we have the quite literal elemental building blocks of life itself reacting with plasma to bring about altered-states of consciousness. This has huge implications for our understanding of the consciousness-reality interface.

Ball lightning has been observed for centuries in many locations. It is usually associated with thunderstorm conditions in the atmosphere, but has also been reported on clear, settled days. Indeed, in one extraordinary case, it was observed inside an aircraft. In the paper, Cooray and Cooray highlight the extraordinary similarities between hallucinations perceived during epileptic aura-states and reports of ball lightning:

> In particular luminous balls of different colours, red, yellow, blue and green, moving horizontally from the periphery of the vision to the centre have been described that may appear to be rotating or spinning. Sometimes, the ball may also appear to have a solid structure surrounded by a thin glow or, in other cases, it appears to generate spark like phenomena. When the ball is moving towards the centre of the vision (Cooray & Cooray, 2008).

Related to visual effects are auditory, olfactory and other sensory sensations such as the smell of burning and, of great significance to this discussion, buzzing sounds and powerful vibrations perceived in the head and body, which are widely reported features of all manner of High Strangeness experiences.

What is of particular importance here is that the authors cite evidence that many people experience undiagnosed "idiopathic" occipital epilepsy, that this can be triggered by external factors and that it is particularly prevalent in children (Taylor, Schaffer & Berkovic, 2003). Indeed, what is even more intriguing is that the seizure threshold is lower for children and adolescents than adults (Hay, Levin, Sondheimer

& Deterding, 2004). This is also reflected in empirical research that shows that 70% of reports of ball lightning encounters collected by a group of researchers in 2002, were described by youngsters under 20 years old, 46% by children under 15 years old and 25% by children under 10 (Abrahamson, Bychkoy & Bychkoy, 2002).

Research has also shown links between geomagnetic disturbances and the experience of epilepsy, revealing a very strong correlation between atmospheric conditions in the 10 kHz region (Ruhenstroth-Bauer, Baumer, Kugler & Spatz, 1984). 10 kHz has an exact resonance with alpha brain waves, associated with relaxed, meditative states of consciousness. This is the state in which hypnogogic and hypnopompic perceptions break through. I suspect that this may be of great significance, as it is during just such altered states that many "egregore" encounters take place.

I believe that over the next few years huge advances will be made with regard to our understanding of the real nature of the physical universe that surrounds us. The shackles of the present materialist-reductionist and eliminative-materialist paradigms will slowly be replaced by a broader and deeper understanding of reality, a new paradigm that will include explanations for the existence of consciousness and an all-encompassing model that will finally bring together quantum mechanics (the physics of the very small) and relativity (the physics of the very large).

We are about to embark on a hugely exciting intellectual adventure in which we may finally discover ourselves, and our role in this fascinating universe.

PANPSYCHISM

Minds in Nature

PETER SJÖSTEDT-HUGHES

Rather than merely asking the perennial question, 'What is mind?,' one ought also ask, 'Where is mind?' If, as Descartes staked, mind is completely non-spatial, inextensive (see for instance Descartes, 1996 [1641], p. 100), then the question makes little sense. Location of the non-spatial appears to be an oxymoron. Not only did Descartes claim that minds, as distinct souls, were inextensive – something William James considered 'absurd'[60] – but also that they pertained only to humans. All other organisms, even pet mammals, were mere lifeless machines in Descartes' *Weltanschauung* (though he once inconsistently attributed feelings to the magpie, see Cottingham, 1978). Thus when asking the question as to where minds[61] are, the Cartesian will only say nowhere yet also paradoxically in mankind only. Man has mind: Nature is a mindless mechanism. The answer I shall proffer to the question – Where is mind? – is that it is everywhere, from mankind to mantis to molecule, and beyond. In this chapter I shall seek to replace the anthropocentric view of mind with an ecocentric one: panpsychism.

---

[60] 'Descartes for the first time defined thought as the absolutely unextended [...] But to argue [...] that experience is absolutely inextensive seems to me little short of absurd' (James, 1904, pp. 488–489). For more on the relation of space to sentience, see Sjöstedt-Hughes, 2021, pp. 155–86.

[61] In this text I use 'mind' synonymously with 'sentience,' 'consciousness,' and the 'mental.'

Despite its weird inconsistencies, Descartes' system fit the West's Christian trajectory: mind was only soul, separate from the matter of Nature, with a destiny beyond Nature in an afterworld. That destiny was determined for the most part by whether the behaviour of the person was in line with Christian prescriptions – commands that were enforced through indoctrination and punishment. Thus the West's metaphysical bifurcation of mind from matter was, in part at least, the outcome of ecclesiastical power structures. This bifurcation was ever present in Christianity from the Platonism that interwove its architecture from Augustine onwards, but Descartes formalised, anthropomorphised, and energised it in the seventeenth century sparking the scientific revolution. Descartes' influence as a philosopher, physicist and mathematician (and Christian) is still deeply felt, albeit unconsciously, throughout the West today. The Church was delegated the role of saving the soul, and science was reborn and delegated the role of understanding and manipulating the lifeless machine that was Nature. The dualism of mind and matter helped engender the dualism of religion and science.

But this whole bifurcation of Nature and social structure – built upon inconsistencies – was one that inevitably led to the cracks that now appear. The most obvious theoretical crack is the so-called 'explanatory gap' (Levine, 1983), or the 'hard problem of consciousness' (Chalmers, 1995). Though both these terms were coined in the late twentieth century, they had also been recognised centuries earlier. For instance, John Locke wrote in 1689: '[We] can by no means conceive how any size, figure, or motion of any particles can possibly produce in us the idea of any colour, taste, or sound whatsoever: there is no conceivable connexion betwixt the one and the other' (p. 366). The problem is the *mind-matter mystery*: what the *relation* is between mind and matter. If the matter of Nature is without mind, as the Cartesian legacy claims, then it becomes a mystery as to how mind emerges from, or is identified with, matter. Correlations between the brain and mind merely present the problem rather than actually solving it: why are there correlations at all? What is the nature of the correlation? As the late great philosopher of mind Jaegwon Kim put it: 'Making a running list of psychoneural correlations does not come anywhere near gaining an explanatory insight into why there are such correlations [...]' (Kim, 2005, p. 13). That is a theoretical crack. The practical cracks include our abstract alienation from Nature (even though this abstraction itself is part of Nature, as we are also part of Nature), and thus our exploitation of Nature (or, its self-exploitation): if Nature is without mind, it is without *intrinsic* value – it only has *instrumental* value to we humans with minds. The exploitation of Nature thus ensues, causative of both ecological destruction and widespread morose. With regard to the latter, the British Idealist philosopher A. E. Taylor bemoaned:

> There is no thought more familiar, and few more disquieting, to the reflective man of to-day than that of the utter deadness and soullessness of the vast world of things around us [...] The cold glare of truth – so we are accustomed to repeat – has long ago dispeopled our valleys, hills and streams of the visions by which they were once filled with a hundred forms of sentient purposeful life [...] (Taylor, 1902, pp. 55–6).

With regard to the former, on the other side of the Channel, the German thinker Ludwig Klages – prefiguring other societally-cognisant environmentalists such as Rachel Carson, Lynn White Jr., Arne Naess, and Carolyn Merchant – lamented in 1913 the destruction of Nature induced by this Christian-Cartesian cut:

> Christianity may mouth such phrases as "the welfare of mankind," or "humanity," but what the voice inside these formulas is really saying is that no other living being has the slightest intrinsic value or purpose, except in so far as it can be forced to serve the purposes of *man*. From time immemorial, the "love" of the Christian has never prevented him from persecuting pagans with murderous hatred; and this same "love" does not prevent him even now from abolishing the sacred rituals of tribal cultures (Klages, 2013 [1913], p. 40).

The Christian cut of mind and Nature is as such opposed to the uncut unity of mind and Nature found in animist cultures, to which Klages alludes. Anthropologist Luis Eduardo Luna sees a direct lineage from the Christian persecution of the animist pagans of Europe to the Roman Catholic conquest of the Americas and the destruction of Amerindian cultures and practices. The conquest and destruction was, therefore, nothing new, but continued the line of Christian expansion. Symbolic of this destruction of Nature worship by the Church was, Luna points out,[62] the felling of the sacred Oak of Thor in Germany by the Christian missionary Saint Boniface in the early eighth century. This killing signifies the time at which the northern pagans became Christianised,

---

[62] From his speech at Psycherence 2018. Online: https://youtu.be/tQTforn4EME

and the anthropocentric turn that elevated – by ideology – the human organism above all others. As well as being the 'Apostle of the Germans,' Saint Boniface became, in 2019, the patron saint of the beautifully-verdant, forest-strewn county of Devon in England where he was born.

We begin to glimpse the path trod hand-in-hand by the Church and science in the West. Western science can be seen as a product of the Church rather than, as is the stereotype, its nemesis. The bifurcation of Nature helped both define their remit: the mind, soul for the Church, and the quantifiable, geometric landscape of dead Nature for science. When science strayed and started to study mind – the scientific study of consciousness really only started properly in the 1990s (before that 'consciousness' was a *faux pas* in science, considered an illusion of some sort, see Yaron *et al.*, 2022) – the troubles amplified, the cracks became more apparent. With implicit, unwitting Christian-Cartesian inheritance, it was – it is – believed that mind only pertains to human-like entities. In other words, to organisms with complex brains. Somehow, it is believed, brains exclusively make, emerge, or are identical with, mind, or consciousness. This is known as *neuroessentialism*. How mind is emergent or identical is the hard problem of consciousness, as mentioned. It is *presupposed – without evidence –* that the rest of (non-brained) Nature is without sentience. The pagan, pre-Christian Greeks did not believe this. As R.G. Collingwood wrote in his grand book, *The Idea of Nature*: 'That vegetables and animals are physically akin to the earth is a belief shared by ourselves with the Greeks; but the notion of a psychical [...] kinship is strange to us' (Collingwood, 2015 [1945], p. 4). Though Plato was a mind-matter dualist, he was not, like Descartes, anthropocentric with regard to mind and matter. In *Timaeus* he explains that: 'The plant [...] is without belief or reason or understanding but has appetite and a sense of pleasure and pain' (Plato, 1965, p. 103).

'Strange' is relative to inculcation. Neuroessentialism is normal to us in the West, though strange not only to the ancient Greeks, but also to non-Western contemporary cultures, such as certain of the indigenous Amerindians who hold an animist metaphysics, which in turn seems strange to most Westerners. We have seen how neuroessentialism has roots in the Church, despite its appearance as a non-dualistic, secular endeavour. Let us now look at its theoretical problems. By exposing these problems, we shall see how an alternate, extended, contrary view of mind – namely that minds are not limited to brain activity but are rather ubiquitous throughout Nature (panpsychism) – is not all that strange.

Neuroessentialism reduces to one essential proposition taken to be true, viz. 'Certain activity in the brain is both necessary and sufficient for sentience.' This means that without a brain, there can be no sentience, no mind. If true, it would mean that Nature is insentient; that minds are a rarity in reality. But can the neuroessentialist proposition be shown to be true? No. Firstly, it is not a tautology, it is not true by definition. If it were, it would simply beg the question as to the existence of minds in Nature. Moreover, it is not conceptually impossible to imagine sentience without brains, whereas it is conceptually impossible to imagine real contradictions, such as a three-sided square. Thus the proposition is not a tautology, and thus its contradiction is not an impossibility. So the proposition is not analytically true. Is it empirically true? Let us begin with the mode of necessity: is certain activity in the brain a *necessary* condition for sentience? How would it be possible to empirically verify or falsify this? How could one observe that a plant or even a machine was not a condition for sentience? It is not possible to verify the claim that certain brain activity is necessary for sentience because of The Problem of Other Minds: if a plant, say, had a basic form of sentience – a primal delight in receiving sunlight, or suchlike – one could not determine this by simply observing its behaviour. One cannot even observe the mental perspective of another human (their thoughts, worries, hopes, etc.), though one can *infer* it from expressions and behaviour, and the fact that the person is a human and thus shares mental features with you the human observer.[63] But inference is not empirical observation. That a plant, or any partly self-sufficient entity, may have sentience is not a matter of empirical observation. It is as logically and empirically viable that a plant has sentience as that a brain and body has. The founder of psychophysics, Gustave Fechner, expressed this point through an analogy:

> If I remove or destroy all the strings of a piano, a violin, a lute, then there will be no tone to the instrument [...] so obviously the strings are the essential means for producing tones; they are so to say the nerves of these instruments [...] But now when I hear that the flute after all

---

[63] With Henri Bergson and A.N. Whitehead, I hold the possibility that one can directly feel another person's feelings rather than infer it. But this only holds in the cases of people in one's near proximity in time and space. We only infer the feelings, etc., of those in the far past and the far regions (that one sees on screens).

does actually produce tones, in spite of my pretty argument, I cannot see why plants might not be able to produce subjective sensations without having nerves. The animals might be the string instruments of sensation, and the plants the wind instruments (Fechner, 1948, pp. 173–174).[64]

That is to say that we cannot determine that neurons are a necessary condition for sentience. Empirical observation cannot show or prove that plants have or have no sentience. Likewise empirical observation cannot show that certain brain activity alone is *necessary* for sentience. When it comes to mind, the empirical method is insufficient. We must rely on inference to the best explanation.

Next, we ask whether certain brain activity is *sufficient* for sentience? The claim that a brain was sufficient but not necessary for sentience would be compatible with certain types of panpsychism. But even this is not an empirically observable proposition. If, as certain thinkers such as Maimonides argue, our minds are part of a greater mind, as our spatial bodies are part of a greater space, then our brain and bodies alone would not be sufficient for sentience. Though I leave this pantheistic question to the side, the essential point for us is that whether or not this is the case, empirical observation cannot determine it: it cannot verify or falsify it. We need not even go so far as pantheism: contemporary 'Extended Mind' theories argue that our brains alone are not sufficient for our consciousness – we must extend mind to our immediate environment, with which we interact (see Noë, 2009, for instance). As well as neural correlates of consciousness, there are, it is argued, environmental correlates of consciousness. Thus the neuroessential proposition that dominates Western thought is merely a speculation that cannot be logically or empirically demonstrated. In fact, if we accept Karl Popper's doctrine that a theory must be in principle falsifiable if it is to be considered 'scientific,' then *the neuroessentialist proposition, that lies at the base of modern scientific views of consciousness, is itself not scientific.* Here again, the religious undercurrents of the modern Western scientific enterprise are glimpsed. Further still, all the main neuroscientific theories of consciousness that have emerged over the past decades contradict one another (Yaron *et al.*, 2022). The mind is not the remit of neuroscience alone, but rather also logic, metaphysics, history, anthropology and a myriad of other disciplines including, perhaps, botany.

---

[64] Specifically the quotation comes from 'The Soul Life of Plants' (1848).

There are therefore reasons not to blindly maintain neuroessentialism, the fundamentally anthropocentric view of the mind. But are there good reasons to maintain a more Greek, more pagan, more ecocentric view of the mind? Is panpsychism plausible?

For a start, we should acknowledge not only that the ancient Greeks and other pagans of Europe held panpsychological views, but also many indigenous peoples living today. Panpsychism is not an alien concept; it is only strange in our monotheistic culture. As well as the destruction and suppression of animist cultures by the Church – one can see animism as the religious side, panpsychism as the secular side, of the same coin – the Church also suppressed panpsychological beliefs in European thinkers. Giordano Bruno was burned alive in 1600 by the Roman Inquisition; Benedict de Spinoza's books were banned by the Church and his pantheistic, panpsychological philosophy was spurned in Europe till the Pantheism Controversy of the 1780s, a century after his death. This controversy was one causative factor for the Romantic movement in Europe, a movement that was ecocentric and that can now be seen as correct in its critique of both the scientific mechanism and restricting religion of its day. Yet still, the word 'Romanticism' is a derogatory term. Other great thinkers of the Western canon who expressed panpsychological insights include Goethe, Leibniz, Schopenhauer, Schelling, W.K. Clifford, A.N. Whitehead, Bertrand Russell, and William James to name but a few. Despite their rational pleas, the anthropocentrism of Church and Lab ploughs on, and ploughs down. Especially noteworthy is the case of Spinoza who died in 1677. He resolved Descartes' dualism of mind and matter into a monism, thereby overcoming many of the difficulties in the Cartesian view. But as he saw mind and matter both as expressions of one substance, a substance that he called both Nature and God, the authorities saw to his demise. When Bruno and Spinoza were suppressed in Europe by the Church, it was concurrently busy in the Americas engaged in the same activity against the animists. The suppression of panpsychism and paganism has been an active directive of the Church.

Thus there are reasons for panpsychism being spurned, but what are the more positive reasons for it being true? The theory of evolution plays its role here. As William James put it:

> Consciousness, however small, is an illegitimate birth in any philosophy that starts without it, and yet professes to explain all facts by continuous evolution. If evolution is to work smoothly, consciousness in some

shape must have been present at the very origin of things (James, 1950 [1890], p. 149).[65]

Rather than a magical jump from non-sentient matter to sentient matter (a tremendous jump, disjunct in the evolution of the cosmos), it appears more parsimonious to accept that just as matter evolves in complexity so too does mind. The complexity of the human body is parallel to the complexity of the human mind, the simplicity of a particle being parallel to the simplicity of the mind associated therewith. A human brain and body may be necessary for human consciousness, but not necessary for non-human forms of consciousness. If mind is an aspect of matter, as in panpsychism, then the evolution of mind and matter is the same thing meaning that there is no need to introduce an 'illegitimate birth,' a magical conjuring of mind, into the development of the universe.

Moreover – as was argued by figures such as F.H. Bradley, William James, A.N. Whitehead, and Karl Popper – the question arises as to why mind would have evolved and maintained itself in multiple organisms if mind had no causal efficacy, no power. Accordingly, mind must play a role in behaviour and evolution beyond sexual selection. Though this may seem obvious to most, such mental causation is in fact a serious problem for those physicalists who reject panpsychism. There are no known laws of nature that accommodate the *power of mentality* in the physicalist, or 'panhylist,' worldview. This is a big problem – the Problem of Mental Causation – because though mental force does not fit into the current physicists' framework, nonetheless epiphenomenalism (the rejection of mental causation) does not fit into the biologists' evolutionary framework. Another crack, as paradox, in the current Western view (see Kim, 2005, for a detailed exposition of such paradoxes). This paradox betrays a deeper mistake: that our idea of the physical is inadequate. In the words of analytic philosopher Galen Strawson:

> At the root of the [mind-body] muddle lies an ability to overcome the Very Large Mistake: [...] to think we know enough about the nature of physical reality to have any good reason to think that

---

[65] As it happens, James criticises panpsychism in this volume, even putting forward the so-called Combination Problem for panpsychism in it. Two decades later, however, he fully endorses panpsychism as can be seen in his book, *A Pluralistic Universe*.

consciousness can't be physical [...] It seems to be stamped so deeply in us, by our everyday experience of matter as lumpen stuff, that not even appreciation of the extraordinary facts of current physics can weaken its hold [...] To see through it is a truly revolutionary experience (Strawson, 2015).

In other words, matter is an abstraction – that is, our concept of 'matter' only reveals some attributes (mass, spin, charge, etc.) of what is in reality a richer concrete reality that may include mind. Descartes gave matter merely the attribute of extension, spatiality, as we saw. Since then physics has added many more properties. But we have no reason to believe that we have reached any final stage in our understanding of matter. Science moves on continually. And indeed there can be no 'theory of everything' until, at the very least, physics and psychology are bridged. If mind is an aspect of matter, à la panpsychism, then all physical causation *is* mental causation (even though it may be determinable and not 'free'). As such, we do away with the incongruence between the physicists' and evolutionists' demands.

We have certain fundamental options regarding the mind-matter mystery. Are mind and matter separate substance? Is mind an illusion? Is matter an illusion? Is mind really reducible to matter, or neural matter? Do mind and matter both emerge from something else? Are mind and matter ultimately the same thing? The last option, panpsychism, seems more parsimonious, ecocentric – mind is everywhere. But wherever the truth of the matter lies it is going to be deeply weird to someone, or something, somewhere.[66]

---

[66] For a less sociological and more analytic argument for panpsychism, see my book, *Modes of Sentience* (2022).

THROUGH A MAGICKAL LENS

Towards an Experimental Model of Conjuring

SUSAN DEMETER

From my earliest childhood memories I recall having strange encounters with what appear to be non-human entities and visions of the dead. And even as a child I knew these events were not normal. I could not share them with my friends from school or my closest relatives because when I tried to share them I felt rejection. I have lived the deep weird; I know it in my soul, but I have very little understanding of what it *is*. Ignoring these experiences in my early adulthood did not make them go away. It intensified them. Peace finally came for me with acceptance and a determination to investigate the deep weird from within boundaries that I learned to create for myself. And the creation of those boundaries – which provide me with the necessary balance needed to comfortably experiment and research deep weird encounters – came to me through my magickal practice. My experiences, both intense and highly personal, have undeniably played a large part in shaping my life. For me, the deep weird counts. And it is from this perspective – as an investigator, a magickal practitioner and an experient of high strangeness – that this chapter has been written.

There is a profound and intrinsic connection between magick, magickal practices and extraordinary experience that can be defined as 'deep weird.' The link between these domains was made by researchers such as Jacques Vallée, John Keel, Jenny Randles and others who have studied esoteric writings and consulted with magickal thinkers as part of their investigations into highly strange experiences. This connection has also been noted by some experiencers who, like me, see their encounters as having informed their spirituality and magickal practice. While contemplating associations between the deep weird and magickal practice, let us begin by reflecting on this quote from author and high strangeness experiencer Whitley Strieber, who in a comprehensive 1998 analysis of close encounter UFO experiencers describes some of the changes that abductees undergo as a result of their deep weird encounters:

> What basically happens is that the witness's whole sense of reality explodes. People become psychic, they begin to believe that they can see into the future, they take spontaneous journeys through time, they begin to see vivid images in the region of the brain known in folklore as the 'third eye,' they levitate, they believe that they take on the appearance of alien forms for periods of time, they acquire wisdom and new compassion, their children become preternaturally brilliant, they take journeys out of the body, they become healers, they acquire relationships with the dead, they become deeply concerned with the welfare of the environment (Strieber, 1998, p. 16).

It is impossible not to note how these descriptions mirror the experiences of practitioners of occult traditions (Harvey-Wilson, 2000).

Deep Weird is the Domain of Magical Thinkers and Practitioners

Historical records of pre-modern and early modern witchcraft in the Western tradition recount initiation into the craft through a compact between humans and non-human agents who inhabit the unseen dimensions of this world and others. These encounters, which were largely considered taboo within the societies where these people lived, have been sought in a variety of forms and ways by humans who would become witches. The gateway into becoming a witch or sorcerer came from meeting with entities in the form of the spirits of the dead, an influence within the local landscape such as an elemental, or some other type of mysterious being or non-human power, and then forming an extraordinary relationship with them (Artisson, 2020, pp. 11-16).

Spontaneous initiations occurred too. There is a vast number of seemingly unprovoked encounters in which people going about their everyday lives describe extraordinary meetings with otherworldly beings or spirits that act as an agent of transformation (Wilby, 2005). These meetings between humans and spirits have always existed on the margins of western society and were never fully acceptable in the mainstream.

In early modern Europe, political upheaval combined with cultural and religious uncertainties led to the pervasive notions that these types of encounters were inherently evil, and that those who participated in or experienced them were a threat to society. This included people who claimed to be in contact with angels and saints. The resulting consequences of torture and execution from this line of reasoning were horrific (Demeter, 2020, pp. 93-104; Hutton, 1999; Behringer, 2004). Forms of persecution, abuse, and ostracism of those who actively and spontaneously experience the other-worldly persist in the present day. This includes groups of UFO or paranormal enthusiasts who lean heavily towards a materialist or quasi-scientific paradigm and who will disregard witness testimony, including levelling accusations of hoaxing and lying when their boggle threshold is surpassed (Demeter, 2021).

This is exactly what happened in the case of Marius Dewilde. Marius was a railway worker when in 1954 in the north of France he had an encounter with a flying saucer piloted by what he described as robots. This extraordinary case was widely covered in the media and he was considered by many to be a very credible witness. Many years later, when he shared subsequent paranormal encounters, he was dismissed as non-reliable. Having more than one strange event exceeded the boggle thresholds of the people who had previously supported him, and he was dumped (Vallée, 1969/1993, pp. 17-19).

For three decades I have conducted in person and online outreach to those who have had spontaneous and deliberately induced extraordinary encounters. My approach to my experiencers and others is phenomenological; acceptance of the reality of the experience without *a priori* judgement on its ultimate nature. Jeff Kripal advocates for this line of inquiry – which he has aptly named "making the cut" – when examining high strangeness:

> The fundamental idea here is to begin any inquiry by taking a set of experiences on their own terms and setting aside, for the time being, the question of their possible external source, cause, or truth value.

The method encourages us to "make a cut" between the appearances themselves and what may, or may not, lie behind them (Kripal & Strieber, 2016).

The following spontaneous high strangeness event is from my own personal case files, and should be read with a view to making the cut.

A Deeply Weird Encounter in the Wild

I'm not drawn by curiosity, nor am I in search of a novel experience. Often I spend my time barefoot and practicing interior prayer. The hollow is a protected place. Its length is owned by a number of affluent families who basically keep people out. At any rate I was walking down this hollow along the stream, my mind was somewhat silent which I think had a lot to do with having had the experience. I was about five or more feet above the stream bed and to my left I saw two somewhat humanoid creatures sitting on a log that had fallen across the stream. I was clearly aware of them before they became aware of me and in the instant they realised I was there, the one sitting closest to me turned instantly into a frog and leapt into the water. The one sitting to his left was clearly confused and mildly panicked. In trying to choose his best avenue of escape I watched him morph through three different animal forms in the span of seconds, a frog, a mouse and finally as a small bird he flew in a small circle and disappeared under the bank. If I were an artist I could easily sketch these two entities. They never stood completely erect but I estimate they were between nine and twelve inches high, their skin was leathery and brown. Their noses were long and large in proportion to their frame. Naked or clothed I cannot say. I know what I saw. And I saw them as clearly as I see anything. However I don't expect ever to see such things again and I'm sure a search would be futile. I saw them morph with my eyes and that explains a lot of how they might exist alongside of us (Demeter, 2013).

Encountering little humanoids in the woods would be a shocking experience for most of us, but witnessing them morph or shape-shift into something else firmly places this story in deep weird territory.

I received this extraordinary account as part of a correspondence with a gentleman who had lived in rural Pennsylvania for four decades. Used to living in isolation he was well acquainted with the hollow described in his encounter, and the surrounding landscape. His life had been dedicated to religious studies, but he was deeply shocked by his odd experience. The encounter with the little shape shifters was something he did not illicit, nor was it something he particularly wanted to revisit. His own boggle threshold had been exceeded and he was "making the cut" by sharing it.

While boggling for the witness I found the similarities of his experience to Indigenous American lore of little people and early modern witchcraft accounts of initiates who entered into pacts with other-worldly spirits in the woods particularly striking (Johnston, 2001).

I thanked the gentleman for his candidness and for entrusting me with his unusual experience, and he gave me permission to publish his encounter on the condition that I would keep his personal details and the exact location of the sighting confidential. This is typical of the many experients of the extraordinary that have contacted me, especially those who have provided me with details that are deeply weird. People do understand what is acceptable and what is not, even in the context of retelling paranormal encounters.

In Jacques Vallée and Paola Harris' recent book *Trinity* (2021) it is revealed that witnesses like Maurice Masse will go so far as hiding evidence of later observations in order to realign their experiences with official statements made by the authorities. Deep weird experiencers intimately know how much the general public is willing to tolerate when it comes to witness testimony because they too are boggled. These experiences, which appear to take place outside of our consensus reality, can be frightening, difficult to process, transformative, and life altering for the experient. And I suspect because of the tendency of witnesses to withhold deep weird details, they are much more widespread than we may realise.

There are, however, groups of people – including myself – who invite and participate in these types of encounters despite the societal taboos and associated unpleasantness that can arise from immersing oneself in the deep weird. Magical practitioners of various traditions, both historically and currently, describe active engagement with human and non-human entities that inhabit the unseen realms. Their testimonies and methods can provide a framework and an engaging tool for studying deep weird encounters by means of what anthropologist Susan Greenwood describes as *"magical consciousness"* – a way of approaching research and the world that can broaden our understanding of reality (Greenwood, 2020).

Psi and Magick as the Foundation for Experimental Conjuring

The position I take for this model is that both spontaneous encounters and magickal practices involving deep weird experiences share the same operational mechanism – namely psi. This knowledge has been utilised by researchers in the past to successfully examine paranormal, or more aptly named super natural, events through experimentation. Examples of these experiments will be presented a little further on.

Let us begin by defining psi and magick.

What is Psi?

Psi as defined by the Society for Psychical Research is the "modern collective term for the psychic functions of telepathy, clairvoyance, precognition and psychokinesis." Parapsychology generally divides psi into two broad types of effects. The first is known as extrasensory perception, which is communication of information without known physical means; this includes telepathy, clairvoyance, mediumship, and premonitions.

The second is known as psychokinesis or PK which is when mental intentions affect matter without known physical means, such as dice rolls, the bending of objects, and levitation. PK differs from other psychic abilities because its effects are physical in nature. It is defined as the ability of a person to influence a physical system without physical interaction. Not only does psychokinetic energy affect matter, but it can affect the information about the matter and has been studied extensively by various military and civilian scientists. Psi in the form of PK is what is operative when magickal rituals are performed because they have a direct effect on living beings, and objects, affecting the information of matter itself (Society for Psychical Research, 2021).

Psi is not fully understood at the time of this writing. It is not directly observable *per se*, but its effects are observable and it has been statistically proven to exist. Therefore it is reasonable to base hypotheses, speculation and models of high strangeness experiences on what we know about psi (Utts, 1991).

What is Magick?

When defining magick, especially in the spirit of this chapter, I recall this quote from modern magician and author Damien Echols. Echols credits magick with helping him survive eighteen years on death row in an American prison for a crime he did not commit. A horrific ordeal that is unimaginable to most. He explains:

> Magick is not a path for followers; it is a path for questioners, seekers, and anyone who has trouble settling for dogma and pre-formulated answers. Magick is for those who feel the desire to peel away the surface of reality and see what lies beneath. Like various persecuted forms of mysticism, magick promotes direct contact with the source of creation (Echols, 2018).

I resonate deeply with Echols' words and they are an apt descriptor for the conjuring model I am working towards.

Magick is a very broad term, and I will defer to western occultist Aleister Crowley to pin it down. Crowley was an English ceremonial magician and founder of the philosophy and system of magick known as Thelema (Churton, 2011). He is arguably the most controversial and influential occultist of modern times. It was he who re-popularised the spelling of magick through his writings in order to differentiate occultists and their practices from stage magicians and performance magic (Hutton, 2012). It should be noted that not all magickal thinkers use this spelling in defining what they do, but for the purposes of this model I believe it will be useful to bring clarity to what is being discussed.

Crowley defined magick as "the science and art of causing change to occur in conformity with Will." In other words – shaping reality to work towards our intentions, goals, and purposes. He was an admirer of science and the scientific method, which he often wrote about in his periodical journal, entitled *Equinox*. He encouraged magicians to keep detailed records of their magickal experimentation, writing "the more scientific the better." He believed that science and older forms of magic could synthesise into magick, which would accept the existence of the supernatural and an experimental methodology simultaneously (DuQuette, 2003; Crowley & Wasserman, 1993).

An Experimental Conjuring Model in Practice

For the purpose of a conjuring model it is not necessary to have any firm belief in the mechanisms or causation, but to approach it with the same mindset as "making the cut." To be open to it, without necessarily explaining it. But, the potential lasting and profound effects a deep weird encounter can have on experimenters must be considered when testing this model.

When I was a teenager I watched a documentary on the lives and work of self experimenting scientists from the eighteenth to early-twentieth century. I recall being enamoured of these true scientific pioneers, but at the same time somewhat disturbed by their methodologies. Many of those self experimenters changed medical science and furthered our knowledge of diseases, benefitting humanity, while others were somewhat misguided, and some even died (Kerridge, 2003).

I keep these cautionary anecdotes in mind when experimenting with conjuration. I set boundaries and know the limits of my own comfort within the space that I purposefully create, which allows for engagement with something that is still very much an unknown. Investigators who undertake this experimental model do have agency. It is important to be coming from a place where the intentions are ethical and responsible, and to be fully transparent about where you will be drawing the line, and what you may include and exclude.

A connection between psi and magick, and their relationship to spontaneous paranormal experiences has been established, and this observation is not new to scholars of high strangeness. In my book *Cosmic Witch* I describe my own personal encounters with the paranormal as an initiation. This is something scholar Jacques Vallée also noted in his research into UFO close encounters:

> Answering such questions could also help us to understand the strong resemblance that anyone who has examined the beliefs of esoteric groups could not fail to note between certain UFO encounters and the initiation rituals of secret societies. This opening of the mind to a new set of symbols that is reported by many witnesses is precisely what the various occult traditions also try to achieve (Vallée, 1989).

Later within the same work Vallée writes: "A study of these [high strangeness] events from the point of view of the esoteric tradition might be rewarding" (Ibid.).

I draw inspiration from scholars such as Vallée, and maintain that a conjuring model can potentially provide useful insights and lead us to better questions about the nature of the deep weird. Having used Aleister Crowley's definition of magick as our starting point, let us now look to him for examples of conjuring up experiences straight out of the deep weird.

The Conjuration of Lam

Crowley was living in New York City in the late 1910s with his lover and magickal partner Roddie Minor when together they embarked on various magickal experiments including one that is known as the Amalantrah Working. This series of magickal rituals was performed in order to gain greater insights into the lives of the practitioners through channelled knowledge and divination. It was from this magickal working that a supernatural being named Lam emerged. Exactly what Lam was or meant to Crowley is unclear and remains a mystery. The most popular interpretations are that Lam represented a cosmic ultra-dimensional entity ushered into our reality through the Amalantrah rituals, or a thought-form conjured from the consciousness of the magicians, or possibly a self-portrait of Crowley himself on the astral plane. Crowley first published a sketched portrait of Lam in 1919, which he entitled 'The Way,' so there is an original representation of what Lam looked like (Evans, 1986, pp. 211-215).

In 1945 Lam reappears in Crowley's writing in a diary entry about Kenneth Grant's interest in the entity. Grant was an occultist and friend of Crowley and he republished the Lam portrait in his own book *The Magic Awakens*, along with his thoughts on what Lam might be and how to connect with it through conjuring. It is at this point that Lam's story becomes relevant for an experimental conjuring model. Grant had a keen interest in Ufology, and reported UFO/alien encounters which he wrote about along with H.P. Lovecraft's cosmic horror, obscuring the boundaries between reality and fiction. Similar techniques of blending fictional narratives with magickal practice have also been successfully utilised in parapsychological research (Grant, 1995).

Over a century after he first appeared in the drawings and writing of Crowley, Lam is still with us today. He continues to hold influence, blurring the lines between magickal conjuring, fiction and reported UFO and abduction experiences. Lam's image has appeared in various publications and has wide circulation on the internet, inspiring both occultists and UFOlogists to make comparisons between Crowley's drawing and UFO witnesses' descriptions of grey aliens (Boudillon, 2003; Evans, 1986, pp. 300-301). Engaging with Lam-like entities can challenge our notions of reality and push the boundaries of believability in the same way that reports of spontaneous confrontations with a telepathic Sasquatch might.

It has been argued that magickal rituals like those performed to engage with Lam produce altered states of consciousness in practitioners, and these types of experiences with otherworldly entities are understood as either hallucinations or illusions created by the magician's state of mind. But, the possibility that something more is occurring remains. There is a large body of reported spontaneous cases of psychic experience, out-of-body journeys, telekinesis, healing, and entity encounters occurring while the experient was in an altered state of consciousness (Luke, 2011). Many of these spontaneous cases resist easy explanations, such as simple hallucinations, and by extension this must also be considered of deliberate attempts at conjuring. In parapsychology it is well understood that altered states of consciousness are an enabling condition for psi effects to occur (Kelly & Locke, 1981; Evans, 1986, pp. 219-220).

Puss in Boots Manifests in Russia

Experimentation in conjuration from an occult-scientific perspective has been occurring since at least the nineteenth century in Russia. One of these early groups "the Brotherhood of the Rising Sun" consisted of scientists, philosophers, and occultists led by a teacher-guru who was described as either Chinese or Tibetan in origin. In December 1912 the group devised an experiment known as the St Petersburg Circle with the intention to see if they could create a thought-form of a fictional being that would become autonomous. They based their ideas on Tibetan Buddhist philosophy and methodology.

The Russians had initially suggested creating a dragon because it was not something that had existed in reality, but their teacher-guru was uncomfortable with creating something viewed as potentially menacing and harmful. It was decided they would work with a puss-in-boots character who was not only comical, but considered to be a helper and therefore controllable. The participants were given a basic description of how the cat should look and instructed on how to use a visualisation technique in order to manifest it. After a period of time the experiment proved successful and the participants reported seeing an apparition of a red cat wearing common Russian boots. The puss-in-boots tulpa was described by participants as looking like a "poorly developed photograph, motionless and of a very short duration before melting away" (Mamontoff, 1960).

The Russian endeavour is reminiscent of Alexandra David-Néel's descriptions of the purposeful creation of a tulpa; an animated thought-form that takes on an autonomous existence. David-Néel was exploring Tibetan magickal traditions including creating tulpas during the same time period that the Russian circle were experimenting with Puss-In-Boots. She gives several examples including her own experiment. Her monk tulpa that she initially describes as "jolly" reportedly travelled with her on horseback and was witnessed by many others. When the tulpa began to take on sinister characteristics and behaviours she describes her decision to destroy it (Ibid.). The book *Magic and Mystery in Tibet*, which chronicles her adventures, was first published 1929 and has since been reprinted several times. Although Alexandra David-Néel is a controversial figure her writings introduced "tulpa" creation to a western readership, and she has had a great influence over modern experiments in conjuring.

Conjuring Philip: An Adventure in Psychokinesis

Decades after the St Petersburg Circle experiment a similar approach was taken in the visionary work conducted in the 1970s by the Toronto Psychical Research Society under the supervision of A.R.G. Owen and Joel Whitton. Unlike the Russian experiment and David-Néel's account, the Philip experiment is relatively recent, was very well documented and corroborated by observers outside of the sitting group.

Owen was a member of the Department for Preventative Medicine and Bio-statistics at the University of Toronto and co-founding member with his wife Iris of the Toronto Society of Psychical Research or TSPR. The Owens were primarily interested in ghost and haunting cases that involved poltergeist activity, and Owen wrote extensively on the subject in his 1964 book *Can We Explain The Poltergeist* (1964). According to Iris Owen and Margaret Sparrow's book *Conjuring Up Philip: An Adventure In Psychokinesis*, after the TSPR was involved in a ghost hunting expedition in 1973, eight of the organisation's members endeavoured to answer the question, what is a ghost? Iris explains that the prevailing thought at the time was that apparitions witnessed by multiple people were a collective hallucination. This notion was supported by telepathy experiments the group had conducted under the guidance of Dr D.H. Lloyd, which had been published in their journal *New Horizons*, volumes 1-2. Telepathy can take place and seems to exist between persons who may not be consciously aware of it, nor identify as having psychic abilities. To the members of the TSPR this made the collective hallucination hypothesis tenable. The next question the group had was how to prove it? (Sparrow & Owen, 1976, pp. 1-6, 40-50, 122-126).

The Owens designed some basic parameters for an experiment. The goal would be to answer the question: "Could they manifest an apparition with their minds?" The group would meet weekly for a period of one year in order to collectively work on visualisation techniques. The work would be done in a lighted room allowing for outside observers to rule out fraud. Participants would be screened to ensure that they were psychologically well, had some creative ability and did not identify as psychically gifted. The latter was of particular importance to their goals of demonstrating that virtually anyone could duplicate their results.

If the experiment was successful and the group members saw a ghost it was imperative that they could determine that it was a product of their own minds and not a conventional ghost or disembodied spirit of a deceased person. In order to prove beyond a reasonable doubt that a ghost was manufactured by the group it was essential to their purpose that they create a fictitious character. Not merely a figment of the imagination, but clearly and obviously so, with a biography full of historical errors.

A basic storyline was created by one of the group's members named only as "Sue" – a retired nurse with the Canadian Armed Forces. The character the group would attempt to conjure was an aristocratic Englishman living in the middle 1600s at the time of Oliver Cromwell. The group named him Philip. Further details including a loveless marriage, a lover who was executed on false charges of witchcraft, and a tragic and mysterious death were added as the group discussed and immersed themselves in Philip's invented biographical data.

Initially the group sat around a table with a drawing they had made of Philip placed at its centre (or a piece of aluminsed cardboard on the floor instead of the table), in the hope of causing Philip to materialise on it. After a period of quiet meditation, they would share what they had felt or experienced during meditation. Iris Owen writes in *Conjuring Up Philip* that in these early stages of the experiment the participants and outside observers witnessed a mist in the room, but very little else. This was disappointing and after a few months there was talk of ending the experiment. It was during this stage of the experiment that Iris Owen read papers by the psychical researcher Kenneth Batcheldor who had carried out successful experiments in PK using techniques found in Spiritualist séances: "the participants sat around in a relaxed and jolly atmosphere, singing songs and hymns, making jokes and carrying on a conversation."

The Owens adapted their experiment to resemble a more traditional nineteenth century parlour séance including a round table. The only differences were that no one participant was named as the officiating medium, and the room was always lighted. The group began to have almost immediate results in the form of psychokinesis. Manifestations included raps, which were used to communicate yes or no responses. The group began to question Philip, whose answers in turn helped them to co-create his fictional story. Belief in the narrative was strengthened and more physical phenomena were manifested, such as varied movements of the table, including its levitation and the flickering of lights on command as the experiment progressed.

One of the more intriguing and disturbing concomitant effects of the Philip experiment is that several of the participants described experiencing poltergeist phenomena in their homes when they took short breaks during the duration of the experiment. These after-effects should be considered for similar experiments and attempts at replication.

The Philip experiment had succeeded well beyond the expectations of the TSPR, albeit in unexpected ways. The initial goal of creating an apparition was not realised, but the manifestations of physical paranormal phenomena via "an invisible communicator" were so pronounced that media were able to record them, including the table levitating during live broadcasts on television. These broadcasts, and a full documentary that was filmed by the Canadian national broadcaster, are available on YouTube at the time of this writing.[67]

Philip's raps were recorded and translated into sound charts by Dr Alan Gauld of the Society for Psychical Research in England, "showing

---

[67] The Philip Experiment https://www.youtube.com/watch?v=X2lGPT2J1cc (Retrieved October 13th 2021).

that they had a different acoustic quality than normally-created raps" (Wehrstein, 2021). Physicists and psychologists invited the group to Cleveland, Ohio for a demonstration, including the original table. One physicist sat on the table and was promptly violently ejected by what remained an unknown force (ibid.).

When the Philip experiment ended the Owens were confident in stating that while they could not rule out the existence of disembodied souls their experiment had proven that "humans can produce spirits through expectation, imagination and visualisation" (Sparrow & Owen, 1976). When reading *Conjuring Up Philip* it is evident to me that if the language of parapsychology is replaced with occult terminology we could easily be reading a magickal how-to manual on conjuring.

Further experiments with a different group were carried out in 1974. The Lilith experiments saw similar results to the Philip one in just five weeks. This was likely due to the fact that the Owens were able to formulate shortcuts in methodology based on the earlier experiment, and the new participants were able to sit in with the Philip group on an individual basis. In 2004 Merseyside Anomalies Research Association, with the support of Liverpool John Moores University Psychology department, conducted an updated version which they named *The Humphrey Experiment*. While it was limited in comparison to the Owens' work it does demonstrate an interest in these types of experiments (Demeter, 2020b).

Manifesting UFOs

Attempts at manifesting aliens and spaceships are not new, but for this chapter I will only outline those I have had direct involvement with. My own experimentation has been inspired by all of the examples given in this chapter as well as by my work with sociologist Dr Eric Ouellet – examining UFOs as a parapsychological event (Ouellet, 2015).

Similar in set up to the Philip experiment, I make use of modern technology and a UFO narrative in my experiments. I have incorporated a number of methods that I have learned and intuited from my personal magickal practice, and I give much consideration to the ethical concerns associated with attempting to create an artificial "alien" entity experience. Everything I do in relation to this work comes from an open, compassionate heart with the utmost respect for the well-being of others, particularly when I work in group experiment settings. I cannot stress enough how imperative it is that this work is carried out ethically and honourably.

I supervised two group experiments in 2017 that ran concurrently using the conjuring model, but with quite different methodologies. Each group was asked for non-disclosure for the duration of the experiment, and each was unaware of the other. The first group were tasked with writing a shared fictional narrative of a pleasant UFO encounter at a specific location known as a UFO hotspot. This can be likened to writing fan-fiction based on a well-known UFO story with the hope of creating a physical effect that will be reported, or somehow shared, by an observer outside of the group. When I devised this experiment I considered the words of German occultist Jan Fries on the importance of storytelling in shaping reality:

> We have taken a look at the way stories were used to shape belief and reality. Some of you may think that the magick of tales is only a minor matter rating on a level with spell-crafting and dowsing. On the contrary I would propose that stories are so magickal that they can shape group reality (Fries, 2005).

Myth and storytelling have a powerful effect in an experimental model of conjuring, as has been shown with the examples given in this chapter. Western esoteric scholar Mark Stavish has written extensively on the subject of *egregores* (group created thought-forms) and fictional storytelling. He asserts that most spiritual practices, are informed by creative fiction and this continues in the modern world through fan fiction and live-action role playing, which can create egregores by blurring the lines between fantasy and consensus reality. The question of where does fantasy end and alternate reality, or new reality, begin must be considered when exploring deep weird experiences through conjuring (Stavish, 2018, pp. 70-73, see also Anthony Peake's chapter in this volume).

The second group I worked with used meditation and visualisation to create a ball of light over the skies of a randomly generated location that they were not aware of. These random locations listed as geographic co-ordinates included known areas of UFO activity mixed with general sites. The exact location where it was that the second group was supposed to manifest their light was also unknown to me.

In my forthcoming book, I will present these experiments in detail and the conjuring model that arises from them – a model that other experimental groups could put into practice. Each group achieved some verifiable successes in what we had set out to accomplish, and I am examining and thinking about them as I work towards developing the model. I invite the reader to think on what I have presented here and consider how you would put forward an experimental model based in psi and magick to engage directly with deep weird experiences?

Conclusions

There are many forms of knowledge from which different truths emerge: some are objective, others are more personal, but they all count. All of our accumulated knowledge counts, including what arises from experiences so weird, and astonishing in their absurdity that they boggle our minds and challenge our convictions.

An experimental conjuring model asks us to see a door where others see a wall. It invites us to cross over the boggle threshold and immerse ourselves in the deep weird. The model I am working towards pushes the boundaries of what is generally accepted as consensus reality. Once again I will invoke the wise words of occultist Jan Fries:

> What is the chief problem in magickal evolution? Not demons or angels, not wrathful deities or wriggly things from in-between. It is simply the ordinary human personality, the mask of identity held together by habitual thinking and rigid belief. This creature can do with a bit of confusion from time to time. How about confusing yourself on purpose? (Fries, 2000).

And this is what deep weird encounters do. They confuse us with their absurdity forcing us outside of our comfort zone, into new lands where evolution might occur. The experimental conjuring model as a non-traditionally accepted way of acquiring knowledge may be exactly what is needed in order to gain a deeper understanding of unusual experiences.

From the examples I have given in this chapter we can discern a few key points for working with an experimental model of conjuring:

1. An open mind with regards to methodology is necessary, but belief in the origin of the phenomena generated is not. The Philip participants had no strong belief as to the causation of ghosts when testing out their hypothesis, nor did they rule out survival of bodily death for some cases of haunting afterwards.

2. Theatre, fiction and a positive and relaxed environment facilitate psi phenomena.
3. We have agency over the space that we create and what we will and will not authorise. We can "make the cut" for ourselves. Recall that the St Petersburg Circle rejected the idea of creating a fictional dragon, opting instead for a helper cat. Iris Owen writes in *Conjuring Up Philip* that when the participants jokingly told Philip that if he did not answer a question the group might send him away the phenomena stopped. The group had to work in subsequent sessions to bring him back. This seems to confirm that a purposefully created thought-form entity can be destroyed if it becomes necessary to do so (Wehrstein, 2021).
4. Expect the unexpected. The Philip group did not create an apparition as they originally set out to do, but they did achieve measurable success with PK.
5. Experiments using the conjuring model can produce physical effects through PK, like the raps produced in the Philip experiment, which are measurable.
6. The language used when framing the experiment – scientific parapsychology or magickal ritual – is irrelevant and both can produce results.
7. All of these experiments, practices and methods – which can be brought together under the term conjuring – hint at a greater reality, unknown intelligences, co-creation, symbolic communication, and a human mind or consciousness that exists outside of the confines of a physical body.

I began this chapter with a quote from Whitley Strieber and I feel that it is also fitting to conclude with one. When confronted with mind-boggling experiences Whitley writes:

> Instead of shunning the darkness, we can face straight into it with an open mind. When we do that the unknown changes. Fearful things become understandable and a truth is suggested: the enigmatic presence of the human mind winks back from the dark (Strieber, 1988).

Strieber is a modern mystic, his experiences exceed most people's boggle thresholds yet he makes no pretence to being a keeper of any one perfect truth beyond that he is a human being and his encounters are part of his life's journey. He is very clear in where he is "making the cut." These events, like those of others who experience high strangeness, invoked a spontaneous hint at a much richer reality than what is currently known and accepted. Magick is a form of knowledge, and its practice through a conjuring model may allow us to glimpse and accept a profound reality where the deep weird is fully engaged.

JIISAKIIWIGAAN

Shaking Tent Ceremony as Sacred Metamorphosis

RENEE E. MAZINEGIIZHIGOO-KWE BEDARD

Entering the Deep Weird of Anishinaabeg[68] Spirituality

Jiisakiiwigaan

Biindigeg, Manidoowag miinawaa Jiibayag!
Biindigeg, Manidoowag miinawaa Jiibayag!
Biindigeg, Manidoowag miinawaa Jiibayag!
Biindigeg, Manidoowag miinawaa Jiibayag!
Come in, Spirit Beings and Ghosts!

Aambe! Aambe! Aambe! Come here!
Boozhoo, indinawemaaganag! Welcome, my relatives!

To the bagone'giizhik, the hole in the sky, they come to.
They are beckoned by Jiisakiid, the seer, the conjurer, the cosmic-traveller, and medicine-keeper.

---

[68] Anishinaabeg are Indigenous peoples from the lands around Nayaano-wiishkbiwii-nibiimaang Gichigamiin (The Five Freshwater Seas; Great Lakes). Our traditional territory crosses the borders of Canada and the United States of America. We have lived on the lands of Turtle Island (North American Continent) since time immemorial.

They come.
They come.
Knock! Knock! Knock!
Biindigeg!

They come through the doorway and into the Jiisakiiwigamig.
Pouring in like water into a bucket.
They are here.
There are so many.
So loud. Talking, talking, talking.
The lodge sways, bends, and jumps as they come in.
There are so many.
"Quiet," shouts Mikinaaak, the wise snapping turtle. All are silent.
They have so much to say to us.
We are grateful.
Miigwech, indinawemaaganag!

The poem written above works to immediately immerse all readers into the Anishinaabeg worldview, and speaks to the wonderfulness, mysteriousness, and strangeness of the deep weird qualities of the Anishinaabeg Jiisakiiwigaan ceremony. In the Anishinaabemowin language, Jiisakiiwigaan refers to the Shaking Lodge ceremony. It is a ceremony that embodies spiritual healing, visioning, mediumship, conjuring, and spirit-communing. The ceremony is used by Anishinaabeg to teach lessons, explore, and come-to-know our cosmic place in the order on Aki (the Earth), in waawiyakamig (the universe), and beyond. The Anishinaabeg welcome the strange and weird as vital to our survival along the journey of our miikana-bimaadizi (path of life). The deep weird is both the space and the method by which the beings of the Spirit World structure communication and give demonstrations of the ever-present intersectionality of everyday reality with the levels of reality that run concurrent to our own Earthly realm. "Deep weird" is a phrase borrowed from the work of Welsh anthropologist Jack Hunter (2021), however, in true trickster – Nanaaboozhoo – fashion, I manipulate, configure, and recreate it for my own purposes: not unlike what my ancestors did with glass beads for our beadwork. I take what does not threaten our traditional knowledge and use it to express Anishinaabeg creative vision.

The Jiisakiiwigaan ceremony and its Jiisakiidjig seer teachings came to the Anishinaabeg thousands of years ago. No one knows exactly when the ceremony came to the Anishinaabeg, but it has always been there for us to seek knowledge, divine the future, acquire healing medicines or ceremonies, and commune with our relatives or spiritual allies in the Spirit World. In this chapter, I share some Jiisakiiwigaan teachings and Anishinaabeg understandings of the deep weird through Anishinaabeg eyes. First, I will provide a summary of the deep weird as witnessed by Anishinaabeg. I will also offer a story of the origins of the Jiisakiiwigaan. Following the story, the nature of the Jiisakiiwigaan ceremony as sacred metamorphosis, or transformation, will be discussed. Then, I will examine the aspects of the Jiisakiiwigaan that manifest sacred metamorphosis as teachings on the complexities and intellectual nuances of Anishinaabeg cultural understandings around the deep weird. I share these teachings to educate, build space, and create conversations with other Indigenous and non-Indigenous peoples about the nature of spiritual knowledge in decolonised contexts. Finally, I will offer some concluding thoughts on the deep weird to summarise the knowledge and teachings I have shared and discussed.

Entering the Deep Weird Through an Anishinaabeg Lens

Anishinaabeg understandings, teachings, and ethical intellectual traditions that relate to the deep weird are rooted in the lands we live on, the animals we live with, as well as from the spirit beings who shared life-knowledge with the Anishinaabeg. Anishinaabeg knowledge of the deep weird arises from the Gichi-inaakonigewinan (Great Laws), which are essential to Anishinaabeg worldview, cosmology, axiology, ontology, and epistemologies. The weird spaces of the spirit realms are the traditional territories of the jiibayag (ghosts; spirits) and manidoowag (Spirit Beings). These realms overlap, weave between, and move through the Earthly realm, to make the weird spaces, feelings, knowledge centres, and meeting places that criss-cross the land. The weird in Anishinaabeg contexts holds distinctive meanings that lie outside of Eurocentric expressions of the numinous and anomalous. We recognise the beings that dwell in the weirdness, weird time, and weird territories, as our relatives in the cosmic order of Creation and not outside the realm of possibility. We do not marginalise weirdness or weird beings. We welcome them and hold complex protocols, duties, and responsibilities to guard their sovereign rights. We acknowledge the presence of weirdness and of Spirit when we lay our semaa (sacred tobacco) down on the land.

In Anishinaabemowin, the words for the deep weird are both animate and inanimate based on the contexts that they manifest or are created from. In inanimate contexts, we use the word maamakaaj-ayi'ii, meaning an inanimate strange, wonderful, mysterious or curious thing or place. In animate contexts, maamakaaj-ayi'aa is used to describe a strange, wonderful and mysterious living being or a curious human being, Spirit Being or place. To understand the mystery of the weirdness as affirmed in our language and cultural traditions, I look to words of wisdom from the Anishinaabeg Gichi-aya'aag (Elders). Anishinaabeg Elder James (Jim) Onaubinisay Dumont says that Anishinaabeg embrace, "the mysterious complement of ordinary and "non-ordinary" reality" (Dumont, 1976, p. 36). Anishinaabeg ways of the mythic, mysterious, and mystical, the strange and deep weird are aspects of those people, places or things that are part of our vision of the complexity of Waawiyekamig (universe; cosmos).

Anishinaabeg fully accept that the deep weird can and will occur at any time, but also that it does so to fulfil a function in our everyday reality: to teach, to reveal, to enlighten, and to transform the mundane into mystery. Anishinaabeg worldview in relation to the deep weird is holistic, inclusive of the spirit, mind, body, and emotional state of being, living, seeing, doing, and relating to the cosmos, as well as all our gindinawemaaganidog (relatives or relations) across the universe and beyond. There are ethical protocols for interaction and stories to record the events where we engage with the deeply weird. The deep weird can become a safe space of learning, growth, evolution, and a metaphysical ground for cosmic creativity to work through and for human beings.

The procedures of how to understand, live with, act upon, and participate with the deep weird are outlined in the stories left behind by the ancient Gete-Anishinaabeg (ancestors), as well as those we create today to leave knowledge behind for the seven generations yet to come. In Anishinaabeg traditional pedagogy, we often begin with a story. Story immerses a listener, or reader in this case, inside a particular worldview. Anishinaabeg storytelling anchors our worldview in the contexts of land, the cosmos, time, space, ancient wisdom, and the language of our ancestors. Encoded in each story is the specific knowledge, traditions, and worldview of those Anishinaabeg who have come before, but also those who still carry and live it today. The knowledge and traditions of Jiisakiiwigaan ceremony were gifted long ago by the Spirits and every time we tell their stories we are given those gifts yet again (Murdoch, 2019, p. 113).

Anishinaabeg refer to these types of gifts as, "gaa-izhi-zhawendaa-goziyang" or "that which is given to us in a loving way (by the Spirits)"

(Geniusz, 2009, p. 12). These gifts were so precious that Anishinaabeg created stories to remember and pass on to our children, and future generations – the intricate details of the ceremonies. As the stories are told over and over, the cycle of gift giving is repeated as a reminder of our relationality. Stories tell us that the ceremonies given by Spirit beings allow us to communicate with Manidoowag (Spirit Beings) and Jiibayag (ghosts) across weird spaces, realities, and territories; and, to understand the nature of the weird phenomena, and to learn from them. This gichitwaa-wiijigaabawidaadiwin (sacred relationship) is anchored in the notion of gichitwaa-aanzinaago'idizowin (sacred metamorphosis or transformation) of the body, mind, emotions, or spirit. The origins of Anishinaabe gikendaasowin (intelligence; knowledge) of the deep weird is shaped by our ever-evolving relationships to the weird, which our ancestors left behind in a variety of stories, so that we can continue to learn about our duties and responsibilities.

Below I offer a retelling of an origin story of the Jiisakiiwigaan ceremony. My retelling is inspired by the stories written down by Anishinaabeg cultural writers Isaac Murdoch (2019, pp. 112-116) and James A. Starkey (2006), along with historical accounts from Chief William Berens and A. Irving Hallowell (1942, 1992), Thor Conway's accounts from Anishinaabeg Elders Dave McGregor and Norma Fox (Conway, 2016, pp. 238-242), and the personal accounts of Anishinaabeg painter and Jiisakiiwigaan practitioner, Miskwaabik Animikii (Copper Thunderbird) Norval Morrisseau (Morrisseau, 1979; Sinclair & Pollock, 1979; Ruffo, 2014). In my story, the traditional teachings are given from a regenerative stance and an Anishinaabeg mother's matricentric perspective. Why do I do this? Why do I retell a story in my own way and words? Anishinaabeg-Mississauga scholar Leanne Simpson explains that when she tells the creation story to her children she places the listener, which is usually her children, into the story:

> We are taught to insert ourselves into the story [...] What does this tell us about Nishnaabeg thought? It is personal [...] By inserting ourselves into these stories, we assume responsibilities – responsibilities that are not necessarily bestowed upon us by the collective, but that we take on according to our own gifts, abilities and affiliations. Nishnaabeg theory has to be learned in the context of our own personal lives, in an emotional, physical, spiritual and intellectual way. Every time I tell my children this story, or they hear this part of it in ceremony, their faces light up. It re-affirms that they are good, and beautiful and perfect

the way they are. Every time I have shared this part of our creation story with Indigenous students, their faces light up as well. When interpreted this way, our stories draw individuals into the resurgence narrative on their own terms and in accordance to their own names, clan affiliations and gifts. For just a moment, they are complete in the absence of want – decolonising one moment at a time. Indigenous thought can only be learned through the person; this is because our greatest influence is on ourselves (Simpson, 2011, p. 41).

In this way, I want you to see the story I share through my own Anishinaabeg mother-centred eyes and to not only understand what the ceremony is, but also the *reality* through which an Anishinaabeg woman and mother contextualises the ceremony.

Maajtaadaa![69]

The Gift of Jiisakiiwigaan (Shaking Lodge Ceremony) Comes to the Anishinaabeg-Nibising[70]: A Nanaaboozhoo Story

Long ago there was an Anishinaabeg-Nibising mother named Waaseyaaban-kwe (Light at Dawn Woman). It was fall in the month of Binaakwe-giizis (Falling Leaves Moon). Waaseyaaban-kwe's twelve-year-old child Bineshiinyens (Little Bird) had become very sick, and it lingered for many days. The sickness had settled in their lungs and they were struggling to breathe.[71] Bineshiinyens became weaker and weaker. Waaseyaaban-kwe had tried all the medicines she knew, plus those of

---

[69] Maajtaadaa translates to "Let's begin!" in Anishinaabemowin.

[70] Nibising is the way those at Nipissing First Nation write the name of their people and ancestors. To honour this and my own ancestors, I have included their dialect and spelling preferences here. The Nibising or Nipissing peoples are located in Ontario, Canada. The reserve, Nipissing First Nations, is on the north shore of Lake Nipissing. The Nbisiing Anishinaabeg, are of Ojibweg and Omàmiwininiwag (Algonquin) descent and have lived in the area of Lake Nipissing and the French River watershed since time immemorial. Chief Shabokishick was one of the signatories of the 1850 Robinson-Huron Treaty with my ancestor Biidwewejiwan (or Petawachuan in some translations), whose English name was Michel Eagle Dokis.

[71] I have chosen not to assign gender to the child so that any child can see themselves reflected in the story and any parent can see their child reflected in this story. The pronouns for this child are their, them, they.

the village mashkikiiwi-kwe (medicine woman), but nothing worked. She feared her child would soon die from the mysterious illness. All day, she busied herself making the wiigiwaam (lodge; home) clean and comfortable for her child.

That night, Waaseyaaban-kwe consulted with the grandmothers of her village and they told her to go into a sweat to pray and ask to receive a vision from the Spirits. If there was a cure the Spirits held the answers. The grandmothers and grandfathers of the village prepared the madoodoowgamig (women's sweat lodge; mother's sweat lodge). Finally, Waaseyaaban-kwe and the grandmothers entered the lodge. Together they all prayed to the Spirits, especially Nookomis Dibik-Giizis (Grandmother moon). Very quickly, Waaseyaaban-kwe saw the smoky figures of the Spirits sit down. A paw rested on her knee. It was large, with claws and soft fur. She could see the outline of the animal and recognised it as Odjig (Fisher).

"Odjig, I need help. My child Bineshiinyens is very ill. I fear they will pass away soon if I cannot find some medicine to give them. Can you help me save my baby?" Waaseyaaban-kwe pleaded with the Spirit. Odjig patted her knee reassuringly but did not speak for a long time.

"All life must pass at some time, good mother," Odjig finally said, denying the young mother the information she sought. This was not what Waaseyaaban-kwe wanted to hear at all and she burst into tears.

"Odjig, I beg you. Please share with me what medicine I might use to cure my child. Bineshiinyens is my heart. I love them dearly. Please help me, I beg you," Waaseyaaban-kwe pleaded yet again.

Odjig was again going to deny Waaseyaaban-kwe the answers because Spirits are sometimes very guarded with their knowledge. However, Nanaaboozhoo in the guise of a Waabooz (hare; rabbit) appeared on the other side of Waaseyaaban-kwe and leaned over her lap to poke a paw at Odjig's chest, "You give her that medicine you stingy Fisher!" Waabooz challenged Odjig.

Odjig huffed and snapped back at the rabbit, "How rude! Who invited you here anyway Nanaaboozhoo? I know it is you. That rabbit costume doesn't fool me one bit. You, cousin, are a thieving rat! You're such a big troublemaker, that's what you are. I don't have to give anybody anything!" Odjig turned its face away stubbornly.

"Yes, I am a troublemaker, but that is beside the point. You, cousin, are an old grump. Nookomis-Dibik-Giizis (Grandmother moon) told me about this good mother's plight. Grandmother heard her prayers and sent me to help her in case you decided to be a pain in everyone's behind about it," Waabooz stated, crossing its arms over its chest like a human being. Odjig squirmed knowing that Nookomis-Dibik-Giizis had sent Waabooz specifically to get the medicines for the girl. He couldn't exactly deny the mother now without upsetting Nookomis-Dibik-Giizis, or other Elder Spirits.

"Okay, Okay. No need to get pushy and involve an Elder in this business. I will tell you what to do. Here are the instructions, good mother, listen very closely and do it exactly as I tell you to do it," said the grumpy Odjig.

Odjig told the mother of a manidookewin (sacred ceremony) called the Jiisakiiwigaan (Shaking Lodge) that would bring knowledge to cure her child. The mother was instructed to go back to her Elders, family, and community after the madoodoowgamig was complete.

Waaseyaaban-kwe was to ask the Elders, family and community to help her build a Jiisakiiwigamig (Shaking Lodge) structure. She was given a long list of items to find for lodge-making: fresh spruce sapling poles, spruce branches, basswood bark fibre strands to act as rope, a large black spirit-stone, bells, deer or moose hides, birch bark blankets or cloth tarps as the tent coverings.

Next, she was told to instruct the assemblers of the lodge to take all of the lodge building materials down to the nearby beach and to build two lodges. The first lodge was to be placed several paces from the water's edge and the second lodge would go several paces out into the water, about waist deep. They were to make sure that there was a clear view of the night sky, with the Bagone'giizhik (Seven Sisters; Pleiades star cluster) visible above the lodge, as the entrance to Sky World.

Waaseyaaban-kwe was told to tell the assemblers to take the poles and drive them deep into the ground, one arm's length so that they are firmly held, and angle the poles slightly outward so that when they are tied together with spruce branches in the shape of rings, they will create a firm tension to give the entire structure strong support. The rings must encircle the standing poles. Odjig also instructed that the assemblers attach bells to the top of the lodge that would make noise when the manidoowag (Spirit Beings) and jiibayay (ancestral ghosts) arrived.

Odjig explained that the lodge should only be as tall as a grown man and only far enough across to sit or curl up on the ground like an infant in its mother's womb. When the Shaking Lodge was completed, the assemblers will then need to cover the poles with the hides, blankets, or tarps, leaving an opening at the top for the passage of the visiting jiibayag or manidoowag from the Bagone'giizik.

Then, Odjig instructed her to make sure that all the participants in the ceremony wait till dark for the Jiisakiid seer to arrive. Only then, could the ceremony begin. Next, she was told to provide oshkaabewisag (helpers) for the Jiisakiid. When the Jiisakiid arrived, they would give further instructions from the Jiisakiid.

With all the knowledge and instructions, Odjig provided one last piece of direction to Waaseyaaban-kwe, "Take all this ceremony back to your people. The Anishinaabeg-Nibising can make this lodge whenever you need answers to life's great questions, cures for illness, divinations for the future, or need guidance of the Spirit World." Odjig patted the woman's knee one last time and as the vision faded, Waaseyaaban-kwe could hear Waabooz shout, "See you soon Waaseyaaban-kwe!"

Waaseyaaban-kwe awoke from her gichitwaa-waasayaa-bindamiwin (sacred vision) to the last round of the sweat lodge ceremony. When the ceremony was finally complete, she consulted with the Gichi-aya'aag (Elders) about her vision and the next steps to take. They said that they would call everyone in the village together and tomorrow they would all gather at the Lake Nipissing beach to begin construction of the lodges.

The next day, Waaseyaaban-kwe's family and community built the strange looking cone-shaped wiigiwaaman with the openings on top. As nightfall came and the stars began to speckle the sky, Waaseyaaban-kwe's people waited for the Jiisakiid's arrival with great anticipation.

When the last speck of light was gone and Nookomis-Dibik-Giizis had come over the treetops, a tall figure wrapped in blankets came out of the forest nearby. The being was strikingly beautiful. Yet, there was something deeply weird about this human-looking entity, they did not seem to walk so much as float over the earth. The strange person glided over to Waaseyaaban-kwe.

"Hello Waaseyaaban-kwe," the stranger whispered to her in a rather familiar tone. "Tonight, I am playing a Jiisakiid. This is going to be so much fun. Hey, where are my oshkaabewisag for the evening?" asked the Jiisakiid looking around.

"Do I know you?" Waaseyaaban-kwe asked nervously.

The stranger laughed. "Yes and no," they replied. "Where are my oshkaabewisag?" they repeated.

"Here Jiisakiid," Waaseyaaban-kwe said, leading the Jiisakiid over to their four helpers. The Jiisakiid put down a bandolier bag and then removed their blankets and stood naked before the moonlight. The Jiisakiid began to quietly explain to the helpers how to bind the basswood ropes around their feet, ankles, legs, buttocks, hands, wrists, arms, back, neck, and finally, the mouth. By the time they were done, the Jiisakiid was tied tightly in a fetal position and head tucked downwards between their legs. Their breathing became laboured and strained. The ropes cut into their skin and caused their hands and feet to become blue from lack of blood circulating. The helpers wrapped the Jiisakiid back up in their original blankets. Next, they picked up the Jiisakiid and walked around the lodge on the beach a sacred number of times. Upon completion of the rotations, the Jiisakiid was placed inside the Shaking lodge with their bandolier bag. The contents were laid out for the Jiisakiid: a rattle, a drum, and sacred medicines. They closed the lodge coverings tight and went to sit down.

Silence followed for a long, long time. Silence always marks the beginning. The beginning of something was coming. The quiet was broken by the sound of a rattle, followed by a steady drumming. Soon, strange noises began to build – louder and louder. The sounds were a mixture of knocking, banging, scraping, cracking, and then, distant voices. The bells sounded. Tinkle! Tinkle! Tinkle! The voices sounded like a cacophony of conversations coming from inside the lodge. Lights appeared through cracks in the lodge coverings and out of the opening at the top of the lodge. Like waawaatesiwag (fireflies), they flew around the opening. The tent began to move in an unnatural way, swaying, bending, bulging outwards, jumping, and seemingly dancing in a wind that could not be felt by the community members outside the lodge. The lodge seemed to want to launch upwards, but the poles held the structure tight to the land.

Then a voice from within the Shaking lodge laughed a joyous belly laugh. "Look at you! What is that get-up you got on? Are you into the kinky stuff now? Who has tied you up my silly cousin?" asked the strange croaking voice of Mikinaak (Snapping Turtle). It was a squeaky quacking voice that sounded oddly like a duck. "Here let me get these off you so we can chat. You should not let them bind you up like this. You are 'so-drama' sometimes. Who tied these knots? Dammit! This one is hard to get out. That has got to hurt your boy parts down there. That is going to leave a mark in a very uncomfortable location," said Mikinaak. A lot of huffing, puffing, and swearing came from inside the lodge, but also so much laughter. Joyous laughter. Then, out of the top of the lodge came flying the basswood ropes, which landed on the attendants of the ceremony. It made everyone laugh, breaking the nervous energy that had been held by the crowd outside the lodge.

"Here, sit on this over here before you drown, cousin," said Mikinaak.

Waaseyaaban-kwe wondered who was helping Jiisakiid get out of those tightly bound ropes? She had not seen anyone go into the lodge and all the helpers were sitting next to her on the beach sand.

"Come forth Waaseyaaban-kwe and ask your questions," said the Jiisakiid. Waaseyaaban-kwe crawled closer and sat next to the lodge coverings and put her head close to the lodge.

"Boozhoo (welcome)," said Waaseyaaban-kwe. "Who am I talking to?" she asked the voice within.

"WE ARE," said a multitude of voices. They were so loud that Waaseyaaban-kwe put her hands over her ears.

"Wow! One at a time dammit, and don't yell for Creator's sake. Be polite!" shouted Mikinaak. There were a bunch of sorries said.

Mikinaak (Snapping Turtle), Makwa (Bear), Mashkode-bizhiki (Buffalo), Animikii (Thunderbird), Nibiinaabe-kwe (Mermaid), Odjig (Fisher), and the jiibay known as Baagak (skeleton), all politely offered a greeting to Waaseyaaban-kwe one at a time.

"Boozhoo, to all of you manidoowag and jiibay," replied Waaseyaaban-kwe.

"Ask your questions Waaseyaaban-kwe," stated the Jiisakiid.

"Jiisakiid, Mikinaak, jiibay miinawaa manidoowag, my people have helped me build this Shaking lodge on the instructions of Odjig, so that I could come ask all of you if you have knowledge of a cure for my child's deathly illness. Please help me indinawemaaganag," Waaseyaaban-kwe pleaded.

"I do not know the cure, but we will consult with one another," replied Mikinaak. Sounds of conversations came from inside the lodge. Lights excitedly zoomed around the lodge opening.

"Waaseyaaban-kwe, we will give you the cure for your child and a new name for them to carry because they will be a new person now. They have undergone a transformation by being so close to the edges of the Spirit World. Their new name will be Dakamose-gashkii-dibik-ayaa (Person Who Walks Across the Darkness of Night)," Mikinaak explained.

"Gchi-Miigwech (Thank you) you all for aiding my family and gifting us this knowledge. We will use it in a good way," Waaseyaaban-kwe said through tears.

Mikinaak explained what plant medicines Waaseyaaban-kwe would need to gather, where to find them, and how to prepare the ingredients for the child to consume. After Mikinaak was finished, he said his parting words and the sounds of the lodge quieted until it was completely silent. The winds that had been shaking the lodge stopped, and the lights above the lodge's opening dimmed out. The silence that followed the dimming lights marked the closing of the ceremony.

Then, the oshkaabewisag got up to assist the Jiisakiid out of the lodge. Instead of going to the lodge on the beach, they walked out to the second lodge in the water and opened the coverings. Out floated Waabooz sitting on a log. Startled, the oshkaabewisag watched as the log floated towards the shore. Once at the shore, the Waabooz jumped off and hopped over to Waaseyaaban-kwe. She smiled at seeing the Waabooz from her vision once again. She knew now why the Jiisakiid had acted so familiarly towards her before the ceremony began.

"Waaseyaaban-kwe! Did you get your cure for your child?" asked the Waabooz excitedly. People in the circle around the lodge let out startled sounds seeing a Waabooz talking to the young mother as if it were a human being.

"Yes, Waabooz. Miigwech for all your help," replied Waaseyaaban-kwe smiling.

"No problem, little sister. Please call me Nanaaboozhoo," they said. The Waabooz turned to the oshkaabewisag and lodge assemblers and asked them to begin removing the lodges. It is protocol to dispose of the poles and put all re-usable materials aside upon completion of the ceremony. Waabooz turned back to the community members and told them to go get the medicines and heal the child. To Waaseyaaban-kwe and her husband, Waabooz privately said they would be back to train the child to perform the Shaking Lodge ceremony and healing arts. To this day, both men and women perform the ceremony of the Shaking Lodge.

Gichitwaa-Aanzinaago'idizowin (Sacred metamorphosis) and the Deep Weird

Gichitwaa-aanzinaago'idizowin – the sacred metamorphosis – is the main teaching of the story of Waaseyaaban-kwe. Her child is undergoing a transformation from sickness to death, and from death to healing. Waaseyaaban-kwe undergoes several ceremonies that alter her physical state of being to enhance her spiritual state of being. The Jiisakiiwigamig structure, like the sweat lodge, becomes a cosmic-vehicle or shuttle to the Bagone'giizhik (Pleiades), the opening to the Spirit World, and a tool for the transformation for the Jiisakiid seer to re-make themselves in order to interact with the beings of the deep weird spaces. The Jiisakiid weakened their body using the wiigob-biiminakwaan (basswood bark ropes) to conversely strengthen their spiritual energies. As such, they became the conduit, or medium, for the manidoowag and jiibayag to commune with the participants of the ceremony. The Jiisakiid literally moved locations from the lodge on the beach sand to the second lodge located offshore in the water. They travelled through weird space – the Spirit World – to arrive in that other location. The space inside the lodge is no longer an entirely Earthly place, but an in-between space facilitating transient movements. Lastly, the Jiisakiid transformed into Waabooz, the being that Waaseyaaban-kwe first met in her sweat lodge vision. In this story, it is the spirit beings who are helping to lead, educate, and aid the human world with coming-to-know the deep weird citizens, territories, and knowledge on an intimate level. Additionally, the jiibayag and manidoowag also transform their spiritual bodies to cross over to the Earthly realm and go back again. Bending and turning their being into something that can enter the lodge space, speak and engage in relationships with human beings.

The land also undergoes many changes to facilitate Anishinaabeg access to the spaces, experiences, inhabitants, and knowledge of the deep weird. Aki (Earth), the land, shares her resources, which are transformed from simple rocks, trees, plant medicines, water, and sand, into a nexus point for the intersection of the mundane, the spiritual, and the extraordinary. The animal beings and plant beings are also transformed in this context: as hide, medicine, rattles, and a drum.

Through Waaseyaaban-kwe's journey – interacting in, through and alongside the deep weird – we see sacred metamorphosis in action and manifested through the aid of the Jiisaakid and the shaking lodge ceremony. To me, this is what Anishinaabeg gikendaasowin (knowledge; intelligence), regarding the deep weird looks like – it takes place in the context of family, community, and relations within the natural and spiritual realms. It lacks overt fear, disregard, distrust, and horror, which are values so normalised with mainstream western pedagogy related to the deep weird. Instead, Anishinaabeg responses emphasise creativity, wonder, mystery, ethical responsibility, relationality, reciprocity, and learning in the context of love.

The process of entering the deep weird and interacting with the beings of these spaces is a "cerebral exercise" (Dumont, 1976, p. 33) and is profoundly spiritual in nature. The deep weird requires human beings to utilise a "total way of seeing" (pp. 32), which Elder Dumont likens to "not only vision before but also vision behind (a three-hundred-and-sixty-degree-vision). This was a circular vision that sought to perceive and understand the whole nature of an object or event – its physical reality as well as its soul" (pp. 31-32). This way of knowing is what Michi-Saagiig-Anishnaabeg scholar Leanne Betasamosake Simpson describes as a "whole body intelligence" that is performed in the contexts of land, family, community, ceremony, language, and spiritual traditions (Simpson, 2014, p. 7).

I am using Waaseyaaban-kwe's story here in the same way that it is used by Anishinaabeg Elders in the lodge spaces during ceremony. Story is a teaching space where Anishinaabeg traditional knowledge travels over time and space for individual and collective consciousness, to pass from learner-to-learner. Every Anishinaabeg story undergoes a birth and rebirth with each re-telling. This gichitwaa-aanzinaago'idizowin or metamorphosis of the sacred, is generated out of the power of the storyteller's words containing pieces of their own spirit to animate each word and generate a spiritual connection to the listener, or reader. Story is relationally generated and regenerated, over and over, from person to person. The weird runs real deep in Anishinaabeg storytelling, as each story allows the spirit beings a presence in our Earthly world, our lives, and represent a way to remind human beings of their responsibilities to the weird.

Jiisakiiwigaan Ceremony: Weird Processes in Anishinaabeg Contexts

Within the Jiisakiiwigaan, a jiisakiid is a deep weird practitioner and trained specialist in the ceremony and healing arts of the Jiisakiiwigaan or Shaking Lodge (or Tent) ceremony. They are considered to have been born with the unique gift of having a psychic, clairvoyant 'vision,' or 'the sight.' In Anishinaabeg culture, they have many descriptors, including: seer, conjurer, sorcerer, medium, clairvoyant, medicine man/woman, diviner of future events (Struthers & Valerie, 2005, p. 82), and even prophet (Hallowell, 1992, pp. 68-71; Vastokas, 1973, p. 36). I do not use the term shaman because of its colonial baggage and its tendency to erase traditional terminology. Anthropologist Harvey A. Feit, who worked closely with the James Bay Cree and sought to understand their Shaking Lodge ceremony through a Cree cultural lens, suggests that:

[...] the generalised use of the category "shamanism" is a product of a colonising form of social analysis wherein shamanism was defined by the features which distinguished it from the great religious traditions, or religions with dogmas. As such, it is a concept which has been associated, implicitly or explicitly, with categorising an "other" by the absence of features of the analysts' cultures, whether or not the differences were valued or denigrated (Feit, 1997, p. 123).

There is power and creativity in prioritising the original Anishinaabemowin terminology.

Jiisakiidjig spend many years training to navigate the weird spaces and properly interact with the manidoowag and jiibayag that dwell in those territories. They apprentice with either a family member or community member that is already initiated into the Jiisakiidjig traditions (Ruffo, 2014, p. 35). They carry honorary degrees in spiritual-research, healing, and cosmic-travel. Jiisakiidjig use their own methodologies, methods, and pedagogies of sacred metamorphosis to aid their nation, communities, and culture. Their tools are plant medicines, ceremonial instruments (rattles, drums, and so on), divination, communing, vision-making, language, song, prayer and chanting. Their healing methods include work both inside and outside of the Shaking Lodge. Healing can be physical, mental, spiritual, or even psychic in nature.

Jiisakiidjig's work with the Shaking Lodge is multifaceted when it comes to working with the deep weird to facilitate the gichitwaa-aanzinaago'idizowin for the purposes of healing, lifting curses (McGuire, 2013, p. 163), knowledge gathering, exploration, or divining the future. The jiisakiid must uphold specific ethical principles and behaviours to work their gifts, such as only eating certain foods, refraining from hunting, or avoiding specific animals (Feit, 1994, pp. 295-296; 1997, p. 125). Feit notes that the spirit-helpers of Cree Shaking Lodge practitioners required them to perform specific duties and responsibilities in order to perform the ceremony. He states that:

> [...] the reciprocal dependency of the performer is symbolised by the obligation that throughout his life he may be required by spirit being helpers to show special forms of respect and abstinence for their help. Nevertheless, the willingness of spirits to come distinguishes the performer from his consociates, and several individuals who decided not to do the shaking tent said they took that decision because they

were not sure that the "tent would shake" – that is, that the spirits would indeed enter their tent (Feit, 1997, p. 125; Conway, 2016, p. 239).

In Anishinaabeg contexts, a manidoo-waawaashkeshi (deer spirit-being) would not be inclined to support the human as their bawaaganag (guardian spirits; dream helper; animal or plant spirit beings; ancestral spirits or ghosts), if they engage in eating their clan members and family. For these reasons, Jiisakiid must uphold very specific ethical ways of living and thinking to be granted access to the beings of the weird, as well as to their territories.

To help them navigate the deep weird – to protect, and offer advice – Jiisakiidjig form close working relationships with manidoowag and jiibayag (Vastokas, 1973, p. 36). A deep connection is established between a Jiisakiid and their bawaaganag. These helpers have a burden placed upon them by aligning with the Jiisakiidjig and participating in the Shaking Lodge ceremonies. They bend and reshape their beings to enter our Earthly reality. For instance, Feit remarks that the Cree Shaking Lodge "is dependent on the spirit beings placing themselves in unusual circumstances," and that "they come into the tent, reversing the usual spatial order in which humans reside in the tents and spirit beings outside" (Feit, 1997, p. 125). Both parties leave their comfort zone to interact in the confined space and walls of the Shaking Lodge. Some of the beings that will enter that space may not exactly be safe to be around psychically, psychologically, emotionally, or even physically (Hallowell, 1992, pp. 68-71). To do this, the Jiisakiid brings with them, and relies upon, their guardians, who protect the jiisakiid's soul-spirit (jichaag), and act for their benefit or protection.

Further, because a Jiisakiid must undergo their own metamorphosis inside the lodge space to be able to interact with the Spirit World – and the beings of those realms – they weaken their physical body almost to the point of death in some cases, and their Spirit becomes stronger, but also vulnerable to attack. In Waaseyaaban-kwe's story, the Jiisakiid is bound in basswood ropes that slow their blood circulation and alter their breathing. Such a practice is used to weaken the Jiisakiid physically, reveal the spiritual power and mystery of the weird energies within the ceremony, and to show that the control of the transformative powers of the ceremony is bound directly to the goodwill of the beings of the spirit world (Ruffo, 2014, p. 36; Starkey, 2006, p. 221; Coleman, 1936, p. 51). The role of the weird-helper-beings is to attend to the spiritual wellbeing of the Jiisakiid during that time when they are weakened

– as they conduct their work, and travel across to the territories-of-the-weird-ones, through it, and back again.

Jiisakiiwigamig or Jiishakaan (Shaking Lodge/Tent)

The structure of the Jiisakiiwigamig, also called Jiishakaan, is the other vital component of the gichitwaa-aanzinaago'idizowin, and its overall contexts of accessing and utilising the vast powers of the deep weird. The Jiisakiiwigamig is a cosmic-shuttle carrying the Jiisakiid up to the Bagone'giizhik to open that 'hole in the sky' like a doorway for the beings of the Spirit-World to gather at, but not pour over into our Earthly realm. The Jiisakiid must invite and open the way for the beings of the Spirit World. The Jiisakiiwigamig is like a meeting room, a classroom, a researcher's lab, and a vast library with countless librarians with access to unknown amounts of knowledge.

Jiisakiiwigamig should be viewed as more than just a mere ceremonial lodge, it is also a vital instrument to transform the human traveller, changing space, time, and reality in the process. Anishinaabeg scholar Patricia D. Kishebakabaykwe McGuire writes that the Shaking Lodge works to "serve as manifestations of ceremonial worlds" (McGuire, 2013, p. 68).

The Jiisakiiwigamig is only ever meant to be used as a spiritual healing or learning space. The lodge is never meant to be used for the hurt or harm of Anishinaabeg or any other living being in the cosmos (McGuire, 2013, pp. 163, 209). Patricia Danielle McGuire notes that, "if someone placed a curse on you, the tent could find the person and find out what it took to lift the curse. It was used only on a very special occasion, when needed" (ibid.). The lodge space is animated by the Jiisakiid, but also simultaneously works independently to animate, manipulate and control aspects of the lodge's interior space for the needs of the weird beings that enter. The lodge, as an animate force, manipulates life and lived experience to create a new state of being, thinking, and living for the Jiisakiid, as well as for the ceremonial participants. This can be seen during ceremony when the lodge or tent moves and shakes due to unseen spiritual forces. The shaking signals for the participants that they are now in the domain of the weird, it moves between and through them, and they are now transformed. This sacred movement is evidenced by the presence of the manidoowag and jiibayag, which forever changes the way the viewer will see and experience the Earthly realm (Hallowell, 1992, pp. 68-70; Feit, 1997, pp. 126-128; Starkey, 2006,

p. 221). Once seen, the viewer is forever aware of the weird, and it is acutely aware of those specific human beings in attendance.

Each component of the structure of the Jiisakiiwigamig, represents a piece of a metaphysical device used to undergo sacred metamorphosis. Without each piece being present and actively used, the structure does not become the Jiisakiiwigamig, the metaphysical meeting place, an entrance into the many realities and inhabitants of the deep weird. The lodge is also a space that can only become active using a trained Jiisakiid. Only a trained Jiisakiid could harness the power of the lodge's space to call forth, contain, manage, and return manidoowag and jiibay back to the Spirit World. The trained Jiisakiid utilises the structure of the lodge like an orchestral conductor asserts control over the musicians in an orchestra.

As seen in Waaseyaaban-kwe's story, the Shaking lodge is designed and engineered for spiritual travel. It is a shuttle for metaphysical journeys upwards to access the Star-Nation and Bagone'giizhik. As it shakes, moves, and bends, it signals a spiritual lift off, contact with the Star-Nation, and gitchitwaa-mawadishiwewin (sacred visitation) by beings that dwell in the Spirit Realm. The lodge is cylindrical in shape, high-domed, tall enough for a grown man to stand, and large enough to hold one person on their cosmic voyage, sitting or lying down. The lodge's interior architecture is constructed using freshly cut gaawaandag-mitigoons (spruce saplings) used as abanzhiin (poles) to create the frame of the lodge (Starkey, 2006, p. 221; Conway, 2016, p. 239). The poles are buried deep into the earth, several feet down, to prevent the structure from being torn out of the ground by the movements of the tent during the ceremony (Struthers & Eschiti, 2005, p. 82; Hallowell, 1992, pp. 68-70; McGuire, 2013, pp. 163, 193). The amount of poles varies, but they act as anchors to tether the entire structure and keep a steady connection to the Earthly realm. Practically, the abanzhiin provide a frame for the coverings that create a space for the weird to enter the Earthly realm, but also for the Jiisakiid to enter a space that is considered as a spiritual matrix for the manifestation of the weird (Starkey, 2006, p. 221; Struthers & Eschiti, 2005, p. 82).

Historically, the frame would be covered or draped with wiigwaas (birchbark), large waawaashkeshiwayaan (deer hide) or moozowayaan (moose hide), but in modern contexts, canvases, blankets or plastic tarps are used to cover the entire lodge, blocking light from the outside; however, some lodges leave a space at the bottom. Struthers and Eschiti share that the poles are arranged with "a centre pole and then the rest of them are all packed around them. Then, this material is wrapped around it, probably as high as this ceiling (room ceiling)" (Struthers & Eschiti, 2005, p. 82).

Near the hole left open at the top of the lodge, the lodge assemblers place bells, pieces of metal, tin (e.g. can lids), or powwow jingle cones, to create noise makers that rattle and jingle, sounding the beginning of the metamorphosis (McGuire, 2013, pp. 163, 193). The presence of weird sounds is critical because sound waves create and recreate life. Our bodies are held together by sound waves, so making a space for weird sounds to be present in the ceremony is a transformative experience. Anishinaabeg are taught in the Creation stories about the birth of the cosmos, that sound is the presence of Gizhew-Manidoo's thoughts manifesting and made real to us (Benton-Banai, 1988, pp. 2-4; Johnston, 1986, pp. 12-13).

The other entrance of importance is the lodge doorway and door. The point of entry into the space where the Jiisakiid enters the aazhawigamig or the between space linking the earth to the realm of the spirit begins with the jiisakiiwigamig gibinde'igan (Shaking Lodge door coverings) and the gibishkwaandem (doorway) as a space protecting our earthly realm and acting as an opening for both humans, jiibay and manidoowag to cross through to attend the ceremony. The Jiisakiid is either placed or crawls inside the lodge through the doorway and coverings (Struthers & Eschiti, 2005, p. 82). The purpose of such a small opening is to seal out the earthly world to create a space of darkness where the jiibay and manidoowag feel comfortable to enter the aazhawigamig space of the Shaking Lodge.

Entering through the door marks the moment when the Jiisakiid seer is transformed from a mere human into a being recognisable to the spirit entities as a Jiisakiid. The action and motion of physically entering the shaking tent as a sacred space is gichitwaa-babaamaadiziwin (sacred travel). The Jiisakiid enters the between-space, moving between the Earthly realm and the Sky World, or World of the Spirit Beings. Aazhawigamig can be used to describe this. Another term is zhegwazowin (to be in-between the folds), where the Jiisakiid undergoes zhaabwiiwin, which is the process of passing through and surviving that spiritual movement. In the case of the Jiisakiid, they also become or transform into a passage space, a conduit, or channel, through and for, the weird beings to communicate with the participants of the Shaking Lodge ceremony. It is a complicated state of transformative intersection and mediumship.

The human being must be transformed into the Jiisakiid 'in-practice,' capable of transforming him/her/themself into a conduit or channel for calling forth jiibay and manidoowag. Entry to the lodge begins the process of Jiisakiid's metamorphosis and can only occur for the human being inside (or around in some cases) that lodge. In his book, *The Ojibwa of Berens River, Manitoba: Ethnography into History*, anthropologist A. Irving Hallowell states that as the Jiisakiid enters, in that moment he/she/they becomes the "conjurer" (Hallowell, 1992, p. 68). Entry into and over to what Elder Dumont called "dream-reality" or space, activates in the jiisakiid special abilities that would not exist in everyday reality, only in another reality concurrent to our own (Dumont, 1976, p. 33). Now the Jiisakiid is no longer bound by the restraints of our everyday human reality (Anishinaabeg gikenjigaadewin). The Jiisakiid travels through the doorway of the lodge and into the Jiibayag miinawaa manidowwag gikenjigaadewin (Ghosts and Spirit Beings reality) located in a dream-space or vision-space, which are places that enable the Jiisakiid to "realise their own ability to be transformed or to transform themselves" (ibid.).

Elder Dumont teaches that in a dream/vision reality, a human being can fly, we can be an eagle, we can change genders, or travel to another part of the Earth (Dumont, 1976, pp. 33-34). He describes the process as taking place on a "level of reality which is concurrent with everyday reality and one of the ways we gain access to this "other reality" is through the dream. So it is, when we travel in dreams, we actually do travel" (Dumont, 1976, p. 33). Elder Dumont defines this as "spirit travel" (ibid.), or in Anishinaabemowin, jiibay-babaamaadiziwin, where the body of the human is weakened so that the spirit can be free, boundless, and untethered to the waking realm. As human beings, most of our dreams and visions take place in the darkness provided by night or ceremonial lodges, and when the Jiisakiid enters the darkness of the Shaking Lodge, they travel into the concurrent reality offered by the dark spaces.

The last aspect of the lodge space that I want to share here is the power of darkness or gichitwaa-dibikad (Sacred Darkness). No discussion of the weird could ever be deemed complete without discussion of darkness. There are different types of gichitwaa-dibikad (sacred darkness) required in the Shaking Lodge ceremony to enact metamorphosis. First, is the darkness that comes with dibikaabaminaagwad (dusk or twilight) and dibikad (night). The darkness of the night is referred to as gashkii-dibikad. Gashkii-dibikad refers specifically to the darkness that comes from the depths of the forest and wraps around you as soon as the sunlight begins to disappear, and it will not return till morning. There is a feeling that arrives with the kind of darkness that does not retreat but envelops everything on the land.

There is also the nighttime darkness that exists between the stars (aazhawi-anangoog) that exists as cosmic-darkness. This darkness reminds Anishinaabeg of the connections between the Shaking Lodge and Star-Nation and the Bagone'giizhig, which is the origin for the Shaking Lodge ceremony. To harness the power of the Bagone'giizhig stars, the ceremony is conducted at night when the stars can be seen. Anishinaabeg people know that everything in Creation, seen and unseen, has Spirit. Holding the Shaking Lodge at night acknowledges the Sky World and Star Nation as animate. All are part of our First Family, the natural ecology of the cosmos. The Stars are paid respect through this ceremony.

There is great significance in the ceremony being held during the dark of night, or at dusk (Struthers & Eschiti, 2005, p. 82; Hallowell, 1992, p. 70; Ruffo, 2014, p. 36; Hill, 2006, p. 183). The key is to create space for darkness inside and outside the lodge because only in the darkness will the jiibayag and manidoowag emerge. The darkness acts as a gitchitwaa-gokokaajigan, meaning sacred bridge between or across to another reality or world. Safety and communing can only happen in that darkened space. Darkness is the facilitator for the azhawigamig (between spaces), enabling engagement, communication, connection, and intimacy between human beings and the manidoowag (Follet, 2005, p. 2; Cook, 1997, p. 58).

We are told in our Anishinaabeg Creation Stories that in the beginning, before there was a beginning, there was only darkness. Everything important begins first in darkness. As Kanien'kehá:ka Elder and traditional midwife, Katsi Cook says, life in a woman's womb begins in total darkness, as the "first environment" (Follet, 2005, p. 2; Cook, 1997, p. 58). Our dreams and visions in a sweat lodge begin in darkness. The darkness of the Shaking Tent evokes the cosmic darkness from which all things and all life begins. Darkness holds the power of the dream-space (or vision-space). In the Creation story, Gizhew-Manidoo existed in darkness and the first thing they saw in the darkness was a dream or a vision of everything that could come about in the cosmos. Out of the darkness, the dream was transformed into life. The darkness is a place Anishinaabeg always return to when we seek answers to life's questions, and to commune with those elements of Creation that exist in those cosmic-creative spaces, such as the other-than-human-beings, or Manidoowag, who naturally dwell within them.

Inside the Shaking Lodge the Jiisakiidjig will partake in the sacred darkness that opens inwards into the metaphysical dark spaces of the cosmic map to reach out to those "other-than-human" realities (Dumont, 1976, p. 33). Hallowell describes this as partaking in the metaphor of the vision (1942, pp. 9-10). To enter the darkness is to begin manifesting the vision. Each Jiisakiid travels into the gashkii-dibikate (dark as night inside the lodge) to sit on the bottom floor of the lodge in the centre as the aabaabika'gan (key) to open the metaphysical doorway at the Bagone'giizhik; and also, the genawenimaad (keeper; protector; guard), so that they can welcome, gather, and manage the company of jiibayag and manidoowag inside the lodge. Sitting on the floor of the lodge in utter darkness – except maybe the light of the stars or moon above – initiates the Jiisakiid to begin to move within the metaphorical vision of the ceremony.

The darkness comes through the floor of the lodge, the ground below, directly from the Anaamakamig (underworld). For this reason, the lodges are often placed near or in the nibi (water) (Starkey, 2006, p. 221; McGuire, 2013, pp. 193, 209). A Jiisakiid can appeal to the Makadeshigan (Black Bass), who is known as a great Spirit Being of the underworld, patron to the deep night and darknesses. He guards the lakes of the underworld and has knowledge of all the dark places. He is described as the "Manidoowid dimiigami, Manidoowid bishagiishkibik, manidoowid dibikadinik, manidoowid giimoodiziwin. Spirit of the deep, spirit of the dark, spirit of the night, spirit of the hidden" (Zhaawano-Giizhik, 2019). According to Anishinaabeg artist Zhaawano Giizhik, Makadeshigan's teachings are about striving to live an honest and humble life (ibid.). Makadeshigan, along with other weird beings of the underworld, such as Mishi-bizhiw (Water Lynx or Underworld Cat) and Gchi-Ginebigoog (Great Water Serpents), act as protectors of the Anishinaabeg, in return Anishinaabeg offered their semaa (sacred tobacco) or kinnikinnik[72] (tobacco mix; medicine offering; mixed medicines), respected their privacy and territories, and protected the wellbeing of the water, along with regularly offering ceremony to the water as an honoured relative (Smith, 1995, pp. 142-143; Conway, 2016, pp. 103-126). These Giigoonhyag Manidoog (Water Spirit beings) of the Underworld are

---

[72] Kinnikinnik is also written as Giniginigeg, which is probably more the way my Elders and language speakers would want it written, but the spelling I have used here is recognised by most Anishinaabeg as the "universally" recognised way to write it.

known for the sacrifices they have made for human beings, not just as food, but as medicine, allies in war, gift-givers (for example, providing ceremonies, medicines, stories), and important teachers on how to safely navigate the complexities of the darkness: physically, mentally, emotionally, and spiritually. Some Spirits found in the Underworld are considered to be the guardians of those who seek to travel through the dark places in this reality and those realities beyond our own (Starkey, 2006, p. 263). In Anishinaabeg oral stories, the manidoowag of the Underworld are known for presenting the Anishinaabeg with methods and methodologies to deal with the harder aspects of the darkness in our lives, to find power in dreams and visions that rise only from within the space of sacred darkness (Geniusz, 2009, p. 10; Hallowell, 1992, pp. 11-12; Benton-Banai, 1988, p. 4). There are benefits – and life even – in the darkness that resides below the ground, which are central to the process of ceremonies like the Shaking Lodge.

Every culture around the world has a relationship with the gichitwaa-dibikad, the darkness, the shadow space where the weird beings live, thrive, and survive despite ongoing colonial genocide to their culture, territories, and life-ways. For Anishinaabeg, the ceremony of the Shaking Lodge celebrates this survival, uses its intelligence, and welcomes the inhabitants as relatives in Creation. For some cultures, the darkness is evil, scary, alien, unknown, and weird. Through the weirdness, strangeness, and mystery, we find creation and valuable experiences to take with us when we are reborn to the light of our everyday lives.

Emerging from the Weird: Final Words Before We Go ...

As Anishinaabeg, the deep weird is our relative, our relation. Interwoven into the reality of our worldview as Anishinaabeg, the deep weird is the presence of the Spirit World that intersects, overlaps, and interweaves into our Anishinaabe mino-miikana bimaadizi. Our ancestors learned to walk, dance, and sing through the deep weird using the ceremonies gifted to them in a loving way by the spirits and those weird beings of the forests, lakes, rivers, night sky, and dreams. Our Shaking Lodge, sweat lodges, fasting lodges, birth ceremonies, marriage ceremonies, death ceremonies, and so many more, are all ways for us to incorporate the beings of the weird, including the manidoowag, jiibayag, bawaaganag, and the bawaajigan mayaajiiging (plant helpers), into our Anishinaabe-bimaadizi (human life). This means we learn to live traveling across our human Earthly realm, or reality, and the concurrent realities, or Spirit realms, because that is our natural state of existing. In this way, we are intimately tied to these relations of the deep weird in ways that other cultures of the world have forgotten, forsaken, or been forced to put aside due to colonisation.

The knowledge shared here does not belong to me, but to all Anishinaabeg. As carriers of ancestral knowledge, we are responsible for passing it forward, so that our descendants can see themselves mirrored in the experiences of their ancestors. These words, teachings, and experiences are meant to educate about Anishinaabeg spiritual traditions and knowledge systems within Anishinaabeg contexts.

The Anishinaabeg have no words or need for conclusions. We have no word for goodbye because we do not believe that anything truly ends. Further, we believe that everything belongs to the deep weird energies of waawiyekamig, our universe, and, to Gizhew-Manidoo, the Great Mystery that guides us all through the mysteries of life. Therefore, as an act of resistance, decolonisation, and destabilisation of settler-colonial narratives about the deep weird in relation to Indigenous intellectual traditions, I offer the following parting Anishinaabeg words to unsettle. When I say these words, it 'weirds people out' with its heaviness and I love it! Somewhere in the darkness Waabooz/Nanaaboozhoo laughs. So, I extend these parting words to all who might read what I have shared:

Baanimaa miinawaa odisaabandamang giga-waabandimin.

The spirits will decide when we will meet each other again.
If we do not see each other in this world then we will see each other in the next.

BIOGRAPHIES

Renée E. Mazinegiizhigo-kwe Bédard, PhD., is of Anishinaabeg ancestry and a member of Dokis First Nation. She holds a doctorate from Trent University and previously worked at Nipissing University as an Assistant Professor in the Department of Native Studies. She is now based at Western University, cross appointed to the Gender, Sexuality and Women Studies Department and Indigenous Studies program. Her area of publication includes work related to Anishinaabeg mothering, maternal education, and contemporary issues facing Anishinaabeg women.

Joshua Cutchin is an author of speculative nonfiction and a professional tuba player based out of Roswell, Georgia. He has appeared on a wide variety of paranormal programs discussing his work, including Coast to Coast AM, Mysterious Universe, Binnall of America, Expanded Perspectives, Radio Misterioso, and the Gralien Report. He is the author of five books: 2015's *A Trojan Feast: The Food and Drink Offerings of Aliens, Faeries, and Sasquatch*; 2016's *The Brimstone Deceit: An In-Depth Examination of Supernatural Scents, Otherworldly Odors, & Monstrous Miasmas*; 2018's *Thieves in the Night: A Brief History of Supernatural Child Abductions*; and 2020's *Where the Footprints End: High Strangeness and the Bigfoot Phenomenon, Volumes I & II*, with Timothy Renner. 2022 saw the release of his two-volume work *Ecology of Souls: A New Mythology of Death & the Paranormal*. Joshua is also a contributor to Robbie Graham's 2017 collection of ufological essays *UFOs: Reframing the Debate*, as well as David Weatherly's 2018 Sasquatch collection *Wood Knocks: Vol. 3*. Excerpts of his work have appeared in *Fortean Times* and *Edgescience*.

Susan Demeter is a Canadian born author, artist, and witch. The themes of her writing, research, art, and spirituality incorporate her lifelong interest in exceptional human experiences, UFOs, nature, social history, mysteries, and cosmic magic. She has conducted PhD supervised research on behalf of the Defence Studies Department of the Canadian Armed Forces College in Toronto, Canada on the topic of UFOs and social psi, and for the The Koestler Parapsychology Unit at the University of Edinburgh on poltergeist activity. Susan has been a member of various paranormal groups and has developed several websites over the years including PSICAN: Paranormal Studies and Inquiry Canada. Susan's first book *Cosmic Witch: Magic Witchcraft and the Supernatural* was published in both English and Italian in August 2020. She has conducted a series of experiments based on and inspired by the work of the late mathematician A.R.G Owen and psychotherapist Joel Whitton, popularly known as "The Philip Experiments," which will be the focus of her forthcoming book tentatively titled *Out of My Mind's Eye: Conjuring UFOs*. She is a co-creator of, and magickal consultant for, the UFOlogy Tarot. Susan lives in the Apennine Mountains near Bologna, Italy with her husband, astrophysicist and electronic musician Massimo Teodorani, and their two cats Pixie and Merry. Her home studio faces a mountain peak that was in ancient times considered to be a holy place by both Pagans and early Christians. It is there that the ultra-terrestrials inspire her witchcraft and her art. Susan can be reached online through her website at susandemeter.com and her socials. She is always keen to hear from other magickal thinkers and experiencers of the deep weird.

Chris Diltz, PhD., was born in Edmonds, Washington. During his youth he became fascinated with science and would spend his free time learning mathematics, astronomy, physics and electronics. Dr Diltz also obtained an interest in the paranormal, including unexplained aerial phenomena, Men in Black and the interdimensional hypothesis. He went to Ohio University to obtain a Bachelor of Science degree in Physics in 2010, and stayed on to obtain a PhD in Astrophysics in 2016, specialising in high energy particle interactions in active galaxies. Through his degrees, Dr Diltz has been able to obtain a broad variety of different computer and programming skills, including data science, machine learning, deep learning and computational physics. Dr Diltz currently resides in Dayton, Ohio where he works as a computer scientist and hardware verification engineer. In his spare time, he enjoys reading historical non-fiction and journal articles on high energy astrophysics, exercising, traveling and seeing family and friends.

Zelia Edgar has had a lifelong interest in the paranormal inspired by the rich history of weirdness throughout her home state of Wisconsin, and has been seriously researching it for over a decade. In that time, her interest has evolved from the conventional to the highly strange, with a special emphasis on cases that transcend the boundaries between different fields of study. She is the creator and presenter of the YouTube channel Just Another Tin Foil Hat. Her first book *Just Another Tin Foil Hat Presents...* was recently published by Beyond the Fray Publishing.

Barbara Fisher was born and raised in West Virginia. She has a degree in professional writing with concentrations and minors in journalism, history, film, and biology from Ohio University. She has studied the paranormal on her own since she could read, spurred on by her own extensive personal experience and communications with non-human intelligences, which began in early childhood. These experiences have influenced her art and writing, and have led to her partnership with data and computer scientists in an attempt to use natural language processing and machine learning to analyse the copious amount of data that has been collected about paranormal experiences over the past several centuries. She also runs a paranormal podcast called *6 Degrees of John Keel*, where she specialises in bringing attention to the stories of experiencers like herself.

Michael Grosso, PhD., is an independent scholar, associated with an ongoing Seminar at Esalen on the role of mind in the cosmos. His latest book focuses on psychic anomalies that challenge reductive materialism. The emphasis is on waking up to the full girth of our potential. He has taught humanities and philosophy at Marymount Manhattan College, City University of New York, and New Jersey City University. He is on the Board of Directors of the American Philosophical Practitioner's Association, and is a past editor of the journal for that association.

Jack Hunter, PhD., is an anthropologist exploring the borderlands of consciousness, religion, ecology and the paranormal. He is an Honorary Research Fellow with the Alister Hardy Religious Experience Research Centre, and a tutor with the Sophia Centre for the Study of Cosmology in Culture, University of Wales Trinity Saint David, where he is lead tutor on the MA in Ecology and Spirituality and teaches on the MA in Cultural Astronomy and Astrology. He is also a lecturer on the Alef Trust's MSc in Consciousness, Spirituality and Transpersonal Psychology. He is a Research Fellow with the Parapsychology Foundation, and a Professional Member of the Parapsychological Association. In 2010 he founded *Paranthropology: Journal of Anthropological Approaches to the Paranormal*. He is the author of *Spirits, Gods and Magic* (2020) and *Manifesting Spirits* (2020), and is the editor of *Mattering the Invisible* (2020), *Greening the Paranormal* (2019), *Damned Facts* (2016), *Strange Dimensions* (2015), and *Talking with the Spirits* (2014). He lives in the hills of Mid-Wales with his family.

Jeffrey J. Kripal, PhD., is the Associate Dean of the School of Humanities and holds the J. Newton Rayzor Chair in Philosophy and Religious Thought at Rice University, where he chaired the Department of Religion for eight years and helped create the GEM Program, a doctoral concentration in the study of Gnosticism, Esotericism, and Mysticism. He is the Associate Director of the Center for Theory and Research at the Esalen Institute in Big Sur, California, where he served as Chair of Board from 2015 to 2020. Jeff is the author or co-author of eleven books including, most recently, a memoir-manifesto entitled *Secret Body: Erotic and Esoteric Currents in the History of Religions* (Chicago, 2017). He specialises in the study of extreme religious states and the re-visioning of a New Comparativism, particularly as both involve putting "the impossible" back on the academic table again. He is presently working on a three-volume study of paranormal currents in the history of religions and the sciences for The University of Chicago Press, collectively entitled *The Super Story*.

David Luke, PhD., is an Associate Professor of Psychology at the University of Greenwich. He is currently a leader on the Psychology of Exceptional Human Experience module, which has been running since 2009, and also teaches on the Introduction to Psychology, and Criminology and Forensic Psychology modules. Dr Luke is also currently an Honorary Senior Lecturer at the Centre for Psychedelic Research, Division of Brain Sciences, Imperial College London, and is a lecturer on the MSc Consciousness, Spirituality and Transpersonal Psychology where he leads and teaches a module on Psychedelics and Entheogens for The Alef Trust via Liverpool John Moores University. He was President of the Parapsychological Association between 2009 and

2011, and received an Early Career Research Excellence Award (2011) and the first Inspirational Teaching Award (2016) from the University of Greenwich.

Leonardo Breno Martins, PhD., is a collaborating Professor at the Institute of Psychology, University of São Paulo. He holds a doctorate and a master's degree in social psychology from the University of São Paulo, as well as a degree in psychology from the Federal University of Minas Gerais. He is a member of Inter Psi - Laboratory of Anomalistic Psychology and Psychosocial Processes (USP). His research interests are in areas related to mental health, social psychology, anomalistic psychology, psychology of magic and the psychology of religion.

Alan Murdie is a barrister who has personally investigated numerous reports of hauntings and poltergeists, in Britain and abroad. He knew both Maurice Grosse and Guy Lyon Playfair for over twenty years and has enjoyed extensive access to their original records, as well as those of other researchers involved with the Enfield case. He has been a member of the Society for Psychical Research since 1997 and is chairman of The Ghost Club. He has written and broadcast extensively on paranormal topics and writes a monthly column on ghosts for the magazine *Fortean Times*.

Anthony Peake is a bestselling author, lecturer, broadcaster and leading thinker in the area of consciousness studies. He studied Sociology and History at the University of Warwick and Human Resources Management at the London School of Economics. He is a member of the Scientific and Medical Network and the International Association of Near Death Studies. His ideas apply scientific reasoning to some of the greatest mysteries of the universe, including what happens when we die. His most recent books include: *Opening the Doors of Perception* (2016), *The Hidden Universe* (2019) and *Cheating the Ferryman* (2022).

Sharon Hewitt Rawlette, PhD., has a doctorate in philosophy from New York University and wrote her dissertation at the Ecole Normale Supérieure in Paris. She was Florence Levy Kay Fellow in Ethics at Brandeis University before launching her freelance writing career. Her essays have appeared in *Salon* and *Orion*, as well as in the peer-reviewed scholarly publications *Philosophical Studies* and the *Journal of Scientific Exploration*. She lives in rural Virginia, and is the author of *The Feeling of Value: Moral Realism Grounded in Phenomenal Consciousness* (2016), *The Source and Significance of Coincidences* (2019), and *Beyond Death* (2022).

Peter M. Rojcewicz, PhD., is a higher education administrator and professor, folklorist, and poet, as well as an executive leadership consultant. He has researched international stories, beliefs, and manifestations of the mythic imagination around the world. Trained in folklore and folk life, English and American literature, and depth psychology, he is an authority on archetypal images and symbols. He has taught the humanities, fairy tales, myths, comparative religions and folk belief systems at several universities, as well as at the C.G. Jung Foundation for Analytical Psychology, New York. Peter is currently Provost and Vice President of Academic Affairs at Pacifica Graduate Institute, Santa Barbara, CA. He served previously as Chief Academic Officer at University of the West, Vice President of Academic Affairs and Dean of Faculty at Antioch University Seattle, and Dean of the School of Holistic Studies, John F. Kennedy University, as well as Professor and Chair of the Department of Liberal Arts at The Juilliard School. He received his doctoral degree in folklore & folk life from the University of Pennsylvania, where he earned the Dean's Award for Distinguished Teaching.

Gregory Shushan, PhD., is the leading authority on near-death experiences and the afterlife across cultures and throughout history. He is the author of *The Next World: Extraordinary Experiences of the Afterlife* (2022), *Near-Death Experience in Indigenous Religions* (2019), and *Conceptions of the Afterlife in Early Civilizations* (2009). He is currently Visiting Fellow at University of Winchester, and Research Fellow at the Parapsychology Foundation. Dr Shushan was previously Honorary Research Fellow at the Religious Experience Research Centre at University of Wales Trinity Saint David, Perrott-Warrick Researcher at University of Oxford's Ian Ramsey Centre for Science and Religion, and Scholar-in Residence at the Centro Incontri Umani (The Cross Cultural Centre), Ascona, Switzerland. He has lectured at universities in the UK, Ireland, and Switzerland and has given numerous talks on his research in nine countries.

Peter Sjöstedt-Hughes, PhD., is a philosopher of mind, research fellow and associate lecturer at the University of Exeter, in the United

Kingdom. Peter is the author of the books *Noumenautics* and *Modes of Sentience*, the TEDx Talker on 'Psychedelics and Consciousness,' and the inspiration for the Marvel superhero, Karnak. Sjöstedt-Hughes has a doctorate in 'Pansentient Monism,' and specialises in philosophies of mind concerning panpsychism, altered states of consciousness, and mental causation – and in the thoughts of Whitehead, Spinoza, and Nietzsche amongst others. Peter, though born in Sweden, lives by the ocean in Cornwall, Britain, with his wife and two children.

Samantha Lee Treasure is a British-Canadian medical anthropology student at SOAS University of London, and is currently based in Busan, South Korea. Inspired by childhood experiences on a (potentially) haunted farm, her research focuses on out-of-body experiences and sleep paralysis, and she has delivered talks on these topics since 2013 in the UK, Japan, Russia, and the UK. Her goal is to help de-stigmatise these experiences, while offering helpful information to people in an ethical and balanced way. Her first book, exploring the effects of technology and fiction on a variety of supernatural and hallucinatory experiences, is due to be released with Inner Traditions in 2023.

Zofia Weaver, PhD., served as Editor of the *Journal of the Society for Psychical Research* in the years 1999-2002 and is currently its Associate Editor. One of her main areas of interest in psychical research is the investigation of famous Polish psychics. Together with Mary Rose Barrington and the late Professor Ian Stevenson she has written a comprehensive study of the Polish clairvoyant Stefan Ossowiecki, published in 2005, and in 2015 she published a book on the Polish physical medium Franek Kluski. She is currently co-authoring a book about clairvoyance and psychic detection.

Simon Young, PhD., is a British folklore historian, based in Italy. He has a longstanding interest in the study of the supernatural. In 2017 he edited *Magical Folk* (2017) with Ceri Houlbrook, and has published dozens of peer-reviewed articles in *Folk Life, Folklore, Gramarye, Supernatural Studies, Tradition Today* and other journals. His most recent book *The Boggart* (2022) is a study of the most feared supernatural being from the north of England, the boggart.

REFERENCES

Abraham, D. (2021). Personal communication.

Abrahamson, J., Bychkoy, A. V., & Bychkoy, V. L. (2002). 'Recently reported sightings of ball lightning: observations collected by correspondence and Russian and Ukrainian sightings.' *Phil Trans R Soc Lond,* A360, pp. 11-35.

Ager, R. (2008). 'Mazes, Mirrors, Deception and Denial: Chapter Four – Around Every Corner.' Available Online: https://www.collativelearning.com/the%20 shining%20-%20chap%204.html [Accessed 8th September 2021].

Alexandrian, S. (1970). *Surrealist Art.* London: Thames & Hudson.

Almeida, A. M. & Lotufo Neto, F. (2003). 'Methodological guidelines to explore altered states of consciousness and anomalous experiences.' *Revista de Psiquiatria Clínica,* Vol. 30, No. 1, pp. 21-28.

Alvarado, C. S. (2002). 'Guest editorial: thoughts on the study of spontaneous cases.' *Journal of Parapsychology,* Vol. 66, pp. 115-125.

Alvarado, C.S. (2019). 'Musings on Materializations: Eric J. Dingwall on "The Plasma Theory."' *Journal of Scientific Exploration,* Vol. 33, No. 1, pp. 73–113.

Alvarado, C. S., Machado, F. R. & Zingrone, N. (1998). 'Research methods in parapsychology (Part II) [Métodos de investigación en parapsicología (Parte II)].' *Boletim Aipa, Buenos Aires,* 2, Vol. 1, No. 3, pp. 9-12.

Anon (1566). *The Examination of John Walsh: Before Maister Thomas Williams.* London: John Awdely.

Anon (1914). *Princess Mary's Gift Book.* London: Hodder & Stoughton.

Appelle, S., Lynn, S. J. & Newman, L. (2000). 'Alien abduction experiences.' In: E. Cardeña, S.J. Lynn, & S. Krippner (eds.) *Varieties of anomalous experience:*

examining the scientific evidence. Washington: American Psychological Association, pp. 253-282.

A.P.R.O. (1972). 'Multiple Witness Case in California.' *The A.P.R.O. Bulletin*, March-April 1972, pp. 1-5.

Arment, C. (2006). *The Historical Bigfoot.* Landisville: Coachwhip.

Artisson, R. (2020) *The Clovenstone Workings: A Manual of Early Modern Witchcraft*: Maine Black Malkin Press.

Athappilly, G., Greyson, B. & Stevenson, I. (2006). 'Do prevailing societal models influence reports of near-death experiences? A comparison of accounts reported before and after 1975.' *Journal of Nervous & Mental Disease*, Vol. 194, pp. 218-222.

Au, R. (2020). 'How I shifted to Hogwarts.' YouTube [online]. Available from: https://www.youtube.com/watch?v=foAf-vOLs_4 [Accessed 18th March 2022].

Badham, P. (1990). *Near-Death Experiences, Beliefs About Life After Death, and the Tibetan Book of the Dead.* Tokyo: Honganji International Buddhist Study Center.

Badham, P. (1997). 'Religious and near-death experience in relation to belief in a future life.' *Mortality*, Vol. 2, No. 1, pp. 7-20.

Barrett, W. (1911). 'Poltergeists Old and New.' *Proceedings of the SPR*, Vol 25, No. 191.

Barrington, M.R. (2018). *JOTT: when things disappear... and come back or relocate - and why it really happens.* San Antonio: Anomalist Books.

Barrington, M.R. (2019). *Talking about psychical research.* Guildford: White Crow Books.

Bastos, M.A.V., Bastos, P.R.H.D.O., Osório, I.H.S., Muass, K.A.R.C., Iandoli, D. & Lucchetti, G. (2016). 'Frontal electroencephalographic (EEG) activity and mediumship: a comparative study between spiritist mediums and controls.' *Archives of Clinical Psychiatry (São Paulo)*, Vol. 43, pp.20-26.

Batcheldor, K. (1984). 'Contributions to the theory of PK induction from sitter-group work.' *Journal of American Society of Psychical Research*, Vol. 78, pp. 105-122.

Bates, B. (2012 [1983]). *The Way of Wyrd: Tales of an Anglo-Saxon Sorcerer.* London: Hay House.

Baxter, R. (1691). *The certainty of the worlds of spirits and, consequently, of the immortality of souls of the malice and misery of the devils and the damned: and of the blessedness of the justified, fully evinced by the unquestionable histories of apparitions, operation.* London: Printed for T. Parkhurst.

REFERENCES

Beardsworth, T. (1977). *A Sense of Presence: The phenomenology of certain kinds of visionary and ecstatic experience, based on a thousand contemporary firsthand accounts.* Oxford: The Religious Experience Research Unit.

Becker, C. (1985). 'Views from Tibet: near-death experiences and the Book of the Dead.' *Anabiosis,* Vol. 5, No. 1, pp. 3-20.

Behringer, W. (2004). *Witches and Witch-hunts: a Global History.* Oxford: Wiley-Blackwell.

Beischel, J. & Schwartz, G. (2007). 'Anomalous information reception by research mediums demonstrated using a novel triple-blind protocol.' *Explore: The Journal of Science and Healing,* Vol. 3, No. 1, pp. 23-37.

Belanti, J., Perera, M., & Jagadheesan, K. (2008). 'Phenomenology of near-death experiences: a cross-cultural perspective.' *Transcultural Psychiatry,* Vol. 45, No. 1, pp. 121–33.

Bender, H. (1969). 'New Developments in Poltergeist Research.' *Proceedings of the Parapsychological Association,* Vol. 6, pp. 81-102.

Bender, H. (1974). 'Modern Poltergeist Research – A Plea for an Unprejudiced View.' In J. Beloff (ed.) *New Directions in Parapsychology.*

Benton-Banai, E. (1988). *The Mishomis Book: The Voice of the Ojibway.* Minneapolis: University of Minnesota Press.

Bertrin, G. (2018 [1908]). *Lourdes: A History of its Apparitions and Cures.* Facsimile Publisher.

Besmer, F. E. (1983). *Horses, musicians, and Gods. The Hausa cult of possession-trance.* New York: Greenwoood.

Beyer, S. (1974). *Magic and ritual in Tibet: The cult of Tara.* Berkeley: University of California Press.

Bishop, G. (2016). *It Defies Language!* Los Angeles: Excluded Middle Press.

Blackmore, S. (1984). 'A psychological theory of the out-of-body experience.' *Journal of Parapsychology,* Vol. 48, No. 3, pp. 201-218.

Blackmore, S. (1984). 'A Postal Survey of OBEs and other Experiences.' *Journal of the American Society for Psychical Research,* Vol. 523, pp. 225-244.

Blackmore, S.J. (1986). 'Spontaneous and deliberate OBEs: A questionnaire survey.' *Journal of the Society for Psychical Research,* Vol. 53, No. 802, pp. 218-224.

Blackmore, S.J. (1993). *Dying to Live: Near-Death Experiences.* London: Grafton.

Bork, E. (2016). 'Keeping it Real.' Available Online: https://www.flyingwrestler.com/2016/10/keeping-it-real/ [Accessed 9th September 2021].

Bosi, E. (2003). *The living time of memory [O tempo vivo da memória]. Ensaios de psi-cologia*. São Paulo: Ateliê Editorial.

Bottazzi, F. (2011 [1909]). *Mediumistic Phenomena*. Princeton: ICRL Press.

Boudillion, D. (2003) 'Aleister Crowley's Lam & the Little Grey Men A Striking Resemblance.' Available Online: http://www.boudillion.com/lam/lam.htm [Accessed 24th September 2021].

Bourdieu, P. (1993). *The misery of the world [La Misère du monde]*. Paris: Le Seuil.

Bourne, H. (1725). *Antiquitates Vulgares: Or, The Antiquities of the Common People*. Newcastle: J. White.

Boyce, Mary (1975). *History of Zoroastrianism, Vol. I*. Leiden: Brill.

Braude, S. E. (2002). 'The problem of super-psi.' In F. Steinkamp (ed.) *Parapsychology, philosophy and the mind: Essays honouring John Beloff*. Jefferson, NC: McFarland, pp. 91-111.

Bregman, L. (1989). 'Dying: A universal human experience?' *Journal of Religion and Health*, Vol. 28, No. 1, pp. 58-69.

Dr Breton, (1906). 'Correspondence.' *Revue Scientifique et Morale du Spiritisme*, Vol. 12, No. 12 pp. 742-4. Available Online: https://drive.google.com/file/d/0Bxmr5kjDLMCvToZsXy1BUS1zYko/view?resourcekey=0-AcS44nTyaUbwPBZyp_O3_A

Breton, A. (1990). *Manifestoes of Surrealism*. Ann Arbor: The University of Michigan Press.

Breysse, D. (1994). 'Case 148.' In A. Rosales (ed.) *1980 Humanoid Sighting Reports*. Available Online: http://www.ufoinfo.com/humanoid/humanoid-1980.pdf [Accessed 5th February 2014].

Briggs, K. (1978). *The Vanishing People: A Study of Traditional Fairy Beliefs*. London: Batsford.

Bugaj, R. (1996). 'Macro-pk in Poland: An account of two cases.' *Journal of the Society for Psychical Research*, Vol. 61, pp. 26-33.

Bullard, T. E. (1989). 'UFO abduction reports: the supernatural kidnap narrative returns in technological guise.' *Journal of American Folklore*, Vol. 102, No. 404, pp. 147-170.

Burton, R. (1881). *Melancholy Anatomised: Showing Its Causes, Consequences, and Cure*. London: Chatto and Windus.

Campany, R.F. (1995). 'To hell and back: death, near-death, and other worldly journeys in early medieval China.' In J.J. Collins & M. Fishbane (eds.) *Death, Ecstasy and Other Worldly Journeys*. Albany: SUNY Press, pp. 343-60.

REFERENCES

Campion, N. (2002). 'Surrealist Cosmology: André Breton and Astrology.' *Culture and Cosmos*, Vol. 6, No, 2, pp. 45-56.

Camus, A. (2000). *The Myth of Sisyphus*. London: Penguin.

Capra, F. (1985). *The Turning Point: Science, Society and the Rising Culture*. London: Flamingo.

Cardeña, E., Krippner, S. & Lynn, S. (2000). *Varieties of Anomalous Experience: Examining the Scientific Evidence*. Washington: American Psychological Association.

Carrington, H. (1931). *The Story of Psychic Science*. London: Rider & Co Ltd.

Carrington, H. (1946). *The Invisible World*. New York: The Beechhurst Press.

Carrington, H. (1954). *The American Séances with Eusapia Palladino*. New York: Garrett Publications.

Carrington, H & Fodor, N. (1951). *Haunted People: Story of the Poltergeist Down the Centuries*. New York: Dutton.

Carruthers, G. (2015). 'Who am I in Out of Body Experiences? Implications from OBEs for the explanandum of a theory of self-consciousness.' *Phenomenology and the Cognitive Sciences*, Vol. 14, No. 1, pp. 183-197.

Cassaniti, J.L. & Luhrmann, T.M. (2014). 'The cultural kindling of spiritual experiences.' *Current Anthropology*, Vol. 55, S10, pp. 333-343.

Caswell, J.M., Hunter, J. & Tessaro, L.W.E. (2014). 'Phenomenological Convergence Between Major Paradigms of Classic Parapsychology and Cross-Cultural Practices: An Exploration of Paranthropology.' *Journal of Consciousness Exploration and Research*, Vol. 5, No. 5, pp. 467-482.

Chalmers, D. J. (1995). 'Facing up to the problem of consciousness.' *Journal of Consciousness Studies*, Vol. 2, No. 3, pp. 200–219.

Chataway, C. J. (2001). 'Negotiating the observer-observed relationship: participatory action research.' In D. Tolman, &

M. Brydom-Miller (eds.) *From subjects to subjectivities – a handbook of interpretative and participatory methods*. New York: New York University Press, pp. 239-255.

Chibbet, H. (1965). *The Prince of Shades*. Unpublished manuscript on the Battersea poltergeist, Alan Murdie's collection.

Chilver, I. (2009). *Oxford Dictionary of Art & Artists*. Oxford: Oxford University Press.

Choucha, N. (1992). *Surrealism and the Occult: Shamanism, Magic, Alchemy, and the Birth of an Artistic Movement*. Rochester: Inner Traditions Bear and Company.

Churton, T. (2011). *Aleister Crowley: The Biography.* London: Watkins Media.

Clark, J. (1980). 'The Ultimate Alien Encounter.' In D. Scott Rogo (ed.) *UFO Abductions.* New York: New American Library.

Clark, J. & Coleman, L. (2006). *The Unidentified & Creatures of the Outer Edge.* Charlottesville: Anomalist Books.

Clark, M. (2017). *The Tawny One: Soma, Haoma and Ayahuasca.* London: Muswell Hill.

Clelland, M. (2015). *The Messengers: Owls, Synchronicity and the UFO Abductee.* New York: Richard Dolan Press.

Clelland, M. (2020). *The Messengers: Owls, Synchronicity and the UFO Abductee.* Beneath the Stars Press.

Clelland, M. (2019). *Hidden Experience: Collected Writings from Ten Years of Blogging 2009-2019: A Personal Journey of Owls, Synchronicity, and UFO Contact.* Beneath the Stars Press.

Cohen, O., Druon, S., Lengagne, S., Mendelsohn, A., Malach, R., Kheddar, A., Friedman, D. (2014). 'fMRI-Based Robotic Embodiment: Controlling a Humanoid Robot by Thought Using Real-Time fMR1.' *Presence,* Vol. 23, pp. 229-241.

Coleman, B. (1936). 'The Religion of the Ojibwa of Northern Minnesota.' *Primitive Man,* Vol. 10, No. 3/4, pp. 33-57.

Coleman, L. (2002). *Mothman and other Curious Encounters.* New York: Paraview.

Coleman, L. (1983). *Mysterious America.* Winchester: Faber & Faber.

Collier, J.P. (1841). *The mad pranks and merry jests of Robin Goodfellow: reprinted from the edition of 1628.* London: Reprinted for the Percy society by C. Richards.

Collier, J.P. (1881). *The History of English Dramatic Poetry to the Time of Shakespeare and Annals of the Stage to the Restoration.* London: John Murray.

Collingwood, R. G. (2014 [1945]). *The Idea of Nature.* Mansfield: Martino Publishing.

Cook, K. (1997). 'Women are the First Environment.' *Native Americas.* Vol. 14, No. 3, p. 58.

Conway, T. (2016). *Discovering Rock Art: A Personal Journey with Tribal Elders.* Garibaldi Highlands: Thor Conway.

Cooper, C.E. (2012). *Telephone Calls from The Dead: A Revised Look at the Phenomenon Thirty Years On.* Portsmouth: Tricorn Books.

Cooper, D.E. (2018). *Senses of Mystery: Engaging with Nature and the Meaning of Life.* London: Routledge.

REFERENCES

Cooper, J. (1990). *The Case of the Cottingley Fairies.* London: Hale.

Cooray, G., & Cooray, V. (2008). 'Could Some Ball Lightning Observations be Optical Hallucinations Caused by Epileptic Seizures?' *The Open Atmospheric Science Journal*, Vol. 2, pp. 101-105.

Cornell, T. (2002). *Investigating the Paranormal.* New York: Parapsychology Foundation.

Cott, A. (1975) *Fasting: The Ultimate Diet.* New York: Eagle Publishing.

Cottingham, J. (1978). '"A Brute to the Brutes?": Descartes' Treatment of Animals.' *Philosophy*, Vol. 53. No. 206, pp. 551–559.

Counts, D. A. (1983). 'Near-death and out-of-body experiences in a Melanesian society.' *Anabiosis*, Vol. 3, pp. 115–35.

Crabbe, J. (2002). 'Some Paracoustics Proposals.' *Journal of the Society for Psychical Research*, Vol 66, pp. 175-9.

Craven, J. (2019). 'Surrealism, the Amazing Art of Dreams.' Available Online: https://www.thoughtco.com/what-is-surrealism-183312 [Accessed 9th September 2021].

Cropper, P. & Healy, T. (2014). *Australian Poltergeist.* Sydney: Strange Nation Publishers.

Crowe, C. (1848). *The Night Side of Nature: Ghosts and Ghost Seers.* London: T.C. Newby.

Crowley, A. & Wasserman, J. (1993). *Aleister Crowley and the Practice of the Magical Diary.* Tempe: New Falcon Publications.

Crowley, M. (1996). 'When the gods drank urine: A Tibetan myth may help solve the riddle of soma, sacred drug of ancient India.' *Fortean Studies*, vol. 3.

Cruz, J.C. (1977). *The Incorruptibles: A Study of the Incorruption of the Bodies of Various Catholic Saints and Beati.* Charlotte: TAN Books.

Cutchin, J. (2016). *The Brimstone Deceit: An In-Depth Examination of Supernatural Scents, Otherworldly Odors, and Monstrous Miasmas.* San Antonio: Anomalist Books.

Cutchin, J. & Renner, T. (2020). *Where the Footprints End: High Strangeness and the Bigfoot Phenomenon. Vol. 1: Folklore.* Red Lion: Dark Holler Arts.

Dale, E. (2019). 'The Owlman of Mawnan Smith.' Available Online: https://cornishbirdblog.com/the-owlman-of-mawnan-smith/ [Accessed 5th March 2022].

David-Neel, A. (2007). *Magic and Mystery in Tibet.* London: Souvenir Press.

David-Neel, A. (2014). *Magic and Mystery in Tibet.* Eastford: Martino Publishing.

Davids, P. & Schwartz, G.E. (2016). *An Atheist in Heaven: The Ultimate Evidence for Life after Death?.* Reno: Yellow Hat Publishing.

Davis, E. (2019). *High Weirdness: Drugs, Esoterica and Visionary Experience in the Seventies.* Cambridge: MIT Press.

De Aguilar, R. (1995). *Las Casas Que Se Incendian Solas: Psicopirosis En Panama.* Panama: Editorial Universitaria.

De Boer, E.M. (2020). 'Out of body, loss of self: Spiritual or scary?' *Religions*, Vol. 11, No. 11, pp. 558.

Degh, L. (1977). 'UFOs and How Folklorists Should Look At Them.' *Fabula*, Vol. 18, pp. 242-248.

Demeter, S. (2013). 'The Little People.' Available Online: http://psican.org/index.php/other/829-the-little-people [Accessed 2nd October 2021].

Demeter, S. (2020a). *Cosmic Witch: Magic Witchcraft and the Supernatural.* Bologna: Le Due Torri.

Demeter, S. (2020b). 'The Philip Phenomenon: Out Of My Mind's Eye.' Available Online: https://susandemeter.com/2021/05/16/the-philip-phenomenon/ [Accessed 10th October 2021].

Demeter, S. (2021). 'Online UFO Witch Hunts.' Available Online: https://susandemeter.com/2021/07/21/online-ufo-witch-hunts/ [Accessed 11th October 2021].

Denton, W. & Denton, E. (1866). *The Soul of Things: Psychometric Researches and Discoveries.* Boston: Walker, Wise.

Descartes, R. (1996 [1641]). *Discourse on Method and Meditations on First Philosophy.* New Haven: Yale University Press.

de Vere Patey, P. (2000). Personal communication with Alan Murdie, 22 April 2000.

Devereux, P. (1982). *Earth Lights: Towards an Explanation of the UFO Enigma.* Northamptonshire: Turnstone Press Limited.

Diamond, S. (1974). *In Search of the Primitive.* New Brunswick: Transaction Books.

Dingwall, E.J. (1948). *Very Peculiar People: Portrait Studies in the Queer, the Abnormal and the Uncanny.* London: Rider and Company.

Dickson, M. (2021). 'Fairy Encounters in 21C England.' *Fairy Investigation Society Newsletter*, Vol. 13, pp. 54-61.

REFERENCES

Doniger, W. (1998). *The Implied Spider: Politics & Theology in Myth*. New York: Columbia University Press.

Doniger O'Flaherty, W. (1986). *Dreams, Illusion, and Other Realities*. Chicago: University of Chicago Press.

Doyle, A.C. (1922). *The Coming of the Fairies*. London: Hodder & Stoughton.

Dundes, A. (1980). 'Text, Texture, Context.' In A. Dundes (ed.) *Interpreting Folklore*. Bloomington: Indiana University Press, pp. 20-32.

Dumont, J. (1976). 'Journey to Daylight-Land: Through Ojibwe Eyes.' *Laurentian University Review*. Vol. 8, No. 2, pp. 31-43.

DuQuette, L.M. (2003). *The Magick of Aleister Crowley: A Handbook of Rituals of Thelema*. San Francisco: Weiser.

Echols, D. (2018). *High Magick: A Guide to the Spiritual Practices That Saved My Life on Death Row*. Louisville: Sounds True.

Eclipsery (2020). 'People believing they can astral project into an anime world?' Available from: https://www.reddit.com/r/witchcraft/comments/ioo4l3/people_believing_they_can_astral_project_into_an/ [Accessed 18th March 2022].

Edgar, Z. (2022). *Just Another Tin Foil Hat Presents ...* San Diego: Beyond the Fray Publishing.

Ehrsson, H.H. (2007). 'The experimental induction of out-of-body experiences.' *Science*, Vol. 317, p. 1048.

Ellwood, R.S. (1973). *Religious and Spiritual Groups in America*. Englewood Cliffs: Prentice Hall.

Eno, P. F. (2006). *Turning Home: God, Ghosts and Human Destiny*. Woonsocket: New River Press.

Esbjörn-Hargens, S. (2020). *Our Wild Kosmos! An Exo Studies Exploration of the Ontological Status of Non-Human Intelligences*. Available Online: https://whatsupwithufos.com/wp-content/uploads/2020/06/Exo_Studies.pdf [Accessed 26/07/2022].

Escobar Uribe, A. (1950). *Mitos de Antioquia*. Bogota: Minerva Editions.

Esman, A.H. (2011). 'Psychoanalysis and Surrealism: André Breton and Sigmund Freud.' *Journal of the American Psychoanalytic Association*, Vol. 59, No. 1, pp. 173-181.

Evans, H. (1986). *Visions, Apparitions, Alien Visitors: A Comparative Study of the Entity Enigma*. Wellingborough: Aquarian Press.

Evans, H. (1987). *Gods, Spirits, Cosmic Guardians: Encounters with Non-Human Beings*. Wellingborough: The Aquarian Press.

Evans-Pritchard, E.E. (1976). *Witchcraft, Oracles and Magic Among the Azande.* Oxford: Clarendon Press.

Evans-Wentz, W.Y. (1909). *The Fairy-Faith in Celtic Countries, Its Psychical Origin and Nature.* Rennes: Thesis.

Evans-Wentz, W. Y. (1911). *The Fairy Faith in Celtic Countries.* Oxford: Oxford University Press.

Fechner, G. T. (1948). *Religion of a Scientist: Selections from Gustav Theodor Fechner.* New York: Pantheon Books.

Feilding, E., Baggally, W.W. & Carrington, H. (1909). 'Reports on sittings with Eusapia Palladino.' *Proceedings of the Society for Psychical Research,* Vol. 23, pp. 305-569.

Feit, H. A. (1994). 'Dreaming of Animals: The Waswanipi Cree Shaking Tent Ceremony in Relation to Environment, Hunting, and Missionization.' In T. Yamada & T. Irimoto (eds.) *Circumpolar Animism and Shamanism.* Sapporo: Hokkaido University Press, pp. 289-316.

Feit, H. A. (1997). 'Spiritual Power and Everyday Lives: James Bay Cree Shaking Tent Performers and Their Audiences.' In T. Yamada & T. Irimoto (eds.) *Circumpolar Animism and Shamanism. 2nd Edition.* Sapporo: Hokkaido University Press,, pp. 129-149.

Fenwick, P. (2005). 'Science and spirituality: a challenge for the 21st century.' *Journal of Near-Death Studies,* Vol. 23, No. 3, pp. 131-157.

Festinger, L., Riecken, H. & Schachter S. (1956). *When prophecy fails: a social and psychological study of a modern group that predicted the destruction of the world.* University of Minnesota Press.

Finucane, R. C. (1996). *Ghosts: Appearances of the Dead and Cultural Transformations.* New York: Prometheus.

Fisher, M. (2016). *The Weird and the Eerie.* London: Repeater Books.

Flohr, C. (2012). *Heaven's Child: A Mother's Story of Tragedy and the Enduring Strength of Family.* Blakely Rock: Blakely Rock Press.

Follet, J. (2005). *Voices of Feminism Oral History Project: Interview with KATSI COOK.* Northampton: Sophia Smith Collection, Smith College.

Forghieri, Y. (1993). *Phenomenological psychology: fundamentals, methods and research.* São Paulo: Pioneira.

Fort, C. (1931). *Wild Talents.* Cosimo Classics.

Fort, C. (2008). *The Book of the Damned: The Collected Works of Charles Fort.* New York: Jeremy P. Tarcher.

REFERENCES

Foster, L. (2019). 'The Invisible Ecosystem.' In J. Hunter (ed.) *Greening the Paranormal: Exploring the Ecology of Extraordinary Experience*. Milton Keynes: August Night Press.

Fowler, R.E. (1980). *The Andreasson Affair*. New York: Bantam Books.

Fowler, R.E. (2020). *UFOs: The Ultimate Abduction – We Are Property*. Portsmouth: Seacoast Press.

Fox, M. (2003). *Religion, Spirituality and the Near-Death Experience*. London: Routledge.

Fox, M. (2003). 'Sharing the Light: An Analysis of RERC Archival Accounts Describing Shared Experiences of Unusual Light.' *RERC Second Series Occasional Paper 39*, pp. 1-16. Available Online: https://repository.uwtsd.ac.uk/id/eprint/451/1/RERC2-039-1.pdf [Accessed 23/02/2021].

Fraser, J. (2020). *Poltergeist! A New Investigation Into Destructive Haunting*. Winchester: John Hunt.

Frecska, E., Móré, C. E., Vargha, A., & Luna, L. E. (2012). 'Enhancement of creative expression and entoptic phenomena as after-effects of repeated ayahuasca ceremonies.' *Journal of Psychoactive Drugs*, Vol. 44, No. 3, pp. 191-199.

French, C. (2003). 'Fantastic memories: the relevance of research into eyewitness testimony and false memories for reports of anomalous experiences.' *Journal of Consciousness Studies*, Vol. 10, No. 6-7, pp. 153–174.

Freud, S. (2003). *The Uncanny*. London: Penguin Classics.

Freud, S. (1930). *Civilization and its discontents*. London: Hogarth Press.

Freud, S. (1961). *Civilization and Its Discontents*. New York: W.W. Norton Books.

Fries, J. (2000). *Visual Magick: A Practical Guide to Trance, Sigils and Visualization Techniques*. Oxford: Mandrake.

Fries, J. (2005). *Cauldron of the Gods: A Manual of Celtic Magick*. Oxford: Mandrake of Oxford.

Gaiman, N., Keith, S., Dringenberg, M., & Jones III, M. (1991). *The Sandman: Preludes and nocturnes*. New York: DC Comics.

Gardner, E.L. (1951). *Fairies: The Cottingley photographs and their sequel*. London: Theosophical Publishing House.

Garrett, E.J. (1939). *My life as a search for the meaning of mediumship*. London: Rider & Co.

Gauld, A. (1968). *The founders of psychical research*. London: Routledge & Kegan Paul.

Gauld, A. (2022). *The Heyday of Mental Mediumship, 1880s-1930s: Investigators, Mediums and Communicators.* Brighton: White Crow Books.

Gauld, A. & Cornell, A.D. (1979). *Poltergeists.* London: Routledge Kegan Paul.

Geley, G. (1924/1927). *Clairvoyance and Materialization.* Whitefish: Kessinger Legacy Reprints.

Geniusz, W.M. (2009). *Our Knowledge is Not Primitive: Decolonizing Botanical Anishinaabe Teachings.* Syracuse: Syracuse University Press.

Gerhard, K. (2013). *Encounters with Flying Humanoids: Mothman, Manbirds, Gargoyles and Other Winged Beasts.* Woodbury: Llewellyn.

Gettier, E.L. (1963). 'Is Justified True Belief Knowledge?' *Analysis,* Vol. 23, No. 6, pp. 121-123.

Giesler, P. (1984). 'Parapsychological anthropology: I. Multi-method approaches on the study of psi in the field setting.' *Journal of the American Society for Psychical Research,* Vol. 78, pp. 287-328.

Glazier, J.W. (2021). 'Decolonizing Parapsychology.' Presentation at *Combined Online Convention of the*

Parapsychological Association & Society for Scientific Exploration, July 23-31, 2021. Available Online: https://www.academia.edu/50715112/Decolonizing_Parapsychology [Accessed 16th March 2022].

Godfrey, L. (2010). *The Michigan Dogman: Werewolves and Other Unknown Canines Across the U.S.A.* Eau Claire: Unexplained Research Publishing Company.

Gordon, S. (2010). *Silent Invasion: The Pennsylvania UFO-Bigfoot Casebook.* Greensburg: Stan Gordon.

Graham, R. (2017). *UFOs: Reframing the Debate.* Brighton: White Crow Books.

Grant, K. (1995). *The Magical Revival.* London: Skoob Books Publishing.

Graves, R. (1961). *The white goddess: A historical grammar of poetic myth.* London: Faber and Faber.

Greely, A.M. (1975). *The Sociology of the Paranormal.* Beverly Hills: Sage Publications.

Green, C. (1968). *Out of the Body Experiences.* London: Hamish Hamilton.

Green, C., & McCreery, C. (1975). *Apparitions.* London: Hamish Hamilton.

Green, C.E. & McCreery, C. (1994). *Lucid Dreaming: The paradox of consciousness during sleep.* New York, NY: Routledge

REFERENCES

Greenwell, R., Lorenzen, J., & Lorenzen, C. (1968). 'Humcat 1952-1953.' Available Online: http://www.cufos.org/HUMCAT/HUMCAT_Index_1952-1953.pdf [Accessed 9th September 2021].

Greenwood, S. (2020). *Magic, Witchcraft and the Otherworld: An Anthropology.* Abingdon: Taylor & Francis.

Gregory, A. (1982). 'London Experiments with Matthew Manning.' *Proceedings of the Society for Psychical Research*, Vol. 56. pp. 282-365.

Gregory, A. (1985). *The Strange Case of Rudi Schneider.* Metuchen: The Scarecrow Press.

Gregory, R. (1998). *The Oxford Companion to The Mind.* Oxford: Oxford University Press.

Grey, M. (1985). *Return from Death: An Exploration of the Near-Death Experience.* London: Arkana.

Greyson, B. (1999). 'Defining near-death experiences.' *Mortality*, Vol. 4, No. 1, pp. 7-19.

Greyson, B. (2006). 'Near-death experiences and spirituality.' *Zygon: Journal of Religion and Science*, Vol. 41, pp. 393-414.

Greyson, B. (2010). 'Seeing people not known to have died: 'Peak in Darien' experiences.' *Anthropology and Humanism*, Vol. 35, No. 2, pp 159–171.

Greyson, B. & Bush. N.E. (1992) 'Distressing near-death experiences.' *Psychiatry*, Vol. 55, pp. 95-110.

Greyson, B., Kelly, E. & Kelly, E. (2009). 'Explanatory models for near-death experiences.' In J.M. Holden, B. Greyson & D. James (eds.) *The Handbook of Near-Death Experiences: Thirty Years of Investigation.* Santa Barbara: Praeger/ABC-CLIO, pp. 213–234.

Grim, J.A. (1983). *The Shaman.* Norman: University of Oklahoma Press.

Grosse, M. (1980). 'The Enfield Poltergeist.' *Alpha magazine UK*, October 1980.

Grosso, M. (2012). *Soulmaking: Uncommon Paths to Self-Understanding.* San Antonio: Anomalist Books.

Grosso, M. (2016). *The Man Who Could Fly: St. Joseph of Copertino and the Mystery of Levitation.* Lanham: Rowman & Littlefield.

Grosso, M. (2020). *Smile of the Universe: Miracles in an Age of Disbelief.* Charlottesville: Anomalist Books.

Guggenheim, B. & Guggenheim, J. (1995). *Hello from Heaven! A New Field of Research – After-Death Communication – Confirms That Life and Love Are Eternal.* New York: Bantam.

Gulyas, A. (2018). 'Encounter 505: Esotericon Saucer Interlude.' Available Online: https://saucerlife.com/2018/05/22/encounter-505-esotericon-saucer-interlude/?fbclid=IwAR3hKHfEyNXazDkikrrWXbWtpoTxcdqwzFX3cPUQTWv9PeWUHCg3AittBEI [Accessed 10th September 2021].

Hall, R.L. (1974). 'Sociological Perspectives on UFO Reports.' In C. Sagan & T. Page (eds.) *UFOs: A Scientific Debate*. Ithaca: Cornell University Press, pp. 213-223.

Hallowell, A.I. (1942). *The Role of Conjuring in Saulteaux Society*. Philadelphia: University of Pennsylvania Press.

Hallowell, A.I. (1992). *The Ojibwa of Berens River, Manitoba: Ethnography Into History*. Fort Worth: Harcourt Brace Jovanovich College Publishers.

Hallowell, M.J. (2007). *Invizikids: The Curious Enigma of 'Imaginary' Childhood Friends*. Loughborough: Heart of Albion Press.

Hallowell, M. & Ritson, D.W. (2006). *The South Shields Poltergeist: One family's fight against an invisible intruder*. London. Sutton.

Hallson, P. & Barrington, M.R. (1982). *Enfield Poltergeist Investigation Committee Report (EPIC)*. London: Society for Psychical Research.

Hampe, J.C. (1979; reprint 2022). *To Die is Gain*. Santa Fe: Afterworlds Press.

Hand, W. (1977). 'Will-o'-the-Wisps, Jack-o'-Lanterns and Their Congeners: A Consideration of the Fiery and Luminous Creatures of Lower Mythology.' *Fabula*, Vol. 18, pp. 226-233.

Hansen, G.P. (1991). 'D. Scott Rogo and his Contributions to Parapsychology.' *The Anthropology of Consciousness*, Vol. 2, No. 3, pp. 32-35.

Hansen, G.P. (2001). *The Trickster and the Paranormal*. Bloomington: Xlibris.

Hanna, J. (1998). 'Alex Grey speaks ...' *The Entheogen Review*, Vol. 7, No. 4, pp. 17-22.

Haraldsson, E. (1985). 'Representative national surveys of psychic phenomena: Iceland, Great Britain, Sweden, USA and Gallup's multinational survey.' *Journal of the Society for Psychical Research*, Vol. 53, pp. 145-158.

Haraldsson, E. (1987). *Miracles Are My Calling Cards*. London: Century.

Haraldsson, E. (2011). 'A perfect case? Emil Jensen in the mediumship of Indridi Indridason, the fire in Copenhagen on November 24th 1905 and the discovery of Jensen's identity.' *Proceedings of the Society for Psychical Research*, Vol. 59, pp. 195-223.

Haraldsson, E. & Gissurarson, L.R. (2015). *Indridi Indridason: The Icelandic Physical Medium*. Brighton: White Crow Books.

Hardy, A. (2006). *The Spiritual Nature of Man: A Study of Contemporary Religious Experience*. Lampeter: Religious Experience Research Centre.

Harris, K. (2019). *Synchronicity: The Magic. The Mystery. The Meaning*. York: Capucia.

Harris, P. L. & Vallée, J.F. (2021). *Trinity: The Best-kept Secret*. New York: StarWorks USA LLC.

Harner, M. (1982). *The Way of the Shaman*. New York: Bantam New Age Books.

Harte, J. (1998). 'Medieval fairies: Now you see them, now you don't.' *At the Edge*, No. 10, pp. 2-3.

Harte, J. (2019). 'A Fairy or Else an Insect: Traditions at Fairy Wells', *Gramarye*, No. 16, pp. 55-59.

Harvey, G. (2005). *Animism: Respecting the Living World*. London: Hurst & Company.

Harvey-Wilson, S.B. (2000). 'Shamanism and alien abductions: a comparative study.' Available Online: https://ro.ecu.edu.au/theses/1389 [Accessed 30th September 2021].

Hasted, J. (1981). *The Metal Benders*. Abingdon: Routledge.

Hay, W.W., Levin, M.J., Sondheimer, J.M. & Deterding, R.R. (2004). *Current Diagnosis & Treatment in Pediatrics*. New York: McGraw Hill.

Haynes, R. (1980). 'The Boggle Threshold.' *Encounter*, August 1980 Issue, pp. 92-96.

Hensley, M.H. (2015). *Promised by Heaven: A Doctor's Return from the Afterlife to a Destiny of Love and Healing*. New York: Atria.

Hill, G. A. (2006). *Norval Morrisseau: Shaman Artist, Exhibition Catalogue*, Ottawa: National Gallery of Canada.

Hodson, G. (2010). *Fairies at Work and Play*. Wheaton: Theosophical Publishing House.

Holden, J. M. (2009). 'Veridical perception in near-death experiences.' In J.M. Holden, B. Greyson & D. James (eds.) *The Handbook of Near-Death Experiences: Thirty Years of Investigation*. Santa Barbara: Praeger/ABC-CLIO, pp. 185–211.

Holroyd, S. (1979). *Alien Intelligence*. Newton Abbot: David & Charles.

Home, Mme. (1888/2006). *D. D. Home: His life and mission*. In: *The Complete D.D. Home*. Vol 2. Worksop: SDU Publications.

Hopkins, B. (1981). *Missing Time: A Documented Study of UFO Abductions*. Berkeley Books, New York.

Howe, L.M. (2002). *Mysterious Lights and Crop Circles*. Los Angeles: Paper Chase Press.

Hufford, D.J. (1982). *The Terror That Comes in the Night: An Experience-Centred Study of Supernatural Assault Traditions*. Philadelphia: University of Pennsylvania Press.

Hufford, D. (1983). 'Folk Healers.' In R.M. Dorson (ed.). *Handbook of American Folklore*. Bloomington: Indiana University Press, pp. 306-13.

Hufford, D. (1985). 'Commentary: Mythical Experience in the Modern World.' In G.W. Foster, *The World Was Flooded with Light*. Pittsburgh: University of Pittsburgh Press.

Hunter, J. (2015a). '"Between Realness and Unrealness": Anthropology, Parapsychology and the Ontology of Non-Ordinary Realities.' Diskus: Journal of the British Association for the Study of Religion, Vol. 17, No. 2, pp. 4-20.

Hunter, J. (2015b). 'Music in Shamanism and Spirit Possession.' In S. Parsons & C. Cooper (eds). *Paracoustics: Sound and the Paranormal*. Hove: White Crow Books, pp. 177-184.

Hunter, J. (2016). *Damned Facts: Fortean Essays on Religion, Folklore and the Paranormal*. Paphos: Aporetic Press.

Hunter, J. (2017a). 'Re-Thinking Charles Fort.' *Bulletin of the British Association for the Study of Religion*, No. 131, pp. 22-24.

Hunter, J. (2017b). 'Ontological Flooding and Continuing Bonds.' In D. Klass & E. Steffen (eds.) *Continuing Bonds in Bereavement: New Directions for Research*. Abingdon: Routledge, pp. 191-200.

Hunter, J. (2019a). 'Religious Experience and Ecological Participation: Animism, Nature Connectedness and Fairies.' *De Numine: The Journal and Newsletter of the Alister Hardy Trust*, No. 67, pp. 4-9.

Hunter, J. (2019b). *Greening the Paranormal: Exploring the Ecology of Extraordinary Experience*. Milton Keynes: August Night Press.

Hunter, J. (2020a). 'Harmony and Ecology.' In N. Campion (ed). *The Harmony Debates: Exploring a practical philosophy for a sustainable future*. Lampeter: Sophia Centre Press.

Hunter, J. (2020b). *Manifesting Spirits: An Anthropological Study of Mediumship and the Paranormal*. London: Aeon Books.

Hunter, J. (2021a). 'Deep Weird: High Strangeness, Boggle Thresholds and Damned Data in Academic Research on Extraordinary Experience.' *Journal for the Study of Religious Experience*, Vol. 7, No. 1, pp. 5-18.

REFERENCES

Hunter, J. (2021b). '"...not the action of mind upon matter, but the action of mind-matter upon matter-mind...": A World of Many Minds in Archaeology and Ethnography.' *Time and Mind: Journal of Archaeology, Consciousness and Culture*, Vol. 14, No. 4, pp. 481-485.

Hunter, J. (2021c). 'Mysterium Horrendum: Exploring Otto's Concept of the Numinous in Stoker, Machen and Lovecraft.' In B. Grafius & J. Morehead (eds.) *Theology and Horror: Explorations of the Dark Religious Imagination*. New York: Lexington Books, pp. 41-54.

Hunter, J. (2022). 'The Folklore of the Tanat Valley: Fairies, Giants and Forgotten Ecological Knowledge.' *Newsletter of the Fairy Investigation Society*, No. 15, pp. 31-47.

Hurd & K. Bulkeley, (2014). *Lucid Dreaming: New Perspectives on Consciousness in Sleep. Vol. I: Science, Psychology, and education*. Santa Barbara: Praeger

Hutton, R. (1999). *Triumph of the Moon*. Oxford: Oxford University Press

Hutton, R. (2012). 'Crowley and Wicca.' In H. Bogdan & M.P. Starr (eds.). *Aleister Crowley and Western Esotericism*. Oxford: Oxford University Press, pp. 285–306.

Hutton, R. (2014). 'The Making of the Early Modern Fairy Tradition.' *The Historical Journal*, Vol. 57, pp. 1135-1156.

Hynek, J.A. (1974). *The UFO Experience: A Scientific Inquiry*. New York: Ballentine Books.

Hynek, J.A. (1979). *The UFO Experience: A Scientific Inquiry*. London: Corgi Books.

Hynek, J. A. & Vallée, J. (1975). *The Edge of Reality: A Progress Report on Unidentified Flying Objects*. Chicago: Henry Regnery Company.

Hyslop, J. (1913). 'Poltergeist Phenomena and Dissociation.' *Journal of the American Society for Psychical Research*, Vol. 7, No. 1, pp. 1-56.

Inglis, B. (1990). *Coincidence: A Matter of Chance – or Synchronicity?* London: Hutchinson.

Irwin, H.J. (1981). 'Some psychological dimensions of the out-of-body experience.' *Parapsychology Review*, Vol. 12, No. 4, pp. 1-6.

Irwin, H.J. (1985). *Flight of Mind*. Metuchen: Scarecrow Press.

Irwin, H. J. (1994). 'The phenomenology of parapsychological experiences.' In S. Krippner (ed.) *Advances in parapsychological* research. Vol 7. Jefferson: McFarland, pp. 10-76.

Ishii, M. (2013). 'Playing with perspectives: spirit possession, mimesis, and permeability in the buuta ritual in South India.' *Journal of the Royal Anthropological Institute*, Vol. 19, No. 4, pp. 795-812.

Jackson, L.L. (2015). *The Light Between Us: Stories from Heaven, Lessons for the Living.* New York: Spiegel & Grau.

Jackson, L.L. (2020). *Signs: The Secret Language of the Universe.* New York: The Dial Press.

Jackson, N., & Howard, M. (2000). *The pillars of Tubal Cain.* Taunton: Capall Bann.

James, W. (1950 [1890[). *The Principles of Psychology, Vol. I.* New York: Dover.

James, W. (1896). 'Presidential Address.' *Proceedings of the Society for Psychical Research*, Vol. 3, No. 77, pp. 881-888.

James, W. (1904). 'Does Consciousness Exist?' *Journal of Philosophy, Psychology, and Scientific Methods*, Vol. 1, No. 18, pp. 477–491.

James, W. (1909). *A Pluralistic Universe.* New York: Longmans, Green, and Co.

James, W. (2003). *Essays in radical empiricism.* New York: Dover.

James, W. (2004). *The Varieties of Religious Experience.* New York: Barnes & Noble.

Jansen, K. (2001). *Ketamine Dreams and Realities.* Santa Cruz: Multidisciplinary Association for Psychedelic Study.

Jeler, A. (2020). 'The Weird Sisters. Historical-Religious Genealogies.' *Studia Universitatis Babes-Bolyai-Dramatica*, Vol. 65, No. 1, pp. 51-68.

Johnson, M. (2014). *From the Lost Archives of the Fairy Investigation Society, Authentic Reports of Fairies in Modern Times.* San Antonio: Anomalist Books.

Johnson, R. (1953). *The Imprisoned Splendour.* London: Hodder Ltd.

Johnson, S. (1834). *A Dictionary of the English Language in which the words are deduced from their originals; and illustrated in their different significations by examples from the best writers.* London: Frederick Westley.

Johnston, B. (1986). *Ojibway Heritage.* Toronto: McClelland & Stewart.

Johnston, B. (1986). *The Manitous: The Spiritual World of the Ojibway.* Minnesota: Minnesota Historical Society Press.

Jones, E. (1780). *A Relation of Apparitions of Spirits in the Principality of Wales.* NP: NP.

Josiffe, C. (2017). *Gef! The Strange Tale of an Extra-Special Talking Mongoose.* London: Strange Attractor Press.

Jung, C.G. (1958). *Psyche and Symbol.* Garden City: Doubleday Books.

Jung, C.G. (2010 [1960]). *Synchronicity: An Acausal Connecting Principle.* Princeton: Princeton University Press.

REFERENCES

Kasprowicz, L. (2018). *Des Coups de Fil de L'AU-DELÀ? Enquête sur un Phénomène Paranormal Incroyable: Sa Folie, Ses Caractéristiques et Son Explication*. Paris: Livre de Poche.

Kastrup, B. (2011). *Meaning in Absurdity: What bizarre phenomena can tell us about the nature of reality*. Alresford: Iff Books.

Keel, J.A. (1970). *Strange Creatures from Time and Space*. New York: Main Street Publishing.

Keel, J.A. (1971). *Our Haunted Planet: Strange truths about the earth and its mysterious inhabitants*. London: Neville Spearman.

Keel, J.A. (1975). *The Eighth Tower*. New York: E.P. Dutton & Co.

Keel, J.A. (1976). *UFOs? Operation Trojan Horse*. New York: Manor Books.

Keel, J.A. (2013). *Operation Trojan Horse: The Classic Breakthrough Study of UFOs*. San Antonio: Anomalist Books.

Keel, J.A. (2002). *The Complete Guide to Mysterious Beings*. New York: Tor.

Keel, J.A. (2002). *The Mothman Prophecies*. London: Hodder & Stoughton.

Keel, J. A. (2013). *The Mothman Prophecies*. New York: Tor.

Keel, J.A. (2013). *The Eighth Tower: On Ultraterrestrials and the Superspectrum*. Charlottesville: Anomalist Books.

Kellehear, A. (1996). *Experiences Near Death: Beyond Medicine and Religion*. Oxford: Oxford University Press.

Kelleher, C. & Knapp, G. (2005). *Hunt for the Skinwalker: Science Confronts the Unexplained at a Remote Ranch in Utah*. New York: Paraview Pocket Books.

Kelly, E.F. (2010). 'Review: Out-of-Body and Near-Death Experiences: Brain-State Phenomena or Glimpses of Immortality?' *Journal of Scientific Exploration*, Vol. 24, No. 4, p. 730.

Kelly, E.F., Kelly, E.W., Crabtree, A., Gauld, A., Grosso, M. & Greyson, B. (2006). *Irreducible Mind: Toward A Psychology For The 21st Century*. Lanham: Rowman & Littlefield.

Kelly, E. F., Locke, R. G. (1981). Altered *States of Consciousness and PSI: An Historical Survey and Research Prospectus*. London: Parapsychology Foundation.

Kent, J. (2005). 'The case against DMT elves.' In C. Pickover (ed.) *Sex, drugs, Einstein, and elves*. Petaluma, Los Angeles: Smart Publications, pp. 102-105.

Kerridge, I. (2003). 'Altruism or reckless curiosity? A brief history of self experimentation in medicine.' *Internal Medicine Journal*, Vol. 33, pp. 203-207.

Kim, J. (2005). *Physicalism, or Something Near Enough.* Princeton: Princeton University Press.

Kimmerer, R.W. (2011). 'Restoration and Reciprocity: The Contributions of Traditional Ecological Knowledge.' In D. Egan, E.E. Hjerpe & J. Abrams (eds) (2011). *Human Dimensions of Ecological Restoration: Integrating Science, Nature and Culture.* Washington: Island Press, pp. 257-276.

Kirk, G.S., Raven, J.E. & Schofield, M. (1957). *The Presocratic Philosophers.* Cambridge: Cambridge University Press.

Klimo, J. (2018). 'A Report on Phase III of FREE's Experiencer Research Study: The Results of a Qualitative Study.' In R. Hernandez, J. Klimo, & R. Schild (eds.) *Beyond UFOs: The Science of Consciousness and Contact with NonHuman Intelligence, Volume I.* Miami: Dr Edgar Mitchell Foundation for Research into Extraterrestrial and Extraordinary Experiences, pp. 121-287.

Klages, L. (2013 [1913]). 'Man and Earth.' In L. Klages, *The Biocentric Worldview: Selected Essays and Poems of Ludwig Klages.* London: Arktos, pp. 26–44.

Kracke, W. (2003). 'Beyond the Mythologies: A shape of dreaming.' In R.I. Lohmann (ed.). *Dream Travelers: Sleep experiences and culture in the Western Pacific.* New York: Palgrave MacMillan, pp. 211-235.

Kripal, J.J. (2010). *Authors of the Impossible: The Paranormal and the Sacred.* Chicago: University of Chicago Press.

Kripal, J.J. (2011). *Mutants and Mystics: Science Fiction, Superhero Comics, and the Paranormal.* Chicago: University of Chicago Press.

Kripal, J.J. (2020). *The Flip: Who you really are and why it matters.* London: Penguin.

Kripal, J.J. & Strieber, W. (2016). *The Super Natural: Why the Unexplained Is Real.* London: Penguin.

Krosnick J.A. & Presser, S. (2018). 'Questionnaire Design.' In: D. Vannette & J.A. Krosnick (eds.) *The Palgrave Handbook of Survey Research.* London: Palgrave Macmillan, pp. 439-455.

Kuhn, T.S. (1962). *The Structure of Scientific Revolutions.* Chicago: University of Chicago Press.

Lambert, G.W. (1955). 'Poltergeists: A Physical Theory.' *Journal of the SPR*, Vol. 38, pp. 49-71.

Lang, A. (1903). 'The Poltergeist Historically Considered.' *Proceedings of SPR*, Vol. 17, pp. 305-326.

Lash, D. (2020). *The Cinema of Disorientation: Inviting Confusions.* Edinburgh: Edinburgh University Press.

REFERENCES

Latham, M.W. (1930). *The Elizabethan Fairies: The Fairies of Folklore and the Fairies of Shakespeare.* New York: Columbia University Press.

Laughlin, C.D. (2011). *Communing with the Gods: Consciousness, Culture and the Dreaming Brain.* Brisbane: Daily Grail Publishing

Lawson, A. (1980). 'Hypnosis of Imaginary UFO "Abductees."' In C.G. Fuller (ed). *Proceedings of the First International UFO Congress.* New York: Warner Books.

Lawson, O.G. & Porter, K.W. (1951). 'Texas Poltergeist, 1881.' *Journal of American Folklore,* Vol. 64, No. 254, pp. 371-382.

Layard, J. (1943). 'Psi Phenomena and Poltergeists.' *Proceedings of the SPR,* Vol. 47, pp. 237-48.

Leary, T., Litwin, G.H. & Metzner, R. (1963). 'Reactions to psilocybin administered in a supportive environment.' *Journal of Nervous and Mental Disease,* Vol. 137, No. 6, pp. 561–573.

Lebiedziński, P. (1921). 'Expériences de matérialisations avec Mme Stanisława P.: Essai d'analyse de la "substance."' *Revue Métapsychique,* Vol. 6, pp. 317–327.

Lecouteux C. (2012). *The Secret History of Poltergeists and Haunted Houses: From Pagan Folklore to Modern Manifestations.* Vermont: Inner Traditions.

LeShan, L. (2009). *A new science of the paranormal.* New York: Quest Books.

Letcher, A. (2001). 'The Scouring of the Shire: Fairies, Trolls and Pixies in Eco-Protest Culture.' *Folklore,* Vol. 112, pp. 147-161.

Levine, J. (1983). 'Materialism and qualia: the explanatory gap,' *Pacific Philosophical Quarterly,* Vol. 64, pp. 354–361.

Levitan, L., LaBerge, S., DeGracia, D.J., & Zimbardo, P.G. (1999). 'Out-of-body experiences, dreams, and REM sleep.' *Sleep and Hypnosis,* Vol. 1, No. 3, pp. 186-196.

Linhart, D. (1995). 'Hausgeister in Franken.' Cited in A. Puhle (1998) 'Ghosts, Apparitions and Poltergeist Incidents in Germany between 1700 and 1900.' *Journal of the Society for Psychical Research,* Vol. 63, No. 857, p. 290.

Locke, J. (1964 [1689]). *An Essay Concerning Human Understanding.* London: Collins Sons and Co.

Lloyd, D. (1967) 'Crawling Lights – A New Development.' *Flying Saucer Review,* Vol. 13, No. 3, pp. 29-30.

Long, J. & Holden, J.M. (2007). 'Does the arousal system contribute to near-death and out-of-body experiences? A summary and response.' *Journal of Near-Death Studies,* Vol. 25, pp. 135–169.

Lorenzen, C. & Lorenzen, J. (1977). *Abducted: Confrontations with Beings from Outer Space*. New York: Berkley Books.

Lorenzen, C. (1977). 'UFO Occupants in United States Reports.' In C. Bowen (ed.) *The Humanoids*. London: Futura Publications.

Lovecraft, H.P. (1927). "The Supernatural in Fiction." In H.P. Lovecraft. *At the Mountains of Madness: The Definitive Edition*. New York: Random House.

Lowe, V. (1979). 'A Brief Look at Some UFO Legends.' *Indiana Folklore*, Vol. 12, pp. 67-79.

Löwy, M. (2009). *Morning Star: Surrealism, Marxism, Anarchism, Situationism, Utopia*. Austin: University of Texas Press.

Lozneanu, E. & Sanduloviciu, M. (2003). 'Minimal-cell system created in laboratory by self-organization.' *Chaos, Solitons & Fractals*, Vol. 18, No. 2, pp. 335-343

Luhrmann, T. (2012). *When God Talks Back: Understanding the American Evangelical Relationship with God*. New York: Knopf.

Luke, D. (2008). 'Disembodied Eyes Revisited: An Investigation into the Ontology of Entheogenic Entity Encounters.' *The Entheogen Review*, Vol. 17, No. 1, pp. 1-9.

Luke, D. (2011). 'Anomalous phenomena, psi, and altered consciousness.' In E. Cardeña & M. Winkelman (eds.) *Altering consciousness: Multidisciplinary perspectives: History, culture, and the humanities; Biological and psychological perspectives*. Santa Barbara: Praeger/ABC-CLIO, pp. 355–374.

Luke, D. (2012). 'Altered states of consciousness, mental imagery and healing.' In C. Simmonds-Moore (ed.) *Exceptional experience and health: Essays on mind, body and human potential*. Jefferson: McFarland, pp.64-80.

Luke, D. (2019). *Otherworlds: Psychedelics and Exceptional Human Experience*. London: Aeon Books.

Luke, D. (2020). 'Anomalous Psychedelic Experiences: At the Neurochemical Juncture of the Humanistic and Parapsychological.' *Journal of Humanistic Psychology*, May 2020, pp. 1-41.

Luke, D. P., & Kittenis, M. (2005). 'A preliminary survey of paranormal experiences with psychoactive drugs.' *Journal of Parapsychology*, Vol. 69, No. 2, pp. 305-327.

Lukoff, D., Lu, F. & Tuner, R. (1992). 'Toward a more culturally sensitive DSM-IV: psychoreligious and psychospiritual problems.' *The Journal of Nervous and Mental Disease*, Vol. 180, No. 11, pp. 673-82.

Machado, F. R. (2010). 'Anomalous experiences (extrasensorymotor) in daily life and their association with beliefs, attitudes and subjective well-being.' *Boletim Academia Paulista de Psicologia*, Vol. 30, No. 79, pp. 462-483.

REFERENCES

MacKenzie, A. (1975). *Riddle of the Future: A Modern Study of Precognition.* New York: Taplinger Publishing.

Mac Manus, D. (1959). *Irish Earth Folk.* New York: Devin-Adair.

Mac Manus, D. (1973). *The Middle Kingdom: the faerie world of Ireland.* Gerrards Cross: Colin Smythe.

Mack, J. E. (1994). *Abduction.* New York: Macmillan Publishing Company.

Mack, J.E. (1999). *Passport to the Cosmos: Human Transformation and Alien Encounters.* New York, NY: Three Rivers Press.

Magliocco, S. (2018). 'Reconnecting to Everything: Fairies in Contemporary Paganism.' In M. Ostling (ed.) *Fairies, Demons and Nature Spirits: Small Gods at the Margins of Christendom.* London: Palgrave Macmillan, pp. 325-347.

Marçolla, B. & Mahfoud, M. (2002). 'The green light from the Red Hill: The elaboration of the supernatural in a traditional community in Minas Gerais [A luz verde do Morro Vermelho: a elaboração do sobrenatural em uma tradicional comunidade mineira].' *Psicologia em Revista*, Vol. 8, No. 12, pp. 83-94.

Marsh, M. (2010) *Out-of-Body and Near-Death Experiences: Brain-State Phenomena or Glimpse of Immortality?* Oxford: Oxford University Press.

Martins, L. B. (2011). *Close encounters: Investigating personality, mental disorders and attribution of causality in subjective UFO and alien experiences.* São Paulo: University of São Paulo. Master thesis.

Masters, R. & Houston, J. (1966). *The Varieties of Psychedelic Experience: The First Comprehensive Guide to the Effects of LSD on Human Personality.* New York: Dell Publishing.

Matlock, J.G. (2019). *Signs of Reincarnation: Exploring Beliefs, Cases, and Theory.* Lanham: Rowman & Littlefield.

Mavromatis, A. (1987). *Hypnogogia: The unique state of consciousness between wakefulness and sleep.* London: Routledge & Kegan Paul.

Maxwell-Stuart, P.G. (2011). *Poltergeists: A History of Violent Ghostly Phenomena.* Stroud: Amberley.

McClenon, J. (1994). *Wondrous Events: Foundations of Religious Belief.* Philadelphia: University of Pennsylvania Press.

McCue, P. (2012). *Zones of Strangeness: An Examination of Paranormal and UFO Hot Spots.* Bloomington: AuthorHouse.

McGuire, P.D. (2013). *Anishinaabe Giikeedaasiwin – Indigenous Knowledge: an Exploration of Resilience.* Saskatoon: University of Saskatchewan.

McKenna, T. (1992). *The Food of the Gods: The Search for the Original Tree of Knowledge.* New York: Bantam.

McNamara, P. & Bulkeley, K. (2015). 'Dreams as a source of supernatural agent concepts.' *Frontiers in Psychology,* Vol. 6, No. 283, pp. 1-8.

Medhurst, R.G., Goldney, K.M. & Barrington, M.R. (1972). *Crookes and the Spirit World: A Collection of Writings by or Concerning the Work of Sir William Crookes, O.M., F.R.S., in the Field of Psychical Research.* New York: Taplinger Publishing.

Melton, J.G. (1980). 'UFO Contactees – A Report on Work in Progress.' In G. Curtis (ed.) *Proceedings of the First International UFO Congress.* New York: Warner Books, pp. 313-18.

Menezes Júnior, A. & Moreira-Almeida, A. (2009). 'Differential diagnosis between spiritual experiences and mental disorders of religious content.' *Revista de Psiquiatria Clínica,* Vol. 36, No. 2, pp. 75-82.

Metzinger, T. (2003). *Being No One. The Self-Model Theory of Subjectivity.* Cambridge: MIT Press.

Metzinger, T. (2005). 'Out-of-Body Experiences as the Origin of the Concept of a 'Soul'.' *Mind & Matter,* Vol. 3, No. 1, pp. 57–84.

Meyer, P. (1994). 'Apparent communication with discarnate entities induced by dimethyltryptamine (DMT).' In T. Lyttle (ed.) *Psychedelics.* New York: Barricade Books, pp. 161-203.

Michel, A. (1963). 'Global Orthoteny: Aime Michel's Latest Discovery.' *Flying Saucer Review,* Vol. 9, No. 3.

Miller, H. (1859). *The Old Red Sandstone.* Boston: Gould and Lincoln.

Monroe, R.A. (1977). *Journeys Out of the Body.* New York: Doubleday Books.

Montenegro, R. (2020). 'The Vibrational State: a Novel Neurophysiological State?' *AutoRicerca* Vol. 20. pp. 191-231.

Moody, R.A (1975) *Life After Life.* New York: Bantam.

Moody, R.A. (1976). *Life After Life.* Harrisburg: Stackpole Books.

Moreira-Almeida, A. (2013) 'Implications of spiritual experiences to the understanding of mind–brain relationship.' *Asian Journal of Psychiatry,* Vol. 6, No. 6, pp. 585–589.

Moreira-Almeida, A. & Santos, F. S. (2012). *Exploring frontiers of the mind-brain relationship.* New York: Springer.

Morriseau, N. (1965). *Legends of my People: The Great Ojibway.* Toronto: The Ryerson Press.

REFERENCES

Morse M.L. (1994). 'Near death experiences of children.' *Journal of Pediatric Oncology Nursing*, Vol. 11, No. 4, pp. 139-145.

Mosha, R.S. (2000). *The Heartbeat of Indigenous Africa: A Study of the Chagga Educational System.* New York: Garland Publishing, Inc.

Muldoon, S. & Carrington, H. (1980 [1929]). *The Projection of the Astral Body.* New York: Samuel Weiser.

Munro, C. & Persinger, M.A. (1992). 'Relative right temporal-lobe theta activity correlates with Vingiano's hemispheric quotient and the 'sensed-presence.' *Perceptual and Motor Skills*, Vol. 75, pp. 899- 903.

Murdoch, I. (2019). *The Trail of Nenaboozhoo and Other Creation Stories.* Neyaashiinigmiing: Kegedonce Press.

Murray, B. (2007). *The Worst It Can Be Is A Disaster.* London: Methuen.

Murdie, A. (1999). 'Psi in Colombia.' Paper to the 23rd Conference of the Society for Psychical Research, Durham, UK 4-5 September 1999.

Murphet, H. (1971). *Sai Baba: Man of Miracles.* York Beach: Samuel Weiser.

Myers, F.W.H. (1895). 'The experiences of W. Stainton Moses.' *Proceedings of the Society for Psychical Research*, Vol. 9, pp. 245-353.

Myers, F. (1903). *Human personality and its survival of bodily death.*

Nadeau, M. (1989). *The History of Surrealism.* Cambridge: Harvard University Press.

Nagata, J.M., Cortez, C.A., Cattle, C.J., et al. (2022). 'Screen Time Use Among US Adolescents During the COVID-19 Pandemic: Findings From the Adolescent Brain Cognitive Development (ABCD) Study.' *JAMA Pediatr*, Vol. 176, No. 1, pp. 94–96.

Nash, T. (1883-1885). *The Complete Works of Thomas Nashe, 6 volumes.* London: private circulation.

Naver, (2007). '유체이탈해서 귀신(?)을 봤어요.' Available Online: https://m.kin.naver.com/mobile/qna/detail.nhn?d1id=3&dirId=316&docId=49986173&qb=7Jyg7LKo7J2o7YOIIOunjO2ZlOy6kOumre2EsA==&enc=utf8&section=kin.ext&rank=1&search_sort=0&spq=0 [Accessed 18th March 2022].

Nebesky-Wojkowitz, R. (1956). *Oracles and demons of Tibet: The cult and iconography of the Tibetan protective deities.* London: Oxford University Press.

Newman, K. (2006). 'Roger Corman and New World.' In L.R. Williams & M. Hammons (eds.) *Contemporary American Cinema.* Maidenhead: McGraw-Hill, pp. 21-25.

Nichols, J. (1788). *The progresses and public processions of Queen Elizabeth.* London: for the author.

Noheden, K. (2017). *Surrealism, Cinema, and the Search for a New Myth.* Cham: Palgrave Macmillan.

Northcote, J. (2004). 'Objectivity and the Supernormal: The Limitations of Bracketing Approaches in Providing Neutral Accounts of Supernormal Claims.' *Journal of Contemporary Religion*, Vol. 19, No. 1, pp. 85-98.

Noë, A. (2009). *Out of Our heads: Why You are not Your Brain, and Other Lessons from the Biology of Consciousness.* New York: Hill and Wang.

Noyes, R., Fenwick, P., Holden, J.M. & Christian, S.R. (2009) 'Aftereffects of pleasurable Western adult near-death experiences.' In J.M. Holden, B. Greyson & D. James (eds.) *The Handbook of Near-Death Experiences: Thirty Years of Investigation.* Santa Barbara: Praeger/ABC-CLIO, pp. 41-62.

O'Connell, S. (2017). What Really Happened When Harrison Ford Gave George Lucas Crap On Set. Available Online: https://www.cinemablend.com/news/1702860/what-really-happened-when-harrison-ford-gave-george-lucas-crap-on-set [Accessed 9th September 2021].

O'Hanlon, J. (1870). *Irish Folk Lore: Traditions and Superstitions of the Country.* Glasgow: Cameron.

Ohayon, M.M., Priest, R.G., Caulet, M. & Guilleminault, C. (1996). 'Hypnagogic and hypnopompic hallucinations: pathological phenomena?' *British Journal of Psychiatry*, Vol. 169, pp. 459-467.

Oesterdiekhoff, G.W. (2015). 'Why Premodern Humans Believed in the Divine Status of Their Parents and Ancestors? Psychology Illuminates the Foundations of Ancestor Worship.' *Anthropos*, Vol. 110, pp. 582-589.

Ohkado, M. (2017). 'Same-Family Cases of the Reincarnation Type in Japan.' Journal of Scientific Exploration, Vol. 31, No. 4, pp. 551-71.

Okołowicz, N. (1926). *Wspomnienia z seansów z medium Frankiem Kluskim.* Warszawa: Książnica – Atlas.

Orloff, J. (2000). *Second Sight: An Intuitive Psychiatrist Tells Her Extraordinary Story and Shows You How to Tap Your Own Inner Wisdom.* New York: Three Rivers Press.

Otto, R. (1958). *The Idea of the Holy.* Oxford: Oxford University Press.

Ouellet, E. (2015). *Illuminations: The UFO Experience as a Parapsychological Event.* San Antonio: Anomalist Books.

Owen, A.R.G. (1964). 'Can We Explain the Poltergeist?' New York: Garrett Publications.

REFERENCES

Owen, E. (1896). *Welsh Folk-lore a Collection of the Folk-Tales and Legends of North Wales.* Wrexham: Woodall & Minshall.

Owen, G. (1964). 'Brownie, Incubus and Poltergeist.' *International Journal of Parapsychology,* Autumn 1964, pp. 455-472.

Owen, I.M. & Sparrow, M. (1976). *Conjuring up Philip: An Adventure in Psychokinesis.* Toronto: Fitzhenry & Whiteside.

Owen, I. M., & Sparrow, M. (1976). *Conjuring up Philip.* London: Harper & Row.

Owl (1995). 'A mushroom entity.' *The Entheogen Review,* Vol. 4, No. 2, pp. 5-6.

Palmer, J. (1978). 'The out-of-body experience: A psychological theory.' *Parapsychology Review,* No. 9, pp. 19-22.

Palmer, J. (1978). 'Extrasensory perception: Research findings.' In S. Krippner (ed.) *Advances in parapsychological research, Vol. 2: Extrasensory perception.* New York: Plenum, pp. 59-243.

Palmer, J. (1982). 'ESP research findings: 1976-1978.' In S. Krippner (ed.) *Advances in parapsychological research. Vol. 3.* New York: Plenum, pp. 41-82.

Parker, A. & Brusewitz, G. (2003). 'A Compendium of the Evidence for Psi.' *European Journal of Parapsychology,* Vol. 18, pp. 33-52.

Parnia, S., Spearpoint, K. & Fenwick, P.B. (2007). 'Near death experiences, cognitive function and psychological outcomes of surviving cardiac arrest.' *Resuscitation,* Vol. 74, pp. 215-221.

Parsons, S. & Cooper, C. (2015). *Paracoustics: Sound and the Paranormal.* Hove: White Crow Books.

Paulson, D.S. (1999). 'The near-death experience: an interpretation of cultural, spiritual, and physical processes.' *Journal of Near-Death Studies,* Vol. 18, No. 1, pp. 13-25.

Peake, A. (2016). *Opening The Doors of Perception.* London: Watkins.

Peake, A. (2019). *The Hidden Universe: An Investigation into Non-Human Intelligences.* London: Watkins.

Peake, A. (2022). *Cheating The Ferryman.* London: Arcturus.

Pearson, J. (2016). 'The Ghost of Col. Bowen: 1655, 1691, 1941/42', *Preternature,* Vol. 5, pp. 86-111.

Pereira, M. E., Silva, J. F. & Silva, B. (2006). 'Psychological research in cyberspace: The role of interest, group adherence and knowledge in accepting ufological beliefs.' *Interação em Psicologia,* Vol. 10, No. 2, pp. 375-384.

Perry, V. (1978). 'The Huron Visitations: A Personal Narrative.' *Awareness*, Vol. 7, No. 1, pp. 5-17.

Platthy, J. (1992). *Near-Death Experiences in Antiquity*. Santa Claus: Federation of International Poetry Associations of UNESCO.

Plato (1965). *Timaeus and Critias*. Harmondsworth: Penguin.

Playfair, G.L. (1980). *This House is Haunted*. London: Souvenir Press Ltd.

Playfair, G.L. (2010). *This House is Haunted*. Guildford: White Crow Books Ltd.

Playfair, G.L. (2012). *Twin Telepathy*. Guildford: White Crow Books.

Podmore, F. (1896). 'Poltergeists.' *Proceedings of the SPR*, Vol 12, pp. 45-115.

Podmore, F. (1902). *Modern Spiritualism: A History and Criticism*. London: Methuen & Co.

Podmore, F. (1910). *The Newer Spiritualism*. London: T. Fisher Unwin.

Poincaré, H. (1902). *La science et l'hypothèse*. Paris: Flammarion.

Popper, K. (1959). *The Logic of Scientific Discovery*. New York: Basic Books.

Price, H. (1945). *Poltergeist Over England*. London: Country Life Books.

Price-Williams, D.R. (1974). 'Psychology and Epistemology of UFO Interpretations.' In C. Sagan & T. Page (eds.) *UFOs: A Scientific Debate*. New York: W.W. Norton and Co, pp. 224-32.

Proudfoot, W. (1985). *Religious Experience*. Berkeley: University of California Press.

Puhle, A. (2013). *Light Changes: Experiences in the Presence of Transforming Light*. Guildford: White Crow Books.

Pup (2006). 'DMT trip accounts.' Available Online: http://dmt.tribe.net/thread/9e832018-5fbc-4ff6-b4e5-e314184f687c (number 246). [Accessed 14th March 2022]

Purkiss, D. (2000). *Troublesome Things: A History of Fairies and Fairy Stories*. London: Penguin.

Radin, D. (2006). *Entangled Minds: Extrasensory Experiences in a Quantum Reality*. New York: Paraview Pocket Books.

Randles, J. (1983). *The Pennine UFO Mystery*. London: Granada Publishing.

Randles, J. (1988). *Abduction: Scientific Exploration of Alleged Kidnap by Alien Beings*. London: Headline.

Randles, J. (1990). *Mind Monsters: Invaders from Inner Space?* Northampton: Aquarian Press.

REFERENCES

Randles, J. (n.d.). 'Essay on the Oz Factor and the Strange Sensations of Altered Reality Reported by UFO Witnesses.' Available Online: http:// alienjigsaw.com/et-contact/Randles-The-Oz- Factor.html [Accessed 9th December 2018].

Rawlette, S.H. (2019). *The Source and Significance of Coincidences: A Hard Look at the Astonishing Evidence.* Virginia: Sharon Hewitt Rawlette.

Rawlette, S.H. (2019). 'Coincidence or Psi? The Epistemic Import of Spontaneous Cases of Purported Psi Identified Post-Verification.' *Journal of Scientific Exploration,* Vol. 33, No. 1, pp. 9-42.

Rawlette, S.H. (2020). 'Essay Review: Phone Calls from the Dead? Exploring the Role of the Trickster.' *Journal of Scientific Exploration,* Vol. 34, No. 1, pp. 116-26.

Rawlette, S.H. (2022). *Beyond Death: The Best Evidence for the Survival of Human Consciousness.* Virginia: Sharon Hewitt Rawlette.

Reintjes, S. (2003). *Third Eye Open: Unmasking Your True Awareness.* Houston: Third Eye Publishing.

Reis, C. & Rodrigues, U. (2009). *The deconstruction of a myth [A desconstrução de um mito].* Juiz de Fora: Livro Pronto.

Rhys, J. (1901). *Celtic Folklore: Welsh and Manx, Volume 1.* Oxford: Clarendon Press.

Richardson, M. (2006). *Surrealism and Cinema.* Oxford: Berg.

Ring, K. (1980). *Life at Death: A Scientific Investigation of Near-Death Experiences.* New York: Coward, McCann and Geoghegan.

Ring, K. (1992). *The Omega Project: Near-Death Experiences, UFO Encounters, and Mind at Large.* New York: William Morrow.

Ring, K. & Cooper, S. (1999). *Mindsight: Near-Death and Out-of-Body Experiences in the Blind.* Palo Alto: William James Centre for Consciousness Studies.

Ritson, D. (2021). *Poltergeist Parallels and Contagion.* Guildford; White Crow Books.

Ritson, D. & Hallowell, M.J. (2014). *Contagion: In the Shadow of the South Shields Poltergeist.* Limbury: The Limbury Press.

Robichaud, P. (2021). *Pan: The Great God's Modern Return.* London: Reaktion Books.

Rodriguez, M. A. (2007). 'A methodology for studying various interpretations of the N,N-dimethyltryptamine-induced alternate reality.' *Journal of Scientific Exploration,* Vol. 21, No. 1, pp. 67-84.

Rogo, D.S. (1978). *Minds and Motion: The riddle of psychokinesis.* New York: Taplinger publishing.

Rogo, D.S. (1979). *The Poltergeist Experience*. Harmondsworth: Penguin Books.

Rogo, D.S. (1990). *Beyond Reality: The role unseen dimensions play in our lives*. Wellingborough: The Aquarian Press.

Rogo, D.S. & Bayless, R. (1979). *Phone Calls from the Dead: The Results of a Two-Year Investigation into an Incredible Phenomenon*. Englewood Cliffs: Prentice-Hall.

Rojcewicz, P.M. (1984). *The Boundaries of Orthodoxy: A Folkloric Look at the UFO Phenomenon*. Ph. D. dissertation, University of Pennsylvania.

Rojcewicz, P. M. (1985). 'The Problems of Definition and Taxonomy in the Study of Belief Materials: UFOs.' Paper presented at the American Folklore Society Annual Meeting, October 18th 1985, Cincinnati.

Rojcewicz, P. M. (1987). 'The "Men in Black" Experience and Tradition: Analogues with the Traditional Devil Hypothesis.' *Journal of American Folklore*, Vol. 100, No. 2, pp. 148-160.

Roll, W.G. (1972). *The Poltergeist*. New York: Nelson Doubleday.

Roll, W. (1977). 'Poltergeists.' In B. Wolman (ed.) *A Handbook of Parapsychology*. New York: Van Nostrand.

Roney-Dougal, S. (2001). *The Faery Faith: An Integration of Science with Spirit*. Langport: Green Magic.

Rosales, A. (2017). *Humanoid Encounters, The Others Amongst Us: 1AD-1899*. Triangulum Publishing.

Rosales, A.S. (2016). *Humanoid Encounters: The Others Amongst Us: 1970-1974*. Triangulum Publishing.

Ross, C. A. and Joshi, S. (1992). 'Paranormal experiences in the general population.' *The Journal of Nervous and Mental Disease*, Vol. 180, No. 6, pp. 357-361.

Rothman, J. (2018). 'Are we already living in virtual reality?' Available online: https://www.newyorker.com/magazine/2018/04/02/are-we-already-living-in-virtual-reality [Accessed 2nd April 2018].

Roxburgh, E. & Roe, C. (2011). 'A survey of dissociation, boundary-thinness, and psychological wellbeing in spirituality mental mediumship.' *Journal of Parapsychology*, Vol. 75, No. 2, pp. 279-299.

Rudgley, R. (2000). *The encyclopedia of psychoactive substances*. New York: Thomas Dunne.

Ruffo, A.G. (2014). *Norval Morrisseau: Man Changing into Thunderbird*. Madeira Park: Douglas and McIntyre, Ltd.

REFERENCES

Ruhenstroth-Bauer, G., Baumer, H., Kugler, J. & Spatz , R. (1984). 'Epilepsy and weather: A significant correlation between the onset of epileptic seizures and specific atmospherics-a pilot study.' *International Journal of Biometeorology*, Vol. 28, pp. 333-340.

Sabom, M.B. (1982). *Recollections of Death: A Medical Investigation*. New York: Harper & Row.

Sabom, M.B. (1998). *Light and Death: One Doctor's Fascinating Account of Near-Death Experiences*. Michigan: Zondervan.

Salway. C. (2015). 'Psychonauts going psychonuts.' Paper presented to the 3rd Breaking Convention: International Conference on Psychedelic Consciousness, University of Greenwich, London, 10-12th July.

Santos, J.P. (2017). 'Intimations of Infinite Entanglement: Notes toward a Prologomenon to any Future Repudiatory Postscript to The Farthest Home Is in an Empire of Fire.' in C. Josefina Merla-Watson and B.V. Olguín (eds.) *Altermundos: Latin@ Speculative Literature, Film, and Popular Culture*. Los Angeles: UCLA Chicano Studies Center Press.

Sartori, P. (2008). *The Near-Death Experiences of Hospitalized Intensive Care Patients: A Five Year Clinical Study*. Lewiston: The Edwin Mellen Press.

Satyananda Saraswati, Swami. (1972). *The pineal gland (ajna chakra)*. Bihar: Bihar School of Yoga.

Satyananda Saraswati, Swami. (1996). *Kundalini tantra*. Munger: Yoga Publications Trust.

Schmeidler, G. R. (1994). 'ESP experiments 1978-1992: The glass is half full.' In S. Krippner (ed.) *Advances in parapsychological research. Vol. 4*. Jefferson: McFarland, pp. 104-197.

Schrenck-Notzing, von A. (1920/1923). *Phenomena of materialisation: A contribution to the investigation of mediumistic teleplastics*. London: E.P. Dutton & Co.

Schroll, M.A. (2019). 'Re-Awakening the Transpersonal Ecosophical Significance of Sacred Places.' In J. Hunter (ed.) Greening the Paranormal: Exploring the Ecology of Extraordinary Experience. Milton Keynes: August Night Press.

Schwartz, G.E. (2011). 'Possible Causal Mechanisms in the Occurrence of Synchronicities: Testing the Spiritual Assistance Hypothesis.' *Journal of Spirituality and Paranormal Studies*, Vol. 34, No. 4, pp. 182-209.

Schwarz, B.E. (1980). 'Psychiatric Aspects of UFOs.' In R.D. Story (ed.) *The Encyclopedia of UFOs*. Garden City: Doubleday Books.

Schwarz, B.E. (1983). *UFO Dynamics*. Moore Haven: Rainbow Books.

Seinfeld, S., Zhan, M., Poyo-Solanas, M., Barsuola, G., Vaessen, M., Slater, M., Sanchez-Vives, M.V., de Gelder, B. (2021). 'Being the victim of virtual abuse changes default mode network responses to emotional expressions,' *Cortex*, Vol. 135, pp. 268-284.

Serdahely, W.J. (1995). 'Variations from the prototypic near-death experience.' *Journal of Near-Death Studies*, Vol. 13, No. 3, pp. 185-196.

Sergent, D. & Wamsley, J. (2002). *Mothman: The Facts Behind the Legend.* Proctorville: Mark S. Phillips Publishing.

Seligman, R., Kirmayer, L.J. (2008). 'Dissociative experience and cultural neuroscience: Narrative, metaphor and mechanism.' *Cultural Medicine and Psychiatry*, Vol. 32, pp. 31-64.

Sheldrake, R. (1988). *The presence of the past.* London: Fontana.

Shelton, H.M. (1978). *Fasting For Renewal of Life.* Chicago: Natural Hygiene Press.

Sheriff, R. (2017). 'Dreaming of the Kardashians: Media Content in the Dreams of US College Students,' *Ethos*, Vol. 45, No. 4, pp. 532-554.

Shiftingwith.lilly. (2021). 'The Julia Method.' Available Online: https://www.instagram.com/p/CNesLvFpXQv/?utm_source=ig_web_copy_link [Accessed 10th April 2021].

Shushan, G. (2009). *Conceptions of the Afterlife in Early Civilizations: Universalism, Constructivism, and Near-Death Experience.* London: Continuum International. Revised edition forthcoming 2023 from Inner Traditions, Rochester, VT.

Shushan, G. (2018). *Near-Death Experience in Indigenous Religions.* Oxford: Oxford University Press.

'Shushan, G. (2022). *The Next World: Extraordinary Experiences of the Afterlife.* Guildford: White Crow Books.

Sidgwick, H. (1891). 'A Census of Hallucinations.' *The New Review*, Vol. 4, No. 20, pp. 52-59.

Simpson, L.B. (2011). *Dancing on Our Turtle's Back: Stories of Nishnaabeg Re-creation, Resurgence, and a New Emergence.* Winnipeg: Arbeiter Ring Publishing.

Simpson, L.B. (2014). 'Land as Pedagogy: Nishnaabeg Intelligence and Rebellious Transformation.' *Decolonization: Indigeneity, Education & Society.* Vol. 3, No. 3, pp. 1-25.

Sinclair, L. & Pollock, J. (1979). *The Art of Norval Morrisseau.* Toronto: Methuen.

Sipos, T.M. (2010). *Horror Film Aesthetics.* Jefferson: McFarland & Company.

Sitwell, S. (1940). *Poltergeists.* London: Faber and Faber Ltd.

REFERENCES

Sjöstedt-Hughes, P. (2022). *Modes of Sentience: Panpsychism, Psychedelics, Metaphysics*. London: Psychedelic Press.

Smith, M. (2019). 'Results of the New Fairy Census.' Fairy Investigation Society Newsletter, No. 10, pp. 26-32.

Smith, S. (2021). 'What is 'reality shifting' and why is it taking over TikTok?' *Vice*. Available Online: https://i-d.vice.com/en_uk/article/y3z8vm/what-is-reality-shifting-and-why-is-it-taking-over-tiktok [Accessed 18th March 2022].

Smith, T. (1995). The Island of the Anishinaabeg: Thunderers and Water Monsters in the Traditional Ojibwe Life-World. Moscow: University of Idaho Press.

Snyder, B. (2005). *Save the Cat!: The Last Book on Screenwriting You'll Ever Need*. Studio City: Michael Wiese Productions.

Sobchack, V. (2014). 'Stop Making Sense: Thoughts on Two Difficult Films from 2013.' *Film Comment*, Vol. 50, No. 1, pp. 50–53.

Society For Psychical Research. *PSI Encyclopedia*. Available Online: https://psi-encyclopedia.spr.ac.uk/ [Accessed 25th September 2021].

Sommer, A. (2012). 'Psychical Research and the Origins of American Psychology: Hugo Münsterberg, William James and Eusapia Palladino.' *History of the Human Sciences*, Vol. 25, No. 2, pp. 23-44.

Soulières, J. (2012). *Les coïncidences*. Paris: Dervy.

Souriau, É. (2015). The Different Modes of Existence. Minneapolis: Univocal.

Southey, R. (1846). *The Life of Wesley and Rise and Progress of Methodism*.

Spencer, J. & Spencer, A. (1996). *The Poltergeist Phenomenon: An Investigation into Psychic Disturbance*. London: Headline Book Publishing.

Spooner, B. (1968). 'The Haunted Style.' *Folklore*, Vol. 79, pp. 135-139.

Starkey, J.A. (2006). *Back to the Blanket: A Native Narrative Of Discovery*. Lincoln: iUniverse, Inc.

Stavish, M. (2018). *Egregores: The Occult Entities That Watch Over Human Destiny*. Vermont: Inner Traditions/Bear.

Steadman, L.B., Palmer, C.T. & Tilley, C.F. (1996). 'The Universality of Ancestor Worship.' *Ethnology*, Vol. 35, pp. 63-76.

Steiger, B. (1976). *Gods of Aquarius: UFOs and the Transformation of Man*. New York: Harcourt.

Steiger, B. (1988). *The UFO Abductors*. New York: The Berkley Publishing Group.

Steiner, J. (1967). *Therese Neumann: A Portrait*. New York: Alba House.

Stevenson, I. (1972). 'Poltergeists are they living or are they dead?' *Journal of the American SPR*, Vol. 66, pp. 232-252.

Stevenson, I. (2001). *Children Who Remember Previous Lives: A Question of Reincarnation.* Jefferson: McFarland & Company, Inc.

Stevenson, I. & Greyson, B. (1996). 'NDEs: relevance to the question of survival after death.' In L.W. Bailey & J. Yates (eds.) *The Near-Death Experience: A Reader.* London: Routledge, pp. 199-206.

Stevenson, I. Kellehear, A., Pasricha, S. & Cook, E.W. (1994). 'The absence of tunnel sensations in near-death experiences from India.' *Journal of Near-Death Studies*, Vol. 13, No. 2, pp. 109-113.

Stevenson, I., Owens, J.E. & Cook, E.W. (1990). 'Features of 'near-death experience' in relation to whether or not patients were near death.' *The Lancet*, Vol. 336, pp. 1175-1177.

Stillman, W. (2006). *Autism and the God Connection: Redefining the Autistic Experience through Extraordinary Accounts of Spiritual Giftedness.* Naperville: Sourcebooks.

Stillman, W. (2017). *The Secret Language of Spirit: Understanding Spirit Communication in Our Everyday Lives.* Newburyport: Career Press.

Storm, L. & Thalbourne, M. (2019). 'Thalbourne's Theory of Psychopraxia.' *Mindfield: Bulletin of the Parapsychological Association*, Vol. 11, No. 1, pp. 8-12.

Strassman, R. (2001). *DMT: The spirit molecule: A doctor's revolutionary research into the biology of near-death and mystical experiences.* Rochester: Park Street Press.

Strawson, G. (2015). 'The Consciousness Myth.' *Times Literary Supplement*, 27th February 2015.

Strieber, W. (1988). *Communion.* New York: HarperCollins.

Strieber, W. (1995). *Breakthrough.* San Antonio: Walker & Collier, Inc.

Strieber, W. (1998) *Confirmation: The Hard Evidence of Aliens Among Us.* London: Simon & Schuster.

Strieber, W. (2021). 'David Metcalfe on UFOs, UAPs, ET Contact, Black Magic and the Secrets of the Ages.' Available Online: https://www.unknowncountry.com/dreamland/david-metcalfe-the-saucers-will-keep-their-secrets-or-will-they/ [Accessed 10th September 2021].

Struthers, R. & Eschiti, V.S. (2005). 'Being healed by an indigenous traditional healer: sacred healing stories of Native Americans. Part II.' *Complementary Therapies in Clinical Practice*, Vol. 11, No. 2, pp. 78-86.

REFERENCES

Sudolski, Z. (ed.) (1996). *Świadek epoki: Listy Elizy z Branickich Krasińskiej z lat 1835-1876*, Vol.3. Warszawa: Wyd. Ancher.

Sullivan, J. (1857). *Cumberland & Westmorland, ancient and modern; the people, dialect, superstitions and customs*. London: Whittaker and Co.

Szwed, J.F. (1970). 'Paul E. Hall: A Newfoundland Song Maker and His Community of Song.' In H. Glassie (ed.) *Folksongs and Their Makers*. Bowling Green, OH: Bowling Green University Popular Press, pp. 147-169.

Taves, A. (1999). *Fits, Trances and Visions: Experiencing Religion and Explaining Experience from Wesley to James*. Princeton: Princeton University Press.

Taylor, A. E. (1902). 'Mind and Nature.' *International Journal of Ethics*, Vol. 13, No. 1, pp. 55–86.

Taylor, I., Schaffer, I.E. & Berkovic, S.F. (2003). 'Occipital epilepsies: identification of specific and newly recognized syndromes.' *Brain*, Vol. 126, pp. 753-69.

Thalbourne, M. & Houran, J. (2000). 'Transliminality, the Mental Experience Inventory and tolerance of ambiguity.' *Personality and Individual Differences*, Vol. 28, pp. 853-863.

Thomas, K. (1971). *Religion and the Decline of Magic*. New York: Charles Scribner's Sons.

Thomas, K. (1973). *Religion and the Decline of Magic Studies in Popular Beliefs in Sixteenth- and Seventeenth-Century England*. London: Penguin.

Thompson, R. (2004). 'The automatic hand: Spiritualism, psychoanalysis, surrealism.' *Invisible Culture: An Electronic Journal for Visual Studies*, Issue 7. Available Online: http://www.rochester.edu/in_visible_culture/Issue_7/Issue_7_Thompson.pdf [Accessed 3rd March 2022].

Thurston, H, (1952). *The Physical Phenomena of Mysticism*. London: Burns Oates.

TikTok (2021). Available Online: https://vm.tiktok.com/ZMLytQBNg/ [Accessed 16th March 2022].

Treasure, S. (2019). *Encountering figures in out-of-body experiences: A qualitative UK study*. [Unpublished bachelor's thesis]. Birkbeck: University of London.

Trip333 (2007). 'A choice between worms and stars.' Available Online: http://www.erowid.org/experiences/exp.php?ID=6217 [Accessed 8th January 2007].

Trungpa, C. (1982). 'Sacred outlook: The Vajrayogini shrine and practice.' In D. E. Klimburg-Salter (ed.) *The silk route and the diamond path*. Los Angeles: UCLA Art Council.

Tucker, S.D. (2020). *Blythe Spirits: A History of the Poltergeist*. Stroud: Amberley Publishing.

Tuhiwai Smith, L. (2012). *Decolonizing Methodologies: Research and Indigenous Peoples*. London: Zed Books.

Turner, D.M. (1995). 'Exploring hyperspace.' *The Entheogen Review*, Vol. 4, No. 4, pp. 4-6.

Turner, E. (1993). 'The Reality of Spirits: A Tabooed or Permitted Field of Study.' *Anthropology of Consciousness*, Vol. 4, No. 1, pp. 9-12.

Utts, J. (1991). 'Replication and Meta Analysis in Parapsychology.' *Statistical Science*, Vol. 6, No.4, pp. 363-403.

Vallée, J. (1969). *Passport to Magonia: From Folklore to Flying Saucers*. Chicago: Henry Regnery.

Vallée, J. (1993) *Passport to Magonia: On UFOs, Folklore and Parallel Worlds*. Chicago: Contemporary Books Inc.

Vallée, J. (1975). *The Invisible College*. New York: E.P. Dutton.

Vallée, J. (1989). *Dimensions: A Casebook of Alien Contact*. New York: Random House Publishing Group.

Vallée, J. (1977). *UFOs: The Psychic Solution: UFO Influences on the Human Race*. St Albans: Panther Books.

Vallée, J. (1988). *Dimensions: A Casebook of Alien Contact*. London: Souvenir Press.

Vallée, J. (1990). *Confrontations: A Scientist's Search for Alien Contact*. New York, NY: Ballantine Books.

Vallée, J. (2014). *Passport to Magonia: From Folklore to Flying Saucers*, 2nd Edition. Brisbane: Daily Grail Publishing.

van Lommel, P. (2007). *Consciousness Beyond Life: The Science of the Near-Death Experience*. New York: HarperOne.

van Lommel, P. (2006). 'Near-death experience, consciousness, and the brain: a new concept about the continuity of our consciousness based on recent scientific research on near-death experience in survivors of cardiac arrest.' *World Futures*, Vol. 62, pp. 134–151.

van Lommel, P., van Wees, R., Meyers, V. & Elfferich, I. (2001). 'Near-death experience in survivors of cardiac arrest: a prospective study in the Netherlands.' *The Lancet*, Vol. 358, pp. 2039-2045.

Vastokas, J. (1973). *The Sacred Art of the Algonkians: A Study of the Peterborough Petroglyphs*. Peterborough: Mansard Press.

Vaughan, A. (1979). *Incredible Coincidence: The Baffling World of Synchronicity*. New York: J. B. Lippincott Company.

REFERENCES

Vézina, J. (2009). *Necessary Chances: Synchronicity in the Encounters That Transform Us.* Pari: Pari Publishing.

Viveiros de Castro, E. (1998). 'Cosmological Deixis and Amerindian Perspectivism.' In M. Lambek (ed.) (2002). *A Reader in the Anthropology of Religion.* Oxford: Blackwell, pp. 306-326.

Wade, J. (2003). 'In a sacred manner we died: Native American near-death experiences.' *Journal of Near-Death Studies,* Vol. 22, No. 2, pp. 83-115.

Wamsley, J. (2005). *Mothman: Behind the Red Eyes.* Point Pleasant: Mothman Press.

Ward, D. (1977). 'The Little Man Who Wasn't There: Encounters with the Supranormal.' *Fabula,* Vol. 18, pp. 212-225.

Watson, L. (1986). *Supernature II.* London: Hodder & Stoughton.

Wehrstein, K. (2021). 'Philip Psychokinesis Experiments.' *The PSI Encyclopedia.* Available Online: https://psi-encyclopedia.spr.ac.uk/articles/philip-psychokinesis-experiments [Accessed 30th September 2021].

Wilby, E. (2005). *Cunning-folk and familiar spirits: shamanistic visionary traditions in early modern British witchcraft and magic.* Eastbourne: Sussex Academic Press.

Willerslev, R. (2004). 'Not Animal, Not Not-Animal: Hunting, Imitation and Empathetic Knowledge among the Siberian Yukaghirs.' *The Journal of the Royal Anthropological Institute,* Vol. 10, No. 3, pp. 629-652.

Wilson, C. (1981). *Poltergeist! A Study of Destructive Haunting.* London: Hodder & Stoughton.

Winkelman, M. (2013). 'The Integrative Mode of Consciousness: Evolutionary Origins of Ecstasy.' In T. Passie, W. Belschner & E. Petrow (eds.) *Ekstasen: Kontexte - Formen - Wirkungen.* Würzburg: Ergon-Verlag.

Winkelman, M. (1982). 'Magic: A Theoretical Reassessment.' *Current Anthropology,* Vol. 23, No. 1, pp. 37-66.

Wiseman, R, (1992). 'The Feilding report: A reconsideration.' *Journal of the Society for Psychical Research,* Vol. 58, pp. 129-152.

r/witchcraft. 'People believing they can astral project into an anime world?' *Reddit.* Available Online: https://www.reddit.com/r/witchcraft/comments/ioo4l3/people_believing_they_can_astral_project_into_an/ [Accessed 18th March 2022].

Weaver, Z. (2015). *Other realities? The enigma of Franek Kluski's mediumship.* Guildford: White Crow Books.

Weaver, Z. (2018). 'Mediumistic Phenomena by Julian Ochorowicz.' *Journal of Scientific Exploration*, Vol. 32, No. 1, pp. 85–160.

White, C.G. (2018). *Other Worlds: Spirituality and the Search for Invisible Dimensions*. Cambridge: Harvard University Press.

Winkler, K. (1982). *Pilgrim of the Clear Light: The Biography of Dr Walter Evans-Wentz*. Gerrards Cross: Colin Smythe.

Yamane, D. (2000). 'Narrative and Religious Experience.' *Sociology of Religion*, Vol. 61, No. 2, pp. 171-189.

Yaron, I., et al. (2022) 'The ConTraSt database for analysing and comparing empirical studies of consciousness theories.' *Nature Human Behaviour*: doi.org/10.1038/s41562-021-01284-5

Young, F. (2019). *Suffolk Fairylore*. Norwich: Lasse Press.

Young, S. (2016). 'Four Neglected Pixy-Led Sources from Devon.' *The Devon Historian*, Vol. 85, pp. 39-49.

Young, S. (2018). *The Fairy Census, 2014-2017*. Available Online: http://www.fairyist.com/wp-content/uploads/2014/10/The-Fairy-Census-2014-2017-1.pdf [Accessed 17/02/2021].

Young, S. (2019). 'When did fairies get wings?' In J.W. Morehead & D. Caterine (eds.) *The Paranormal and Popular Culture*. Abingdon: Routledge, pp. 253-274.

Young, S. (2022a). *The Wollaton Gnomes: A Nottingham Fairy Mystery*. Pwca Press.

Young, S. (2022b). *The Nail in the Skull and Other Victorian Urban Legends*. Jackson: University of Mississippi Press.

Yunkaporta, T. (2019). *Sand Talk: How Indigenous Thinking Can Save the World*. Melbourne: The Text Publishing Company.

Zaleski, C. (1987). *Otherworld Journeys: Accounts of Near-Death Experiences in Medieval and Modern Times*. Oxford: Oxford University Press.

Zangari, W. (2005). 'A psychosocial interpretation of the phenomenon of mediumship in umbanda [Uma leitura psicossocial do fenômeno da mediunidade de umbanda].' *Boletim da Academia Paulista de Psicologia*, Vol. 3, No. 5, pp. 70-88.

Zangari, W. & Maraldi, E. (2009). 'Psychology of mediumship: from the intrapsychic to a psychosocial approach.' *Boletim Academia Paulista de Psicologia*, Vol. 77, No. 2, pp. 233-252.

INDEX

A

Absurd, vii, 2, 25, 27, 28, 30, 40, 219, 284,285, 307
After-death communication (ADC), 54
Altered States of Consciousness, 111, 155, 229, 300, 326, 365
Ager, Robert, 280
Animism, 34, 313
Artificial Intelligence (AI), 264
Astral Projection, 42, 102, 104, 106,108, 110

B

Bigfoot, viii, 6, 15,16, 25, 28, 32, 43, 211, 214, 269, 285,286, 359
Bishop, Greg, vii, 16, 277, 282,283
Boggle Threshold, 1, 21, 45, 130, 132, 147, 208, 319, 321, 332

C

Cinema, x, 273,277, 281,282, 286, 288
Clelland, Mike, viii, 14,15, 31, 71, 73, 277

Co-creation, 333
Coincidence, 50, 54,55, 60, 65, 69, 126, 153
Conjuring, x, 45, 137, 314, 317, 319, 321,327, 329,334, 336, 360
Consciousness, 3, 29, 33-34, 45, 82-83, 95, 108, 110, 117, 125, 299, 302, 307, 310, 312-314
Cosmology, 33, 337, 361
Crowley, Alister, 178,179, 293, 323, 325, 326
Cryptids, 213
Cryptozoology, 212, 214, 222, 285
Cutchin, Joshua, x, 2, 16, 27, 31,32, 35, 44,45, 273, 286, 359

D

Death, 11, 25
Decolonisation, 40, 358
Deep Weird, 6-8
Dimensions, 35, 170
Dimethyltryptamine (DMT), 42, 170,175, 177,178, 180,183, 188
Dolly zoom, 278
Doniger, Wendy, 2,3

D

Dreams, 13-14, 18, 26-27, 32, 53, 56-57, 81, 90-96, 177, 257, 273-274, 354-355, 357

E

Ecology, 355, 359, 361, 362
Ecstatic Experience, 13, 19, 21, 23, 26, 118, 122, 254, 257
Ectoplasm, ix, 2, 129, 131, 133, 135, 137, 139, 141, 143, 145, 147
Egregor, 292, 293, 300, 303, 305e
Enstatic Experience, 254
Entity encounters, ix, 2, 7, 43, 44, 211, 215, 217, 219, 221, 223, 225, 326
Evolution, 2, 42, 71, 114-117, 121-122, 126, 166, 202, 313-315, 332, 338
Experiment, 13, 32, 45, 82, 94, 117, 119, 130, 136-138, 141, 146-147, 157, 163, 298, 322-340
Extrasensory Perception (ESP), 116, 125

F

Fairy Faith, 196, 220, 222
Fear, 8, 9, 25, 28-30, 45, 72, 77, 80, 177, 278, 300-301, 347
Fisher, Mark, x, 24, 44, 90, 93, 259, 267, 341, 345, 361
Folklore, 2, 10, 24, 43, 150, 164-165, 170, 190, 196, 205, 219-222, 237, 245-246, 255, 257, 291, 318
Fort, Charles, 5, 13, 16, 22, 108, 157, 281, 282
Freud, Sigmund, 25, 26, 232, 236, 257
Fruits of religious experience, 81

G

Gnomes, 14, 21, 24, 163, 165, 202

H

Hallucination, 105, 152, 157, 232, 294, 296, 328
Hansen, George P., 16, 34, 286
High Strangeness, 15-17, 21-23, 29-30, 32-36, 39-40, 52, 149-150, 157-158, 160-161, 215, 217, 219, 260, 273-279, 278, 281-288, 303, 317-320, 324
History of Religions, 2, 362
Home, Daniel Dunglas, 131-132, 135-136, 139-140, 144, 147, 162
Humanoids, 21, 23, 43, 89, 193, 203, 205, 211, 212, 245, 260, 262, 269, 320
Hynek, J. Allen, 15, 30, 40, 220, 245, 251

I

Inedia, 121, 122
Indridason, Indridi, 135, 137, 147, 148
Intellect, 147, 291
Imagination, 2, 42, 85, 90-91, 93, 102, 105, 109, 113, 126, 136, 138, 147, 160, 157, 276, 284, 285, 294, 297, 299, 328, 330
Interviews, 43, 83, 230, 232, 237, 239-240

J

James, William, 8-9, 11-13, 20, 22, 28, 33, 81, 93, 131-132, 175, 257, 307, 313, 314
Jung, Carl, vii, 7, 53, 54, 246, 276, 291, 364

K

Kastrup, Bernardo, 28

INDEX

Keel, John, 14, 16, 32, 35, 52, 213, 216,218, 222, 224, 248, 256,257, 261, 267,268, 287, 318, 361
Kluski, Franek, 135,137, 143,147, 365
Kripal, Jeffrey J., ix, 1, 3, 17, 35, 39, 282, 319,320, 362

L

Lam, 325,326
Lash, Dominic, 185, 277, 281, 286,288
Light phenomena, 212, 217, 268
Lovecraft, H.P., 24,25, 325
LSD, 11,12, 175, 180, 278, 296
Lynch, David, 62, 288

M

MacGregor, Trish, 51
Mack, John, 32, 234, 240, 288
Magick, 45, 293, 317, 322,325, 331,332, 334
Magician, 119, 323, 326
Materialisation, 42, 119,120, 144
Meditation, 82, 90, 92, 102, 104, 106, 109, 197, 297, 329, 331
Mediumship, 33, 36-38, 127, 156, 229, 303, 322, 336, 353
Men in Black, 16, 21, 22-24, 28, 52, 250, 286, 360
Metachoric hypothesis, 294
Metalepsis, 277, 286, 288
Mothman, 14, 16, 24,25, 32, 43, 213, 216,217
Multiverse, 35
Myers, F.W.H., 132, 136, 138, 141, 146, 157,
Mysterium tremendum et fascinans, 22, 29-30
Mysticism, 127, 197, 257, 323, 362

N

Neuroessentialism, 310,311, 313
Numinous, vii, 1, 22,25, 27, 30, 42, 171, 185,186, 254, 279, 337

O

Occult, 26,27, 103, 177, 197, 212, 221, 281, 291, 298, 318, 324, 326, 330
Ontological Flooding, 36
Otto, Rudolf, vii, 22,25, 30
Out-of-Body Experience (OBE), 7, 13, 20, 42, 77, 89-90, 96-97, 99, 101-106, 109-111, 248, 251, 253, 288, 295, 303, 365
Owlman, 27
Owls, viii, 14, 27, 71
Oz Factor, viii, 1, 22, 28, 30,31, 280

P

Painlevé, Jean, 281
Palladino, Eusapia, 132, 135,137, 141, 162
Panpsychism, x, 34, 44,45, 307, 309,315, 365
Parapsychology, iv, 16,17, 22, 32,33, 37, 157, 214, 285, 300, 322, 326, 330, 333, 360, 362, 364
Permanent Paranormal Object, 144
Philip Experiment, 297, 299, 327, 329,330, 333
Physical Mediumship, 129-148
Poltergeist, 16, 32, 42, 130, 133, 135, 137, 147, 149,158, 160,167, 213,214, 274, 283, 327, 329, 360
Popielska, Stanisława, 133
Possession, 5, 36,37, 86, 119, 154, 163, 214, 217

Psi, 13, 32,34, 38, 53,54, 113, 115,116, 121, 123, 129, 150, 156,157, 161, 229,230, 238, 274, 286, 322, 324, 326, 332,333, 360, 363

Psilocybin, 12, 174,175, 180

Psychokinesis (PK), 32, 53, 115,116, 150, 156, 158, 160, 229, 300, 322, 327, 329

R

Recurrent Spontaneous Psychokinesis (RSPK), 32, 156

Reincarnation, 59,60, 96, 127

Religious Experience, 5, 8,11, 17,19, 21,23, 28, 33, 40, 81, 87, 93, 361, 364

Richardson, Michael, 281,284

Ring, Kenneth, 76,77, 79, 83, 253, 279

Rogo, David Scott, 16, 35, 58, 163, 299,300

S

Sasquatch, 189, 206, 208, 211,212, 217,218, 222, 224,225, 326, 359

Schneider, Rudi, 135,137, 142, 146

Séance, 37, 42, 129, 131-132, 134-135, 137, 139, 141-146, 148, 162, 329

Shifting, 106,110, 170, 206, 209

Sidgwick, Henry, 18

Simulpathity, 62

Spirits, 28, 33, 38, 75, 85, 91, 131, 138, 140-141, 146, 156-157, 162-165, 172, 179, 184-185, 191-192, 195, 197-198, 200, 203-204, 208, 212, 215, 256, 283, 318-319, 321, 330, 337-338, 341-342, 349, 357-358

Spirit possession, 5, 36, 154, 163

Stainton Moses, William, 135,138, 141, 145,147

Strieber, Whitley, 17, 279, 287, 318, 320, 333

Superspectrum, 35

Surrealism, 26,27, 277, 281,284,

Synchronicity, viii,ix, 2, 7, 14, 39, 49,55, 57,59, 61, 63, 65,71, 73, 166,167

T

Technology, 115, 243, 274, 330, 365

Telepathy, iv, 32, 53, 62, 91, 116, 126, 150, 292, 322, 328

Television, 53, 60, 102, 111, 120, 172, 216, 329

Thelema, 323

Toronto, 297, 299, 327, 360

Trance, 42, 82, 92, 106, 135, 139, 147, 254

Trickster, 34, 36, 39, 180, 286, 336

Tulpa, 103, 293, 327

Twins, 60, 62,63

U

UFOs, vii,viii, 1, 16, 35, 71, 73, 115, 213, 216, 218, 237, 243,247, 250, 257,258, 260, 268,269, 274, 280, 283, 285,287, 303, 330, 359,360

UFO occupants, 212, 254, 268

Uncanny, vii, 7, 14, 25,26, 30, 116, 187, 206, 260, 275

V

Vallée, Jacques, 35, 149, 220-221, 245, 248, 274-275, 318-319, 321, 324

Vampire, 284, 287

Vardøger, 66

Visualisation, 106, 109, 265, 299, 327,328, 330,331

W

Weird, 24
Wide angle lens, 278
Witch, 45, 108, 163, 190, 193, 318, 324, 360
Witness effects,
Wyrd, 6,7

Z

Za, 42, 172,173, 177,180, 184, 187,188

Lightning Source UK Ltd.
Milton Keynes UK
UKHW011258310123
416239UK00004B/225